CERTIFIED

Developer Study Guide

Ben Forta

Macromedia ColdFusion MX 7 Certified Developer Study Guide

Ben Forta

Published by Macromedia Press, in association with Peachpit, a division of Pearson Education.

Macromedia Press
1249 Eighth Street
Berkeley, CA 94710
510/524-2178
Fax: 510/524-2221 (fax)

Find us on the World Wide Web at: www.peachpit.com www.macromedia.com

To report errors, please send a note to errata@peachpit.com

Macromedia Press Editor: Angela Kozlowski
Technical Editor: Demian Holmberg
Production Coordinators: Myrna Vladic, Jeffrey Sargent
Index: Julie Bess, JBIndexing Inc.
Interior Design: Happenstance Type-O-Rama
Cover Design: Happenstance Type-O-Rama
Page Layout: Happenstance Type-O-Rama

ISBN 0-321-33011-0

9 8 7 6 5 4 3 2 1

Printed and bound in the United States of America

ABOUT THE AUTHOR

Ben Forta is Macromedia Inc.'s Senior Technical Evangelist, and has over two decades of experience in the computer industry in product development, support, training, and marketing. Ben is the author of the best-selling ColdFusion book of all time. Macromedia ColdFusion Web Application Construction Kit and its sequel Advanced Macromedia ColdFusion Application Development, as well as books on SQL, JavaServer Pages, Windows development, Regular Expressions, WAP, and more. Over ½ million Ben Forta books have been printed in more than a dozen languages worldwide. Ben helped drive the features in ColdFusion MX 7, and co-authored the official Macromedia ColdFusion training material, as well as the certification tests and Macromedia Press study guides for those tests. He writes regular columns on ColdFusion and Internet development, and now spends a considerable amount of time lecturing and speaking on application development worldwide. Ben welcomes your e-mail at ben@forta.com and invites you to visit his web site at http://forta.com/ and his blog at http://forta.com/blog.

ACKNOWLEDGMENTS

First and foremost, thanks to all of you who reviewed and commented on the previous three editions of this book—your feedback (both positive and otherwise) is always welcomed and helped shape this new edition. Thanks to Demian Holmberg for being brave enough to sign up as my technical editor again. A very special thank you to my acquisitions editor, Angela Kozlowski, for still putting up with me. And finally, thanks to Marcy and the kids, for so much love, support, encouragement, and pride.

CONTENTS

Introduction

IN THIS INTRODUCTION

What Is the Certified ColdFusion Developer Exam?

The popularity of Macromedia's products continues to grow, and along with it, so has the demand for experienced developers. Once upon a time (Internet time, that is, but actually not that long ago in conventional time), claiming to be a ColdFusion developer was easy; the product was simple enough that, with a minimal investment of time and energy, developers could realistically consider themselves experts.

That is not the case anymore. The product line has grown both in actual products and in their complexity, and the levels of expertise and experience among developers are diverse. Claiming to be an expert is not that easy anymore, and recognizing legitimate expertise is even harder.

The Macromedia Certified Professional Program

This is where certification comes into play. Formal, official certification by Macromedia helps to mark a threshold that explicitly separates developers by their knowledge and experience, making it possible to identify who is who.

The *Certified Macromedia ColdFusion Developer* certification is part of a series of certification tracks from Macromedia—this one concentrating on developers who use Macromedia's flagship product, ColdFusion. Additional exams and certification programs concentrate on other products and areas of expertise.

Reasons to Get Certified

There's really only one important reason for ColdFusion developers to become certified (aside from the goodies you'll receive): Being able to call yourself a *Macromedia*

Certified ColdFusion Developer means that you can command the respect and recognition that goes along with being one of the best at what you do.

Just as has happened with other products and technologies in this space, certification is becoming a prerequisite for employers—an additional barometer by which to measure the potential of candidates and applicants.

Whether being certified helps you find a new (or better) job, helps persuade your boss that the pay raise you want is justified, helps you find new clients, or gets you listed on Macromedia's Web site so that you can attract new work or prospects—whatever the reason—it will help you stick out from the crowd.

About the Exam

Becoming a *Certified Macromedia ColdFusion Developer* involves being examined on your knowledge of ColdFusion and related technologies. As far as exams go, this one is not easy—nor should it be. In fact, more than a third of all examinees fail their first test. This is not a bad thing; on the contrary, this is good because it means that you really have to know your stuff to pass. You do not merely receive a paper certificate; the exam and subsequent certification have real value and real significance. "Very challenging but fair" is how many examinees describe the exam itself.

The Exam Itself

The exam itself is a set of multiple-choice questions that you answer electronically. A computer application issues the test, and you'll know whether you passed immediately upon test completion.

You are presented with questions and possible answers. Some questions have a single correct answer; others have two or more (you'll be told how many answers to provide). If a question stumps you, you can skip it and come back to it later.

After you have answered all the questions, you can review them to check your answers. And after you are done (or when the time is up; yes, the test has a 70-minute limit), you'll get your results. You need at least 65 percent correct to pass. If you do not pass, you'll need to wait at least 30 days before you can try again. You may take the test no more than three times in a single year (starting from the date of your first test).

Examinees who score at least 80 percent on the test are certified with *Advanced ColdFusion Developer* status. So to stand out from the crowd, you need to know your stuff, and know it well.

The test is available a variety of languages. The questions are the same in each language, so content studied using this book is applicable regardless of the language you are being tested in.

What You'll Be Tested On

Being a ColdFusion expert requires that you know more than just ColdFusion. As such, the exam includes questions on related technologies. The subjects you'll be tested on are as follows:

- ColdFusion functionality
- ColdFusion Markup Language (CFML) usage and syntax
- Internet and Web fundamentals
- ColdFusion extensibility features and technologies
- Basic Hypertext Markup Language (HTML) and related client technologies
- Database fundamentals and concepts
- Structured Query Language (SQL)

Every question counts, and you cannot assume that one particular topic is more or less significant than others. You need to know it all, and you need to know it all well.

Preparing for the Exam

Obviously, the most important preparation for the exam is the use of ColdFusion itself. If you do not use ColdFusion regularly, or have not done so for an extended period, then you probably will not pass.

Having said that, we can tell you that many experienced ColdFusion developers still find the exam challenging. Usually, they say this because they don't use some features and technologies, or because they have learned the product but have never paid attention to changing language and feature details (and thus are not using the product as effectively as they could be).

And that is where this book fits in. This book is not a cheat sheet. It will not teach you ColdFusion from scratch, nor will it give you a list of things to remember to pass the test. What it will do is help you systematically review every major (and minor) feature and technology of the product—everything that you need to know to pass the test.

Where to Take the Exam

To offer the exams in as many locations as possible, Macromedia has partnered with a company called Virtual University Enterprises (VUE). VUE offers exams and certification programs for a wide range of companies and products, and it has more than 2,500 regional testing facilities in more than 100 countries.

You can take the *ColdFusion Certified Developer* exam at any VUE testing center. For a list of current locations, visit the following Web site:

```
http://www.vue.com/macromedia/
```

How Much It Costs

The fee to take the exam in North America is $150. Pricing in other countries varies. The fee must be paid at the time you register. If you need to cancel, you must do so at least 24 hours before the exam, or the fee will not be refunded.

How to Use This Book

This book is designed to be used in two ways:

- To prepare for your exam, you should start at the beginning of the book and systematically work your way through it. The book flow, layout, and form factor have all been specially designed to make reviewing content as pleasant an experience as possible. The content has been designed to be highly readable and digestible in small, bite-size chunks so that it will feel more like reading than studying.
- After you have reviewed all content, reread the topics that you feel you need extra help brushing up on. Topics are covered in highly focused and very manageable chapters so that you can easily drill down to the exact content you need. And extensive cross-referencing allows you to read up on related topics as needed.

Even after the exam, you'll find that the style and design of this book makes it an invaluable desktop reference tool as well.

Contents

The book is divided into eight parts, each containing a set of highly focused chapters. Each chapter concludes with a summary and sample questions (the answers to which are in the Appendix).

Part I: The Basics

This part covers the basics of Internet development in general and ColdFusion development in particular, and includes chapters on the following topics:

- Web Technology and Terminology
- Working with Variables and Expressions

- Conditional Processing
- Looping
- Redirects and Reuse
- The Application Framework
- Using Databases

Part II: Variables and Expressions

This part covers the use of different variable types, scopes, and expressions, and includes chapters on the following topics:

- `URL` Variables
- `FORM` Variables
- `APPLICATION` and `SERVER` Variables
- Session State Management
- Locking

Part III: Data Types

This part covers the data types supported by ColdFusion, and includes chapters on the following topics:

- Lists
- Arrays
- Structures

Part IV: User Interface & Data Presentation

This part covers the ColdFusion features used to collect and present data, and includes chapters on the following topics:

- Flash Forms
- XForms
- Printing
- Reporting
- Graphing

Part V: Advanced ColdFusion

This part covers a wide range of advanced development technologies and features, and includes chapters on the following topics:

- Scripting
- Dynamic Functions
- Stored Procedures
- Transactions
- Debugging
- Error Handling
- Application Security

Part VI: Extending ColdFusion

This part covers ColdFusion's extensibility features, and includes chapters on the following topics:

- Custom Tags
- Advanced Custom Tags
- User-Defined Functions
- ColdFusion Components
- Web Services
- Java, COM, & CORBA
- XML
- WDDX
- Flash Remoting
- Event Gateways

Part VII: Services and Protocols

This part covers the services and protocols supported by ColdFusion, and includes chapters on the following topics:

- Full-Text Searching
- System Integration
- Scheduling and Event Execution

- Email Integration
- LDAP
- Other Internet Protocols

Part VIII: Databases

This part covers database concepts and terminology, and includes chapters on the following topics:

- Basic SQL
- Joins
- Aggregates
- Advanced Database Features
- Improving Performance

Part IX: Tuning and Optimization

This part covers tuning and performance-optimization techniques, and includes chapters on the following topics:

- Application Performance Tuning and Optimization
- Server Performance Tuning

Conventions Used in This Book

The publishers have spent many years developing and creating computer books designed for ease of use and filled with the most up-to-date information available. With that experience, we've learned what features help you the most. Look for these features throughout the book to help enhance your learning experience and get the most out of ColdFusion.

- Screen messages, code listings, and command samples appear in `monospace` type.
- URLs that identify pages on the Web and values for ColdFusion attributes also appear in `monospace` type.
- Terms that are defined in the text appear in *italics*. *Italics* are sometimes used for emphasis too.

> **TIP**
>
> Tips give you advice on quick or overlooked procedures, including shortcuts.

> **NOTE**
> Notes present useful or interesting information that isn't necessarily essential to the current discussion, but which might augment your understanding with background material or advice relating to the topic.

> **CAUTION**
> Cautions warn you about potential problems that a procedure might cause, such as unexpected results or mistakes that could prove costly.

Cross-references are designed to point you to other locations in this book that will provide supplemental or supporting information. Cross-references appear as follows:

➜ Arrays and structures are covered in detail in Chapter 14, "Arrays," and Chapter 15, "Structures."

The Accompanying Web Site

To further assist you in preparing for the exam, this book has an accompanying Web site. This site contains the following:

- Updated exam information, should there be any
- Links to other exam-related sites
- Book corrections or errata, should there be any
- A sample interactive test that can help gauge your exam readiness

The URL is `http://www.forta.com/books/0321330110/`

In addition, book support is available via an online forum at `http://forums.forta.com/`

Where to Go from Here

Now you're ready to get started. If you think you're ready for the exam, start with the sample questions (in the book or online) to find out for sure. If you're not ready (or if the sample questions indicate that you might not be as ready as you thought), make sure to pay close attention to the areas you need to focus on most by reading the documentation and actually writing appropriate applications.

When you're ready, work through this book to review the content and prepare for the exam as described here.

And with that, we wish you good luck!

PART 1 The Basics

IN THIS PART

CHAPTER 1

Web Technology and Terminology

IN THIS CHAPTER

The Basics

Effective ColdFusion development requires a solid understanding of Internet and Web concepts, terms, and technologies. So, in this first chapter, we'll start with a brief review of these.

The Internet

The Internet is simply the world's biggest computer network. It connects millions of hosts (computers, servers, devices, and so on) to each other so that they can communicate and interact.

The Internet is not a physical entity, nor is it any particular host or set of hosts. You could never point to a machine and identify it as the Internet, nor could you ever turn the Internet on or off. The Internet is a living entity, and one that is evolving and changing all the time.

IP

The Internet is held together by IP, the Internet Protocol, and every host connected to the Internet must be running a copy of IP.

IP requires every host to have a unique address by which to identify it. The unique identifiers are IP addresses that (in the current version of IP) are made up of four sets of numbers separated by periods—for example, `65.36.166.120`. Some hosts have fixed (or *static*) IP addresses; others have dynamically assigned addresses. Regardless of how an IP address is obtained, no two hosts connected to the Internet may use the same IP address at any given time. (The exception to this rule is the addressing used in a private network, which needs to be unique only within that network.)

> **NOTE**
> The IP address `127.0.0.1` always points to the local machine.

DNS

IP addresses are the only way to uniquely specify a host. When you want to communicate with, for example, a Web server host, you must specify the IP address of the Web server you're trying to contact. Similarly, when you connect to an FTP server, or specify the SMTP and POP servers in your mail client, you must specify the name of the host to which you want to connect.

As you know from browsing the Web, you rarely specify IP addresses directly. You do, however, specify a host name, such as `www.forta.com`. If hosts are identified by IP address, how does your browser know which Web server to contact when you specify a host name?

The answer is the Domain Name Service (DNS), a mechanism that maps host names to IP addresses. When you specify the destination address of `www.forta.com`, your browser sends an address resolution request to a DNS server, asking for the IP address of that host. The DNS server returns an actual IP address—in this case, `65.36.166.120`. Your browser can then use this address to communicate with the host directly.

DNS is rarely required. Users can usually specify the name of a destination host by its IP address to connect to the host. There are, however, some very good reasons not to use the IP address:

- IP addresses are hard to remember and easy to mistype. Users are more likely to find `www.forta.com` than they are `65.36.166.120`.
- IP addresses are subject to change. For example, if you switch service providers, you might be forced to use a new set of IP addresses for your hosts. If users identified your site only by its IP address, they could never reach your host if the IP address changed. Your DNS name stays the same, even if your IP address switches. You need to change only the mapping so that the host name maps to the new, correct IP address.
- Multiple hosts, each with unique IP addresses, can all have the same DNS name. This allows load balancing between servers, as well as the establishment of redundant servers.

- A single host, with a single IP address, can have multiple DNS names. This enables you to create aliases if needed. For example, `ftp.forta.com` and `www.forta.com` might point to the same IP address, and thus the same server.

> **NOTE**
> The host name `localhost` always points to the IP address `127.0.0.1`, the local machine.

The World Wide Web

The Web is what put the Internet on the map and made it a household word. Many people mistakenly think the Internet is the Web. The truth, however, is that the Web is merely an application that sits on top of the Internet.

The Web is built on the Hypertext Transfer Protocol (HTTP). HTTP is designed to be a small, fast protocol that is well suited for distributed multimedia information systems and hypertext jumps between sites.

Information on the Web is stored in pages. A page can contain any of the following:

- Text
- Lists
- Tables
- Graphics
- Headers
- Menus
- Forms
- Multimedia
- Embedded objects and plug-ins (like Macromedia Flash)

Each Web page is an actual file saved on a host. When a Web page is requested, the file containing the Web page is read and its contents are sent to the host that asked for it.

A *Web site* is simply a collection of Web pages along with any supporting files (such as GIF or JPEG graphics). Creating a Web site thus involves creating one or more Web pages and linking them. The Web site is then saved on a Web server.

Web Servers

The Web consists of pages of information stored on hosts running Web server software. The host is often referred to as the *Web server*, which is technically inaccurate. The Web server is actually software, not the computer itself. Versions of Web server software can run on almost all computers, and although most Web server applications do have minimum hardware requirements, no special computer is needed to host a Web server.

Originally, all Web development was performed under different flavors of Unix. While most Web servers still run on Unix boxes, this is changing. There are now Web servers for most major operating systems. Web servers hosted on high-performance operating systems, such as Windows 2000 and Windows 2003, are becoming more and more popular because Unix can be more expensive to run than Windows, and is also more difficult to use for the average user. Windows 2000 and 2003 have proven themselves to be efficient, reliable, and cost-effective platforms for hosting Web servers. As a result, the Windows slice of the Web server operating system pie is growing dramatically.

So what exactly is a Web server? It's a program that serves up Web pages upon request. Web servers typically don't know or care what they're serving. When a user at a specific IP address requests a specific file (a Web page, or a part thereof), the Web server tries to retrieve that file and send it back to the user. The requested file might be the HTML source code for a Web page, a GIF image, a Flash movie, an AVI file, and so on. The Web browser, not the Web server, determines what should be requested. The Web server merely processes that request.

Pages are stored on the Web server beneath the Web *root*—a directory or folder designated to contain all the files that make up the Web site. When a request is made for a specific page within a specific directory, that page is retrieved from the appropriate directory beneath the Web root.

Web servers enable administrators to specify a default Web page, a page that is sent back to the user when only a directory is specified. These default pages are often called `index.html` or `default.htm`. If no default Web page exists in a particular directory, the server returns either an error message or a list of all available files (depending on how the server is set up).

Web Browsers

A Web browser is the program used to view Web pages. The Web browser has the job of processing received Web pages, parsing the HTML code, and displaying the page to users. The browser attempts to display graphics, tables, forms, formatted text, and whatever else the page contains. The most popular Web browsers are Microsoft Internet Explorer and various Mozilla based browsers (like Firefox).

Web page designers must pay close attention to the distinctions between browsers because various Web browsers behave differently. Web pages are created using HTML (a language that we'll look at in a few moments). Unfortunately, not all browsers implement all of HTML consistently. Furthermore, the same Web page often looks different on two separate browsers because every browser renders and displays Web page objects in its own way.

For this reason, most Web page designers use multiple browsers and test their pages in every one to ensure that the final output appears as intended. Without this testing, some Web site visitors can't correctly see the pages you publish.

To request a Web page, the browser user must specify the page's address. The address is known as the *URL*.

> **NOTE**
>
> Web browsers communicate with Web servers and provide information about themselves to the servers. That information is then made available to application servers (such as ColdFusion). Within ColdFusion code, these variables are accessed using the `CGI` scope.

URLs

Every Web page (and indeed every object, even individual graphics) on the Web has an address. That is what you type into your browser to instruct it to load a particular Web page.

URLs are made up of as many as five parts:

- The protocol to use to retrieve the object. This is always `http` for objects on the Web (or `https` for requests over secure connections).
- The Web server from which to retrieve the object. This is specified as a DNS name or an IP address.
- The host machine port on which the Web server is running. If omitted, the specified protocol's default port is used; for Web servers, this port is `80`.
- The file to retrieve or the script to execute. The filename often includes a complete file path.
- Optional script parameters, also known as the *query string*.

There are generally two ways to go to a specific URL. The first is typing the URL in the Web browser's address field (or selecting it from a saved bookmark or favorite). The second is clicking a link within a Web page—a link is simply a reference to another URL. When a user clicks a link, the browser requests whatever URL it references.

HTML

Web pages are plain text files constructed with HTML. HTML is implemented as a series of easy-to-learn *tags*, or instructions. Web page authors use these tags to mark up a page of text. Browsers then use these tags to render and display the information for viewing.

HTML tags are always placed between < and >. For example, to force a paragraph break, you would specify `<P>`.

> **NOTE**
> Even though HTML is tag-based, it is not strictly typed as XML is. For example, HTML is case-insensitive, not all tags have matching end tags, and most browsers accommodate badly formed HTML rather well.

Some tags take one or more parameters in the form of attributes. Attributes are used to specify optional or additional information to a tag. Some tags have no attributes, while some have many. Attributes are almost always optional and can be specified in any order you want. Attributes must be separated from each other by a space, and attribute values should ideally be enclosed within double quotation marks.

HTML is constantly being enhanced with new features and added tags. To ensure backward compatibility, browsers must ignore tags they don't understand. For example, if you were to use the `<marquee>` tag to create a scrolling text marquee, browsers that don't support this tag will still display the marquee text, but it won't scroll. (And no, don't use the `<marquee>` tag, that was just an example).

Web browsers ignore white space, so the following two lines will be displayed identically:

```
My name is Ben
My      name      is      Ben
```

Many characters have special significance to HTML. For example, the double quotation mark character is used to delimit fields and should therefore not be used in plain text. To display these characters, *entity references* are used; for example, `"` for a double quotation mark character. Entity references always begin with an ampersand character (`&`), so to display an ampersand, the entity reference `&` is used. Entity references are available for all special characters, including formatting and international characters.

JavaScript

Most current Web browsers allow the execution of JavaScript within Web pages. JavaScript is used to programmatically control the browser and the content it displays. JavaScript cannot be used to access the file system or to perform system-level operations—its scope is limited to the browser.

JavaScript plays an important part in usable and intuitive Web design in that it allows for more sophisticated and interactive user interface design, which in turn results in a richer and more rewarding user experience.

> **NOTE**
> JavaScript is not Java, and has nothing to do with Java. JavaScript is a scripting language, and Java is a true development language.

VBScript is another scripting language, but for the most part it is supported only by Microsoft Internet Explorer and is used far less than JavaScript.

Cascading Style Sheets

Cascading Style Sheets (often referred to as CSS) provide a mechanism by which to separate content from presentation. Instead of embedding HTML formatting in your text, you can create style definitions that the browser applies automatically when content is displayed.

Styles are associated with HTML types, so body text, links, headers, tables, and more can have associated attributes (everything from colors, fonts, and spacing to special effects that are not available using inline formatting). Additional styles can be created, too, so that developers can have maximum control over generated output.

All current browsers support CSS, although there are differences in the support. As such, any time CSS is used, thorough testing must be performed in as many browsers as possible.

Dynamic HTML

Dynamic HTML (or DHTML) is actually not a feature; it's a collection of features that when used together facilitates powerful browser UI control. DHTML combines HTML, scripting (usually JavaScript), CSS, and the DOM (document object model—a convention that provides naming and programmatic access to every element of every page within a browser) to enable developers to write code that can be used to create very rich and sophisticated user interfaces.

The biggest problem with DHTML is that it is dependent on all of the aforementioned technologies, and their support differs dramatically from one browser to the next. As such, effective DHTML development often requires creating multiple versions of pages (or parts of pages) and intelligently including the appropriate ones as needed.

Application Servers

As explained earlier, Web servers don't do that much—they serve content that is read from disk. Application servers are software applications that extend Web servers, allowing them to do things they couldn't do on their own. These include:

- Accessing databases
- Sending and receiving email
- Manipulating XML data
- Personalizing content
- Building ecommerce applications
- Powering rich Internet applications
- Much more

Application servers usually rely on the underlying Web servers for all host-to-host communication (sending data to and from the browser, for example). When a request is to be processed by an application server, the Web server receives the request from the client, hands it to the application server for processing, and then returns the output from that processing to the client.

Web servers are primarily used to serve static content. Static content is usually stored in HTML files directly (and supporting image files perhaps). These files are created in editors, and they are rendered and displayed just as they were created.

Application servers are used to provide dynamic content. Dynamic content is built at run time based on external criteria. Information could be retrieved from databases, user input could be solicited, and more. All this information is then used to build an application that generates output that could be different each time it is requested.

Static content is essentially the electronic form of print-based publishing. The true power of the Web is realized in dynamic content.

ColdFusion Fundamentals

ColdFusion behaves as an application server, and it functions as described in the previous section. ColdFusion runs on all major operating systems, but regardless of the operating system used, it functions the same way. The core services (or *daemons*) are always running, and requests are submitted to them for processing as they come in.

> **NOTE**
>
> I stated that ColdFusion behaves as an application, and not that it is an application server. The distinction is subtle, but is one worth noting. Earlier versions of ColdFusion were indeed application servers themselves, but not anymore. As of ColdFusion MX, ColdFusion is a J2EE application that is deployed on top of industry standard J2EE servers. ColdFusion thus behaves like a server (in that it responds to incoming requests and returns results) but is actually an application running on an underlying J2EE server.

How ColdFusion Works

ColdFusion processes requests when instructed to do so by the Web server. ColdFusion processes scripts (usually `.cfm` files) and generates output, which is then sent to the client.

ColdFusion is completely client agnostic, and thus supports every client technology (including HTML, JavaScript, and VBScript). The ColdFusion instructions within the scripts are processed on the server and are never sent to the client. The generated client code is sent to the client as is.

ColdFusion provides interfaces to all major back-end technologies, including:

- Databases (via JDBC or other drivers)
- Email (POP and SMTP)
- Internet protocols (HTTP, FTP, and LDAP)
- XML and Web Services
- Any other technology that can be accessed via Java, C/C++, COM, or CORBA

ColdFusion applications are made up of sets of `.cfm` files, just like Web sites are made up of sets of HTML files. ColdFusion applications are simply sets of scripts in a directory structure of your choice (usually under the Web root).

> **NOTE**
>
> `.cfm` files are plain-text files and are usually stored and deployed as such. However, it is possible to compile ColdFusion source into Java bytecode which can be deployed and distributed without the original source code, providing a degree of code protection.

CFML

ColdFusion code is written in CFML—the ColdFusion Markup Language. This is a tag-based language (much like HTML), and tags are used to perform everything from conditional processing to database integration and more. In addition, ColdFusion developers can extend the CFML language by writing their own tags.

CFML also features a rich set of functions that can be used for all sorts of data manipulation. Unlike tags, which perform specific operations, functions return data (or manipulate data). ColdFusion developers can also create their own functions.

Summary

Effective ColdFusion development requires a solid understanding of Internet and Web-related technologies. The Internet provides the backbone on which to build Web-based applications, and ColdFusion is an application server that extends the capabilities of the Web.

Sample Questions

1. Which of the following are valid parts of a URL? *(select three)*
   - **A.** Protocol
   - **B.** Port
   - **C.** CGI variables
   - **D.** Query string
2. Which protocols may be used to access ColdFusion? *(select two)*
   - **A.** `ftp`
   - **B.** `http`
   - **C.** `https`
   - **D.** `pop`
3. Which of the following can ColdFusion access? *(select three)*
   - **A.** Databases
   - **B.** Client-side files
   - **C.** XML data
   - **D.** Microsoft Word
4. The CFML language is made up of *(select two)*
   - **A.** Tags
   - **B.** XML
   - **C.** Functions
   - **D.** JavaScript

CHAPTER 2

Working with Variables and Expressions

IN THIS CHAPTER

Understanding Variables and Expressions

Simple in concept, ColdFusion variables are key to building dynamic Web pages. They provide placeholders in which to put different values. ColdFusion variables are used in expressions. Expressions are generally used in two ways: inside a `<cfoutput>` block to build output on a Web page, and to the right of equals signs (=) in `<cfset>` statements.

> **NOTE**
>
> Remember the following rules when naming ColdFusion variables:
>
> - Names must contain letters, numbers, and the underscore characters only.
> - Each name must start with a letter.
> - Spaces and any special characters besides the underscore are not allowed.

But what exactly is an expression? The ColdFusion documentation says that expressions are "language constructs that allow you to create sophisticated applications." The best way to define an expression is to say it is simply a combination of the following:

- Operands such as integers, strings, real numbers, arrays, query results, and variables
- Operators such as +, `MOD`, and `AND`
- Functions that return changed data such as `UCase()` and `DateFormat()`

In other words, the following is an expression:

```
#var#
```

as is

```
100
```

Expressions can also include calculations, like this:

```
var2-var1
```

Expressions may be used with CFML tags as well as in output, so this is valid:

```
<cfset result=var2-var1>
```

as is

```
<cfoutput>#var2-var1#</cfoutput>
```

> **TIP**
>
> ColdFusion variable names can be variables themselves. If you want to assign a value to a variable, simply use `<cfset>` with the variable name to the left of the = and quotation marks and #s as follows:
>
> ```
> <cfset "#TheVar#"=15>
> ```

Variables and Type

ColdFusion variables are *typeless*. Unlike many other computer languages, ColdFusion does not require that you tell it what type of data will be stored in the variable before it is used. So how does ColdFusion know what type of data a variable holds? The decision is made when you use the variable in an expression.

First, consider the assignment statement below:

```
<cfset TheVar="10">
```

This statement sets a *typeless* variable equal to `10`. Is it the number `10` or the string `10`? It does not matter at this point.

Now look at the variable in another assignment statement below:

```
<cfset TheNumber=TheVar+5>
```

The arithmetic operator + is used here. It dynamically casts the type of `TheVar` to be a number. `TheNumber` is set to equal the number `15`.

Now consider the variable again in another assignment, this time concatenating strings:

```
<cfset TheString="The number is " & TheVar>
```

This time a variable called `TheString` is set equal to the text `"The number is "` and then concatenated with `TheVar`. This assignment dynamically sets the type of `TheVar` to be a string. `TheString` is set equal to `"The number is 10"`.

> **NOTE**
> ColdFusion variables are typeless when created. The type is cast when the variables are later used with an operator.

→ Although ColdFusion expressions are typeless, not all variables in a ColdFusion template can be used as such. When writing SQL, you must surround strings with single quotes. For more information on using SQL with ColdFusion, see Chapter 7, "Using Databases."

Variable Prefixes

ColdFusion supports many different variable types, and when referring to variables the type may be specified as a prefix in the format `prefix.variable`. Many developers believe the best practice is to always use prefixes, but prefixes actually are not required in every instance. The following variables do not need to have a prefix:

- Query result variables (if in a `<cfoutput>` loop)
- Local variables
- `CGI` variables
- File variables
- `URL` variables
- `FORM` variables
- `COOKIE` variables
- `CLIENT` variables

> **NOTE**
> A variable's scope determines where it exists, how long it exists, and where its values are stored. The variable's prefix determines its scope.

Reason One to Use Prefixes: Performance

The first reason to use a variable prefix is performance. Consider a variable called `TheVar` that is used in an expression and not prefixed. ColdFusion must find the value for that variable. ColdFusion must look in each variable scope for the `TheVar` variable and its associated value. The closer the variable is to the bottom of the order of evaluation hierarchy, the longer it will take to retrieve the value of the variable.

> **TIP**
>
> For variable scopes that do not require prefixes, the order of evaluation is as follows:
>
> 1. Query result variables (if in a `<cfoutput>` loop)
> 2. Function local variables (with user defined functions and ColdFusion Component methods)
> 3. `ARGUMENTS` (within a user-defined function or ColdFusion Component)
> 4. Local variables
> 5. `CGI` variables
> 6. `URL` variables
> 7. `FORM` variables
> 8. `COOKIE` variables
> 9. `CLIENT` variables

Reason Two to Use Prefixes: Avoiding Ambiguity

Problems can arise when the same variable name comes from two different scopes. Consider the following two assignment statements:

```
<cfset TestVar="Local">
<cfcookie name="TestVar" value="Cookie">
```

The variable will be displayed using this statement:

```
<cfoutput>#TestVar#</cfoutput>
```

When evaluated, the value `"Local"` would be displayed. The `COOKIE` variable called `TestVar` is set after the local variable `TestVar`, but because of the order of evaluation, the local variable's value is displayed when the expression is evaluated. If you want to display the value of the `COOKIE` variable, you have to use the `COOKIE` prefix.

A Reason Not to Use Prefixes: Flexibility

Consider a template that is both the action page of a form and the target of a URL. A variable of the same name is passed in from each page. In this scenario, by not using a prefix, the template would work in both cases. The nonprefixed variable could act as both a `FORM` and `URL` variable.

Using Local Variables

As you can see from this chapter so far, `<cfset>` is very helpful in assigning values to variables. If the variable already exists, `<cfset>` resets the value.

A common problem in Web development is using variables when you are not sure they exist. The `<cfparam>` tag can assist you in this situation. If the tag:

```
<cfparam name="TheVar" default="Default Value">
```

did not exist, you could replace it with the following code:

```
<cfif NOT IsDefined("TheVar")>
 <cfset TheVar="Default Value">
</cfif>
```

A lesser-known use of `<cfparam>` is checking the data type of a variable. The `type` attribute checks the data type, and if it is not of the type specified, an error is thrown. For example, if a variable is assigned using the statement:

```
<cfset TheVar="Hello">
```

the following `<cfparam>` would generate an error:

```
<cfparam name="TheVar" type="numeric" default="15">
```

The following values are valid for use with the `type` attribute:

- `any`
- `array`
- `binary`
- `boolean`
- `creditcard`
- `date` (may also be specified as `usdate`)
- `email`
- `eurodate`
- `float`
- `guid`
- `integer`
- `numeric`
- `query`
- `regex` (may also be specified as `regular_expression`)
- `ssn` (may also be specified as `social_security_number`)
- `string`
- `struct`
- `telephone`

- `time`
- `url`
- `uuid`
- `variableName`
- `xml`
- `zipcode`

➜ Generating an error is not always a bad thing. In Chapter 26, "Error Handling," you'll see how you can catch the error and programmatically deal with it.

> **CAUTION**
> When you're using `<cfparam>` and no prefix is used with the variable whose existence you are checking, remember that the tag looks through all scopes that do not require a prefix for a variable of that name. You may think you are checking for the existence of `VARIABLES.TheVar`, but if `FORM.TheVar` exists, `<cfparam>` assumes the variable exists.

Using #s

In the examples shown so far in this chapter, no prefixes have been used with `<cfset>` or `<cfparam>`. This creates a variable, called a "local" variable, whose scope is only the local page. The `VARIABLES` prefix is used with local variables.

> **NOTE**
> Remember that local variables can also be used in included templates.

When you use local variables, you sometimes must use the number sign (#) around them. The pair of #s basically tells ColdFusion that what is inside them must be processed, or the variable needs to be distinguished from plain text. Some common uses of local variables are displaying them within `<cfoutput>` tags and using them in expressions.

> **TIP**
> Because of the ambiguity over when to use #s in early versions of ColdFusion, they are sometimes overused. If you're unsure whether to use `#s`, remember the following rules:
>
> - #s are always needed when ColdFusion variables are used outside or between pairs of ColdFusion tags.
> - #s are never needed when used inside ColdFusion tags, unless the variable is inside quotation marks.

Variables and the REQUEST Scope

One limitation of local variables is that they can be used only in the page where they are created (and in any included page), but not within other code being executed (for example, Custom Tag code). To create variables that can be used by all code being processed use the REQUEST scope. Because the scope is the entire page request, the values are carried through to nested tags, such as custom tags. So instead of continually passing the same value to custom tags, you put in the REQUEST scope.

→ A great place to set these REQUEST scope variables is in the Application.cfc or Application.cfm files.

→ You'll see how to use custom tags and pass data to them in Chapter 28, "Custom Tags," and Chapter 29, "Advanced Custom Tags."

You therefore can set a variable using the REQUEST scope and then use that variable in custom tags. You create a variable in the REQUEST scope as shown in the following example:

```
<cfset REQUEST.AppDSN="StoreData">
```

Dumping Variable Contents

When debugging, it is often useful to be able to inspect the contents of a variable. Simple variables can be displayed by merely enclosing them within <cfoutput> tags, but more complex variables (for example, arrays and structures, which are explained in Chapters 14 and 15 respectively) cannot be displayed in this way.

To solve this problem, you may use the <cfdump> tag, which displays a variable (even a complex nested variable) in a clean, easy-to-read format. You'd never actually use <cfdump> in final production code, but this tag is invaluable during development and debugging. For example, to display a single variable you could use the following code:

```
<cfdump var="#TestVar#">
```

You may also use this tag to display sets of variables. For example, to display all variables in the REQUEST scope, you could do the following:

```
<cfdump var="#REQUEST#">
```

> TIP
>
> <cfdump> takes an expression as the value passed to VAR, not a variable name. To refer to a variable within the specified expression, #s must be used.

Functions

Functions return manipulated values for use in, for example, expressions. The functions do not change the data they are acting on; rather, they produce a result or return a value for output.

ColdFusion functions take the form `FunctionName(argument)`. The argument may be nothing, like when you're using the function `Now()`, which returns the current date and time.

For a simple example, consider this assignment:

```
<cfset Convert=UCase("hello")>
```

The function used here is `UCase()`, which converts a string into all uppercase characters. The argument is the string `"hello"`. The function does its work, and the assignment statement stores the string `"HELLO"` into the local variable `Convert`.

> **NOTE**
>
> #s can sometimes be confusing when you're using functions with ColdFusion variables. The proper way to use #s with a function and variable is as follows:
>
> `#DateFormat(SellDate)#`
>
> not:
>
> `#DateFormat(#SellDate#)#`

Nested Functions

Functions can also be nested. This means the argument of a function can be another function itself. A very common example of nesting is using the `DateFormat()` function with the `Now()` function, as follows:

```
DateFormat(Now())
```

Functions with Masks

Some functions also have another option called a *mask*. Functions that do formatting often have masks so that they can be tailored to an individual developer's needs. Again, consider the `DateFormat()` function. Say you want to change the default format to a date in the form `mm/dd/yy`. You do so as follows:

```
DateFormat(Now(),"mm/dd/yy")
```

The mask appears in quotation marks, separated from the argument by a comma.

Strings

Strings are text values, which, when used, can be surrounded by either single or double quotation marks.

String manipulation is part of any Web developer's task. You can manipulate strings in two ways in ColdFusion: constant string manipulation and regular expression string manipulation. ColdFusion offers a complete set of string functions to aid in this task.

Constant String Manipulation

If you know the exact string you want to work with—even if it is part of a bigger string—you can use constant string manipulation. Constant string manipulation tasks can range from the simple, such as being sure no blank spaces are part of a string, to the complex, such as searching a page of text for the last example of an HTML table and extracting that table for use in another page.

Using the powerful string functions helps make your life simpler when you're faced with these kinds of tasks. For instance, when you're pre-filling a form control, you might need to be sure that no leading or trailing spaces are included with the value in the form control. The `Trim()` function, which follows, fits the job perfectly:

```
<input type="Text" name="FName" value="#Trim(FName)#">
```

Regular Expression String Manipulation

If you know only the pattern of the string you want to work with, you need to use regular expression string manipulation. A subset of the string functions deals with regular expressions. You can recognize them by the `RE` in front of the expression names. For instance, you might see a `Replace()` function and a `REReplace()` function.

An example of regular expression string manipulation is looking for a dollar amount in some text when the exact dollar amount is not known. You need to write a regular expression and then use it with one of the appropriate functions.

The appropriate regular expression to find all dollar amounts is as follows:

```
$[0-9,.]*
```

Then, to find the location of the first instance of a dollar amount, you use the following statement:

```
<cfset TheLocation=REFind("$[0-9,.]*",TheString)>
```

> **NOTE**
>
> For an introduction to regular expressions, see my *Sams Teach Yourself Regular Expressions in 10 Minutes* (Sams, ISBN 0672325667).

Summary

ColdFusion variables and expressions are the building blocks of most ColdFusion development. ColdFusion variables are *typeless* upon creation, and the type is then cast when used with an operator. Variable prefixes determine the scope of the variable, and using them is almost always a good idea. `<CFSET>` and `<CFPARAM>` are essential tools in creating variables. Using the request scope is a very helpful way to extend the places where local variables can be used. Functions can be used to return manipulated variable values. Both constant and regular expression string manipulation are possible in ColdFusion.

Sample Questions

1. Expressions are a combination of operands, operators, and functions. Which of the following are operands? *(select two)*

   A. ColdFusion variables

   B. `MOD`

   C. `34`

   D. `LCase()`

2. When no prefix is used, which scope would be used if values existed in all of the following for a variable of the same name?

   A. `FORM`

   B. `URL`

   C. `CLIENT`

   D. `COOKIE`

3. Which of the following is the best syntax for an assignment statement?

   A. `<cfset #PassingDate#=#DateFormat(Now())#>`

   B. `<cfset PassingDate=#DateFormat(Now())#>`

   C. `<cfset #PassingDate#=DateFormat(Now())>`

   D. `<cfset PassingDate=DateFormat(Now())>`

4. Which tag provides the greatest flexibility in verifying the presence of a variable and determining that its contents are valid?

   A. `<cfif>`

   B. `<cfdump>`

   C. `<cfparam>`

   D. `<cfoutput>`

5. What would the following code snippet display?

   ```
   <cfset name="Ben">
   <cfdump var="name">
   ```

   A. The name `Ben`

   B. The word `VAR`

   C. The word `name`

CHAPTER 3

Conditional Processing

IN THIS CHAPTER

What Is Conditional Processing?

Conditional processing is the result of code reacting to specified conditions and behaving differently based on those conditions. When application behavior depends on data that is not known at the time of development, such as user data or query information, conditional processing is an essential tool.

Performing Conditional Processing

ColdFusion employs a number of tags to implement conditional processing. The simplest is the `<cfif>`/`<cfelse>` tag set. In addition, in some situations the `<cfswitch>` tag is a better choice.

`<cfif>`

The `<cfif>` tag can take various forms. The simplest is as follows:

```
<cfif expression>
 Code performed if condition true
</cfif>
```

The expression must evaluate to `TRUE` or `FALSE`. Usually, this is some condition using an operator—for example, `TheVar IS 40`. Regardless of the outcome of the evaluation of the expression (either true or false), program flow continues after the `</cfif>` tag.

> **TIP**
>
> Remember that ColdFusion's operators are different to what you may be used to in other programming languages. For example, a condition cannot use the = sign, but instead uses the word `IS`. The operators are shown in the following table.

Table 3.1 lists the supported `<cfif>` operators:

Table 3.1 `<cfif>` Operators

COLDFUSION OPERATOR	SYMBOL
IS, EQUAL, EQ	=
IS NOT, NOT EQUAL, NEQ	<>
GT, GREATER THAN	>
LT, LESS THAN	<
GTE, GREATER THAN OR EQUAL	>=
LTE, LESS THAN OR EQUAL	<=

Expressions to be evaluated as TRUE or FALSE can take many different forms, not just a condition using an operator. Many ColdFusion functions return a value that can be evaluated to TRUE or FALSE. Remember that numbers are inherently TRUE or FALSE in ColdFusion.

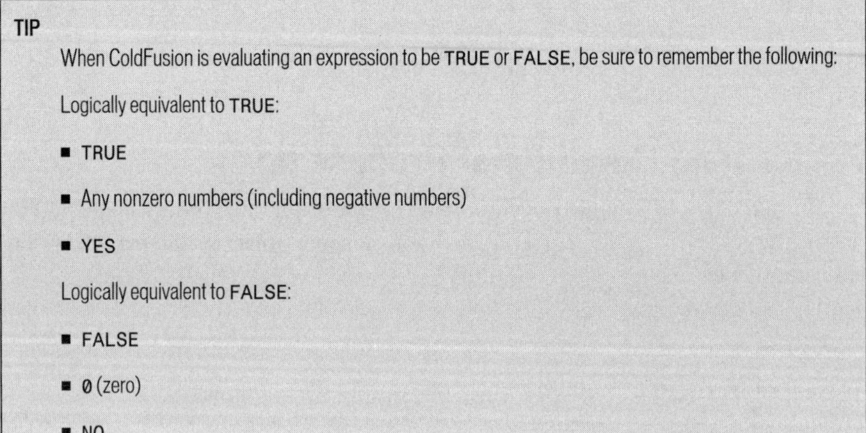

TIP

When ColdFusion is evaluating an expression to be **TRUE** or **FALSE**, be sure to remember the following:

Logically equivalent to **TRUE**:

- TRUE
- Any nonzero numbers (including negative numbers)
- YES

Logically equivalent to **FALSE**:

- FALSE
- 0 (zero)
- NO

The next step in using `<cfif>` is to add an *else* clause. The logic then becomes an either/or situation. The general format is shown here:

```
<cfif expression>
 Code performed if expression is true
<cfelse>
 Code performed if expression is false
</cfif>
```

With a single else clause, still only one expression is evaluated. The `<cfif>` statement can be extended in yet another way, using `<cfelseif>`. This method offers the opportunity to have multiple conditions. The general format is as follows:

```
<cfif expression1>
 Code performed if expression1 is true
<cfelseif expression2>
 Code performed if expression2 is true
<cfelse>
 Code performed if no expressions are true
</cfif>
```

Note that the `<cfelse>` is always optional.

> **TIP**
>
> If you put the most common cases in the first **`<cfelseif>`**, the amount of processing is minimized and performance can be improved.

<cfswitch>

If you have a long list of condition values to be tested, you might be better off using `<cfswitch>`. Many languages refer to this logic as a `CASE` statement. The general format is as follows:

```
<cfswitch expression="expression">
 <cfcase value="value">
 HTML and CFML tags
 </cfcase>
 additional <cfcase></cfcase> tags
 <cfdefaultcase>
 HTML and CFML tags
 </cfdefaultcase>
</cfswitch>
```

With this control structure, you specify the value in each `<cfcase>` statement that will possibly match the expression in the `<cfswitch>` line. The following is a very simple example:

```
<cfswitch expression="World">
 <cfcase value="Hello">
 Hello was matched
 </cfcase>
 <cfcase value="World">
 World was matched
 </cfcase>
 <cfdefaultcase>
 Neither Hello nor World was matched
 </cfdefaultcase>
</cfswitch>
```

In this case, the code would display `"World was matched"`. If neither `Hello` nor `World` were the expression in the `<cfswitch>`, the `<cfdefaultcase>` would apply. Just as `<cfelse>` is optional in `<cfif>`, so `<cfdefaultcase>` is optional when you're using `<cfswitch>`.

The value passed to `expression` is just that, an expression. In the previous example, the `expression` was a string; to use a variable, it must be enclosed within pound signs (#).

NOTE

In the `<cfcase>` statement, equality is the only valid operator. You cannot use `GT` or `LTE`, for example, as the operator.

- Multiple values can be listed for one case.
- A `delimiters` attribute with `<cfcase>` specifies the character that separates multiple entries in the list of values. The default delimiter is the comma.

TIP

As with `<cfif>`, it is best to put the most common cases at the top of the `<cfswitch>` to increase performance.

NOTE

Not every `<cfif>` statement can be replaced with a `<cfswitch>` statement (although every `<cfswitch>` can be replaced by `<cfif>`). The big difference between `<cfif>` and `<cfswitch>` is in what you can test for. `<cfswitch>` can only test for different values in the same expression, whilst `<cfif>` has no such restrictions.

Nested Statements

Both the `<cfif>` and `<cfswitch>` tags can be nested. In `<cfif>`, one of the true conditions can be code that uses another `<cfif>`. Likewise, in `<cfswitch>`, the code executed when a case is true can be another `<cfswitch>`.

More Details of Boolean Expressions

Boolean expressions are expressions that will be evaluated to either TRUE or FALSE. We've already discussed some details concerning the evaluation of Boolean expressions, but other details are essential to understand.

Logical Operators

ColdFusion has a set of logical, or Boolean, operators that are used with Boolean operands. They perform logical connective and negation operations. The most common of them are AND, OR, and NOT.

The AND operator returns TRUE if both operands are true; otherwise, FALSE is returned.

The OR operator returns TRUE if either operand is true. FALSE is returned only if both operands are false.

The NOT operator negates the operand. For instance, NOT FALSE returns TRUE.

Other logical operators are XOR, EQV, and IMP.

Parentheses

The standard rules for operator precedence (the level of priority in which operators are performed) are enforced in ColdFusion. If you want to change the priority, you must use parentheses. For instance, AND is evaluated before OR. If you want to change this in an expression, you could use parentheses as follows:

```
(A OR B) AND C
```

If parentheses are nested, the innermost set is evaluated first.

Short-Circuit Evaluation

When you use the logical operator AND, ColdFusion doesn't really need to do any further evaluation if the first operand is false because when FALSE is joined with any operand using the AND operator, the expression is going to be false. ColdFusion realizes this and uses *short-circuit evaluation*, which means that the logical expression is evaluated only as far as necessary to determine the true value of the whole expression.

Summary

Conditional processing is essential in the development of ColdFusion applications, and several tools are available to help you use it. `<cfif>` is often the best tool , but `<cfswitch>` is easier to read and performs better under certain circumstances.

Sample Questions

1. Which operators are used to test for equality? *(select two)*

   A. `==`

   B. `IS THE SAME AS`

   C. `IS`

   D. `=`

   E. `EQ`

2. Which of the following is logically equivalent to `TRUE`? *(select all that apply)*

   A. `-1`

   B. ON

   C. `1`

   D. YES

3. What output would the following code generate?

```
<cfset name="Ben">
<cfswitch expression="name">
 <cfcase value="Ben">
 Hello Ben.
 </cfcase>
 <cfcase value="Angela">
 Hello Angela.
 </cfcase>
 <cfcase value="Jeff">
 Hello Jeff.
 </cfcase>
 <cfdefaultcase>
 I have no idea who you are.
 </cfdefaultcase>
</cfswitch>
```

   A. `Hello Ben.`

   B. `Hello Angela.`

   C. `Hello Jeff.`

   D. `I have no idea who you are.`

CHAPTER 4
Looping

IN THIS CHAPTER

What Is Looping?

Looping is the use of any control structure to cause a program to repeatedly execute a block of code. You can use many kinds of loops in ColdFusion. The one you choose to implement depends on how you want to loop and on whether you are looping over a data structure. Loops repeat a specific number of times or until a certain condition is met.

Index

Index loops are used to execute a block of code a specified number of times. The number of times a loop repeats is determined by a range of numeric values. In many other languages, index loops are referred to as *for loops*.

> **NOTE**
>
> If you have a condition in which you want to jump out of the Index loop, it's best to use a Conditional loop instead. Although you can use ColdFusion's `<cfbreak>` tag, which permits jumping out of the loop, when it comes to style you are better off not doing so.

The Index loop's attributes are shown in Table 4.1.

Table 4.1 Index Loop Attributes

ATTRIBUTE	DESCRIPTION
`index`	The name of the variable to hold the current loop value.
`from`	The beginning value of the index.
`to`	The ending value of the index.
`step`	An optional attribute that controls the increment of the index each time through the loop. The default is `1`.

To loop from 1 to 10, you would use the following statement:

```
<cfloop index="i" from="1" to="10">
 <cfoutput>#i#</cfoutput><br>
</cfloop>
```

To create a loop that starts at 10 and steps backward in 2s to 4, you would use the following statement:

```
<cfloop index="i" from="10" to="4" step="-2">
 <cfoutput>#i#</cfoutput><br>
</cfloop>
```

Conditional

You use the Conditional loop when you want to loop during the time that a certain condition is true. In many other languages, conditional loops are referred to as *while loops*.

The conditional loop has only one attribute: condition. In it, you place the expression that will be evaluated by ColdFusion as true or false, and thus determines when the loop terminates. Because the condition is checked at the entrance to the loop, the loop may not be executed at all. When you're considering how the loop will behave, it is a good idea to consider how the loop will be entered the first time, and how the loop will terminate.

➜ For a complete discussion of writing expressions that will be evaluated as true or false by ColdFusion, see Chapter 3, "Conditional Processing."

A sample conditional loop follows:

```
<!--- Set up variables for condition --->
<cfset NumToGet=4>
<cfset i=0>
<!--- Now loop --->
<cfloop condition="i LTE NumToGet">
 <cfset i=i+1>
 <cfoutput>#i#</cfoutput><br>
</cfloop>
```

NOTE

The loop does not exit at the instant the condition becomes FALSE. It finishes all the statements between the <cfloop> and </cfloop> before terminating.

CAUTION

In the conditional loop shown here, the output is from 1 to 5, not from 0 to 4 as you might expect. The output goes to 5 because of the order in which the increment is done. If the two lines inside the loop were reversed, the output would be from 0 to 4. Be sure to consider this result when using conditional loops.

Query

The query loop loops over a block of statements once for every record read from a query.

> **TIP**
>
> The function of the query loop is similar to that of `<cfoutput>` with a `query` attribute.

The query loop has the attributes shown in Table 4.2.

Table 4.2 Query Loop Attributes

ATTRIBUTE	DESCRIPTION
`query`	The name of the query to loop over
`startrow`	An optional attribute that determines the first row of the query that will be included in the loop
`endrow`	An optional attribute that determines the last row of the query that will be included in the loop

A sample query loop follows:

```
<cfloop query="MyData">
 <cfoutput>#MyData.MyColumn#</cfoutput><br>
</cfloop>
```

> **NOTE**
>
> As is the case within a `<cfoutput>` block, the use of the query name as a prefix is optional. However, `<cfloop>` does not automatically act as `<cfoutput>`, so those tags are required, as shown in the example.

List

Lists in ColdFusion are simply sets of data separated by one or more delimiters. You can use a list loop to step over the elements of the list one at a time.

➜ For further information on lists, see Chapter 13, “Lists.”

When using a list loop, use the attributes shown in Table 4.3.

Table 4.3 List Loop Attributes

ATTRIBUTE	DESCRIPTION
`index`	The name of the variable to hold the current element of the list
`list`	The list to be stepped through
`delimiters`	An optional attribute that specifies the delimiter or delimiters used to separate items in the list

An example of a list loop follows:

```
<!--- Create a list --->
<cfset Months="Jan,Feb,Mar,Apr">
<!--- Loop over the list --->
<cfloop index="i" list="#Months#">
 <cfoutput>#i#</cfoutput><br>
</cfloop>
```

The index of the loop, here the variable `i`, will contain the values of the list `Months`. Specifically, `Jan`, `Feb`, `Mar`, `Apr`, and those months' abbreviations will be displayed.

List looping can also be used to loop through words in a sentence, paragraphs in a story, and more by specifying the appropriate `delimiters`.

Collection

Collection loops allow looping over key-value pairs in structures. Each time through the loop, the variable specified in the `item` attribute takes the value of successive key names. To display the value of the key-value pairs, you use the `item` with associative array notation. The following example helps clarify the situation:

```
<!--- Create and fill the structure --->
<cfset product=StructNew()>
<cfset product.Name="Ball">
<cfset product.Color="Red">
<!--- Display the key-value pairs --->
<cfloop collection="#product#" item="TheKey">
 <cfoutput>#TheKey#: #product[TheKey]#</cfoutput><br>
</cfloop>
```

The preceding code creates and populates a structure. In the loop, the variable `TheKey` takes the values `Name` and `Color`, which are the keys in the structure. Associative array notation, `#product[TheKey]#`, is used to display the values in the structure, `Ball` and `Red`.

➜ You can find a complete discussion of structures in Chapter 15, "Structures."

> **NOTE**
> In index and list loops, the attribute that holds the current loop value is `index`. With collection loops, it is called `item`.

> **TIP**
>
> The collection loop is built to loop over key-value pairs of a structure. When you're looping over arrays, use an Index loop with the `TO` attribute set equal to `#ArrayLen(My_Array)#`.

Using <cfloop> with <cfoutput>

When a `<cfloop>` is used in any of its variations, it does *not* preclude the need for a `<cfoutput>` block around ColdFusion variables inside the loop. If you scan back through all the code examples in this chapter, you will see that a `<cfoutput>` block is used.

Nested Loops

One loop placed inside another creates a *nested loop*. Generally speaking, the inside loop completely iterates for every single iteration of the outside loop. The following nested Index loops help clarify the situation:

```
<cfloop index="Outside" from="1" to="2">
 <cfloop index="Inside" from="7" to="9">
 <cfoutput>
 Outside is: #VARIABLES.Outside#
 Inside is: #VARIABLES.Inside#<br>
 </cfoutput>
 </cfloop>
</cfloop>
```

The outside loop initializes to `1`, followed by the inside loop initializing to `7`; then the output is displayed. The first `</cfloop>` causes the inside, or nested, loop to increment to `8`, and the output is displayed. This process continues until the inside loop terminates. Then the second `</cfloop>` is processed and increments the outer loop to `2`. When the inside `<cfloop>` is seen this second time, it is as if it has not been seen before, so it initializes the variable `Inside` to `7`. The output of the loops is as follows:

```
Outside is: 1 Inside is: 7
Outside is: 1 Inside is: 8
Outside is: 1 Inside is: 9
Outside is: 2 Inside is: 7
Outside is: 2 Inside is: 8
Outside is: 2 Inside is: 9
```

You can nest other types of loops by applying the same logic.

> **TIP**
>
> You can place code between the two beginning `<cfloop>` and/or the `</cfloop>` tags that create the nested loops. This capability can be especially helpful for formatting issues such as building HTML tables.

Summary

ColdFusion can do the following: iterate through a set of numeric values; loop while a condition is true; loop over the records of a query; loop over elements of a list; and loop over key-value pairs of a collection. Loops can also be nested.

Sample Questions

1. Which one of the following is *not* true of index loops?

   A. They can iterate over numeric values.

   B. The loop value variable is assigned using the `index` attribute.

   C. They can iterate over the alphabet.

   D. They can step by negative increments.

2. What is the output from the following loop?

```
<!--- Set up variables for condition --->
<cfset NumToGet="3">
<cfset i="1">
<!--- Now loop --->
<cfloop condition="i LTE NumToGet">
 <cfset i=i+1>
 <cfoutput>#i#</cfoutput>
</cfloop>
```

   A. `1 2 3`

   B. `2 3`

   C. `1 2`

   D. `2 3 4`

3. A Collection loop is used to loop over a structure that contains key-value pairs of `Animal-Cow`, `Legs-4`, and `Tail-Yes`. What is the value of the attribute `item` in the loop?

   A. `Animal, Legs, Tail`

   B. `Animal. Cow, Legs. 4, Tail. Yes`

   C. `Cow, 4, Yes`

   D. `Cow, 4, Tail`

4. The loop variable is assigned using the `index` attribute in which types of loops? *(select two)*

   A. Conditional

   B. Index

   C. Collection

   D. List

CHAPTER 5 Redirects and Reuse

IN THIS CHAPTER

Redirects

At some point on a page, you might want to send the user to another page. You can do so by using *redirection*. This means that although the browser requests one page, it is actually sent another (or is sent an instruction to load another). Using redirection, the browser never sees the requested page's HTML. This is true even if the HTML is above the tag that performs the redirection.

Using Redirection

ColdFusion allows you to programmatically implement browser-side redirection using the `<cflocation>` tag. This tag has the two attributes shown in Table 5.1.

Table 5.1 `<cflocation>` Tag Attributes

ATTRIBUTE	DESCRIPTION
`url`	The URL the browser should be redirected to.
`addtoken`	An optional attribute that is either `Yes` or `No`. If the value is `Yes`, ColdFusion appends browser identification information to the URL you specify in the `URL` attribute. The default value is `Yes`.

→ See Chapter 6, "The Application Framework," and Chapter 11, "Session State Management," for further information on maintaining client state.

The `url` attribute is simply set equal to the HTML file or CFML template the browser should be redirected to.

> **TIP**
>
> A query string may be added to the end of the URL listed in the `url` attribute. This permits variables and their associated values to be passed to the redirection page.

The `ADDTOKEN` attribute warrants further explanation. Clients are identified in one of two ways:

- If standard ColdFusion session state management is used, two variables are created: `CFID` and `CFTOKEN`. The combination of these two variables uniquely identifies a client.
- If J2EE session state management is used, a single variable named `jsessionid` is used to identify clients.

If you are using session state management, the variables (whichever are used) must be present for each and every request. If you are redirecting requests with `<cflocation>`, the session identifiers should be added to the URL. Using `addtoken="yes"` ensures that the necessary values are appended.

Using HTTP Headers

An HTTP header passes information about requests by the browser and responses from the server. The information needed for the exchange to take place is included in the header without being displayed.

The `<cfheader>` tag sets attribute/value pairs in the response header. The attributes of the tag are shown in Table 5.2.

Table 5.2 `<cfheader>` Tag Attributes

ATTRIBUTE	DESCRIPTION
`name`	The name of the attributes to set
`value`	The value associated with the corresponding `NAME`

A common use of the `<cfheader>` tag is to prevent a Web page from being cached by the browser. This caching can cause a problem if the Web page is used to display data that is being updated in some way. If database data is inserted, updated, or deleted, and the page to display that data is cached by the browser, the database records might not be shown accurately on the page. The Web browser has an `EXPIRES` attribute, which you can set to some time in the past so that the page will always be expired. The code to do so is as follows:

```
<cfheader name="Expires" VALUE="#Now()#">
```

The entry created in the header would look something like this:

```
Normal Expires: {ts '2006-01-01 19:34:42'}
```

> **TIP**
>
> If you run into a situation in which you need to prevent a page from being cached (for example, if proxy servers are being used), you must take into account different browsers and browser versions. The example shown here may not cover all possibilities. You might also want to test the following to be sure you get the best results for the range of browsers you are considering:
>
> ```
> <meta http-equiv="Pragma" content="No-Cache">
> <meta http-equiv="Expires" content="0">
> <cfheader name="Pragma" value="no-cache">
> <cfheader name="cache-control"
>  value="no-cache, no-store, must-revalidate">
> ```

Reuse

Imagine building a Web site with thousands of pages and a copy of the header on each page. Sometime during the life of a successful Web site, changes will be wanted or needed. The developers must go in and change the header code on every page. Obviously this is not a position in which you want to find yourself.

Code reuse has many benefits, one of the most important of which occurs when you need to change code that is viewed on many pages. Other obvious benefits include using code that is already written, tested, and debugged.

Reuse and Including Files

One way to implement reuse in ColdFusion is to use the `<cfinclude>` tag. In essence, this tag takes code from one page, called the *included page*, and puts it into the page that contains the `<cfinclude>` tag, called the *calling page*. Therefore, the code for a header could be stored in a central location and included in every page where it is needed. The `<cfinclude>` tag has only one attribute, `template`, which is the path to the page to include.

The path can be specified either as a relative path or as a ColdFusion mapping. If the first character after the quotation mark in the `template` attribute is a forward slash (`/`), the path uses a ColdFusion mapping.

The included page assumes the directory of the calling page. This means that you must be very careful using relative paths in the included code because they are often used at many different directory levels in the Web site. You can find solutions to this issue in the next two sections of this chapter.

Variables are not protected in the calling or included pages. This means that a variable in the calling page can be directly displayed and manipulated in the included page. Conversely, any variables from the included code can later be displayed and manipulated in the calling page after the `<cfinclude>`. Later in this chapter, you will see that this capability can work to your advantage.

ColdFusion Mappings

ColdFusion mappings are directory aliases created in ColdFusion Administrator. A virtual directory name can be associated with an actual physical directory path. For example, a ColdFusion mapping called `udfs` can be mapped to the physical directory `c:\cfusionmx7\wwwroot\udfs\`. You then could write a `<cfinclude>` tag as follows:

```
<cfinclude template="/udfs/string.cfm">
```

The use of a ColdFusion mapping offers some advantages. No matter where in the directory structure of your Web site the header is called, the path specified in the template attribute of the `<cfinclude>` can be the same. You don't need to worry about a relative path to the header. If the Web page is moved in the directory structure, you don't need to change the path to the header.

If a mapping isn't used and a major overhaul of the site changes the actual directory where the templates are stored, you would have to edit every `<cfinclude>`. If a mapping is used, you would need to make only one change in ColdFusion Administrator.

Web Server Mappings

ColdFusion mappings are only seen by ColdFusion and may only be used within ColdFusion code. This means that they cannot be used outside of ColdFusion, for example, in an `<img src>` tag. As images are served by the Web server (and not by ColdFusion), a ColdFusion mapping would not be of any use, The solution is to use Web server mappings. Just as ColdFusion mappings allow a virtual name for a physical directory that can be used in ColdFusion tags, so can Web server mappings be used with HTML tags where needed.

Consider a Web server mapping, or *virtual directory* as it is called in some Web server software, named `images`. Say it is mapped to the physical directory of `c:\cfusionmx7\wwwroot\imgs\`. You then can use this mapping in the header code where needed to be sure the images are correctly found and no broken links appear. For example, you could use the following:

```
<img src="/images/car.gif">
```

If this tag is used in the header, it does not matter where it is included—the link will function correctly.

Variable Scoping and <cfinclude>

Remember that variables are not protected either in calling or included pages, meaning that a variable from one page can be displayed or manipulated by the other. At first, this capability may seem like a negative factor, but sometimes it is just what you need.

Some search engines use the HTML title as part of the search report. If you include the header as suggested earlier, every title will be the same. Remember that variables set in the calling page can be used in the included page. So you could build something like this for the header:

```
<html>
<head>
 <title>
 <cfoutput>#VARIABLES.TheTitle#</cfoutput>
 </title>
</head>
```

Then, when you're building the home page, you could use this code:

```
<cfset TheTitle="PassThatTest.com Home Page">
<cfinclude template="/templates_mapping/header.cfm">
```

That way, every page would simply set the title before using the `<cfinclude>` tag.

If many parts of the header are changeable, as in a navigation system, a query could be performed before the `<cfinclude>` and the information from the database used in the header.

> **CAUTION**
>
> When you include a page, the `<cfoutput>` block does not carry into the included page. This means that if the `<cfinclude>` is inside a `<cfoutput>` block, any ColdFusion variables to be displayed on the included page must be surrounded with another `<cfoutput>` block.

Generating Non-HTML Content

Using `<cfcontent>`, you can send documents to the client browser. The attributes you use with this tag are shown in Table 5.3.

Table 5.3 `<cfcontent>` Tag Attributes

ATTRIBUTE	DESCRIPTION
`type`	The MIME type of the document being sent.
`file`	The file to be sent to the browser. This attribute is mutually exclusive of the `reset` attribute.

Table 5.3 (CONTINUED)

ATTRIBUTE	DESCRIPTION
`deletefile`	An optional attribute, which defaults to `NO`, that controls whether the file should be deleted after the download operation.
`reset`	An optional attribute, which defaults to `YES`, that determines whether any output before the `<cfcontent>` tag should be discarded. This attribute is mutually exclusive of the `file` attribute.

CAUTION

The `reset` attribute should be set to `NO` if the `<cfcontent>` tag is used in a custom tag. If this attribute is not set, all output from the page before the custom tag call will be discarded.

This example sends a Microsoft Word document to a browser:

```
<cfcontent type="application/msword"
           file="C:\MyWork.doc"
           deletefile="No">
```

In addition to sending a file that is already created, you can send a document that is built on the fly. For instance, you might want to build an Excel spreadsheet to send to users, but with the absolutely latest data. You could use the following example. Assume that the ColdFusion variables `Test.Name` and `Test.Price` are read from the query:

```
<cfcontent type="application/vnd.ms-excel"
           reset="Yes">"Name","Price"
<cfoutput query="Test">"#Test.Name#","#Test.Price#"
</cfoutput>
```

TIP

The `reset` attribute is very helpful in this example because it cleans up any text that might exist on the page before you start the spreadsheet. It is also helpful for cases in which XML packets are being produced and sent.

Also, the lack of a new line after the `<cfoutput query="Test">` is intentional. All characters after `<cfcontent>` are used in the file, so a carriage return in this location would put a blank line between each row of data in the spreadsheet. Tabs separate the two labels that are the column heading names. Tabs also separate the two actual data column names.

NOTE

You can disable the `<cfcontent>` tag's functionality in ColdFusion Administrator.

Summary

To have the browser request one page but be redirected to another, you can use `<cflocation>`. `<cfheader>` allows ColdFusion to create attribute/value pairs in HTTP's response headers. You might practice code reuse for many reasons, and using the `<cfinclude>` tag is a way to do so in ColdFusion. `<cfcontent>` sends non-HTML files, either existing or built dynamically, to a browser.

Sample Questions

1. What does the `<cflocation> addtoken` attribute do?

   A. Forces a page redirect.

   B. Creates `SESSION` variables.

   C. Appends client identification information to the redirected URL.

   D. Creates identification cookies in the client browser.

2. Which of the following are true about `<cfheader>`? (*select two*)

   A. It creates attribute/value pairs in the request header.

   B. It creates attribute/value pairs in the response header.

   C. It can be used to prevent a browser from caching a page.

   D. It can be used to prevent a server from caching a page.

3. The following `<cfinclude>` tag uses what kind of path?

   ```
   <cfinclude template="/templates_mapping/header.cfm">
   ```

   A. Relative

   B. ColdFusion mapping

4. What is displayed from the following line of code?

   ```
   ABC<cfcontent type="text/html" reset="Yes">DEF
   ```

   A. `ABC`

   B. `ABCDEF`

   C. `ABEF`

   D. `DEF`

CHAPTER 6

The Application Framework

IN THIS CHAPTER

What Is the Application Framework?

ColdFusion provides a framework for combining application pages or templates into a single coherent application. This *application framework* provides three basic sets of functionality:

- Application-wide variables and code
- Client and application state management
- Error-handling services

The topmost parent in the application directory tree is known as the *application root*. This directory is usually located within a branch of the Web document root. The subdirectories below this are typically used to separate code templates and other media based on their functionality. For example, included files such as headers might be found in an `../includes` directory, and images in a separate `../images` directory, depending on your development methodology.

> **NOTE**
>
> The Web document root is the directory that has been mapped to the base Web site URL, such as `www.forta.com`. The location of this directory is configured in the Web server administration interface and can be different for each Web site hosted on your server. For example, the default Web document root for ColdFusion's integrated HTTP server (on a Windows machine) is `c:\cfusionmx7\wwwroot\`.

Global variables and application-wide functionality can be implemented within an application by the use of special files named `Application.cfc` or `Application.cfm` (the latter may also have an accompanying `OnRequestEnd.cfm` file).

NOTE

`Application.cfm` has been supported since early versions of ColdFusion. `Application.cfc` was first introduced in ColdFusion MX 7. Both are, and will continue to be, supported, but for new development you are generally advised to use `Application.cfc` which provides for far greater functionality.

→ Client state management is covered in detail in Chapter 10, "`APPLICATION` and `SERVER` Variables," and Chapter 11, "Session State Management." Error handling is covered in Chapter 26, "Error Handling."

Whenever a page is to be executed, the ColdFusion checks the page's local directory for either of the `Application` files. Keep the following in mind:

- If an Application file doesn't exist, the server looks in the parent directory, and then the parent's parent, and so on up the directory tree until one is found or until the drive root directory is reached.
- If more than one `Application` file exists in the directory tree, ColdFusion uses only the first one it finds.
- If there is no `Application` file, the template page executes as per normal.
- If both an `Application.cfc` and an `Application.cfm` exists, `Application.cfc` will be used.

CAUTION

Many developers incorrectly assume that the ColdFusion application server searches only to the document root of the Web server for an `Application` file. In fact, the server searches all the way up the directory tree to the hard drive's root directory.

Typical application uses of the `Application` files include:

- Defining the application name.
- Defining default variables and global constants such as data source names, and absolute file paths for image and file libraries.
- Custom error handling for general exceptions.
- Default style settings such as fonts or colors using the local or request scope (perhaps saved into structures for simplified organization and management).
- Application-wide security code (such as requiring logins and redirecting to a login page if needed).

It is impossible to prevent `Application` files from being executed, if they are present ColdFusion will find them and process them.

On some operating systems (such as Solaris, Linux, and HP-UX), filenames are case sensitive. Therefore, `Application.cfc`, `Application.cfm` and `OnRequestEnd.cfm` must be named with exactly the right casing; capital `A` for `Application` and capital `O`, `R`, and `E` for `OnRequestEnd.cfm`. Although Windows NT, Windows 2000, and Windows XP have case-insensitive file systems, it is good practice for portability of the code to stick to the correct casing when you create these files.

> **NOTE**
>
> As a security measure, `Application` files cannot be called directly from a URL on the Web browser. They can be executed only in the context of another page in the application.

> **CAUTION**
>
> Presentation code such as HTML, JavaScript, and other client-side technologies should not be placed in the `Application` files. `Application` files are designed specifically as a globally included template for application-wide logic, and are not appropriate for any aspect of your application's presentation layer.

Application.cfc

As a ColdFusion Component, `Application.cfc` has a very specific format. The contents of the file must be enclosed within `<cfcomponent>` and `</cfcomponent>` tags.

➜ `Application.cfc` is a special ColdFusion Component. ColdFusion Components in general is discussed in Chapter 31, "ColdFusion Components".

Application settings are defined in the constructor portion of the component (within the component but not within any specific method),. For example, to enable session state management the following `Application.cfc` could be used:

```
<cfcomponent>
  <cfset THIS.name="MyApp">
<cfset THIS.sessionManagement="true">
<cfset THIS.sessionTimeout=CreateTimeSpan(0,0,30,0)>
</cfcomponent>
```

In this example an application name is specified in property `THIS.name`, `THIS.sessionManagement` is used to enable session state management, and the session timeout is set to `30` minutes. Table 6.1 lists the supported application properties (settings).

Table 6.1 `Application.cfc` Properties

PROPERTY	DESCRIPTION
`applicationTimeout`	Application timeout interval (specified as a time span). The default is the interval specified in the ColdFusion Administrator.
`clientManagement`	Whether or not to enable `CLIENT` variable support. Defaults to `FALSE`.
`clientStorage`	Where to store `CLIENT` variables. Default value is `COOKIE`.
`loginStorage`	Where to store login information. Default value is `COOKIE`.
`name`	The application name. This must always be provided.
`scriptProtect`	Whether or not to enable protection against cross-site scripting attacks. Defaults to whatever is specified in the ColdFusion Administrator.
`sessionManagement`	Whether or not to enable `SESSION` variable support. Defaults to `FALSE`.
`sessionTimeout`	Session timeout interval (specified as a time span). The default is the interval specified in the ColdFusion Administrator.
`setClientCookies`	Whether or not to save client identification tokens as cookies. Default is `TRUE`.
`setDomainCookies`	Whether or not to set domain cookies (usually only needed if an application is running on a cluster of servers). Default is `FALSE`.

`Application.cfc` can also contain code to be executed when specific events occur (for example, when an application starts up, or before and after every page request, or when an error occurs). Table 6.2 lists the support methods.

Table 6.2 `Application.cfc` Methods

METHOD	DESCRIPTION
`OnApplicationEnd`	Executed on server shut-down or on application timeout.
`OnApplicationStart`	Executed the first time code within an application is executed (after server start-up, or after application timeout).
`OnError`	Executed whenever an error not explicitly trapped with `<cftry>/<cfcatch>` code occurs.
`OnRequest`	Executed in lieu of the page requested.
`OnRequestEnd`	Executed after each and every page request.

Table 6.2 (continued)

METHOD	DESCRIPTION
`OnRequestStart`	Executed before each and every page request.
`OnSessionEnd`	Executed whenever a session expires.
`OnSessionStart`	Executed whenever a new session is created.

The following example defines an application, sets two variables upon application startup, and initializes a shopping cart when a new session is created.

```
<cfcomponent>

  <!--- Set up app --->
  <cfset THIS.name="MyApp">
  <cfset THIS.sessionManagement="true">
  <cfset THIS.sessionTimeout=CreateTimeSpan(0,0,30,0)>

  <!--- When application starts --->
  <cffunction name="onApplicationStart">
    <cfset APPLICATION.FileLibrary="d:\lib">
    <cfset APPLICATION.DataSource="ows">
  </cffunction>

  <!--- When new session starts --->
  <cffunction name="onSessionStart">
    <cfset SESSION.cart=StructNew()>
    <cfset SESSION.cart.items=ArrayNew(1)>
  </cffunction>

</cfcomponent>
```

Order Of Processing

When multiple methods are defined within `Application.cfc`, there are evaluated in the following order:

1: `onApplicationStart()`

2: `onSessionStart()`

3: `onRequestStart()`

4: `onRequest()`

5: `onRequestEnd()`

The remaining three event methods are called when specific events occur, when an application or session times out or the server is shutdown, or when an error occurs.

> **TIP**
>
> Generally, use `onApplicationStart()` to set `APPLICATION` data, `onSessionStart()` to set `SESSION` data, and `onRequestStart()` to set `REQUEST` data.

Using `onRequest()`

`onRequest()` is a little different from the other `Application.cfc` methods in that it is not executed when as event occurs, rather it is executed in lieu of an event. If present, `onRequest()` will be executed instead of the page that was requested, and the requested pages name is passed to `onRequest()` as an attribute. This allows developers to trap page requests if needed.

Possible uses for `onRequest()` include:

- Temporarily blocking application access during maintenance.
- Restricting access based on IP address or subnet.
- Grabbing generated output and performing processing on it, including stripping whitespace or compressing data.

It is important to note that if `onRequest()` is used then ColdFusion will not automatically execute the requested page. If that page is to be executed that it must be explicitly included using `<cfinclude>`.

➔ Included files are covered in detail in Chapter 5, "Redirects and Reuse."

> **NOTE**
>
> `onRequest()` cannot be used if Web Services or Flash Remoting are needed.

`Application.cfm`

The `Application.cfm` file behaves in the same way as a standard `<cfinclude>` in that it is run as if it were cut and pasted into the top of the executing template. Local variables defined in the `Application.cfm` file are unprotected and are available to the rest of the code template. An `Application.cfm` file placed in the application root is implicitly included at the top of every page in the application. Therefore, it is an ideal place to assign global variables such as file paths and data source names, and to implement application-wide functionality such as security authentication.

The following example is the `Application.cfm` equivalent of the previously seen `Application.cfc` example:

```
<!--- Set up app --->
<cfapplication name="MyApp"
```

```
                sessionmanagement="Yes"
                sessionTimeout="#CreateTimeSpan(0,0,30,0)#">
<!--- When application starts --->
<cfif NOT IsDefined("APPLICATION.settings")
  <cflock type="exclusive" scope="application">
    <cfset APPLICATION.FileLibrary="d:\lib">
    <cfset APPLICATION.DataSource="ows">
    <cfset APPLICATION.settings="true">
  </cflock>
</cfif>

<!--- When new session starts --->
<cfif NOT IsDefined("SESSION.cart")
  <cflock type="exclusive" scope="session">
    <cfset SESSION.cart=StructNew()>
    <cfset SESSION.cart.items=ArrayNew(1)>
  </cflock>
</cfif>
```

Local or request-scope variables that are set in `Application.cfm` are available in all pages that include the file. Such variables do not need to be locked. However, `Application.cfm` is often used for the setting of `SERVER`, `APPLICATION`, and `SESSION` variables, and careful consideration must be given to the appropriate locking of these shared variable types.

➜ Client state management is covered in detail in Chapter 10, "`APPLICATION` and `SERVER` Variables," and Chapter 11, "Session State Management." The importance of locking in ColdFusion is discussed in Chapter 12, "Locking."

In the same way that `Application.cfm` is executed at the beginning of every page in the application, you can create a file called `OnRequestEnd.cfm` that is executed at the end of every page. However, unlike `Application.cfm`, `OnRequestEnd.cfm` must be located in the same directory as the calling page's `Application.cfm`. It will not be executed if it is placed in another directory. If you choose to use `OnRequestEnd.cfm` files in your application, they are in effect linked to the `Application.cfm` file residing in the same directory.

`OnRequestEnd.cfm` can be useful in a multitude of ways for more advanced ColdFusion implementations: for example, to control debugging directives or to manage the logging of code that responds to specific page settings.

```
<!--- OnRequestEnd.cfm example --->
<!--- suppress debugging output --->
<cfsetting showdebugoutput="No">

<!--- activate logging module --->
<cfif request.logpage>
 <cf_log_module>
</CFIF>
```

Multiple `Application` Files

Although you can use a single `Application` file to govern an entire application, it is often useful to break up an application into individual sections or modules. In these instances, you might need to define a different `Application` for each section of code in order to provide different global variables and functions.

If you place an `Application` file in the application root of your Web application, the file will be automatically included in all files throughout the branches of the subdirectory tree. However, by placing an `Application` file in a subdirectory below the application root, it is possible to define different parameters and functionality for all the pages in that specific branch of the directory structure. Remember that ColdFusion will execute only one `Application` file per page and will look in the current directory first.

- If using `Application.cfc`, the `<cfcomponent>` extends attribute can be used to extend another `Application.cfc`. The methods and settings in the `Applciation.cfc` being extended will be executed unless overwritten in the new `Application.cfc`.
- If using `Application.cfm`, `<cfinclude>` can be used to include another `Applciation.cfm`. Care must be taken to use the same application name in `<cfapplication>` or `APPLCIATION` and `SESSION` data will not be shared.

Summary

The `Application` files are an integral parts of the ColdFusion development environment application framework, transforming sets of files into a cohesive application. `Application.cfm` is executed before every page request, `Application.cfc` supports a variety of methods for far greater control.

Sample Questions

1. Which of the following `Application.cfc` methods is executed first?

   A. `onRequest()`

   B. `onRequestStart()`

   C. `onRequestEnd()`

   D. `onRequestNew()`

2. Where must `OnRequestEnd.cfm` be in order to be executed?

   A. In the current directory

   B. In the Web root

   C. In the application root

   D. In the same directory as the executed `Application.cfm`

3. When should `onRequest()` not be used? *(select two)*

   A. When Web Services are being used

   B. When locking is being used

   C. When Flash Remoting is being used

   D. When `onRequestStart()` is being used

   E. When Flash is being used

4. When using `Application.cfc`, which method can be used to set local `VARIABLES` that can be used within the page being requested?

   A. `onRequestStart()`

   B. `onRequest()`

   C. `onRequestEnd()`

   D. None, local variables set within a CFC are local to the CFC

CHAPTER 7 Using Databases

IN THIS CHAPTER

How to Connect to Databases

To access a database using ColdFusion, you need a defined data source. A *data source* is a named configuration (driver and settings) that points to a specific database. The database can be located on the same server as ColdFusion or on another server elsewhere in the network.

The connection behind the data source acts as a gateway or translator to the database that is servicing the application. Each database has its own particular format and mechanisms for storing and retrieving data. To make application development easier, a data source is defined using a database *driver* (software that knows how to talk to a specific database). A driver and associated configuration is known as a *data source*. Database connectivity in ColdFusion is possible through JDBC. The included JDBC drivers allow developers to pass Structured Query Language (SQL) statements to databases and retrieve results (if appropriate).

NOTE

Structured Query Language (SQL) is a standard programming language for interacting with a database. Interactions include retrieving, adding, updating, and deleting information. SQL also can be used for restructuring or modifying the schema and indexing properties of a database.

Although SQL is an ANSI standard, many database products support SQL with proprietary extensions to the standard language, known as a dialect. Examples include Oracle's PL-SQL and MS SQL Server's Transact-SQL.

Adding a Data Source

Data sources to be used with ColdFusion are defined in ColdFusion Administrator (or via the Administration API). You can also use ColdFusion Administrator to view and modify details of the data source connections registered for your server. The type of data source determines what options are available and to what extent they can be modified through the ColdFusion Administrator interface.

A logical name is assigned to a data source so that you can refer to it within tags (e.g., the `<cfquery>` tag). When processing a query, the data source informs ColdFusion which database to connect to and which default attributes to use for the connection.

ColdFusion data sources should abide by the following naming conventions:

- Data sources must be uniquely named.
- As with other ColdFusion variables, a data source name should begin with a letter.
- A data source name can contain any combination of letters, numbers, and underscores.
- A data source name should not contain any special characters (including spaces and periods).

Obviously, a data source must be visible in ColdFusion Administrator before you attempt to reference it within an application page.

The data source configuration options make reference to the location of the underlying database. In addition, they provide Administrator with the capability to set a series of default values for connection parameters. Several of these parameters are specific to the driver in question and can be used to tweak the performance and reliability of the database connection.

User name and password details define the default authentication for the ColdFusion server in the absence of any other instructions. A default password can be defined at the level of the driver, and it is superseded by anything placed in the ColdFusion login fields of Administrator. Administrator is, in turn, overridden by the use of a `username` or `password` attribute in the `<cfquery>` tag.

> **CAUTION**
>
> Do not specify the database administrator password as the authentication to be used for the data source. A malicious developer with the ability to modify code on the ColdFusion server would have total control of the database.
>
> The best practice is to set up a user account for ColdFusion on the database with specific permissions for your application. These permissions should enable your code to perform only the required database operations on the application database, and nothing more.

SQL operations can be restricted through the data source. This enables administrators to grant access to the database but to restrict the types of SQL statements that can be passed. For example, you could enable SELECT statements for retrieving information but not allow any updates or deletions. Security-conscious administrators might prefer to implement these types of restrictions at the database level instead.

What About ODBC?

As of ColdFusion MX, ColdFusion is built on underlying Java technologies, and thus the data sources and drivers used are Java database drivers (JDBC).

Another very common database driver format is ODBC, originally popularized by Microsoft but now supported by numerous products and vendors. Although ColdFusion no longer uses ODBC drivers (prior versions of ColdFusion did), access to ODBC drivers is still possible via a bridge—a special JDBC adapter. To use an ODBC driver via the bridge, that driver must already be defined—perhaps by using the Windows Control Panel applet—and then the virtual data source (using the included JDBC-ODBC driver) should be defined in ColdFusion Administrator.

> **NOTE**
>
> ODBC support is provided primarily for backward compatibility, so as to support databases that lack JDBC drivers. For performance reasons, direct JDBC use is usually the best choice.

Connecting to the Database

<cfquery> is used to prepare and submit an SQL statement to a data source. <cfquery> and its attributes also can be used to override the default settings on the data source connection to the database. Any SQL statement that can be interpreted by the database and its driver can be sent, including SELECT, UPDATE, and INSERT statements:

```
<cfquery name="users"
         datasource="dsn">
SELECT LastName, FirstName, EmpID
FROM Users
</cfquery>
```

SQL is used to communicate with the database through the data source. ColdFusion does not perform SQL validation, so you can use any syntax that is supported by your data source. Check your database documentation for details on the usage of nonstandard SQL code.

➜ Interactions with the database are covered in detail throughout Part VII, "Databases." Chapter 44, "Basic SQL," offers an introduction to SQL.

➜ The <cfquery> attributes `cachedwithin` and `cachedafter` are used to improve query performance and implement dynamic caching. These attributes are covered in detail in Chapter 48, "Improving Performance."

When <cfquery> performs a `SELECT` operation on the database and records are found, a record set is returned. This record set is converted into a ColdFusion query object. The query object is neither an array nor a structure but a special variable in its own right. Although it does exhibit array-like properties, the query object has its own set of ColdFusion functions, such as `QueryAddColumn()` and `QueryAddRow()`.

➜ Arrays are discussed in Chapter 14, "Arrays," and structures are covered in Chapter 15, "Structures."

A query object is referenced by the `name` attribute specified in the <cfquery> tag. This tag stores the complete record set returned by the SQL statement and several additional variables that might be of use, as shown in Table 7.1.

Table 7.1 <cfquery> Variables

VARIABLE NAME	DESCRIPTION
`RecordCount`	The total number of records in the query. If no records were returned, this is 0.
`ColumnList`	A comma-delimited list of all column names in the query (returned in no particular order)
`CurrentRow`	The current row of the query. This is relevant when the result set is being processed by a tag such as <cfoutput> that loops over the rows in the record set.
`ExecutionTime`	The time taken to execute the query on the database and return the results to ColdFusion, in milliseconds. (This variable is returned as `cfquery.executionTime`).

The variables listed in Table 7.1, and additional information, can also be accessed as a result structure. To do so simply specify the name of a structure to be created in the <cfquery> result attribute, as in `result="cfqueryResults"`. ColdFusion will create and populate the named result structure.

> **TIP**
>
> Additional information about query contents may be obtained using the `getMetaData()` function.

You can generate dynamic queries within <cfquery> by using variables and conditional logic. <cfquery> processes any ColdFusion code or variables first, before submitting the resulting SQL code to the database:

```
<cfquery name="users"
         datasource="dsn">
```

```
SELECT LastName, FirstName, EmpID
FROM Users
<cfif FORM.EmpID IS NOT "">
 WHERE EmpID = #FORM.EmpID#
</cfif>
</cfquery>
```

➜ Conditional processing is covered in Chapter 3, "Conditional Processing."

Care must be taken when building dynamic SQL because of the following:

- Unlike CFML, SQL is not typeless. Variables passed to SQL must be *cast* to the appropriate type (for example, strings must be surrounded with single quotes).
- SQL is very picky about the order of clauses; when statements are being built dynamically, all possible statements must be syntactically correct.

Simplified Database Connectivity

`<cfinsert>` and `<cfupdate>` are tags that simplify the process of database inserts and updates, respectively. They effectively build a dynamic SQL statement based on the `FORM` variable structure and submit it like a standard `<cfquery>` with the appropriate SQL statement. Consequently, they are easier to use than `<cfquery>` and SQL code, but they are also less flexible and have some limitations. Only `datasource` and `tablename` are required attributes. `<cfinsert>` and `<cfupdate>` are used like this:

```
<!--- inserting a record --->
<cfinsert datasource="dsn"
          tablename="users"
          formfields="LastName, FirstName">

<!--- updating a record --->
<cfupdate datasource="dsn"
          tablename="users"
          formfields="LastName, FirstName">
```

`<cfinsert>` and `<cfupdate>` have the following restrictions:

- They can submit only `FORM` variables.
- The form field names must be the same as the corresponding column names in the database table.
- `<cfupdate>` must include values for all the columns that make up the table's primary key.

The `formfields` attribute acts as a mask, allowing only specified form fields to be included in the operation. If `formfields` is not present, all the form fields are submitted. Other tag attributes are available to override default settings in the data source connection.

> **TIP**
>
> `<cfparam>` can be used to create default form fields for use with `<cfinsert>` and `<cfupdate>`.

Displaying Data

`<cfoutput>` is used to resolve and display dynamic ColdFusion variables. Coupled with a query object such as the result of a `<cfquery>` and `SELECT` statement, `<cfoutput>` can be used to loop over results, once per record in the record set:

```
<cfquery name="users"
         datasource="dsn">
SELECT LastName, FirstName, Phone
FROM Users
</cfquery>

<table>
  <tr bgcolor="#cccccc">
    <th>Name</th>
    <th>Phone</th>
  </tr>
  <cfoutput query="users">
    <tr bgcolor="#IIF(users.CurrentRow MOD 2,
                     de("##ededed"),
                     de("##ffffff"))#">
      <td>#LastName#, #Firstname#</td>
      <td>#phone#</td>
    </tr>
  </cfoutput>
</table>
```

`<cfoutput>` loops over the block of code contained within the opening and closing tags once per record in the record set of the query nominated in the `query` attribute. The column name in the query is prefixed with the name of the query itself to define the variable. The value of the variable changes with each iteration to reflect the value of the column for the current row in the record set. The dynamic `IIf()` function uses the `users.CurrentRow` variable of the query to alternate the background color of the table rows, and the `users.CurrentRow` variable changes with every iteration to reflect the current record number.

➜ `<cfoutput>` is also covered in Chapter 2, "Working with Variables and Expressions."

➜ `IIf()` and `DE()` are covered in Chapter 22, "Dynamic Functions."

> **NOTE**
>
> Query variables don't always need the query name prefix. If the variable is referenced inside `<cfoutput>` tags with the same query object specified in the `query` attribute, you do not need the query name as a prefix. The `<cfoutput>` query variables are the first to be resolved, so there is no chance of a variable name conflict.

Referencing a query variable from within `<cfoutput>` tags without a `query` attribute specified, or indeed with a different query name nominated, is still possible:

```
<cfoutput>#users.LastName#</cfoutput>
<cfoutput query="users">#departments.DeptName#</cfoutput>
```

The variable resolves the value of the first record in the query only.

> **NOTE**
>
> To reference a specific record in the record set of a query object, you can use the row number in the same way as an array position. For example, to reference the `LastName` column of the second row of the query `users` with array syntax, use this:
>
> `#users.LastName[2]#`

Grouping Data with `<cfoutput>`

`<cfoutput>` also can be used to group data according to a specific column for reporting purposes by using the `group` attribute. `<cfoutput>` does not sort data, so the data in the query object must already be appropriately ordered. After `group` is specified, the `<cfoutput>` statement loops only once per distinct value in the grouped column. A second, nested `<cfoutput>` statement can be used to loop over every record in a particular group, including the first record in the group:

```
<!--- order results by department --->
<cfquery name="users" datasource="dsn">
SELECT EmpID, LastName, FirstName, Phone, DeptID
FROM users
ORDER BY DeptID
</cfquery>
```

This query returns data sorted by `DeptID`. There will be at least one user per retrieved `DeptID`, and possibly more too.

The following report uses the `DeptID` column in the `group` attribute of `<cfoutput>` to generate an HTML table:

```
<table>
  <cfoutput query="users" group="DeptID">
    <tr>
      <td colspan="3" bgcolor="##cccccc">#DeptID#</td>
    </tr>
    <cfoutput>
      <tr>
        <td>#LastName#, #FirstName#</td>
        <td>#Phone#</td>
      </tr>
    </cfoutput>
  </cfoutput>
</table>
```

The first `<cfoutput>` tag loops only once for each distinct value in the `DeptID` column, so if there were ten users in three departments, the outer `<cfoutput>` loop would be processed three times and the inner `<cfoutput>` loop would be processed a total of ten times.

> **NOTE**
>
> The `group` attribute of `<cfoutput>` is different from the SQL command `GROUP BY`. SQL's `GROUP BY` is used to provide a variety of aggregate functions on sets of records in a database query result. In comparison, `group` in `<cfoutput>` is used only to modify the output and looping behavior of the ColdFusion query object.

➜ `GROUP BY` and aggregate functions are discussed in Chapter 46, "Aggregates."

Multiple levels of grouping are allowed as long as each has a unique `group` attribute and the data is sorted in the `<cfquery>` correctly. When grouping data, regardless of the number of levels used, `group` is used in every `<cfoutput>` except the innermost one.

Querying Queries

The result of using `<cfquery>` is effectively a record set sitting in memory on the application server. This query might be available only for the current page execution, or it might be placed into a more permanent memory scope, such as the application, session, or server scope. It could even be a temporarily cached query, by way of the `cachedwithin` and `cachedafter` attributes. Although a query's information might be readily available to the application server, developers typically go back to the database if they need to manipulate the query data in some way (for example, to re-sort or filter the record set).

➜ Shared variable scopes are covered in Chapter 10, "Application and Server Variables," and Chapter 11, "Session State Management."

➜ Query caching is discussed in Chapter 48, "Improving Performance."

ColdFusion allows developers to reuse existing queries by running queries against them in memory. This gives you the advantage of being able to avoid the often costly performance hit of going back to the database to manipulate data that the application server has already recently called. A standard `<cfquery>` statement can be used to call a query variable in memory as though it were simply a table of data in an available data source. Query variables can even be joined, which provides interesting possibilities for joining data from disparate information sources.

Manipulating Existing Queries

You query existing queries by using `<cfquery>` with the `dbtype="query"` attribute set (and no `datasource` attribute specified). You form the query SQL in exactly the same way you would expect to interrogate a data source, except that the data source table name is replaced with the name of the query:

```
<!--- load the entire Employee table into memory --->
<cfquery name="users"
         datasource="dsn">
 SELECT *
 FROM Users
</cfquery>

<!--- grab a subset of the data from users --->
<cfquery name="managers"
         dbtype="query">
 SELECT *
 FROM Users
 WHERE manager = 1
</cfquery>
```

The query can be placed in any scope available to the page that is calling the `<cfquery>` tag.

Although the feature is powerful, it supports a subset of the available `SELECT` syntax. The usable SQL functions are:

- `FROM`
- `WHERE`
- `GROUP BY`
- `UNION`
- `ORDER BY`
- `HAVING`
- `AS`
- `DISTINCT`

Boolean Predicates

- `LIKE`
- `NOT LIKE`
- `IN`
- `NOT IN`

- BETWEEN
- NOT BETWEEN
- AND
- OR
- IS
- IS NOT
- IS NUL

Aggregate Functions

- Count([DISTINCT][*] expr)
- Sum([DISTINCT] expr)
- Avg([DISTINCT] expr)
- Max(expr)
- Min(expr)

Comparison Operators

- <=
- >=
- =
- <
- >
- <>

Conversion Functions

- Cast()
- Lower()
- Upper()

Concatenation

- +
- ||

The *query of queries* feature allows you to reorder the record set in memory without going back to the database. The column name that is being sorted by must be specified in the `SELECT` statement, as well as in the `ORDER BY` statement. This is slightly different from normal SQL code. For example, this works:

```
SELECT EmpID, StartDate
FROM Users
ORDER BY StartDate
```

but this fails:

```
SELECT EmpID
FROM Users
ORDER BY StartDate
```

Query of queries can generate computed columns (for example, by concatenating strings or through the use of aggregate functions):

```
<!--- count the number of employees in each department --->
<cfquery name="DeptUsers"
         dbtype="query">
 SELECT COUNT(DeptID) AS emp_count, DeptID
 FROM Users
 GROUP BY DeptID
</cfquery>
```

➜ `GROUP BY` and aggregate functions are discussed in Chapter 46, "Aggregates."

TIP

When you're using aggregate functions, it's good practice to alias the computed column name to something intuitive. For example, in the `DeptUsers` query, if the alias `emp_count` were not specified, the variable name would become `COMPUTED_COLUMN_1`.

NOTE

ColdFusion variables are supposed to be typeless; however, SQL is not. Use the `Cast()` function to cast ColdFusion variables to specific data types if needed.

NOTE

When you are performing string comparisons, query of queries is case sensitive. For example, the result returned from this:

```
WHERE firstname LIKE 'G%'
```

will be different from the result returned from this:

```
WHERE firstname LIKE 'g%'
```

Joining Different Data Sources

Query of queries can perform a single join of two query variables in memory by using standard SQL. ColdFusion is unconcerned with the origin of the data, and thus any two record sets can be joined—even those from completely different information resources. This allows you to, for example, join tables or views from two different databases, LDAP or POP email queries, and so on.

➜ POP email is discussed in Chapter 41, "Email Integration."

➜ LDAP queries are covered in Chapter 42, "LDAP."

➜ Information about table joins can be found in Chapter 45, "Joins."

An application might need to combine the customer information in a relational database with email received in a POP account after an online marketing campaign. Both the database and the POP server could be queried, and the individual result sets could be combined into a unified query variable for reporting:

```
<!--- get emails from campaign account --->
<cfpop action="GETHEADERONLY"
       name="GetMail"
       server="mail.forta.com"
       username="username"
       password="password">

<!--- get customer records from database --->
<cfquery name="users"
         datasource="dsn">
 SELECT *
 FROM Users
</cfquery>

<!--- join record sets on email address --->
<cfquery name="Responses"
         dbtype="query">
SELECT
 Users.Email AS Email,
 Users.FirstName AS FirstName,
 Users.LastName AS LastName,
 GetMail.Subject AS Subject,
 GetMail.Date AS Date
FROM Users, GetMail
WHERE Users.email = GetMail.from
</cfquery>
```

Any ColdFusion query can be used in query-of-queries processing. This includes the following:

- `<cfcollection>`
- `<cfdirectory>`
- `<cfftp>`
- `<cfhttp>`
- `<cfindex>`
- `<cfldap>`
- `<cfpop>`
- `<cfprocresult>`
- `<cfquery>`
- `<cfsearch>`
- `<cfstoredproc>`
- `<cfwddx>`
- Queries created using `QueryNew()`

Summary

A data source is needed in order for ColdFusion to communicate with a database. The data source is effectively a driver that acts as a translator for communicating SQL statements to the database back end. `<cfquery>` is used to prepare the SQL statements and send them through to the data source with the appropriate connection settings. `<cfquery>` can pass any SQL statement that the data source can handle.

A record set passed back to `<cfquery>` is converted into a query object. The query object can be looped over for each individual record, and the values of the various columns can be output by using `<cfoutput>`. `<cfoutput>` has a `group` function that provides additional output options for record sets ordered by a particular column.

Query variables can be manipulated and joined on the application server by using a subset of the `SELECT` SQL commands. Query of queries can be used to reduce the number of required lookups on any information resource that generates query variables. Record sets from disparate information resource types can be joined as required.

Sample Questions

1. What variables does a `<cfquery>` query object contain?

   A. `RecordCount`

   B. `ColumnList`

   C. `ExecutionTime`

   D. `DBTYPE`

2. `<cfoutput>` with the `GROUP` attribute requires which SQL clause in the SQL query?

   A. `WHERE`

   B. `GROUP BY`

   C. `ORDER BY`

   D. `JOIN`

3. What combination of attributes in `<cfquery>` does a query of queries require?

   A. `name` and `datasource`

   B. `dbtype` and `datasource`

   C. `name` and `query`

   D. `name` and `dbtype`

4. Which of the following SQL operations can be performed by using `<cfquery>`?

   A. `SELECT`

   B. `INSERT`

   C. `UPDATE`

   D. Stored procedure

PART 2

Variables and Expressions

IN THIS PART

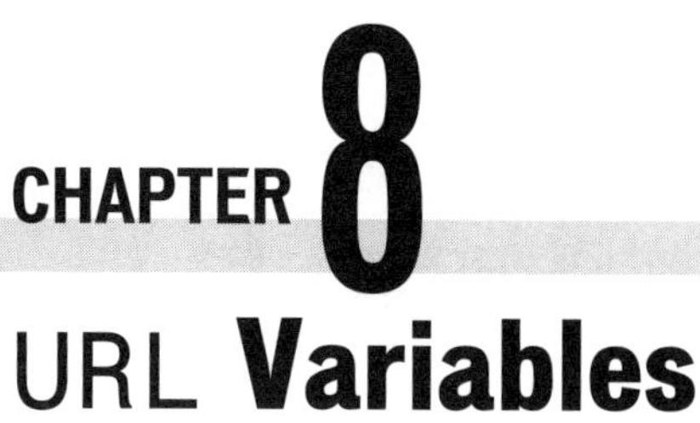

CHAPTER 8 URL Variables

IN THIS CHAPTER

What Is a URL Variable?

URL variables are variables that are created by passing data on the end of a hypertext link.

→ Local variables were introduced in Chapter 2, "Working with Variables and Expressions."

How Are URL Variables Created?

URL variables are not created by ColdFusion; they are created when browsers request URLs and specify parameters. To create a URL variable, you must first create a hypertext link like so:

```
<a href="index.cfm">Click Me</a>
```

URL variables are specified in the *query string* portion of a URL (the text after a ? character). You add URL variables to the link by first typing a question mark and then adding the `name=value` pair as follows:

```
<a href="index.cfm?FName=Emily">Click Me</a>
```

Now when the link is clicked, a variable called `FName`, with a value of `Emily`, is passed to the `index.cfm` page.

> **NOTE**
> You can make a hypertext link from an image as easily as you can from text. The same rules for creating URL variables apply to links around images. Just add the `name=value` pairs to the HTML `<a>` tag as shown in the preceding example. When the image is clicked, the variables are passed as normal.

Passing Multiple Variables at Once

You can pass multiple variables on the end of one link by separating each `name=value` pair with an ampersand (`&`). The following code passes three variables to the `index.cfm` page:

```
<a href="index.cfm?FName=Emily&MInit=B&LName=Kim">Click Me</a>
```

> **CAUTION**
>
> You can pass a lot of information in a query string; however, all browsers impose a length limit on URLs. Typically, older browsers allow approximately 254 characters to be passed in a URL; newer browsers' limits are higher. You should use this variable type with care because long URLs can become unsightly if used excessively.

Passing Complicated Strings

Sometimes you need to pass URL-unfriendly characters in your `URL` variables. For instance, spaces are not allowed in a URL. A ColdFusion function called `URLEncodedFormat()` is very useful in such a scenario.

`URLEncodedFormat()` accepts a single parameter, as shown in the following code snippet:

```
<!--- using URLEncodedFormat() with a string --->
<cfoutput>
<a href="index.cfm?Name=
 #URLEncodedFormat("Emily Kim")#">Click Me</a>
</cfoutput>
<!--- using URLEncodedFormat() with a variable --->
<cfset MyName="Emily Kim">
<cfoutput>
<a href="index.cfm?Name=
 #URLEncodedFormat(Variables.MyName)#">Click Me</a>
</cfoutput>
```

> **NOTE**
>
> The `<cfoutput>` tags are necessary in either case because `URLEncodedFormat()` is a ColdFusion function that must be evaluated by the ColdFusion server even if its parameter is a string.
>
> Also note that quotation marks appear around the string but not around the variable name in the function parameter. Quotation marks denote a string, whereas the lack of quotation marks in this case tells the ColdFusion server to evaluate the variable.

In either case, the function converts the space into its ASCII equivalent (in this instance, `%20`), which allows the variable's value to be passed successfully. Without this function, the part of the string after the space would be lost.

> **NOTE**
>
> When working with some newer browsers, you will often find that the string is passed successfully regardless of whether you use the function `URLEncodedFormat()`. This is because the browsers are forgiving and convert the special characters for you. However, you should not depend on this feature unless you're sure that your Web audience will be using such browsers.

> **TIP**
>
> When you're passing `URL` variables, using `URLEncodedFormat()` is usually a good idea even if you don't think it's necessary. Later, we will discuss dynamically created `URL` variables, whose values can often be unpredictable.

What Is the Scope of a URL Variable?

`URL` variables are not available for use on the page in which they are first defined. Rather, they are available on the page to which the link points.

Because of this fact, using URL variables is the simplest way of maintaining state on a Web site. *State* refers to the capability of a Web server to remember things from one page to the next. For instance, local variables do not help the programmer maintain state because they are available only locally on the page in which they are created; they are not available on any other page in the Web site. URL variables allow you to pass information from one page to another when the user clicks a link.

`URL` variables do not provide a total solution to the state problem because they have a limited scope. They are available only on the page to which they have been passed. After that page is processed by the ColdFusion server, the variables expire. However, while they exist, they can be used like local variables.

> **TIP**
>
> You can also create `URL` variables by using the `<cfparam>` tag. You usually do so on the page to which the link points in order to create a default value for a `URL` variable that is expected for the processing of the page. You can create `URL` variables this way:
>
> ```
> <cfparam name="URL.FName" default="Emily">
> ```

➜ `<cfparam>` was introduced in Chapter 3, "Conditional Processing."

Using URL Variables

So far, we have passed only *static* URL variables. The values of static variables remain constant. What is far more useful to you as a ColdFusion developer is to create *dynamic* URL variables, which are usually generated from the results of a database query.

> **NOTE**
>
> It is worth noting that URL is actually a ColdFusion structure, and URL variables may there be accessed as structure members. Chapter 15, "Structures," reviews structures in detail.

The following example creates a page that queries all the countries from the database. Each country name is displayed as a link. When a link is clicked, the user is sent to the corresponding target page, which displays the names of all employees in that country.

The following query pulls all the country names out of the database:

```
<cfquery name="GetCountries"
         datasource="Employees">
SELECT *
FROM Countries
</cfquery>
```

> **TIP**
>
> Some databases pad retrieved data to column width. To avoid filling URLs with blank spaces, use the `Trim()` function to remove leading and trailing whitespace.

You can then use the results of this query to print the names of all the countries as HTML links:

```
<cfoutput query="GetCountries">
<a href="index.cfm?CID=#CountryID#">#CountryName#</a><br>
</cfoutput>
```

> **TIP**
>
> Long documents often use URL bookmarks, which are links presented in a list at the top of a document. When clicked, these bookmarks jump the user down the page to a specific location. Creating these bookmarks involves first naming the points to which you would jump by using the `<a name="somename">` syntax. To create the URL bookmark to reference that location, you use the syntax `<a href="#somename">`. Note the use of the number sign (#) to tell the browser to jump to the spot on the page with the specified name. If you were dynamically generating this list of URL bookmarks, the # would be located inside the `<cfoutput>` tags and would cause the ColdFusion server to throw an error message essentially stating that it doesn't understand the use of the #. To correct this syntax, you would have to escape the #, thereby rendering it usable by the ColdFusion server. To escape a #, you double it. The correct code would read `<a href="##somename">`.

As each country name is printed, its associated country ID is coded as a `URL` variable called `CID`. When the user clicks any of the links, the country ID associated with the country name on which he or she clicked is passed to the target page. That target page can now use the country ID to query the database for more specific information.

The following query uses the country ID, passed in the variable `URL.CID`, to query the database for all the employees in that country:

```
<cfquery name="GetEmployees"
         datasource="Employees">
SELECT *
FROM Employees
WHERE CountryID = #URL.CID#
</cfquery>
```

Passing the primary key field of a database table is very useful for affecting the results of the target page.

CAUTION

As a rule, passing primary keys as URL parameters is dangerous, as it allows URL tampering to occur. At a minimum, this could allow a user to change a URL to refer to another record, and depending on the database drivers used, it could also allow users to create malicious SQL statements.

➜ Chapter 47, "Advanced Database Features," discusses using bind parameters and the `<cfqueryparam>` tag. This tag will also protect you from the potential security issue mentioned earlier.

Summary

Using `URL` variables is the easiest method for maintaining state in a Web environment. However, `URL` variables' scope is limited because they can pass variables only from one page to a specific target page. Nevertheless, they give you some level of interactivity with the Web visitor by allowing you to present the visitor with a list of dynamically generated hypertext links that are coded to pass information on to the target page. The variables being passed can then direct the target page to display information about the item selected by the visitor.

Sample Questions

1. Which character is used to separate URL variables?

   A. `?`

   B. `=`

   C. `&`

   D. `%`

2. Which function should be used to ensure that URL variables contains only safe text?

   A. `Trim()`

   B. `URLEncodedFormat()`

   C. `URLDecodedFormat()`

   D. `Val()`

3. Which of the following is a valid method for creating `URL` variables?

   A. `<a href="index.cfm?#URLEncodedFormat("Emily Kim")#">`

   B. `<cfset URLVar.FName="Emily">`

   C. `<cfparam name="URL.FName" default="Emily">`

   D. `<a name="index.cfm?#URLEncodedFormat("Emily Kim")#">`

CHAPTER 9 FORM Variables

IN THIS CHAPTER

What Is a FORM Variable?

URL variables allow you to interact with Web visitors in a limited fashion. However, the most common and useful method for providing visitors with an interactive experience is through HTML forms. Examples of the usefulness of forms include collecting user information, letting users enter criteria to search a database, giving users the ability to respond to polls, presenting visitors with options for printing reports, and allowing users to select personalization requirements.

It's important to remember that two pages are involved in using FORM variables: *form* and *action*. The form page has the HTML form elements on it. After a user enters or chooses her information in the form and submits it, and all this information is passed on to the action page, which then performs actions based on that information.

> **NOTE**
>
> In concept, working with FORM variables is the same as working with URL variables. Both have a display page and a processing page. In a URL scenario, the display page lists all the hypertext links. In a form scenario, the display page is the HTML form. The action page in both scenarios merely takes the variables that are passed to it and uses them to perform some action.

→ URL variables were introduced in Chapter 8, "URL Variables."

How Are FORM Variables Created?

As with `URL` variables, you do not create `FORM` variables by explicitly declaring `name=value` pairs. To create a `FORM` variable, you must first create an HTML form, name all the controls in that form, and then submit it. The data entered or selected on a form by the Web visitor are the values for the `FORM` variables.

➔ Local variables were introduced in Chapter 2, "Working with Variables and Expressions."

> **NOTE**
>
> This study guide is written to help you review your ColdFusion knowledge and to fill in some of the gaps. In other words, we are assuming that you are a seasoned developer and have a good working knowledge of ColdFusion and Web development. Therefore, we will assume you know how to create HTML form controls and will not discuss them in detail here.

The following sample code creates a short form:

```
<form action="actionpage.cfm" method="post">
First Name: <input type="text" NAME="FName"><br>
Favorite Color:
 <input type="checkbox" name="FavColor" value="R">Red
 <input type="checkbox" name="FavColor" value="G">Green
 <input type="checkbox" name="FavColor" VALUE="B">Blue<BR>
<input type="submit">
</form>
```

> **NOTE**
>
> You may have multiple forms on the form page, but only one can be submitted at a time. As soon as you click a Submit button, the `FORM` variables are passed on to the action page referenced in this form's `ACTION` attribute.
>
> You can also have more than one submit button per form. If you click either of the submit buttons, the `FORM` variables are passed on to the action page. The trick to determining which submit button was clicked is to give each button a unique `name` or `value`. Only the `name` and `value` of the clicked button will be passed to the action page.

Be sure to note these important points about the above code:

- The `action` attribute of the `form` tag specifies to which page the information from the form will be submitted.
- The text box is named `FName`.
- The checkboxes are all named `FavColor`.
- No ColdFusion functions or tags appear in this code.

> **CAUTION**
>
> When you're working with HTML forms in ColdFusion, it's a good idea to always make sure that the `method` attribute is set to `post`, not `get`. By HTML rules, if `method` is not declared, its value defaults to `get`. You will find that if you have `method="get"`, your `FORM` variables are actually sent instead as `URL` variables. (You can verify this by looking in your server debugging information.) Additionally, if you misspell the words `method` or `post`, you will find that the form submission automatically defaults to `get`.

➜ Debugging is discussed in Chapter 25, "Debugging."

In this section we describe how to create `FORM` variables. Even though you've created HTML form elements, you have not yet actually created any `FORM` variables. `FORM` variables don't exist until they get to the action page. Really, you're just naming the variables when you create the form element. A user enters the values when she types data into the form fields. It's not until she submits the form that the values she entered are matched up with the name of the field, and then the `name=value` pairs are actually created as `FORM` variables and passed on to the action page.

So, in the preceding example, if the user entered the name `Emily` into the text box, selected the `Blue` checkbox, and clicked the submit button, the `FORM` variable `name=value` pairs passed on to the action page would be `FName=Emily, FavColor=B`.

> **NOTE**
>
> Because the submit button was not named, it is not passed as a `FORM` variable.

> **NOTE**
>
> The name you assign to a form control is very important. When many form controls on a page have the same name (as in the case of checkboxes or radio buttons), ColdFusion compiles the submitted values and converts them into a list. Consider the following code:
>
> ```
> <input type="checkbox" name="FavColor" value="R">Red
> <input type="checkbox" name="FavColor" value="G">Green
> <input type="checkbox" name="FavColor" value="B">Blue
> ```
>
> If the user checked the checkbox for `Red` and `Blue`, the action page would receive the `name=value` pair `FavColor=R,B`.
>
> You can use what you know about ColdFusion lists to work with this data

➜ You'll learn about lists in Chapter 13, "Lists."

> **TIP**
>
> When you create a form, you are usually creating it to gather information that will be inserted into a database. Therefore, it is recommended that you name your form fields with the same name as the corresponding database column, or the name of the component or tag to which the fields will be submitted.

As we just discussed, the `name=value` pair for each form element is passed to the action page. However, if you just want a list of all the names of all form elements passed to the action page, you can access the list using the variable `FORM.fieldnames`. The ColdFusion application server automatically generates this variable for you when the form is submitted. It is a very useful variable for dynamically determining the names of all form elements. Again, you can use what you know about lists to manipulate this information.

> **NOTE**
>
> `FORM` itself is a ColdFusion structure which can be accessed like any other structure as will be explained in Chapter 15, "Structures."

Building Database-Driven Form Elements

Earlier you saw that the form page didn't have any ColdFusion functions or tags in it. In this section, you'll see how to use ColdFusion to dynamically generate a `SELECT` (drop-down list) form control from a database query to display a list of options—in this case, colors.

The first step in this process is to perform the query on the form page to grab the color information that you want displayed in the drop-down list:

```
<cfquery name="GetColors"
         datasource="MyDSN">
SELECT ColorID, ColorName
FROM Colors
ORDER BY ColorName
</cfquery>
```

After you have the query, you just need to loop over the query result to print the variables in place of the hard-coded elements:

```
<select name="ColorID">
  <cfoutput query="GetColors">
    <option value="#ColorID#">#ColorName#</option>
  </cfoutput>
</select>
```

> **TIP**
>
> If you find that the dynamically generated form elements are not being created properly, you can always run the page in your browser and view the source. That way, you can see the generated HTML code. Looking at it should help you figure out what is wrong.

Validating Form Fields

Data entered into HTML forms must usually be validated so ensure that required values are specified and that the correct data types are used. There are two basic types of validation employed in HTML form development:

- Client-side validation occurs within the Web browser, usually before form submission. This form of validation requires that client-side code (usually JavaScript) be executed within the browser.
- Server-side validation occurs after the form has been submitted. This form of validation requires server-side code (CFML code in our case).

Client-side validation is primarily used to create a better user experience, whereas server-side validation is what actually enforces data integrity. As such, ideally, both forms of validation should be used.

The simplest way to perform validation is to have ColdFusion do all the hard work for you. The `<cfinput>` tag (and the CFML equivalents of all of the HTML form tags) support the use of additional attributes that instruct ColdFusion to generate validation code for you automatically. Table 9.1 lists these attributes.

Table 9.1 Form Field Validation Attributes

ATTRIBUTE	DESCRIPTION
`mask`	Input mask (only used with client-side validation)
`maxlength`	Maximum number of characters allowed (supported in text fields in HTML, CFML adds support for `<textarea>` fields too)
`message`	Message to be displayed if validation fails
`pattern`	Regular expression validation pattern
`range`	Range of valid values
`required`	Whether or not the field is required
`validate`	Data validation type (types are listed in Table 9.2)
`validateAt`	Where to validate, `onBlur` for immediate client-side validation, `onServer` for server-side validation, `onSubmit` for pre-submission client-side validation

TIP

To perform both client-side and server0side validation, pass multiple values (comma delimited) to `validateAt`.

`validate` is the type of data to be validated, as seen in Table 9.2

Table 9.2 Data Validation Types

TYPE	DESCRIPTION
boolean	Boolean values (yes, no, true, false, number)
creditcard	Credit card number (mod10)
date	US formatted date
email	Well formed e-mail address
eurodate	European formatted date
float	A number (same as numeric)
guid	Microsoft/DCE format unique identifier
integer	Integer value
maxlength	Check for maxlength value
noblanks	Allow no blank values
numeric	A number (same as float)
range	Range of values (specified in range attribute)
regex	Regular expression pattern (same as regular_expression)
regular_expression	Regular expression pattern (same as regex)
social_secutity_number	US social security number (same as ssn)
ssn	US social security number (same as social_secutity_number)
submitOnce	Only allow a single form submission (only used with type="submit" and type="image")
telephone	US format phone number
time	Time in hh:mm:ss format
url	Well formed URL
usdate	US formatted date
uuid	Unique identifier
zipcode	US format zip code

To use ColdFusion generated validation, the `<cfform>` family of tags is used, as seen in the following example:

```
<cfform action="actionpage.cfm"
        method="post">
id:
<cfinput type="text"
         name="id"
         message="You must enter your id to proceed."
         required="yes"
         validate="integer"
         validateat="onsubmit,onserver">
<br>
<input type="submit">
</cfform>
```

In this example a single field is defined as required and as being an `integer`. Validation occurs both client-side and server-side, and an error message (to be displayed if validation fails) is specified.

> **CAUTION**
>
> ColdFusion generated server-side validation is not foolproof. It works by embedding hidden form fields containing validation rules within the form. This means that a user could possibly edit out those rules so as to submit the form without them. Best practices dictate that all passed data be manually validated when received (`<cfparam>` is ideally suited for this task).

What Is the Scope of a FORM Variable?

As stated earlier in this chapter, `FORM` variables are very similar to `URL` variables. That means they can be used as a short-lived method of maintaining state on a Web site.

The scope of `FORM` variables is the action page, and, also like `URL` variables, they expire after the page is processed.

> **TIP**
>
> You can pass `URL` variables at the same time you pass `FORM` variables. Just add them to the end of the `action` attribute of your `form` tag.

➜ You'll review `SESSION` and `COOKIE` variables in Chapter 11, "Session State Management."

The Action Page

After the form data is entered and validated, it is pushed to the action page for processing. You can use `FORM` variables on the action page in much the same way that you would use `URL` or even local variables. Consider this example:

```
<cfquery name="GetEmployees"
         datasource="MyDSN">
SELECT *
FROM Employees
WHERE EmployeeID = #FORM.EmployeeID#
</cfquery>
```

`FORM` variable `name=value` pairs for text boxes, text areas, and drop-down lists always exist on the action page even if the user didn't enter any information. For instance, if a text box named `FName` was left empty upon form submission, the action page would get `FName=`.

This point is important because some form controls—namely checkboxes, radio buttons, multiple select controls, and submit buttons that are not clicked—are not passed at all if they are not selected. So if a form has a set of checkboxes named `FavColor`, and the user doesn't check any of them, *nothing* is sent to the action page.

It is very important that you do the following on your action page:

- Set default values for form controls that could potentially not exist by using `<cfparam>`.

  or

- Use the `IsDefined()` function in your conditional statements to perform validation to ensure that a variable exists before you use it.

→ `<cfparam>` was introduced in Chapter 2, "Working with Variables and Expressions."

TIP

We've stated before that it is always a good idea to prefix your ColdFusion variables. However, it's OK not to prefix your variables if you want to intentionally leave your code flexible. For instance, consider this example:

```
<cfquery name="GetEmployees"
         datasource="MyDSN">
SELECT *
FROM Employees
WHERE EmployeeID = #EmployeeID#
</cfquery>
```

If this code were in the action page, it could use either a `FORM` variable or a `URL` variable in the `WHERE` statement.

Summary

HTML forms are used to collect data from application users. In this chapter, you reviewed the concepts necessary for creating, validating, and using FORM variables. Once FORM elements are named, and the user fills in the value and submits the form, you can have the ColdFusion application server perform either server-side or client-side validation on the entries. You also have the option of creating your own custom validation before performing any other processing on the action page.

Sample Questions

1. What is the recommended METHOD to use when submitting forms to ColdFusion pages?

   A. get

   B. action

   C. post

   D. head

2. Which of the following is an example of a form control that does *not* pass a value to the action page by default?

   A. Text box

   B. Text area

   C. Checkbox

   D. Drop-down select control

3. Consider the following checkboxes:

```
<input type="checkbox" name="FavCountry" value="US">United States
<input type="checkbox" name="FavCountry" value="CAN">Canada
<input type="checkbox" name="FavCountry" value="ENG">England
<input type="checkbox" name="FavCountry" VAlUE="FRA">France
```

   If you check France and Canada, what would your FORM variable look like?

   A. FavCountry=CAN,FRA

   B. FavCountry=CAN

   C. FavCountry=FRA

   D. FavCountry=CAN&FRA

4. Which form of validation is the most secure?

   A. Client-side

   B. Auto-generated server-side

   C. Manual server-side

CHAPTER 10 APPLICATION and SERVER Variables

IN THIS CHAPTER

Understanding APPLICATION and SERVER Variables

This chapter discusses both APPLICATION and SERVER variables. Both types of variables are very important to maintaining state on a server.

→ State maintenance was briefly mentioned in Chapter 8, "URL Variables."

Using these variables, you can *remember* things on a Web site over multiple pages and multiple applications because they are stored in memory on the ColdFusion server.

APPLICATION variables can be set for one application on a server. By doing so, you can create variables that are universal to an entire application (but that cannot be used by other applications).

SERVER variables are set for the entire server and are available to every application on that server. You can add to the server scope or use variables that are already available in the scope.

→ Some default variables that are available in the server scope are listed in Table 10.1, later in this chapter.

APPLICATION Variable Scope

After you create an APPLICATION variable, it is immediately available to every page in your application. You can store simple variables or complex data types such as structures and arrays in it. Query record sets can also be stored in APPLICATION variables.

> **TIP**
>
> `APPLICATION` variables are great places to store queries that are used in many pages of your Web site. For instance, many forms that collect user information have a drop-down list of U.S. states. Querying the database every time you want to display this list can be a waste of valuable resources. Instead, write the query directly to the `APPLICATION` scope, and it will be stored in memory.
>
> You will see an example of the code to put a query record set into the `APPLICATION` scope in the next section, "Creating `APPLICATION` Variables."

By default, `APPLICATION` variables are stored in the ColdFusion server's memory for two days. You can see and change the default and maximum time out for these variables by looking in ColdFusion Administrator. After you log into Administrator, look in the `Server` section at the top and find a link called Memory Variables. You may use this screen to set the default and maximum time-out values.

> **TIP**
>
> If you're worried about `APPLICATION` variables gobbling up all of your extra RAM, you can always turn them off using ColdFusion Administrator. On the Memory Variables page of ColdFusion Administrator, you will see a checkbox labeled `Enable Application Variables`. If you uncheck it, your developers will be restricted from using these variables.

Creating `APPLICATION` Variables

If you plan to use `APPLICATION` variables, each page of your Web site must belong to a specific application. Coding this information on each individual page can be time-intensive and a maintenance headache. Therefore, the `Application` pages are the perfect location to put this information.

➜ `Application` pages was discussed in Chapter 6, "The Application Framework."

To use `APPLICATION` variables the application must be named (as seen in Chapter 6).

> **CAUTION**
>
> Be careful when naming your application. If you give the same name to two different applications on the same server, the server will treat them as if they were the same application and will allow one to see the other's `APPLICATION` variables.

> **TIP**
>
> On the converse of that caution, you can use the naming of your application to your advantage. If the framework of your application requires that you put associated files in widely separated directories, you can still treat the files as part of the same application by naming them accordingly.

Creating APPLICATION variables is very similar to creating local variables. The only addition required is the proper scope, as shown here:

```
<cfset APPLICATION.FName="Emily">
```

This code creates a variable called FName with a value of Emily and places it in the APPLICATION scope. Now it can be used everywhere in your application until it hits its time limit.

Complex data can also be stored in APPLICATION variables. In the following code, the query is created as normal but placed into the APPLICATION scope by prefixing it:

```
<cfquery name="APPLICATION.GetStates"
         datasource="Employees">
SELECT StateAbbreviation, StateName
FROM States
</cfquery>
```

Now the query result set will be available in memory. You can use the query as usual, but with the addition of the scope as shown here:

```
<cfoutput query="APPLICATION.GetStates">
#StateAbbreviation#
#StateName#<br>
</cfoutput>
```

CAUTION

APPLICATION variables are great places to store some query record sets, but others should not be placed in them. For instance, personalized user information should not be stored in APPLICATION variables. Because APPLICATION variables are available to the entire application, they apply to all users. Personalized information is better stored in COOKIE, CLIENT, or SESSION variables.

→ COOKIE, CLIENT, and SESSION variables are discussed in Chapter 11, "Session State Management."

Because APPLICATION variables stay in memory for the specified period of time, it doesn't make sense for you to run the query against the database every time the page is accessed. You should run the query only if it has expired in memory.

If using Application.cfc, use the onApplicationStart() method to ensure that APPLICATION variables are not reinitialized unnecessarily. If using Application.cfm, a conditional statement is placed around the query (as seen in this example):

```
<cfif not IsDefined("APPLICATION.GetStates")>
 <cfquery name="APPLICATION.GetStates"
          datasource="Employees">
 SELECT *
 FROM States
 </cfquery>
</cfif>
```

→ <cfif> was discussed in Chapter 3, "Conditional Processing."

CAUTION

APPLICATION variables persist on the server for a given length of time and are not refreshed until their time limit has been reached. Therefore, if you need to refresh the APPLICATION variables, you must do so programmatically using conditional processing.

TIP

Checking for the existence of APPLICATION variables before you use them is always a good idea. Not only do they expire naturally, but they also are lost if the server is ever rebooted.

Creating SERVER Variables

Much of what you know about APPLICATION variables can be applied to SERVER variables. The most obvious deviation, however, is the fact that the use of special tags or files is not required to enable them. SERVER variables are automatically available to any page in any application on the server.

Table 10.1 lists some default SERVER variables. To see a list of all SERVER variables, you can use the following code snippet:

```
<cfdump var="#SERVER#">
```

Table 10.1 Default SERVER Variables

SERVER VARIABLE	DESCRIPTION
SERVER.ColdFusion.AppServer	Contains the name of the application server being used by ColdFusion (will be JRun4 if standalone ColdFusion is used)
SERVER.ColdFusion.Expiration	Holds the server expiration date (if an evaluation version is being used)
SERVER.ColdFusion.ProductLevel	Stores the ColdFusion Product level (such as Standard or Enterprise)
SERVER.ColdFusion.ProductName	Contains the name of the ColdFusion product
SERVER.ColdFusion.ProductVersion	Holds the ColdFusion version information
SERVER.ColdFusion.RootDir	Stores the ColdFusion root (installation) directory
SERVER.ColdFusion.SerialNumber	Holds the ColdFusion server serial number

Table 10.1 (CONTINUED)

SERVER VARIABLE	DESCRIPTION
`SERVER.ColdFusion.SupportedLocales`	Holds the comma-delimited list of locales that ColdFusion supports
`SERVER.OS.AdditionalInformation`	Additional information as provided by the operating system
`SERVER.OS.Arch`	Processor architecture
`SERVER.OS.BuildNumber`	Operating system build number
`SERVER.OS.Name`	Stores the name of the operating system
`SERVER.OS.Version`	Stores the version information for the operating system

Variables in the `SERVER` scope can be read and written to, but generally the `SERVER` scope should not be used for storage in your own applications.

CAUTION

Overwriting default system `SERVER` variables is a bad idea. Usually, the manipulation of `SERVER` variables is performed only during debugging.

CAUTION

Don't arbitrarily reference `SERVER` variables listed in Table 10.1–always first use `IsDefined()` to check that they exist. Macromedia reserves the right to change these as it sees fit.

NOTE

`APPLICATION` and `SERVER` variables are structures. Therefore, you can also use the structure functions to manage them.

➜ Structures and their functions are discussed in Chapter 15, "Structures."

Summary

`APPLICATION` and `SERVER` variables are wonderful tools for making information widely available throughout an application or server. Although they do take up space in memory, they can decrease the need for calls to the database, which is often the most taxing function of your application.

Sample Questions

1. Which of the following statements is true?

   A. The use of `SERVER` variables must be explicitly enabled in ColdFusion Administrator.

   B. `SERVER` variables may always be used and cannot be disabled.

   C. `SERVER` variables may be used as long as an `Application` file is present.

2. Where are `APPLICATION` variables stored?

   A. Server memory

   B. Server cookies

   C. Client cookies

   D. Database

3. Which `Application.cfc` method should be used to set `SERVER` variables?

   A. `onApplicationStart()`

   B. `onServerStart()`

   C. `onRequestStart()`

   D. `onRequest()`

   E. none of the above

CHAPTER 11

Session State Management

IN THIS CHAPTER

What Is Session State Management?

Earlier in this book, you learned about how FORM and URL variables can be used to pass variables from one page to another. Later, in the chapter on custom tags, you will learn of a tag called <CF_EmbedFields>, which allows you to simulate the passing of form variables across multiple pages. Although these techniques leave the impression of state maintenance, they are, at most, a poor man's version of it.

→ URL and FORM variables were discussed in Chapters 8 and 9, respectively. Custom tags are discussed in Chapter 28, "Custom Tags."

True state maintenance requires that information be stored in a way such that it exists outside the scope of variables that must be passed manually from page to page.

In the previous chapter, you learned about APPLICATION and SERVER variables. These are true state-maintenance variables that are saved in the server's memory.

→ APPLICATION and SERVER variables were discussed in Chapter 10, "APPLICATION and SERVER Variables."

In this unit we learn about three more state-maintenance variables: COOKIE, SESSION, and CLIENT. The difference between these variables and APPLICATION and SERVER variables is that these are used specifically to maintain state about one user, rather than just information that is global to the application or server.

Cookies

Cookies are simply stored variables. The main difference between cookies and ColdFusion variables is that they are saved on the client machine. The ColdFusion server writes cookies to the browser, which then saves them to specific, files in the browser's file system.

> **NOTE**
>
> Different browsers use different storage locations for cookies, but regardless of how they are stored, the behave the same way as far as your ColdFusion code is concerned..

Making Cookies

Cookies are server specific: They can be retrieved only by the server that set them. Cookies can be made to be domain specific, in which case they are accessible to all domain servers.

Within your application, you can create cookie variables by using the `<cfcookie>` tag, as shown here:

```
<cfcookie name="FirstName" value="Emily" expires="10">
```

The preceding code creates a cookie called `FirstName` with a value of `Emily`. It is set to expire in `10` days.

The `expires` attribute can be set as shown in Table 11.1.

Table 11.1 Values for the `<cfcookie>` `expires` Attribute

ATTRIBUTE VALUES	DESCRIPTION
`expires="5"`	Cookie will expire in five days.
`expires="1/1/2006"`	Cookie will expire on January 1, 2006.
`expires="never"`	Cookie will never expire.
`expires="now"`	Cookie will expire immediately. Use this setting to delete a cookie.
No `expires` attribute	Without an `expires` attribute in the `<cfcookie>` tag, you are creating a browser session cookie (one that is never saved to disk), that will expire when the browser is closed.

Cookies are not actually set in the browser until ColdFusion request processing has completed. However, ColdFusion allows you to use cookies in the same page that creates them (it does this be creating temporary cookies internally).

Using Cookies

A cookie can be used like any other variable in ColdFusion. To use a cookie, you simply call it with the `COOKIE` prefix, like this:

```
<cfoutput>#COOKIE.FirstName#</cfoutput>
```

Depending on your browser, you might be confined to 20 cookies per domain, or 4 Kbytes' worth of information. Twenty cookies is quite limiting. Just collecting the user's first name, last name, email address, phone number, and other personal information can easily use up half of your cookie allotment very quickly.

You can bypass this limit with a little creativity and by employing *cookie crumbs*, or *cookie chips*, which take multiple `name=value` variable pairs, combine them into one variable, and use a delimiter to separate the sets of pairs:

```
<cfcookie name="ContactInfo"
          value="fn=emily;ln=kim;e=emily@trilemetry.com">
```

There is nothing exceptional about this technique. When you want to use this cookie, you just access it and parse out the values using list techniques.

➜ Lists are introduced in Chapter 13, "Lists."

A Cookie's Scope

Cookies are available provided that the browser is set to use them and that they have not expired or been deleted.

> **TIP**
>
> Some Web visitors configure their browsers so that cookies are not accepted. If you depend upon cookies in your application, you should use a detection script to display a message to such visitors. Depending on your application, it might not actually break without cookies enabled–it might merely act weird. Don't ever assume that a cookie will be present just because you set it.

Users can (and do) delete cookies. To ensure that they are actually there before you use them, be sure to check that they exist:

```
<cfif IsDefined("COOKIE.FirstName")>
 <cfoutput>#COOKIE.FirstName#</cfoutput>
</cfif>
```

> **CAUTION**
>
> Cookies have always received a bad rap. They are seen as a threat to public safety because they can store personal information about users and can be retrieved by servers. Much of this fear is unfounded because only the server that sets a cookie can retrieve it. However, some of this fear is reasonable because cookies are just text files on the client machine and can be opened easily.
>
> Some responsibility lies in the hands of the programmer. Highly sensitive information–passwords or credit card numbers, for example–should never be stored in cookies.

SESSION Variables

SESSION variables are memory-resident variables that are saved in the server's memory (just like APPLICATION and SERVER variables). However, although SESSION variables maintain information about one user rather than an entire application or server, they are still tied to one application.

Preparing to Use SESSION Variables

SESSION variables track a user through an application, and their use is intrinsically tied to the application. To use SESSION variables you must enable them:

- If using Application.cfc, use <cfset THIS.sessionManagement="true"> to enable session use, and THIS.sessionTimeout to specify the timeout value.
- If using Application.cfm, use <cfapplication sessionManagement="true"> to enable session use, and the sessionTimeout attribute to specify the timeout value.

By enabling sessionManagement, you tell the ColdFusion server to allow you to use SESSION variables. The sessionTimeout uses the CreateTimeSpan() function to declare how long you want SESSION variables to stay in the server's memory.

> **NOTE**
>
> By specifying a sessionTimeout value you can set how long you want your SESSION variables to persist. However, when using this attribute, you can never exceed the maximum time limit set in the ColdFusion Administrator.

When a new session is created, ColdFusion assigns an id to it. ColdFusion supports two forms of SESSION variables (and thus IDs):

- If using ColdFusion-managed SESSION variables, two variables are automatically created: CFID and CFTOKEN. Both of these variables are used to identify specific sessions.
- If using J2EE-managed SESSION variables, a single variable named jsessionid is used to identify specific sessions.

The type of SESSION variable used is a server-wide setting specified in ColdFusion Administrator.

> **TIP**
>
> One benefit of J2EE-managed sessions is that they may be shared with Java code (servlets, for example). Another important benefit is that J2EE servers can replicate SESSION data across servers (including ColdFusion data if the J2EE server manages sessions).

> **NOTE**
>
> SESSION variables use cookies to store copies of the ID in order to track the user to one particular browser. However, no other information is stored in cookies.

Using cookies to store the ID is the preferred and easiest way to use SESSION variables. However, some applications are built for an audience whose browsers do not accept cookies. In that case, you will have to pass both variables manually using URL and FORM variables.

> **NOTE**
>
> If you use <cflocation>, you can have ColdFusion pass the ID for you by using the attribute addtoken and setting it to yes.

> **TIP**
>
> If you are working with multiple subdomains and need the SESSION variables to be available to all of them, you can set the setdomaincookies attribute (in the Application.cfc or the of the <cfapplication> tag) to true. The setdomaincookies attribute tells the server to allow the CFID and CFTOKEN to be recognized by both all hosts within a domain. This attribute is also useful in a clustered environment.

Creating SESSION Variables

After you have prepared the environment to use SESSION variables, you create them using <cfset>, just as with local variables, except that you add the prefix SESSION to them:

```
<cfset SESSION.FirstName="Emily">
```

After you create the SESSION variable, it is available until the session expires.

> **TIP**
>
> You can also use <cfparam> to create and set default values for SESSION variables.

➜ <cfparam> was introduced in Chapter 2, "Working with Variables and Expressions."

The ColdFusion server stores all SESSION variables in structures. Therefore, you should use the structure functions to maintain your SESSION variables.

> **NOTE**
>
> COOKIE variables are also stored as structures.

➜ Structures are discussed in Chapter 15, "Structures."

Using `SESSION` Variables

`SESSION` variables can be simple (numbers, text) or complex (arrays, queries, structures, and more). As they are tied to clients, are so simple to set and edit `SESSION` variables, and they can store just about any type of data, they plan an important role in user settings, application security, and application optimization.

Some common uses for `SESSION` variables include:

- Managing logins and logouts, `SESSION` variables maintain the login state.
- Storing shopping carts.
- Remembering user options (colors, language choices, and more).
- Storing search results.

As already explained, `<cfset>` can be used to both create and update `SESSION` variables. To delete session variables use the `StructDelete()` function (specifying `SESSION` as the name of the structure from which to delete a member).

> **TIP**
>
> ColdFusion session variables persists even after the browser is closed. If you close your browser before the timeout period is up and then reopen your browser to access the site again, you will find that the session is still active. This could be a problem if there is a chance that another user could access the program within the time-out period. You can rectify this problem by converting the ID variables into browser-session cookies. J2EE session variables do not behave this way, and will not persist after the browser is closed.

`CLIENT` Variables

Like `COOKIE` and `SESSION` variables, `CLIENT` variables are specific to one user. However, rather than being stored on the client machine or in the server's memory, `CLIENT` variables are stored elsewhere.

`CLIENT` variables can store only simple data (like numbers and strings), not complex data (like arrays, structures, and queries).

Preparing `CLIENT` Variable Storage

`CLIENT` variables, like `SESSION` variables, are also tied to an application and must be enabled before they can be used:

- If using `Application.cfc`, use `<cfset THIS.clientManagement="true">` to enable client use, and `THIS.clientStorage` to specify their storage location.

- If using `Application.cfm`, use `<cfapplication clientManagement="true">` to enable client use, and the `clientStorage` attribute to specify their storage location.

There are three locations where you can store `CLIENT` variables. They are discussed in Table 11.2 and can be set in the ColdFusion Administrator.

Table 11.2 Storage Locations for CLIENT Variables

STORAGE LOCATION	DESCRIPTION
Data source	A specific data source can be used to store `CLIENT` variable data.
Registry	`CLIENT` variables can be stored in the Registry (Windows only).
Cookie	`CLIENT` variables can be stored in cookies.

> **CAUTION**
> Your system can become unstable or unusable if your registry holds too much data. As a general rule, registry use should be avoided.

If you set `CLIENT` variable storage to a data source, you will find that the ColdFusion application server creates two tables called `CDATA` and `CGLOBAL` in the data source for this purpose.

Cookies can be a good place to store `CLIENT` variable IDs, but all the limitations you have learned about cookies remain true in this case.

There is one special advantage to `CLIENT` variables: Because they can be stored in a database, they can be used by multiple servers (perhaps in a cluster), since those servers can share the same database. As such, `CLIENT` variables are invaluable in the right situation.

Creating `CLIENT` Variables

`CLIENT` variables are the only way to reliably store information about one user over multiple sessions. Although you can do this with cookies, the fact that `COOKIE` variables can be easily deleted or modified makes them less reliable.

You create `CLIENT` variables using `<cfset>` and prefixing the variable name with `CLIENT`:

```
<cfset CLIENT.FirstName="Emily">
```

You can also use `<cfparam>` to set default values for this variable.

Using CLIENT Variables

To use CLIENT variables, you just prefix them appropriately:

```
<cfoutput>#CLIENT.FirstName#</cfoutput>
```

The output of the preceding line will display the name Emily.

Which Variables Should I Use?

In this chapter you reviewed COOKIE, SESSION, and CLIENT variables. They overlap in some uses, but there is a specific time and place for each.

COOKIE variables are often used for non-secure data that can be lost without consequence to the application. Because the variables are tied to one particular browser, if a user were to use the same application at home and at work, her data would have to be re-created in both places.

SESSION variables are usually used for sensitive information because that information remains on the server and is never transmitted to the client machine. As mentioned earlier, SESSION variables are often used for authentication as well. SESSION variables can store complex data (something COOKIE and CLIENT variables cannot do).

CLIENT variables are usually used for site-personalization efforts. CLIENT variables may store only simple data, but because that data can be stored to disk (a database), it can be shared across servers in a cluster (something SESSION variables cannot do). In either case, it is on the server and available to the user from any computer.

Remember that within one application, you might find it useful to use more than one of these types of variables to accomplish your tasks.

Summary

Session state management takes advantage of COOKIE, SESSION, and CLIENT variables, which are essential to an application that needs to work with persistent data.

Sample Questions

1. What value would you assign to the expires attribute of the <cfcookie> tag if you wanted to create a browser session cookie?

   A. session

   B. browser

   C. now

   D. Don't set the expires attribute

2. Which variable types can be shared among clustered servers? *(select two)*

   A. `CLIENT`

   B. `COOKIE`

   C. ColdFusion `SESSION`

   D. J2EE `SESSION`

   E. `SERVER`

3. Which of the following variables may store a ColdFusion query?

   A. `SESSION`

   B. `CLIENT`

   C. `COOKIE`

CHAPTER 12
Locking

IN THIS CHAPTER

Understanding Locking

The concept of locking is well established in multi-user environments. File locking prevents multiple users from editing a file at the same time. Database management systems also use locking by allowing different users to access the same records without interference. In a ColdFusion environment, locking is used to explicitly manage the sequence in which concurrent requests are processed.

There are generally two reasons to use locks within ColdFusion:

- To prevent simultaneous access to code—for example, if you were writing a file with `<cffile>`, you wouldn't want another process reading that same file while it was being written.
- To ensure that a block of code is executed as a group—for example, if you were updating ten `APPLICATION` variables, you wouldn't want other requests to read five old variables and five new ones (you'd want other requests to pause until all ten were written).

> **NOTE**
>
> As of ColdFusion MX, opting not to lock access to shared scopes (`SESSION`, `APPLICATION`, and `SERVER`) will not cause memory corruption.

Using `<cflock>`

Locking in ColdFusion is implemented using the `<cflock>` tag—the code between `<cflock>` and `</cflock>` is managed by the lock.

The <cflock> tag has two mutually exclusive attributes: name and scope (both of which identify a lock). In addition to name and scope, two other attributes need attention.

The first is the timeout attribute, which throws a lock error if a procedure exceeds the value or if two locks are contentious. Contentious locks, which are also known as *deadlocks*, will be reviewed later in this chapter.

The other <cflock> attribute is type, which specifies whether the lock is readonly or exclusive. exclusive locks are used to prevent other access while a lock is in place, while a readonly lock allows read operations but not writes (in other words, readonly allows processing if no exclusive lock is open). readonly locks are faster than exclusive ones.

Using the name Attribute

The NAME attribute of the <cflock> tag uniquely identifies a lock around a specific variable, file system, or custom tag call. This name is referenced in all locations where the lock needs to be obeyed. The name attribute is useful for custom tag calls that are not thread-safe, or for file access locks. Specific SESSION, APPLICATION, or SERVER variables can also be locked using the name attribute.

The following code using the name attribute to lock a <cffile> call (so as to prevent concurrent writes to the same file):

```
<cflock name="fileWrite"
        timeout="15"
        type="exclusive">
  <cffile action="write">
          file="#outFile"
          output="#data#">
</cflock>
```

By locking this block of code, all subsequent requests (using the same lock name) will wait until the initial request finishes running the custom tag. Because the timeout attribute was set for 15 seconds, an error will be thrown if the lock exceeds this period of time.

> **TIP**
>
> You should use exclusive locks whenever custom tags or file access is locked. This makes the lock a single-threaded operation. All calls to the same tag should use the same lock name.

Using the scope Attribute

The scope attribute is the alternative to the name attribute. This attribute has three possible values: SESSION, APPLICATION, or SERVER. Setting one of these values through the SCOPE attribute locks all the variables of that scope at the same time. A locked SESSION scope automatically applies to a single SESSION and does not lock any other sessions.

> **TIP**
>
> When locking the APPLICATION or SERVER scopes it is vital to keep lock time down to the absolute minimum.

readonly Locks

The alternative to using an exclusive lock is to use a readonly lock. A readonly lock will permit two requests to run simultaneously as though no lock existed. But if an exclusive lock is active, any readonly locks will wait until that lock is released.

Dealing with Deadlocks

One potential hazard of using <cflock> is that nested locks can lead to a *deadlock*. A deadlock occurs when two or more locks are initiated on separate templates. Say that you have two pages that lock both the APPLICATION and SESSION scope. The first page, named login.cfm, records a user's name in a SESSION variable and then appends the name to an APPLICATION variable. The APPLICATION variable contains an embedded structure of users who are currently logged in. A second page, logout.cfm, clears the SESSION structure and removes the user's name from the embedded structure in the APPLICATION scope.

These pages behave perfectly if the scopes are locked and nested in the same order. If, however, the locks are nested in a different order, the potential for a deadlock exists. The following code causes a deadlock:

```
login.cfm:
    <cflock scope="session"
            type="exclusive"
            timeout="15">
     <!---
     locked the session scope - now set a session variable
     --->
     <cfset SESSION.userName=FORM.userName>
     <cflock scope="application"
             type="exclusive"
             timeout="15">
     <!---
     a nested lock since we are dealing with both scopes at once
     --->
     <!---
     note that this structure was defined on another page somewhere
     --->
```

```
 <cfset APPLICATION.loggedInUsers[SESSION.userName]
        = SESSION.userName>
 </cflock>
</cflock>
```

```
logout.cfm:
    <cflock scope="application"
            type="exclusive"
            timeout="15">
     <!---
     locked the application scope FIRST, opposite of the login page!!!
     --->
     <!---
     then we nest a second lock since the session scope is used
     --->
     <cflock scope="session"
             type="exclusive"
             timeout="15">
     <!--- get rid of the user from the application scope--->
     <cfset StructDelete(APPLICATION.SESSION.userName)>
     <!--- kill the session --->
     <cfset structClear(SESSION)>
     </cflock>
    </cflock>
```

Although this code may appear to be sound, it is not. If the `login.cfm` page runs and is then interrupted by another thread that runs the logout page, a fatal deadlock may occur. The `login.cfm` page could lock the `SESSION` scope at the same time the `logout.cfm` page locks the `APPLICATION` scope. Then the nested locks will demand exclusive access to the nested scopes. `login.cfm` will wait for `logout.cfm` to release the application scope, while `logout.cfm` will wait for `SESSION` scope to be released. Both would wait forever if there were not a time-out, but because there is a time-out, a fatal error will occur instead. Regardless, the deadlock causes one of the pages to fail.

To avoid deadlocks, you should always lock and unlock in a controlled and ordered sequence. The recommended order is not arbitrary and is based on the underlying architecture of the ColdFusion engine. Locks should be declared in terms of specificity, moving from most specific (`SESSION` scope) to least specific (`SERVER` scope).

You need to declare nested locks in this order:

1. `SESSION` scope
2. `APPLICATION` scope
3. `SERVER` scope

You should unlock in the reverse order:

1. `SERVER` scope
2. `APPLICATION` scope
3. `SESSION` scope

To solve the deadlock in the previous code example, you could simply reverse the order of locking in the `login.cfm` page so that the `APPLICATION` scope is locked first rather than second. Finally, you could place all the `<cfset>` tags on `login.cfm` in the nested lock.

Summary

Locking is an essential element to any production application. Locking is implemented using the `<cflock>` tag. The `name` and `scope` attributes are mutually exclusive and have various pros and cons. Deadlocks can occur if the locks are nested and not locked in a specific order.

Sample Questions

1. Choose the legal `<cflock>` statement.

   A. `<cflock timeout="16">`

   B. `<cflock name="myLock" scope="session" timeout="16">`

   C. `<cflock scope="myLock" timeout="16" type="readonly">`

   D. `<cflock name="myLock" timeout="16">`

2. Which variable scopes should be locked to ensure controlled access? *(select all that apply)*

   A. `REQUEST`

   B. `CLIENT`

   C. `SESSION`

   D. `APPLICATION`

   E. `SERVER`

3. When can deadlocks occur? *(select two)*

   A. When locks are nested

   B. When locks are in a different order on different pages

   C. When locks wait for each other and are not nested

   D. When `readonly` locks are declared against the `CLIENT` scope

PART 3
Data Types

IN THIS PART

CHAPTER 13

Lists

IN THIS CHAPTER

Understanding Lists

A list is one of the most basic variable types in ColdFusion—although, in truth, a list is not a type per se. A list is a simple set of data separated by one or more delimiters. The following is a simple list of six American states (in this example, the list is delimited by commas):

```
CA,FL,MA,MI,NY,WA
```

The individual items in a list are known as *elements*, and unless a list is an empty string, it always contains at least one element. By default, lists are delimited by commas, but ColdFusion allows you to specify any character (or multiple characters) as the delimiter. The following is the same list, this time delimited by spaces:

```
CA FL MA MI NY WA
```

In fact, any variable that is not a complex type (like an array or a structure) is a list, regardless of whether you use it that way. Unlike an array or a structure, a list is not actually a data type. Rather, it is nothing more than a simple string, and ColdFusion treats it as such internally. When you access a specific element in a list (we'll get to that topic in a moment), ColdFusion performs basic string processing for you because that's all lists are—strings.

→ Arrays and structures are covered in detail in Chapter 14, "Arrays," and Chapter 15, "Structures."

NOTE

ColdFusion stores arrays and structures in memory in special formats designed specially for structured data. This makes accessing and manipulating arrays and structures far quicker than accessing and manipulating lists that are simply strings. List processing is essentially the processing of strings and substrings.

Working with Lists

Lists are extremely easy to use and even easier to create. For this reason, many of ColdFusion's internal data sets are stored as lists, and several CFML functions (and variables) return data in this format too.

Lists are accessed via a set of special CFML functions, all of which begin with the word `List` and take a list as the first attribute.

Creating Lists

CFML functions are generally not used to create a list (in contrast to arrays and structures, both of which require the use of special functions). The following `<cfset>` statement creates the list of states shown at the beginning of the chapter:

```
<!--- States list --->
<cfset states="CA,FL,MA,MI,NY,WA">
```

> **TIP**
>
> You can also use `<cfparam>` to create lists, and you can use the assignment operator in a `<cfscript>` block as well.
>
> You can create lists using any of the functions that update lists (for example, `ListAppend()`) by passing an empty string to the function as the existing list.

Accessing List Elements

You access and manipulate lists by using the list functions. For example, to determine the number of elements in a list, you can use the `ListLen()` function as follows:

```
<!--- Display number of states in list --->
<cfoutput>#ListLen(states)#</cfoutput>
```

> **NOTE**
>
> Empty elements are ignored by the list functions, so list `a,,b` contains just two elements (not three). However, white space is not ignored, so list `a, ,b` contains three elements.

To access a specific list element, use the `ListGetAt()` function as follows:

```
<!--- Display the third state --->
<cfoutput>#ListGetAt(states, 3)#</cfoutput>
```

ColdFusion provides special functions to quickly access the first and last elements in a list (the `ListFirst()` and `ListLast()` functions, respectively), as well as to return all elements after the first element (the `ListRest()` function).

> **CAUTION**
>
> Be careful never to refer to an element that does not exist (for example, trying to retrieve the sixth element in a five-element list) because doing so throws an error. It's a good practice to always check the length of a list (using `ListLen()`) before accessing specific elements.

> **NOTE**
>
> List elements are numbered starting from `1` (not `0`, as in other development languages and platforms).

You also can search lists to find the first element that matches or contains specific text. Use `ListFind()` to perform an *element match* (the element matches if it equals the exact search text and nothing more) and `ListContains()` to perform a *contains match* (the element matches if it contains the search text). Both functions return the position of the first matching element (not the element itself) and `0` if no match is found. The following code snippet checks to see whether a state is in a list (using the `ListFind()` function) and displays one of two messages based on the result:

```
<!--- Is user's state in the taxable state list? --->
<cfset match=ListFind(states, user.state)>
<!--- "match" will be greater than 0 (TRUE) if in "states" list --->
<cfif match>
 <!--- Yes, tell user that it is taxable --->
 <cfoutput>Sales to #user.state# residents are taxable</cfoutput>
<cfelse>
 <!--- No, tell user that tax will not be added --->
 <cfoutput>No tax is added for #user.state# residents</cfoutput>
</cfif>
```

> **TIP**
>
> List searches (exact or partial matches) are case sensitive. To perform searches that are not case sensitive, use the `ListFindNoCase()` and `ListContainsNoCase()` functions.

Modifying Lists

You can modify lists as you create them—directly using standard CFML assignment tags and operators. A more efficient way to modify them is to use functions designed for just that purpose. To update an element in a list, for example, use the `ListSetAt()` function, and to delete an element from a list, use `ListDeleteAt()`.

You can add new elements to a list at any time. The `ListPrepend()` function inserts an element at the beginning of a list; `ListAppend()` adds an element at the end of a list; and `ListInsertAt()` inserts an element at a specific location.

> **NOTE**
>
> The list functions do not modify lists; rather, they return modified lists. If you want to modify a list, you must use the same list as the list parameter and the variable being assigned, as follows:
>
> ```
> <cfset states=ListAppend(states, "WY")>
> ```
>
> Here, an element is added to the `states` list, so the value returned by `ListAppend()` (the new list) is assigned to `states`.

Specifying Delimiters

By default, lists use commas as delimiters, which you saw in the previous examples. But as we explained at the beginning of this chapter, ColdFusion allows you to use any characters as list delimiters. You therefore can use list functionality in interesting ways. For example, to determine the number of words in a string, you could treat that string as a list delimited by spaces, as follows:

```
<!--- How many words in "text"? --->
<cfoutput>#text# contains #ListLen(text, " ")# words</cfoutput>
```

Because the default delimiter is a comma, alternative delimiters must be explicitly specified. Every list function takes an optional final attribute—the delimiter to be used. If you specify `" "` (a string containing only a space) as the delimiter, the elements in the preceding list are the words in the variable `text` (words separated by a space).

You can specify multiple delimiters, in which case *any* of the specified characters acts as a delimiter (rather than all of them). In other words, to count the number of words in a string separated by spaces, periods, commas, or hyphens, you could do the following:

```
<!--- How many words in "text"? --->
<cfoutput>#text# contains #ListLen(text, " .,-")# words</cfoutput>
```

> **NOTE**
>
> To change the delimiter used in a list (returning a copy of the list using the new delimiter), use the `ListChangeDelims()` function.

Using Lists

As you have seen thus far, lists are very easy to use and are well suited for simple access to grouped data. Lists were designed to be simple; they were not designed to be efficient. Therefore, it is important to know when to use lists and when not to.

When to Use Lists (and When Not To)

Lists are designed primarily to be used with data that is already in list format. Two key examples are as follows:

- HTML form field values are returned in list format when multiple values exist for the same field name (for example, two HTML form controls have the same name, or a control allowing multiple selections is used).
- SQL uses the list format for sets of values (for example, in an `IN` clause).

➔ Form controls and variables are covered in detail in Chapter 9, "`FORM` Variables." The SQL `IN` clause is covered in Chapter 44, "Basic SQL."

When data is already in a list format, or needs to be, you should use lists and list functions.

Lists are not designed for complex or frequent processing; they just don't perform well enough for that. Arrays and structures are far better suited for that task.

> **TIP**
>
> You can convert lists into arrays and back again by using the `ListToArray()` and `ArrayToList()` functions.

Sorting Lists

You can sort lists by using the `ListSort()` function, and you must specify one of three sort types:

- `numeric` should be used for lists containing only numbers (and should never be used if any elements are not numeric).
- `text` performs case-sensitive alphabetical sorting (`A` before `a`, `1` before `10`, `2` after `1` but before `20`, and numbers before letters).
- `textnocase` performs an alphabetical sort that is not case sensitive.

An optional sort order may also be specified; the default is `asc` (ascending), and the alternative is `desc` (descending).

Looping Through Lists

In addition to accessing lists via functions as shown previously, you also can use CFML to loop through lists with `<cfloop>`. Like the list functions, `<cfloop>`

supports alternative (and multiple) delimiters. The following code snippet displays the `states` list in an HTML unordered list:

```
<!--- Start unordered list --->
<ul>
<!--- Loop through "states" --->
<cfloop index="i" list="#states#">
 <!--- Write this element --->
 <cfoutput><li>#i#</li></cfoutput>
</cfloop>
<!--- End unordered list --->
</ul>
```

The list must be passed to `<cfloop>` in the `list` attribute; the variable name specified in the `index` attribute will contain the appropriate element in each loop iteration.

➜ Looping and the `<cfloop>` tag were covered in detail in Chapter 4, "Looping."

> **TIP**
>
> Another way to apply formatting to list elements (without needing to loop through them) is to use the `Replace()` and `ReplaceList()` functions to replace all delimiters with appropriate HTML code.

Nested Lists

Although the ColdFusion documentation states that lists cannot be nested, technically they actually can. The trick is to use different delimiters for the inner and outer lists. For example, the following list has three elements if the default delimiter is used, and seven elements if a space is used as the delimiter:

```
<cfset list="a b c,1 2 3,x y z">
```

But accessed within nested `<cfloop>` tags, the same list can be used as a nested list—three lists each with three elements. The outer list is delimited by commas, and each inner list is delimited by spaces.

> **TIP**
>
> This kind of list processing is especially useful when you're working with comma-delimited imported data files (sometimes called CSV files). A file can be read into a variable (using `<cffile>`), and the entire file can be treated as a list delimited by carriage-return and line-feed characters (ASCII characters 13 and 10, respectively). This way, each line in the file can be accessed individually as a list element. The data format within each line is comma delimited, so the list functions can be used to process and extract the individual elements easily.

Special Lists

Several CFML functions return data in list format (comma delimited). They include `ValueList()` and `QuotedValueList()`, which return query columns in list form so that they can be easily used in additional SQL statements, and functions like `GetClientVariableList()`, which returns a list of all `CLIENT` variables for the current user.

In addition, several variables are always formatted as lists (again, for simplicity's sake). They include `query.ColumnList`, which lists the columns returned in a query, and `SERVER.ColdFusion.SupportedLocales`, which lists the locales supported by ColdFusion.

You can manipulate all these lists by using the functions and loops discussed earlier.

> **TIP**
>
> Lists that need to be accessed frequently, particularly those that persist across requests, should be converted into arrays (or structures) to improve performance.

Summary

Lists are an important and highly flexible ColdFusion data type. Lists are very well suited for use with HTML form fields, SQL statements, and any other data that is delimited by common characters. But lists should not be overused because they do not perform as well as more advanced data types (specifically arrays and structures).

Sample Questions

1. Which of the following are lists? (*select two*)

   A. Dates

   B. Arrays

   C. Structures

   D. Strings

2. Which of the following are valid list delimiters?

   A. `","`

   B. `""`

   C. `"#Chr(13)##Chr(10)#"`

   D. `"-"`

3. How many elements are in the list `"Ben Forta"`?

   A. 0

   B. 1

   C. 2

   D. 3

CHAPTER 14
Arrays

IN THIS CHAPTER

Understanding Arrays

Arrays, like lists, store multiple values within a single variable. Arrays differ from lists in two important ways:

- Arrays, unlike lists, are an actual data type, with a special internal format that ensures that they perform very efficiently.
- Although arrays can be used to store multiple strings or numbers (like lists), they can also be used to store complex data like arrays, queries, or structures.

> **NOTE**
> ColdFusion stores queries, structures, and arrays as complex data. ColdFusion stores strings and numbers as simple data.

When to Use Arrays

You should use arrays when the order of something is crucial. A shopping cart, for example, is the perfect candidate for an array because each item is referenced according to the order in which the buyer chose it. Arrays should also be used where descriptive statistics (average, sum, min/max, count) need to be performed on a series of values.

When Not to Use Arrays

Arrays are not ideal for all situations. Because arrays are complex data, a complete array can't be printed or passed without the use of `<cfloop>`. For situations in which you need to pass a set of data between HTML form pages or print it on an HTML page, lists are preferred.

For situations in which the order of values does not matter and simple calculations such as averaging or summation are not necessary, a structure is a better alternative. Similarly, if array members (elements) must be named explicitly, then structures should be used.

Arrays are best suited for grouping related data (for example, names of students, grocery lists, and clothing sizes).

> **CAUTION**
> You may hear the term associative array used—these are structures, not arrays.

→ Structures will be covered in detail in Chapter 15, "Structures." `<cfloop>` was described in Chapter 4, "Looping," and lists were discussed in Chapter 13, "Lists."

Using Arrays

Arrays are easy to use, but like all complex data, they must be created and initialized before they can be accessed. The array function `ArrayNew()` creates an array and takes one required argument. After you create the array, you must initialize it.

Creating Arrays

The `ArrayNew()` function creates an array and specifies the number of dimensions the array can hold. Passing an argument of `1` to `ArrayNew()`, as shown in the following example, creates a one-dimensional array. Multidimensional arrays will be discussed later in this chapter. After you create an array, you can access it by using functions or setting values directly.

```
<!--- Create the grocery array --->
<cfset groceries = ArrayNew(1)>
```

Populating Arrays

You can populate an array in a number of ways. The most specific way is to reference the index directly:

```
<!--- Grocery list --->
<cfset groceries = ArrayNew(1)>
<cfset groceries[1] = "Bread">
<cfset groceries[2] = "Cheese">
```

> **TIP**
>
> Array indexes may consist of any ColdFusion expression. For instance, you can reference an element at index `[Q+1]` by using `groceries[Q+1]`. To append a value to an array, you could use `groceries[ArrayLen(groceries)+1]`.

An explicit reference to the array index works for simple initialization. To programmatically and dynamically populate an array, use the `ArrayAppend()` or `ArrayPrepend()` functions, which place values at the end or beginning of the array, respectively. Note that these functions, like most array functions, return `TRUE` in the variable to the left of the equals sign but perform their task against the array referenced in the array function.

```
<cfset groceries = ArrayNew(1)>
<cfset tmp = ArrayAppend(groceries,"Bread")>
```

> **NOTE**
>
> Because it is not necessary to actually save any value returned by `ArrayAppend()`, the following code also would work:
>
> ```
> <cfset ArrayAppend(groceries,"Bread")>
> ```

Accessing Array Values

Array values (or members) are accessed by an index that is specified within square brackets. The first value in an array could be accessed like this:

```
groceries[1]
```

To display the first grocery item, you could do the following:

```
<cfoutput>#groceries[1]#</cfoutput>
```

Printing all values in the array requires that you use the `ArrayLen()` function to determine the array length. The loop is a standard `<cfloop>` that uses the attributes `from`, `to`, and `index`. Because `ArrayLen()` returns the highest index in the array, this combination renders each value for every index:

```
<ul>
<cfloop from="1" to="#ArrayLen(groceries)#" index="i">
 <li><cfoutput>#groceries[i]#</cfoutput></li>
</cfloop>
</UL>
```

> **CAUTION**
>
> Although most programming languages start arrays at position `0`, ColdFusion begins at array position `1`. Attempting to loop, set, or read from position `0` throws an error.

You may not display arrays directly (as in `<cfoutput>#groceries#</cfoutput>`) because this throws an error. However, arrays may be passed to functions or tags if needed.

Converting Between Arrays and Lists

Because HTML forms and `URL` variables frequently pass lists to the Web server, being able to switch back and forth between complex data (arrays) and simple data (lists) is handy. The functions `ArrayToList()` and `ListToArray()` achieve these goals.

These functions are equally useful when you're working with SQL statements. For example, to use an array to populate a SQL `IN` clause (which expects a list), you could use `ArrayToList()`.

Empty Array Indexes

An array may have a missing index, as in this code snippet:

```
<!--- Grocery list --->
<cfset groceries = ArrayNew(1)>
<cfset groceries[1] = "Bread">
<cfset groceries[2] = "Cheese">
<cfset groceries[4] = "Eggs">

<ul>
<cfloop from="1" to="#ArrayLen(groceries)#" index="i">
 <li><cfoutput>#groceries[i]#</cfoutput></LI>
</cfloop>
</ul>
```

In this example, `<cfloop>` would attempt to loop from `1` to `4`, but the `<cfoutput>` would fail on iteration `3` because `#groceries[3]#` is not a valid array index.

Obviously, if the array had been built dynamically (rather than by using explicit indexes), this would not have been a problem. But when indexes are explicitly created, use the `ArraySet()` function to initialize the indexes with values (even if the value is `""`).

Arrays and Memory

In ColdFusion, as with any server-side scripting language, performance is always a consideration. In most languages—Java, for example—arrays must be given a certain size before they are populated. ColdFusion does not require that a size be given because the array is dynamically resized. As data is placed into the array, ColdFusion appropriates memory along the way. Although this makes ColdFusion arrays very easy to use, this highly dynamic behavior can have performance implications.

For large arrays, it is recommended that the array be sized ahead of time so as to pre-allocate the memory that will be needed. That can be done using this `ArrayResize()` function:

```
<cfset ArrayResize(groceries, 500)>
```

> **TIP**
>
> The ColdFusion documentation recommends that an array be resized if it is likely to hold more than 500 indexes.

A resized array actually has multiple empty values in it. This means that a resized array should be initialized with `ArraySet()` if looping is likely to occur:

```
<!--- Init list --->
<cfset groceries = ArrayNew(1)>
<cfset ArrayResize(groceries, 500)>
<cfset ArraySet(groceries, 1, 500, "")>
```

Compressing Arrays

The solution for getting rid of empty values within an array is to compress the array by using the `ArrayDeleteAt()` function. This function not only deletes any value within a given index, but also compresses the array so that its length decrements by one. Compressing an array is a good practice to avoid some of the problems with empty values.

However, when you delete members from an array, keep in mind that indexes will change; thus no assumptions should be made about the array length or the specific index location.

Array Calculations

ColdFusion provides functions that may be used to sum array values; find minimums, maximums, and averages; and even sort values.

For example, you can sort arrays by using the `ArraySort()` function; one of the ollowing three sort types must be specified:

- `numeric` should be used for arrays containing only numbers (and should never be used if any elements are not numeric).
- `text` performs case-sensitive alphabetical sorting (`A` before `a`, `1` before `10`, `2` after `1` but before `20`, and numbers before letters).
- `textnocase` performs an alphabetical sort that is not case sensitive.

An optional sort order may also be specified; the default is `ASC` (ascending), and the alternative is `DESC` (descending).

The following code snippet sorts the grocery list before displaying it:

```
<!--- Grocery list --->
<cfset groceries = ArrayNew(1)>
<cfset groceries[1] = "Bread">
<cfset groceries[2] = "Cheese">
<cfset groceries[3] = "Milk">
<cfset groceries[4] = "Eggs">

<!--- Sort list --->
<cfset ArraySort(groceries, "textnocase")>

<ul>
<cfloop from="1" to="#ArrayLen(groceries)#" index="i">
 <li><cfoutput>#groceries[i]#</cfoutput></li>
</cfloop>
</ul>
```

NOTE

These functions may only be used on single-dimensional arrays and not on multidimensional arrays (which will be explained next).

Multidimensional Arrays

The arrays seen thus far have been single-dimensional, but ColdFusion also supports multidimensional arrays. To understand the need for multidimensional arrays, consider the previously used grocery list, which contains items but no quantities. To store a quantity along with each item (and maybe additional information), a two-dimensional array could be used.

Two-Dimensional Arrays

A two-dimensional array is similar to a grid, each item of which must be referenced by two indexes (the row and column). Index `[1][1]` would refer to row `1` and column `1`, while `[3][2]` would refer to row `3`, column `2`.

The following code defines a two-dimensional array—think of it as a grid in which the left column contains the item and the right column contains the quantity:

```
<!--- Grocery list --->
<cfset groceries = ArrayNew(2)>
<cfset groceries[1][1] = "Bread">
<cfset groceries[1][2] = 3>
<cfset groceries[2][1] = "Cheese">
<cfset groceries[2][2] = 2>
<cfset groceries[3][1] = "Eggs">
<cfset groceries[3][2] = 12>
```

```
<ul>
<cfloop from="1" to="#ArrayLen(groceries)#" index="i">
 <li>
 <cfoutput>
 #groceries[i][1]# - #groceries[i][2]#
 </cfoutput>
 </li>
</cfloop>
</ul>
```

This code will loop through `3` times (the length of the array as returned by the `ArrayLen()` function). On each iteration, `#groceries[i][1]#` displays the item and `#groceries[i][2]#` displays the quantity.

> **CAUTION**
> When an array is two-dimensional, it must be referenced using both indexes. If the second index is omitted in `<cfoutput>`, an error occurs.

Three-Dimensional Arrays

ColdFusion also supports three-dimensional arrays. To create a three-dimensional array, use:

```
<cfset myarray=ArrayNew(3)>
```

When using three-dimensional arrays, specific elements must be referenced using all three indexes:

```
#myarray[2][3][2]#
```

> **NOTE**
> ColdFusion officially supports arrays of up to three dimensions, which is more than most developers will ever need. However, it is indeed possible to create even more complex multidimensional arrays by nesting arrays within arrays.

Summary

Arrays are an important type of complex data. They allow you to group and order data and perform easy calculations on data sets. Arrays are useful for embedding other arrays and complex data. Special attention must be given to resizing arrays and empty values within them.

Sample Questions

1. What function do you use to create an array? *(select two)*

   A. `ArrayNew()`

   B. `ListToArray()`

   C. `ArrayCopy()`

   D. `NewArray()`

2. Why will the following code fail?

```
<cfset items=ArrayNew(1)>
<cfset items[1]=100>
<cfset items[2]=150>
<cfset items[4]=75>
<cfset total=ArraySum(items)>
```

   A. `Items` is not an array.

   B. `Items` is missing index 3.

   C. `ArraySum()` can't sum one-dimensional arrays.

   D. `ArraySum()` is not a valid function.

3. Why will the following code fail? *(select two)*

```
<cfset a = ArrayNew(1)>
<cfset ArrayResize(a, 400)>
<cfset LoopUntil = ArrayLen(a)>
<cfloop from="1" to="#LoopUntil#" index="i">
 <cfset ArrayDelete(a, i)>
</cfloop>
```

   A. `<cfset>` requires an equals sign.

   B. An array must be resized to a size greater than 500.

   C. The index passed to `ArrayDelete()` will be invalid.

   D. The loop will go past the array's length.

4. Which of the following statements are false? *(select two)*

   A. An associative array is a form of array.

   B. Multidimensional arrays are "arrays in arrays."

   C. Arrays can have a maximum of three dimensions.

   D. One-dimensional arrays can contain simple values.

CHAPTER 15

Structures

IN THIS CHAPTER

Structures Defined

Like arrays, structures are complex variables capable of holding multiple values simultaneously. One of the big differences between structures and arrays is that arrays are ordered, whereas structures are not. Another major difference is that while arrays are indexed, structures are accessed by a *key*. A key is more flexible than an array index because it can be any combination of numbers, letters, or special characters.

When to Use Structures

Almost any ColdFusion task could be accomplished without structures, but the programming logic would not be as readable or concise. Structures can improve your code by allowing you to group related data cleanly and easily.

- Data made up of multiple parts (a user record, for example) is ideally suited for storage as a structure.
- Any time that related data must be passed to a custom tag or user-defined function, it may be passed as a structure (allowing a single value to be passed even though it may contain multiple values).
- Within ColdFusion itself, many special variables are exposed as structures.

Creating and Populating Structures

Structures are created using the `StructNew()` function, as seen here:

```
<cfset user=StructNew()>
```

After you create the structure, you may specify members. Structure members are made up of a *key* (the name) and a value. There are two ways to refer to structure members. The first is *dot notation* (sometimes called *object/property syntax*):

```
<cfset user.FirstName="Ben">
<cfset user.LastName="Forta">
<cfset user.age="21">
<cfset user.email="ben@forta.com">
```

The alternative syntax places the key name in brackets (this is sometimes known as *array syntax*):

```
<cfset user["FirstName"]="Ben">
<cfset user["LastName"]="Forta">
<cfset user["age"]="21">
<cfset user["email"]="ben@forta.com">
```

As a rule, dot notation is easier, but using brackets has one important benefit—it allows the use of names that contain *invalid* characters. For example, the following creates keys with spaces in their names, which would not be possible using dot notation:

```
<cfset user=StructNew()>
<cfset user["First Name"]="Ben">
<cfset user["Last Name"]="Forta">
```

> **NOTE**
> Creating a variable with a period in it actually creates a structure with a member. For example, `<cfset user.FirstName="Ben">` would assign the value `Ben` to the structure member `FirstName`, and would also create the structure `user` if it did not already exist.

Using Structures

Structure members may be used like any other variables, simply by referring to their key names. For example, the following creates an email link that displays a user's first and last name:

```
<cfoutput>
<a href="mailto:#user.email#">#user.FirstName# #user.LastName#</a>
</cfoutput>
```

As you can see, structure members may be accessed using dot notation.

In addition, ColdFusion provides an entire set of structure-manipulation functions (the names of which all begin with `Struct`) for more advanced structure processing. `StructFind()` uses the names of a structure and key to return a value:

```
E-Mail: #StructFind(user, "email")#
```

Other functions can check for the existence of keys, sort keys, return a list of key names, add and delete keys, and more.

> **TIP**
>
> Many of the `Struct` functions are not that useful for simple structures (the type used here), but are invaluable for more complex nested structures.

Looping Over Structures

When looping over a structure using `<cfloop>`, you have no control over the order of the structure's keys. If order is an important factor, an array should be used instead. To loop over a structure, pass the structure to the `<cfloop> collection` attribute. The `item` attribute steps through the keys of the structure with each loop as follows:

```
<cfset user=StructNew()>
<cfset user["FirstName"]="Ben">
<cfset user["LastName"]="Forta">
<cfset user["age"]="21">
<cfset user["email"]="ben@forta.com">

<cfloop collection="#user#" item="i">
 <cfoutput>#i#: #user[i]#<br></cfoutput>
</cfloop>
```

`<cfloop>` loops through the keys one at a time. In each iteration, `i` will contain the key name and can thus be used within brackets to access the values.

Key names are case insensitive and unordered. Never make any assumptions about case or the order in which keys will be returned.

> **TIP**
>
> Keys are rarely printed. Instead, you use keys to access or print values. Also, you rarely loop through a collection to print data, but rather to find a certain key or value. For these reasons, the case and order limitations are of little practical significance.

Internal Structures

Due to their speed and versatility, structures are employed by ColdFusion for much of its internal data. The following variable prefixes are structures in ColdFusion:

- `APPLICATION`
- `ATTRIBUTES`
- `CFCATCH`
- `CFERROR`

- CFFILE
- CFFTP
- CFHTTP
- CGI
- CLIENT
- COOKIE
- FORM
- REQUEST
- SERVER
- SESSION
- THIS
- THISTAG
- URL
- VARIABLES

You may use `<cfdump>` to display the members of any structure. For example, to dump all `CGI` variables, you can use the following:

```
<cfdump var="#CGI#">
```

> **TIP**
>
> Knowing about structures translates into a stronger grasp of ColdFusion in general. You can flush `SESSION` variables, for example, by issuing `StructClear(session)`.

→ `SESSION` variables were covered in Chapter 11, "Session State Management."

Combining Complex Data

As was the case with multidimensional arrays, you can combine complex data with itself. Rather than make arrays of arrays, as detailed in the preceding chapter, you can combine arrays with structures and structures with themselves.

Structures of Arrays

Combining structures with arrays supplies you with a perfect combination. You use arrays for their capability to maintain order. You use structures for their capability to store information by logical key names rather than numbers. By combining the two, you can create an ordered array of structures.

The following example contains sales figures by quarter for 2005 and 2006. `sales` is the structure containing two arrays (one for each of the two years). Each array contains four members (one per quarter) that store the sales figures.

Here is the code:

```
<!--- Sales structure --->
<cfset sales=StructNew()>

<!--- 2005 sales --->
<cfset sales.year2005=ArrayNew(1)>
<cfset sales.year2005[1]=300000>
<cfset sales.year2005[2]=475000>
<cfset sales.year2005[3]=285000>
<cfset sales.year2005[4]=575000>

<!--- 2006 sales --->
<cfset sales.year2006=ArrayNew(1)>
<cfset sales.year2006[1]=425000>
<cfset sales.year2006[2]=325000>
<cfset sales.year2006[3]=185000>
<cfset sales.year2006[4]=450000>
```

To refer to sales from 2006's third quarter (Q3), you'd use this element:

```
#sales.year2006[3]#
```

The advantage of this type of organization is that it simplifies the manipulation of data. For example, to display the sum of all sales in 2005, you could do the following:

```
<cfoutput>
#ArraySum(sales.year2005)#
</cfoutput>
```

Arrays of Structures

Shopping carts are often implemented as arrays of structures. The cart itself is an array (it holds a series of items), with each item a structure that provides maximum flexibility. Here is an example:

```
<!--- Create shopping cart --->
<CFSET SESSION.cart=ArrayNew(1)>

<!--- Add first item --->
<cfset SESSION.cart[1]=StructNew()>
<cfset SESSION.cart[1].item="T-shirt">
<cfset SESSION.cart[1].color="red">
<cfset SESSION.cart[1].size="XL">
<cfset SESSION.cart[1].quantity="50">

<!--- Add second item --->
<cfset SESSION.cart[2]=StructNew()>
```

```
<cfset SESSION.cart[2].item="cap">
<cfset SESSION.cart[2].color="navy">
<cfset SESSION.cart[2].size="adult">
<cfset SESSION.cart[2].quantity="25">
```

The shopping cart here is created in the `SESSION` scope, so that it persists. The cart is an array; each time an item is added to the cart, an array index is added to hold it. Individual cart items are structures that contain the item details.

➜ Session state management and `SESSION` variables were covered in Chapter 11, "Session State Management."

Structures of Anything

Structures can contain arrays, and arrays can contain structures. But it doesn't stop there: Structures may also contain structures, as well as queries and any other data type.

In fact, some of the ColdFusion internal structures mentioned previously are structures that contain other elements.

Structures as Pointers

In many programming languages, the term *pointer* signifies that multiple variables can all share the same memory space. With pointers, the variables may have different names, but the values will always be the same because they refer to the same place in memory. ColdFusion stores all structures as pointers.

Although ColdFusion's structure storage does not effect most ColdFusion templates, there are significant consequences when structures are copied because what is made is not actually a copy, but a new way to point to the same values.

Look at the following example:

```
<cfset user.FirstName="Ben">
<cfset user.LastName="Forta">
<cfset user.age="21">
<cfset user.email="ben@forta.com">

<cfset usercopy=user>
<cfset usercopy.age="22">
```

The above code snippet creates a structure named `user`, places several keys in it, then copies it using a `<cfset>` tag and changes the `age`. Although `user.age` should be `21` and `usercopy.age` should be `22`, if you were to execute the code, you'd find out that when `usercopy.age` changed, `user.age` changed too. This is because `user` and `usercopy` actually both refer to the same structure internally.

To create an entirely new structure based on the original, use the `Duplicate()` function.

Queries as Structures

ColdFusion query record sets are complex data types. Although they are neither structures nor arrays, they do have similarities to both. You can refer to a query using the standard `queryname.columnname` syntax, much as with a structure. Yet because there are multiple records within a query, you also can refer to a query as `queryname.columnname[recordnumber]`. Consider the following example:

```
<cfquery name="users"
         datasource="dsn">
SELECT LastName, Firstname
FROM users
ORDER BY Lastname, FirstName
</cfquery>

<!--- <cfloop> through the results --->
<cfloop from="1" to="#users.RecordCount#" index="i">
 <cfoutput>
 #i#: #users.LastName[i]# #users.FirstName[i]#
 </cfoutput><br>
</cfloop>
```

Here the record set is being treated as if it were a structure of arrays. This syntax makes it possible to directly access database results as needed.

Summary

Structures provide a way to group related information for quick and easy access. They may be accessed using dot notation and bracket notation (like arrays). Structures may contain arrays, other structures, and more—and may themselves be part of arrays. Many internal ColdFusion variables are structures and may be accessed as such.

Sample Questions

1. Choose the output of the following code:

   ```
   <cfset a = StructNew()>
   <cfset b = a>
   <cfset a.myVar = 1>
   <cfset b.myVar = 2>
   <cfset c = a.myVar + b.myVar>
   <cfset c = c * b.myVar>
   <cfoutput>#c#</cfoutput>
   ```

   A. 4

   B. 8

   C. 16

   D. 36

2. Choose the correct syntax for looping over a structure.

   A. `<cfloop collection="struct" item="i">`

   B. `<cfloop collection="#struct#" item="s">`

   C. `<cfloop from="#struct#" to="#StructLen(struct)#" index="i">`

   D. `<cfloop collection="#struct#" index="i">`

3. In the following code, which line will throw an error?

```
<cfset car=StructNew(1)>
<cfset car.make="Acura">
<cfset car.model=TL>
<cfset car.year=2005>
```

   A. 1

   B. 2

   C. 3

   D. 4

4. Which of these assignments are valid? (*select two*)

   A. `<cfset user.last name="Forta">`

   B. `<cfset user[lastname]="Forta">`

   C. `<cfset user.lastname="Forta">`

   D. `<cfset user."lastname"="Forta">`

PART 4

User Interface & Data Presentation

IN THIS PART

CHAPTER 16 Flash Forms

IN THIS CHAPTER

Understanding Flash Forms

HTML forms are pretty easy to create and work with, but they are also very limited and not overly capable. For example:

- Making fields required, or enforcing data validation, requires the user of client-side scripting (which may not be supported or enabled) or server-side processing (which is not very user-friendly).
- There is no easy way to extend data types, for example, to display a pop-up calendar to allow simple date selection (and to ensure that dates are entered correctly).
- Form presentation tends to be very tied to form contents. Changing form layout (adding or reordering fields, for example) often requires lots of tinkering with presentation code.
- It is very difficult to reuse form layout and presentation, and even more difficult to simply make changes to the presentation of all forms (maybe to change color schemes or label alignment).

The truth is, the HTML forms specification leaves much to be desired, and Web developers have developed something of a love-hate relationship with forms, both appreciating their simplicity but despising the lack of functionality that that simplicity causes.

There are alternatives. XForms is the next generation of HTML forms, and XForms can help solve lots of the problems with HTML forms. In addition, plug-in technologies like Macromedia Flash can dramatically improve the forms you create and use. And ColdFusion makes leveraging both of these technologies both easy and productive.

➜ Flash Forms are covered in this chapter, XForms is covered in Chapter 17, "XForms."

Anyone who has spent time online has encountered Macromedia Flash. Be it animated site intros, pop-up advertisements, video, or games, Flash is prevalent and ubiquitous. In fact, you'd be hard pressed to find any computer that does not have a Flash player installed.

But as the term *Flash* is often misused, a brief terminology clarification is called for:

- Flash applications (often called *movies*) are run in a special environment called the Flash Player. This is free software available from Macromedia (the single most installed piece of software on the Internet) and it is available for all major computing platforms (and lots of lesser used platforms too). Within the Flash Player, all platforms and devices look the same. This makes it possible for Flash developers to create applications that run identically on Windows machines and Linux boxes and Mac's. End users typically don't pay a whole lot of attention to the Flash Player itself as their Web browsers load the player as needed creating the impression that the Flash application is running in the browser.
- The Flash application (which is run within the Flash Player) is called a SWF file (usually pronounced *swiff*). When Flash developers build applications what they end up with is a SWF file (which can be embedded in Web pages, for example).
- Flash is a tool, a development environment for creating Flash movies. Flash users work with assets (images, icons, sounds, etc.) and manipulate them in the Flash development environment (using timing sequences and/or ActionScript code) to create an application. Flash users create a work file (called a FLA file), and when they have finished their development the create a SWF from that FLA file.
- It is also possible to create applications using a server product called Macromedia Flex. Flex developers write Flash applications in code (instead of using the interactive Flash IDE) using a combination of MXML (an XML language) and ActionScript. These files are compiled and a SWF file is created.

So, to summarize, Flash is a tool and Flex is a server, and both are used to create SWF files which run inside of a Flash Player. If you want to create Flash applications you'll need a copy of Macromedia Flash or Macromedia Flex (depending on the type of application you are building, and how you will go about building it).

> **NOTE**
>
> Users often use the term Flash to refer to the player on the actual SWF. Technically this is inaccurate, Flash is the IDE used to create Flash applications.

Using Flash Forms

Flash applications can be embedded in any Web pages, including pages generated by ColdFusion. If you were to create a Flash animation using Macromedia Flash, for example, you could embed it in the generated page so that it would be displayed within the browser. Similarly, applications created using Macromedia Flex could integrate with ColdFusion applications.

But it is also possible to leverage Flash (without owning Macromedia Flash or Macromedia Flex) without writing anything more than CFML code. ColdFusion has the ability to write Flash for you, allowing you to use CFML tags to create complete Flash applications. These are not general purpose applications, only a very specific type of Flash application can be created this way, namely forms. Using the same `<cfform>` and `<cfinput>` used previously, ColdFusion can do the following:

- Generate ActionScript code to create your form.
- Compile that ActionScript code into a SWF.
- Embed the generated SWF in your ColdFusion generated page.

In other words, using ColdFusion you can build forms that leverage the power and usability of Flash while retaining the development experience that is uniquely ColdFusion.

To create Flash Forms, the `<cfform>` tag is used, specifying `format="flash"`. This instructs ColdFusion to generate a Flash Form instead of an HTML form.

> **NOTE**
>
> It is also possible to embed Flash Form controls within an HTML form. To do this, simply specify `format="flash"` in the control tag instead of in the `<cfform>`.

Flash Form Controls

Within a Flash Form all of the standard HTML form controls can be used, along with additional controls. Table 16.1 lists the controls that may be used within Flash Forms.

Table 16.1 Flash Forms Controls

CONTROL	SYNTAX	NOTES
Button	`<cfinput type="submit">`	Functions just like HTML `<input type="submit">`.
Calendar	`<cfinput type="datefield">`	Not supported in HTML. Functionally similar to `<cfinput type="datefield">` but calendar is open and no text field is displayed.
Check Box	`<cfinput type="checkbox">`	Functions just like HTML `<input type="checkbox">`, but name must be unique in each.
Combo Box	`<cfselect editable="true">`	Not supported in HTML.
Data Grid	`<cfgrid>`	Not supported in HTML.
Date Field	`<cfinput type="datefield">`	Not supported in HTML.
Password	`<cfinput type="password">`	Functions just like HTML `<input type="password">`.
Select	`<cfselect>`	Functions just like HTML `<select>`.
Text	`<cfinput type="text">`	Functions just like HTML `<input type="text">`.
Textarea	`<cftextarea>`	Functions just like HTML `<textarea>`.
Tree	`<cftree>`	Not supported in HTML.

NOTE

The controls listed in Table 16.1 are the ones supported by Flash Forms, and it is not possible to create your own controls for using with this feature. If you need to create customer controls you will need to use Macromedia Flash or Macromedia Flex instead of ColdFusion generated Flash Forms

The following simple form uses a popup date control to prompt for a date of birth:

```
<cfform format="flash"
        action="process.cfm"
        width="200">

<cfinput name="dob"
         label="Date Of Birth:"
         type="datefield">
```

```
<cfinput name="btnSubmit"
         type="submit"
         value="Submit">

</cfform>
```

One important point to note is that every Flash Form control needs a name, even buttons. This name must be unique within the form (with the exception of `type="radio"` where all the related radio buttons must have the same name to function correctly).

> **TIP**
>
> By default, Flash Forms will use all available browser width (possibly resulting in elongated controls). Specifying a `width` in `<cfform>` solves this problem.

The following example uses `<cfgrid>` to create a Flash grid:

```
<!--- Get data --->
<cfquery datasource="myDsn" name="users">
SELECT nameFirst, nameLast, eMail, phone
FROM users
ORDER BY nameLast, nameFirst
</cfquery>

<!--- Display data grid --->
<cfform format="flash">

<!--- Data grid --->
<cfgrid name="gridUsers"
        query="users" />

</cfform>
```

The grid created by this code snippet would be scrollable, sortable, and columns would also be resizable. Additional attributes (and child tags) provide even greater control. This next snippet created an editable grid:

```
<!--- Get data --->
<cfquery datasource="myDsn" name="users">
SELECT nameFirst, nameLast, eMail, phone
FROM users
ORDER BY nameLast, nameFirst
</cfquery>

<!--- Display data grid --->
<cfform format="flash" action="process.cfm">

<!--- Data grid --->
<cfgrid name="gridUsers"
        selectmode="edit"
        query="users"
        insert="yes"
        delete="yes" />

</cfform>
```

To make a `<cfgrid>` editable, `selectmode` must be `"edit"` (instead of the default `"browse"`). In addition, to allow insertions `insert="yes"` is specified, and to allow deletions `delete="yes"` is specified.

> **NOTE**
>
> `<cfgrid>` supports a whole range of attributes for greater control over grid contents. Two child tags may also be used, `<cfgridcolumn>` lets you control the look and behavior of each column, and `<cfgridrow>` can be used to explicitly provide row values (instead of passing a query).
>
> In addition, another tag named `<cfgridupdate>` can be used to simplify processing grid updates in a form `action` page.

Including Other Form Items

Within a `<cfform format="flash">` any HTML tags or plain text is ignored. This means that you cannot use `<br>` for line breaks, `<a>` for links, and the like. To embed line breaks, literal text, spaces, lines, and more, use `<cfformitem>` (the supported types of which are listed in Table 16.2).

Table 16.2 `<cfformitem>` Types

TYPE	DESCRIPTION
hrule	Horizontal line.
html	Embed HTML text in form, text is specified between `<cfformitem type="html">` and `</cfformitem>` tags, supports only the following HTML tags: `<a>`, `<b>`, ` `, `<font>`, `<i>`, `<img>`, `<li>`, `<p>`, `<textformat>`, `<u>`.
spacer	Space between controls.
text	Displays text in form, text is specified between `<cfformitem type="text">` and `</cfformitem>` tags.
vrule	Vertical line.

Form Layout Options

The default layout generates by Flash Forms is a long list of controls, one beneath the other, with labels and controls left-aligned. As HTML layout tags cannot be used within Flash Forms, the `<cfformgroup>` tag provides support for control grouping, alignment, and layout. Table 16.3 lists the supported grouping types.

Table 16.3 `<cfformgroup>` Types

TYPE	DESCRIPTION
`accordion`	Places child pages within a vertical accordion control, use `<cfformgroup type="page">` to define the child pages.
`hbox`	Align horizontally, use only with nested groups and not for form controls.
`hdividedbox`	Align horizontally and allow box resizing, use only with nested groups and not for form controls.
`horizontal`	Align horizontally.
`panel`	Creates a box containing other controls, with a label on a title bar.
`page`	Creates child pages within accordion and tab controls.
`repeater`	Crates child containers dynamically for each item within a query.
`tabnavigator`	Places child pages within a tabbed control, use `<cfformgroup type="page">` to define the child pages.
`tile`	Places child controls in a grid.
`vbox`	Align vertically, use only with nested groups and not for form controls.
`vdividedbox`	Align vertically and allow box resizing, use only with nested groups and not for form controls.
`vertical`	Align vertically.

The following code snippet modifies the date of birth example seen earlier in this chapter, and includes a `<cfformgroup>` tag set so as to display the date control and button aligned horizontally (side-by-side).

```
<cfform format="flash"
        action="process.cfm"
        width="200">

  <cfformgroup type="horizontal">

    <cfinput name="dob"
             label="Date Of Birth:"
             type="datefield">

    <cfinput name="btnSubmit"
             type="submit"
             value="Submit">

  </cfformgroup>

</cfform>
```

> **NOTE**
>
> `<cfformgroup>` tags may be nested as needed. The only type that must always be nested is `type="page"` which is used to create pages within a `<cfformgroup>` of `type="accordion"` or `type="tabnavigator">`

Controlling Form Appearance

By default, all Flash Forms have a similar color and look. This is the Macromedia "Halo" look, and it is the default used by ColdFusion generated Flash Forms. It is implemented as a *skin* and the following skins are supported:

- `haloBlue`
- `haloGreen` (the default)
- `haloOrange`
- `haloSilver`

To specify an alternate skin use the `<cfform>` `skin` attribute, as follows:

```
<cfform format="flash"
        action="process.cfm"
        skin="haloOrange">
```

> **NOTE**
>
> It is not possible to define your own skins, although this functionality may be added in the future. However, form appearance can still be controlled using `style` attributes as explained below.

For more granular control, `style` values may be used. `style` values may be specified at various levels:

- In the `<cfform>` tag, in which case the style will apply to all form groups and controls unless overridden at the group or control level.
- In `<cfformgroup>` tag, in which case the style will apply to all controls unless within the group overridden at the control level.
- In specific controls.

`style` names and values are modeled on HTML CSS styles, and Flash controls supports lots (although not all) of the styles supported by CSS. Styles are specified as `name:value` pairs divided by semicolons, as seen in this snippet:

```
<cfinput type="text"
         name="nameFirst"
         label="First Name:"
         style="fontSize:12; backgroundColor:##FF9900">
```

> **TIP**
>
> When specifying RGB values, or any text containing # chars, be sure to escape # characters as ##.

> **NOTE**
>
> A full list of all supported styles is beyond the scope of this book. Refer to the online Flash and Flex documentation at http://livedocs.macromedia.com, or consult any book on Flash or Flex controls.

> **NOTE**
>
> Unlike CSS styles which may be defined externally and linked to, Flash styles must be specified inline.

Using Data Bindings

In addition to the controls, layout, and consistency advantages to Flash Forms, there is one other very important feature that must be mentioned. *Binding* allows controls to be connected to each other, so that they are aware of values or changes in other controls and can react or change accordingly.

Using bindings requires referring to other controls and properties within them. These are specified using ActionScript syntax (as the bindings you create are executed in the Flash Player). ActionScript uses `{` and `}` to delimit expressions (in much the same way as ColdFusion uses `#`).

Here is a simple binding example:

```
<cfform format="flash" action="formdump.cfm">

 <cfcalendar name="dob">
 <cfinput name="displaydob"
          type="text"
          label="You selected:"
          bind="{dob.selectedDate}">

</cfform>
```

The code defines two controls, a calendar and a text field. The text field contains the following binding:

```
bind="{dob.selectedDate}"
```

This tells Flash to bind the text field to the calendar, populating the text field with whatever the currently selected date is in the calendar. `dob.selectedDate` means the `selectedDate` in the control named `dob`.

Bindings like this can be made between all sorts of controls, even controls on different pages within an accordion or tab navigator. To refer to values in other controls you need to use the syntax listed in Table 16.4 (replacing `control` with the name of the actual control).

Table 16.4 Control Bind Sources

CONTROL	SOURCE
`<cfcalendar>` and `<cfinput type="datefield">` selected date	`{control.selecteddate}`
`<cfgrid>` selected item	`{control.selectedItem.COLUMN}`
`<cfinput>`	`{control.text}`
`<cfinput>` selected radio button	`{control.selectedData}`
`<cfselect>` selected item	`{control.selectedItem.data}`
`<cftextarea>`	`{control.text}`
`<cftree>` selected item	`{control.selectedNode.getProperty('data').value}`

Usage Notes

Before wrapping this review of Flash Forms, it is worthwhile to note some important points pertaining to their use:

- Although Flash Form controls may be embedded in HTML forms, the preferred use case is to create an entire Flash Form. The size of a single Flash Form control won't be much less than a full form, and using Flash for specific controls precludes the use of bindings and other functionality.
- All Flash Form controls must be named.
- It is a good idea to always specify the `width` of the `<cfform>`.
- Like HTML forms, Flash Forms do not need an `action`, and can therefore be used for display (this is particularly useful when using `<cfgrid>` and `<cftree>`).
- When using multi-page forms, form submission does not occur when pages are changed, and only upon final form submission.
- Flash Forms does not support server-side events via AMF (Flash Remoting) or SOAP (Web Services), to do this Flash or Flex are needed.
- Flash Forms support embedded ActionScript expressions, but do not support the creation of new objects or functions or the like.

- The one big limitation of Flash Forms (over HTML forms) is that as the Flash Player has not access to the file system, `<input type="file">` cannot (at this time) be supported by Flash Forms.

> **NOTE**
> If you are looking for additional examples of Flash Forms use, visit http://www.cfform.com/.

Summary

Flash Forms can be used to create a better forms experience for your users. In addition to providing additional control types and sophisticated layout control, Flash Forms also support data bindings, styling, and inline ActionScript expressions while ensuring platform compatibility (thanks to Flash and the Flash Player).

Sample Questions

1. Which of the can be used in Flash Forms?

   A. `<cftextarea>`

   B. `<cfinput type="submit">`

   C. `<cfinput type="file">`

   D. `<cfslider>`

   E. `<cfselect>`

2. Which tag is used to align and place form controls?

   A. `<cfform>`

   B. `<cfformitem>`

   C. `<cfformgroup>`

   D. `<cfformalign>`

3. Which of the following require the use of Macromedia Flash or Macromedia Flex (instead of Flash Forms)?

   A. Bindings

   B. Server-side events

   C. Embedded expressions

   D. Custom controls

   E. Control styling

CHAPTER 17
XForms

IN THIS CHAPTER

Understanding XForms

XForms is the *new* standard way to create forms (the specification is actually not that new, but it is definitely new to almost all developers, few of whom have ever used it). Understanding XForms a better understanding of the worlds of XML and XSL.

XML is simply a way to share structured data. XML documents are each of a specific type which defines what fields and information need to be in XML documents of that type. XForms is an XML type used to define what forms contains. That is important to understand. Unlike HTML forms which contain form controls and presentation, XForms forms contain only form controls.

Or put differently, forms contain controls (the form fields themselves) as well as presentation information (where the label should be displayed, HTML tables, and so on). An XForms form only contains controls, a list of controls and what their attributes are. Attributes include things like:

- Field name
- Field type
- Field label
- Level of nesting (if using fields within groups)
- Type of validation required

There is no presentation at all in the XForms, just lots of information that could be used by whomever (or whatever) needs to provide the presentation.

XSL stands for Extensible Stylesheet Language, it is a language used to provide processing rules for XML. If you had an XML file containing raw movie information and you wanted to convert that data into the format your database needed, you would write an XSL file that provided the translation rules, defining how XML data is to be processed and what any generated output should look like. The XSL file is then applied, and the output you need is generated.

When working with XForms you then need to document:

- The XForm definition of your form
- An XSL file that defines how that form is to be rendered

The big idea is to explicitly divorce form contents from form presentation. Why is this a good thing? Consider the following scenarios:

- You need to reorder form fields, instead of having to fight with `<tr>` and `<td>` tags you simply move the fields around, there is no presentation code to worry about.
- You need to copy and paste parts of one form into another, without presentation code in the way it really is a simple matter of copy and paste.
- You need a common look for all your forms, instead of having presentation code in every form you have a single XSL file that all forms use.
- And when that look and feel needs to change, you now have a single file to change, and all forms will inherit that change automatically.
- It makes a lot of sense. And yet very few developers use XForms. Why is that?

Barriers To XForms Adoptions

There have been three primary barriers to XForms adoption:

- Unlike HTML forms, XForms syntax is very rigid and strict, and creating the well formed XML that XForms requires is not trivial.
- Creating XSL is even less trivial. It is not an easy language to learn and use.
- And worst of all, many browsers won't know what to do with XForms and XSL, and won't apply the transformation for you.

All things considered, it is easy to see why XForms adoption has been slow. And yet XForms does indeed have value, as already explained.

ColdFusion and XForms

ColdFusion can't solve all of the above problems, but it can make using XForms far easier and more manageable:

- ColdFusion can automatically create the XForms XML, all you need to do is use `<cfform>` tags (the same tags you've been using in this and previous chapters), and ColdFusion will figure out what the XML you need should look like and will generate it for you.
- ColdFusion can also apply XSL transformations on the server so that what gets sent to the browser is regular browser code. As such, browsers need know nothing about XForms and XSL because browsers never see the XForms or XSL.
- The only problem ColdFusion can't solve for you is writing the XSL. But fortunately ColdFusion does come with some basic XSL files to get you started, and more will be made available for download.

> **NOTE**
>
> If you intend to use XForms extensively, you'll want to pick up a book on XSL.

Using XForms

To generate XForms XML simple specify `format="xml"` in the `<cfform>` tag. Here is a simple example:

```
<cfform format="xml"
        action="process.cfm">

<cfinput name="nameFirst"
         label="First Name:"
         type="text">

<cfinput name="nameLarst"
         label="Last Name:"
         type="text">

<cfinput name="btn"
         type="submit"
         value="Process">

</cfform>
```

The above code contains no formatting, and yet if processed by ColdFusion would generate a form formatted and laid out in an HTML table. As no skin was specified, the default skin was used, and if you look at the generated source (do a View Source in the browser) you will see that an HTML table was generated automatically (by the XSL transformation).

Applying XSL Skins

To use one of the provided skins, the `<cfform>` can be modified so that it reads:

```
<cfform format="xml"
        skin="silver"
        action="process.cfm">
```

This will generate a nicely formatted form using a silver theme. By simply specifying an alternate `skin` a different output could be generated. The following skins are included with ColdFusion:

- `basic.xsl`
- `basiccss.xsl` (basic alignment using CSS instead of tables)
- `beige.xsl`
- `blue.xsl`
- `bluegray.xsl`
- `red.xsl`
- `silver.xsl`

The provided skins are intended to be examples and starting points for your own skins. And once written, your own skins can be used just as easily. Consider the following example:

```
<cfform format="xml"
        skin="mySkin"
        action="process.cfm">

  <cfformgroup type="myLayout">

    <cfinput name="nameFirst"
             label="First Name:"
             type="text">

    <cfinput name="nameLarst"
             label="Last Name:"
             type="text">

    <cfinput name="btn"
             type="submit"
             value="Process">

  </cfformgroup>

</cfform>
```

In this example a skin named `mySkin` is being used, and any and all formatting and presentation is included within that XSL file. A `<cfformgroup>` is used to group fields together, and ColdFusion allows any group type to be used because it actually does nothing with the specified type, other than simply include it in the generated XML (which is then translated by the XSL skin). The XSL file would have to know what to do with a type of `myLayout` and would render presentation accordingly.

XSL Skin Locations

XSL skins can be shared *system* skins or *application specific* skins.

- Any skins saved in `/cfide/scripts/xsl` (under the Web root) are system skins. These can be shared by all developers, and are referred to by the file name (without the `.xsl` extension).
- Skins may also be located in the current directory (where it can be referred to by name) or in any other directory (where it must be referred to using a path). These skins may not be available to all developers, and when used the full file name (including the `.xsl` extension) must be used.

Usage Notes

A few important notes pertaining to XForms and their use within ColdFusion:

- ColdFusion can help generate the XForms XML and can apply the transformation server-side, but XSL creation is left to the developer.
- XForms can support any client-side technology, including HTML, JavaScript, DHTML, and more.
- ColdFusion generated XForms does not write any client code for you, it simply generates the client code that you specify. In other words, you have to write exactly what you write now, but instead of placing it all in a single file it is now broken into two parts (the form contents and the form presentation).
- The real value of XForms becomes apparent with the XSL contains not just colors and layout, but also form intelligence and logic (via scripting, perhaps).

NOTE

If you are looking for additional examples of XSL skins and use, visit http://www.cfform.com/.

Summary

XForms is the new standard for form creation. ColdFusion dramatically simplifies XForms use by both generating XForms XML and by applying transformations on the server (thus eliminating browser dependencies).

Sample Questions

1. Which of the can be used in ColdFusion XForms?

   A. <cftextarea>

   B. <cfinput type="submit">

   C. <cfinput type="file">

   D. <cfslider>

   E. <cfselect>

2. What is the minimum number of files needed to use XForms in ColdFusion?

   A. 1

   B. 2

   C. 3

   D. 4

3. What belongs in an XSL file?

   A. Form action

   B. Colors

   C. Client-side JavaScript

   D. Submit button

CHAPTER 18

Printing

IN THIS CHAPTER

Introducing <cfdocument>

The inability to be able to easily generate printable content from within Web pages has long been a source of serious aggravation for Web application developers (all developers, not just ColdFusion developers). And considering that a very significant chunk of Web application development tends to be data reporting and presentation type applications, this is even a bigger problem.

The truth is, Web browsers just don't print Web pages properly, and so developers have had to resort to complex and painful workarounds so as to generate content in a format that is indeed printable.

ColdFusion solves this problem simply with the `<cfdocument>` family of tags, as seen in this snippet:

```
<cfdocument format="pdf">
Hello world!
</cfdocument>
```

By wrapping text in between `<cfdocument>` and `</cfdocument>` tags, content between those tags is converted into a PDF file on-the-fly, and embedded in the page.

> **NOTE**
> When generating printable output using `<cfdocument>` it is not necessary to set the MIME type using `<cfcontent>`, ColdFusion does this automatically.

In addition to PDF, ColdFusion can generate Flash paper, a lightweight alternative to PDF, and one that only requires that the Flash Player be present on the browser. To generate FlashPaper, simple change `format="pdf"` to `format="flashpaper"`.

Printable content is not limited to static text, and can use dynamic CFML within the document content too. `<cfdocument>` thus makes generating printable versions of existing pages (static or dynamic) incredibly easy.

> **TIP**
>
> The easiest way to create both screen and print versions of the same page is to create the page as you'd do now, and then create a print version which contains `<cfdocument>` and `</cfdocument>` tags with a `<cfinclude>` in between them (including the page to be printed).

Using `<cfdocument>`

`<cfdocument>` is one of a family of three tags supports all sorts of attributes for sophisticated printed output control. An understanding of these tags and attributes, as well as the scope and limitations of this functionality, is important.

What Is Supported by `<cfdocument>`?

The `<cfdocument>` tag supports all of the following:

- HTML 4
- XML 1
- DOM level 1 and 2
- CSS1 and CSS2

Some elements, however, are not supported:

- JavaScript and DHTML is not supported by `<cfdocument>`. As such, page elements that are rendered programmatically will not be rendered in the generated printable output.
- Plug-ins are not supported, and so embedded Flash, ActiveX, applets, etc., will not be printed.

> **TIP**
>
> `<a href>` tags are supported, and links within the generated PDF and SWF output will work correctly.

`<cfdocument>` should thus be more than able to convert all sorts of pages into printable PDF or FlashPaper.

Greater Output Control

`<cfdocument>` supports a whole series of attributes to give you greater control over printed output. Table 18.1 lists the supported attributes.

Table 18.1 `<cfdocument>` Attributes

ATTRIBUTE	DESCRIPTION
`backgroundvisible`	Whether or not to display page background, default is `no`.
`encryption`	Optional encryption, `128-bit` or `40-bit` (used by PDF only).
`filename`	Optional file name, if specified document is saved to disk instead of being served in the browser.
`fontembed`	Whether or not to embed used fonts, `yes`, `no`, or `selective` (default).
`format`	`pdf` or `flashpaper`, this attribute is required.
`marginbottom`	Page bottom margin, use `unit` to specify unit of measure.
`marginleft`	Page left margin, use `unit` to specify unit of measure.
`marginright`	Page right margin, use `unit` to specify unit of measure.
`margintop`	Page top margin, use `unit` to specify unit of measure.
`name`	Optional variable name to contain generated output.
`orientation`	Page orientation, `portrait` (the default) or `landscape`.
`overwrite`	Whether or not to overwrite existing documents (if using `filename`).
`ownerpassword`	Optional owner password (used by PDF only).
`pageheight`	Page height (used if `pagetype="custom"`), use `unit` to specify unit of measure.
`pagetype`	Page size, supports `legal`, `letter`, `A4`, `A5`, `B5`, and `custom`.
`pagewidth`	Page width (used if `pagetype="custom"`), use `unit` to specify unit of measure.
`scale`	Scaling factor, default is calculated by ColdFusion automatically.
`unit`	Unit of measure, `in` (inches) or `cm` (centimeters).
`userpassword`	Optional user password (used by PDF only).

Saving Generated Output

<cfdocument> embeds generated output in your Web page. You may opt to save the generated files to disk instead of serving them in real-time. Reasons to do this include:

- Caching, so as to not have to regenerate pages unnecessarily
- E-mailing generated content
- Generating pages that may be served statically

To save generated output simple provide a filename in the `filename` attribute. The specified file name must be fully qualified (with a complete path). Here is a simple example:

```
<cfset filePath=ExpandFile("output.swf")>
<cfdocument format="flashpaper"
            filename="#filePath#"
            overwrite="true">
Hello world!
</cfdocument>
```

> **NOTE**
>
> If `overwrite="false"` (the default), and the destination file already exists, an exception will be thrown.

> **TIP**
>
> Use the `ExpandPath()` function to convert file names to fully qualified paths.

<cfdocument> Child Tags

<cfdocument> can be used without any child tags, as seen previously. But two child tags provide greater control over generated output:

- <cfdocumentitem> is used to define headers, footers, and page breaks.
- <cfdocumentsection> is used to define sections within a generated document.

Controlling Output Using The <cfdocumentitem> Tag

<cfdocumentitem> is used within a <cfdocument> tag set to embed additional items. <cfdocumentitem> requires that a type be specified. Table 18.2 lists the supported types.

Table 18.2 `<cfdocumentitem>` Types

TYPE	DESCRIPTION
`footer`	Page footer.
`header`	Page header.
`pagebreak`	Embed a page break, this type takes no body.

> **NOTE**
> Page breaks are calculated automatically by ColdFusion. Use `<cfdocumentitem type="pagebreak">` to embed manual breaks.

The following examples uses all three types to generate a printable employee directory with a cover page, and page headers and footers:

```
<!--- Get data --->
<cfquery datasource="myDsn"
         name="users">
SELECT NameLast, NameFirst, Phone, EMail
FROM users
ORDER BY NameLast, NameFirst
</cfquery>

<!--- Generate document --->
<cfdocument format="pdf">

<!--- Header --->
<cfdocumentitem type="header">
Employee Directory
</cfdocumentitem>

<!--- Footer --->
<cfdocumentitem type="footer">
<p align="center">
<cfoutput>
#CFDOCUMENT.currentpagenumber# of #CFDOCUMENT.totalpagecount#
Printed #DateFormat(Now())#
</cfoutput>
</p>
</cfdocumentitem>

<!--- Title --->
<div align="center">
<h2>Employee Directory</h2>
</div>

<!--- Page break --->
<cfdocumentitem type="pagebreak" />
```

```
<!--- Details --->
<table>
 <tr>
  <th>Name</th>
  <th>Phone</th>
  <th>E-Mail</th>
 </tr>
 <cfoutput query="users">
  <tr>
   <td>#NameLast#, #NameFirst#</td>
   <td>#Phone#</td>
   <td>#EMail#</td>
  </tr>
 </cfoutput>
</table>

</cfdocument>
```

The `<cfdocument>` content contains the following code:

```
<!--- Header --->
<cfdocumentitem type="header">
Employee Directory
</cfdocumentitem>
```

This code defines a page header, text that will be placed at the top of each page. A footer is also defined as follows:

```
<!--- Footer --->
<cfdocumentitem type="footer">
<p align="center">
<cfoutput>
#CFDOCUMENT.currentpagenumber# of #CFDOCUMENT.totalpagecount#
Printed #DateFormat(Now())#
</cfoutput>
</p>
</cfdocumentitem>
```

This page footer contains two special variables. Within a `<cfdocument>` tag a special scope exists named `CFDOCUMENT`. It contains two variables, as listed in Table 18.3. These variables may be used in headers and footers, as seen in this example.

Table 18.3 `CFDOCUMENT` Scope Variables

TYPE	DESCRIPTION
`currentpagenumber`	Current page number.
`totalpagecount`	Total number of generated pages.

In addition, the code embeds a manual page break using this code:

```
<!--- Page break --->
<cfdocumentitem type="pagebreak" />
```

<cfdocumentitem> must always have an end tag, even when no body is used. The trailing / is a shortcut that you can use. In other words, the above tag is functionally identical to:

```
<!--- Page break --->
<cfdocumentitem type="pagebreak"></cfdocumentitem>
```

Defining Sections With <cfdocumentsection>

As you have seen, you have a lot of control over generated pages using the <cfdocument> and <cfdocumentitem> tags. But sometimes you may want different options in different parts of the same document. For example, you may want a title page to have different margins that other pages. Or you may want different headers and footers in different parts of the document.

To do this you use <cfdocumentsection> tags. A <cfdocument> tag pair may contain one or more sections, each defined using <cfdocumentsection> tags. Within each section you may specify alternate margins, and may use <cfdocumentitem> tags to specify headers and footers for each section.

> **NOTE**
> When using <cfdocumentsection>, all content must be in sections. Any content outside of sections is ignored by ColdFusion.

Summary

The <cfdocument> family of tags makes it easy to generate printable output (as well as printable versions of existing pages). Child tags provide support for page headers and footers, manual page breaks, and document sections. Output may be generated in PDF and FlashPaper formats.

Sample Questions

1. Which of the following tags will *not* generate printable output?

   A. <a href>

   B. <p>

   C. <script>

   D. <b>

   E. <embed>

   F.

   G. <em>

2. Which tags are used to set page margins?

   A. `<cfdocument>`

   B. `<cfdocumentmargin>`

   C. `<cfdocumentitem>`

   D. `<cfdocumentsection>`

3. What printable formats are supported by `<cfdocument>`?

   A. Excel

   B. FlashPaper

   C. HTML

   D. PDF

   E. RTF

CHAPTER 19
Reporting

IN THIS CHAPTER

Understanding <cfreport> and the ColdFusion Report Builder

<cfdocument> is designed to create printable versions of Web pages, free-form unstructured web pages. Of course, not all printable pages meet that description, and sometimes more structured output is needed, real reporting with features like:

- Banded reports
- Calculated totals and sums
- Repeating and non-repeating regions
- Embedded charts
- And more

→ <cfdocument> was covered in Chapter 18, "Printing."

While these reports can indeed be created manually, there is a better way, using the ColdFusion's <cfreport> tag and accompanying ColdFusion Report Builder.

It is important to understand that the Report Builder is just that, a builder, an application that allows you to create and manipulate .cfr files. The .cfr files themselves are processed (when requested) by a reporting engine built into ColdFusion itself. This high-performance multi-threaded engine processes .cfr files, executing queries if required, generating charts, laying out pages, performing aggregate calculations, and more, and finally generating complete reports (that may be viewed online or printed).

> **NOTE**
>
> ColdFusion Standard uses a single thread for reporting, whereas ColdFusion Enterprise allows the administrator to allocate as many threads as needed.

Reports created using the ColdFusion Report Builder may be generated in three formats:

- FlashPaper
- PDF
- Excel (Microsoft Excel spreadsheet)

Installing The Report Builder

Unlike ColdFusion itself (which need only be installed on computers processing ColdFusion code), the ColdFusion Report Builder must be installed on every computer on which reports will be designed.

If the ColdFusion Report Builder is not installed on your machine, run the installer named `CFReportBuilder.exe` (it can be found in `/CFIDE/installers` under the ColdFusion web root).

Running The Report Builder

The ColdFusion Report Builder is a standalone program used to define ColdFusion Report templates. It can be run standalone, and also directly from within Dreamweaver by double-clicking on a report file.

> **TIP**
>
> To launch the Report Builder select ColdFusion Report Builder from the Windows Program > Macromedia > ColdFusion MX 7 program group.

Configuring The Report Builder

When first run, the ColdFusion Report Builder launches a wizard that prompts for important initial settings. These include RDS connection information, and default settings.

> **TIP**
>
> You can rerun the setup wizard any time from the File, New menu.

Using The ColdFusion Report Builder

The ColdFusion Report Builder creates and edits a special ColdFusion file with a `.cfr` extension. Unlike `.cfm` and `.cfc` files, `.cfr` files cannot be edited with a text editor, and the ColdFusion Report Builder must be used. `.cfr` files are report templates that may be used as is, or invoked from CFML code as needed (as will be explained below).

> **NOTE**
> The ColdFusion Report Builder is a Windows only utility. Reports created using the Report Builder can be processed by ColdFusion on any platform, and reports can be viewed on all platforms too. However, at this time reports can only be created on Windows machines.

Report Builder Features

Key ColdFusion Report Builder features include:

- Familiar report designer interface.
- Tabbed MDI interface (allows for multiple reports to be edited at once).
- Data grouping via bands.
- Subreport support.
- SQL query builder (requires an RDS connection).
- Charting wizard (requires an RDS connection).
- Report preview (is using an embedded query).
- Access to CFML expressions (with integrated expression builder),
- Styles to manage output.
- Extensive integrated help.

Navigating The Report Builder

The ColdFusion Report Builder screen looks a lot like other report writing tools that you may have used. The screen contains several sections that you should be aware of:

- The large open space in the middle of the Report Builder is where reports are defined and edited.

- On the left is a toolbox containing buttons to insert images, fields, subreports, and more into reports, as well as buttons used to manage element alignment.
- On the top of the screen are toolbars for file opening, editing, fonts, etc.
- On the upper right is the Properties panel, this displays the properties for any report item, and allows for quick property editing.
- On the bottom right is the Fields and Parameters panel, used to access query columns, calculated fields, and input parameters.

Creating A Report

To create a new report, click on File, New to display the ColdFusion Report Builder Gallery dialog box. (This box will be displayed automatically if the Report Builder is started without clicking on a `.cfr` file).

You will be presented with two options:

- **As A Blank Report:** Select this option to create a blank report for you to work with.
- **Report Creation Wizard:** Use this option to launch an interactive Wizard that will prompt you for the SQL, grouping, layout, and more, generating a complete usable report (that you can then edit and tweak as needed).

Whichever option is used, the first task will be to specify the SQL query columns to be used within the reports. This can be via an actual SQL statement (entered manually or created via the SQL Query Builder) or a list of column names manually specified in the Fields and Parameters panel. Once query column have been defined they can be used within the report.

NOTE

Embedded SQL is the default report SQL statement, and it can be overridden at runtime via `<cfreport query="">`.

TIP

It is only necessary to actually embed SQL within the `.cfr` file if you want to support direct execution of the `.cfr` file (as opposed to programmatic execution via `<cfreport>`). However, there is one big advantage of embedding SQL (regardless of the planned invocation method), previewing of the report from within the Report Builder is only possible if a default SQL statement exists.

Editing A Report

To edit an existing `.cfr` file, either double-click on it (from within Dreamweaver or Windows Explorer), or launch the Report Builder and select the `.cfr` file from the recent list (or simply browse to it and open).

Report elements may be edited and modified as needed. To rerun the wizard that created the report (assuming that the wizard was in fact used), Report, Report Wizard For This Report.

> **TIP**
>
> It is generally not a good idea to rerun the wizard after you have made changes to a report. If you need access to the SQL Query Builder portion of the wizard, use Report, Report Query. If you need access to the report orientation, margins, columns, page sizes, and more, use Report, Report Properties.

Running Your Reports

Once reports (`.cfr` files) have been created they must be deployed to the ColdFusion server (just like `.cfm` and `.cfc` files). Once deployed, there are two ways to generate reports, direct invocation, and via the `<cfreport>` tag. The latter is what developers will typically use as it provides far greater control over the report and report data.

Direct Report Invocation

To run your report, simply invoke the full URL to it from within your browser. The report will be displayed, exactly as it was when previewed in the ColdFusion Report Builder. The SQL used will be the default SQL (see the note and tip in *Creating A Report* above), and the output format will be the default format specified in the report properties.

> **NOTE**
>
> By default, the default output format is FlashPaper.

> **TIP**
>
> Direct `.cfr` invocation may be disabled in the report properties.

Invoking Reports From Within ColdFusion Code

Being able to run reports in browsers is useful, but other reporting tools can do that too. What makes ColdFusion reports unique is their ability to be altered at runtime. Here is an example:

```
<!--- Get data --->
<cfquery datasource="myDsn"
        name="users">
SELECT NameLast, NameFirst, Phone, EMail
FROM users
ORDER BY NameLast, NameFirst
</cfquery>

<!--- Generate report --->
<cfreport template="userList.cfr"
         query="users"
         format="PDF" />
```

➜ `<cfquery>` was covered in Chapter 7, "Using Databases."

A `<cfquery>` tag is used to create a database query, and then passes that query to the `<cfreport>` tag overriding the query within the report. Of course, queries can be constructed dynamically, allowing for report data to be changes at runtime based on user access, prior data entry, and more.

> **NOTE**
>
> Any ColdFusion query objects can be passed to `<cfreport>`, including those returned by stored-procedure invocation, those created with `QueryNew()`, and any queries returned by ColdFusion Component and Custom Tag invocation.

This functionality (the ability to invoke reports programmatically) is so important that the ColdFusion Report Builder can actually automatically create calling CFML code fore you. To use this feature, open a report in the ColdFusion Query Builder, and click on the Code Snippet button (the one with tags on it). You will see a screen that contains calling CFML code, either a single `.cfm` or a `.cfc` and `.cfm`.. You can select the code style using the radio buttons at the bottom of the page, and then click Save to save the generated ColdFusion code read for you to use (and modify, if needed).

Additional Reporting Options

Beyond the basic reporting functionality reviewed this far, the ColdFusion Report Writer and the reporting engine also supports a wide range of reporting features (more than can be included in this review chapter). Here are some key features worth noting:

Saving Generated Reports

Like printable pages generated using `<cfdocument>`, reports generated via `<cfreport>` may be saved (instead of served) by specifying a `filename`.

Passing Input Parameters

In addition to being able to pass a query to `<cfreport>` at runtime, `name=value` variable pairs may also be passed in one of two formats, as `<cfreport>` attributes:

```
<!--- Generate report --->
<cfreport template="userList.cfr"
          query="users"
          format="PDF"
          title="Sales Department Employees" />
```

or via `<cfreportparam>` tags:

```
<!--- Generate report --->
<cfreport template="userList.cfr"
          query="users"
          format="PDF">
  <cfreportparam name="title"
                 value="Sales Department Employees" />
</cfreport>
```

These examples are functionally identical, and both pass a input parameter named `title` to the report.

To use this input parameter is must be defined in the report (in the Fields and Parameters panel). Once defined, input parameters can be used like any other report fields or expressions.

Conditional Element Processing

All report element (fields, labels, embedded charts, and more) are included by default (after all, if they are defined in the report then they should be included in it). But all report elements may be included or excluded at runtime based on a CFML expression. To do this, click on an element and specify a condition in the Print When property. For example, to include a chart only on Monday's, embed the chart, and then associate this condition with it:

```
DayOfWeek(Now()) IS 2
```

Report elements can also be included or excluded based on input parameters. For example, to conditionally include or exclude a logo add define an input parameter named `dispLogo` of type `boolean` with a default of `1`, and then use the following as the Print When condition:

```
param.dispLogo
```

This way the logo will be included in the report unless `dispLogo=false` is passed at runtime.

Embedding Subreports

To embed a subreport within a report, click on the subreport button and define where within the report it is to be placed. You will be prompted to either create a new report or to select an existing report. Either way, the subreport will be opened in a second tab allowing you to work on both the main report and the subreport simultaneously.

> **NOTE**
>
> It is not yet possible to pass queries at runtime to subreports, subreports always use embedded SQL.

Using Text Styles

Text styles allow styles to be used for text and labels instead of hard-coding these settings. Text styles are defined in the Text Styles tab, and are associated with report elements by selecting the style from the Text Styles drop down list in the Properties panel.

> **NOTE**
>
> `<cfreport>` still supports the use of Crystal Reports `.rpt` files as it did in previous ColdFusion versions. However, that support is primarily for backwards compatibility, and the primary reporting emphasis now is on the reporting engine and the ColdFusion Report Builder.

Summary

The ColdFusion Report Builder is used to construct report templates processed by the ColdFusion reporting engine. This templates may be invoked directly or programmatically as needed, and reports may be generated in PDF and FlashPaper formats, as well as Excel spreadsheets.

Sample Questions

1. Which files are required to execute reports generated using the ColdFusion Report Builder?

   A. `.cfc`

   B. `.cfm`

   C. `.cfr`

2. What type of data can be passed to reports at runtime?

   A. Arrays

   B. Dates

   C. Queries

   D. Numbers

   E. Strings

   F. Structures

3. What output formats are supported by `<cfreport>`?

   A. Excel

   B. FlashPaper

   C. HTML

   D. PDF

   E. RTF

4. Which of the following can be used to pass query data to `<cfreport>`?

   A. `<cfpop>`

   B. `<cfstoredproc>`

   C. `<cfsearch>`

   D. `<cfdocument>`

   E. `<cffile>`

   F. `<cfoutput>`

CHAPTER 20 Graphing

IN THIS CHAPTER

Introducing ColdFusion Graphing

We'll start with an overview of the charting features included in ColdFusion. ColdFusion comes with a series of tags that will allow you to:

- Create many different types of graphs, including pie charts, bar graphs, line graphs, and scatter charts.
- Format your graphs with an extensive number of formatting options for controlling fonts, colors, labels, and more.
- Display the graphs on any ColdFusion page as JPEG images, PNG images, or interactive Flash charts.
- Allow users to *drill down* on data shown in your charts. For instance, you could allow people to click the wedges in a pie chart, revealing the data represented in that wedge.
- Combine several different charts, displaying them together on the page. For instance, you might create a scatter chart that shows individual purchases over time, and then add a line chart on top of it that shows average spending by other users.
- Save the charts to the server's drive for later use.

Building Basic Charts

Now that you have an idea of what you can do with ColdFusion's charting features, it's time to get started with some basic examples. Most of the time, you will create charts with just two CFML tags, `<cfchart>` and `<cfchartseries>`.

Introducing <cfchart> and <cfchartseries>

To display a chart on a ColdFusion page, you use the `<cfchart>` tag. The `<cfchart>` tag is what controls the height, width, and formatting of your chart, but it doesn't actually display anything. Within the `<cfchart>` tag, you use the `<cfchartseries>` tag, which determines the type of chart (like `bar` or `pie`) and the actual data to show on the chart.

> **NOTE**
> Actually, you will occasionally want to place multiple `<cfchartseries>` tags within a `<cfchart>` tag. See the "Combining Multiple Chart Series" section, later in this chapter.

Table 20.1 shows the most important attributes for the `<cfchart>` tag, and Table 20.2 shows the most important attributes for `<cfchartseries>`.

> **NOTE**
> Because these tags have a large number of attributes (more than 40 in all), we are introducing only the most important attributes in this table. Others are introduced later in this chapter.

Table 20.1 Basic `<cfchart>` Tag Syntax

ATTRIBUTE	DESCRIPTION
`chartwidth`	Optional. The width of the chart, in pixels. The default is `320`.
`chartheight`	Optional. The height of the chart, in pixels. The default is `240`.
`xaxistitle`	Optional. The text to display along the chart's x-axis.
`yaxistitle`	Optional. The text to display along the chart's y-axis.
`rotated`	`Yes` or `No`. If yes, the chart is rotated clockwise by 90 degrees. You can use this to create bar charts that point sideways rather than up and down, and so on. The default is `No`.
`url`	Optional. The URL of a page to send the user to when various sections of the chart are clicked. You can pass variables in the URL so you know what part of the chart the user clicked. See "Drilling Down from Charts," later in this chapter.
`format`	Optional. The type of image format in which the chart should be created. The valid choices are `flash` (the default), `jpg`, or `png`.
`seriesplacement`	Optional. For charts that have more than one data series, you can use this attribute—`cluster`, `stacked`, `percent`, or `default`—to control how the series are combined visually. Use `cluster` if the data series represent related pieces of information that should be presented next to one another, rather than added together visually. Use `stacked` or `percent` if the data series represent values that should be added up to a single whole value for each item you are plotting. See "Combining Multiple Chart Series," later in this chapter.

Table 20.2 Basic <cfchartseries> Syntax

ATTRIBUTE	DESCRIPTION
`type`	Required. The type of chart to create. One of `area`, `bar`, `cone`, `curve`, `cylinder`, `horizontalbar`, `line`, `pie`, `pyramid`, `scatter`, `step`.
`query`	Optional. The name of a query that contains data to chart. If you don't provide a `query` attribute, you will need to provide `<cfchartdata>` tags to tell ColdFusion the data to display in the chart.
`valuecolumn`	Required if a `query` is provided. The name of the column that contains the actual value (the number to represent graphically) for each data point on the chart.
`itemcolumn`	Required if a `query` is provided. The name of the column that contains labels for each data point on the chart.

NOTE

In this chapter, you will see the term data point often. Data points are the actual pieces of data that are displayed on a chart. If you are creating a pie chart, the data points are the slices of the pie. In a bar chart, the data points are the bars. In a line or scatter chart, the data points are the individual points that have been plotted on the graph.

NOTE

You don't have to have a query object to create a chart. You can also create data points manually using the `<cfchartdata>` tag. See "Plotting Individual Points with `<cfchartdata>`," near the end of this chapter.

Creating A Chart

The following example creates a simple bar chart using `<cfchart>` and `<cfchartseries>` to create a simple bar chart.

```
<!--- Get information from the database --->
<cfquery datasource="myDsn"
        name="chartQuery">
SELECT movietitle, amountbudgeted
FROM movies
WHERE active=1
ORDER BY movietitle
</cfquery>

<h2>Chart: Film Budgets</h2>
```

```
<!--- This defines the size and appearance of the chart --->
<cfchart chartwidth="750"
         chartheight="500"
         yaxistitle="Budget">

 <!--- within the chart --->
 <cfchartseries type="bar"
                query="chartquery"
                valuecolumn="amountbudgeted"
                itemcolumn="movietitle">

</cfchart>
```

The `<cfchart>` tag is used to establish the size of the chart, and to specify that the word `Budget` appear along the y-axis (that is, at the bottom of the chart). Within the `<cfchart>` block, a `<cfchartseries>` tag is used to create a bar chart. ColdFusion is instructed to chart the information in the `ChartQuery` record set, plotting the data in the `AmountBudgeted` column and using the `MovieTitle` column to provide a label for each piece of information.

The above code will create a Flash chart, as that is the default chart format generated by ColdFusion. Charts may also be generated as static images (in JPG and PNG formats), although static charts are not as functional or feature rich.

Changing the Chart Type

The previous example created a bar chart. To create a different chart (perhaps a pie chart, simply change the type to one of the values listed in Table 20.2.

Formatting Charts

ColdFusion supports numerous options for fine-tuning and controlling the look of generated charts, both via skins, and via explicitly specified attributes.

Using Skins

Skins are XML files that contain chart color schemes. The following default skins are provided with ColdFusion:

- `beige`
- `blue`
- `default`
- `red`
- `silver`
- `yellow`

These skins are located in `{cfusion root}/charting/styles`, and you may define additional skins simply by placing them in these folder. Skins contain:

- Colors to be used
- 3D effect details
- Font information
- Label formatting
- Animation effects and timings
- …and more

To use a skin, simply specify its name (minus the .xml extension) in the `<cfchart style="">` attribute.

> **NOTE**
> There are two skins for each defined skin, one for pie charts and one for all other charts. These are identically named, except that the pie chart skin has `_pie` in it's name, for example, `red.xml` and `red_pie.xml`.

Controlling Fonts and Colors

ColdFusion provides a number of formatting attributes that you can use to control fonts, colors, and borders. Some of the attributes are applied at the `<cfchart>` level and others at the `<cfchartseries>` level, as listed in Table 20.3 and Table 20.4, respectively.

> **NOTE**
> All of the attributes that control color can accept Web-style hexadecimal color values, such as `FFFFFF` for white or `0000FF` for blue. In addition, any of the following named colors can be used: `Aqua`, `Black`, `Blue`, `Fuchsia`, `Gray`, `Green`, `Lime`, `Maroon`, `Navy`, `Olive`, `Purple`, `Red`, `Silver`, `Teal`, `White`, and `Yellow`.

Table 20.3 `<cfchart>` Formatting Options

ATTRIBUTE	DESCRIPTION
`showborder`	Whether a border should be drawn around the entire chart. The default is `No`.
`showlegend`	Whether to display a legend that shows the meaning of each color used in the graph. This is applicable only to pie charts, or charts that use more than one `<cfchartseries>` tag. The default is `Yes`.

Table 20.3 (CONTINUED)

ATTRIBUTE	DESCRIPTION
`backgroundcolor`	The background color of the portion of the chart that contains the actual graph (that is, excluding the space set aside for axis labels and legends).
`databackgroundcolor`	The background color of the space set aside for axis labels and legends (everywhere except the part where the actual graph is shown).
`tipbgcolor`	The background color for the pop-up tip window that appears when you hover the pointer over a data point.
`foregroundcolor`	The foreground color to use throughout the chart. This controls the color of all text in the chart, as well as the lines used to draw the x- and y-axes, the lines around each bar or pie slice, and so on.
`font`	The font to use for text in the chart, such as legends and axis labels. In ColdFusion MX, you can choose between `arial`, `times`, and `courier`. In addition, you can choose `arialunicodeMS`, which you should use when using double-byte character sets. The default is `arial`.
`fontsize`	The size of the font, expressed as a number. The default is `11`.
`fontbold`	Whether text is displayed in bold. The default is `No`.
`fontitalic`	Whether text is displayed in italics. The default is `No`.
`tipstyle`	Optional. Can be set to `mouseOver` (the default), `mouseDown`, or `off`. By default, a hint or tip message will display when the user hovers her pointer over a data point in a graph (an example of this is shown in Figure 25.1). The tip message includes the label and value of the data point, as well as the series label, if given (see Table 25.5). If you want the tip to be shown only when the user clicks a data point, you can use `tipstyle="mouseDown"`, but this works only if `format="flash"`. If you don't want any tip to be shown at all, use `tipstyle="off"`.
`pieslicestyle`	Relevant only for pie charts. If `sliced` (the default) is used, the pie is shown with its slices separated by white space (this effect is sometimes called exploded). If `solid` is used, the pie is shown with its slices together in a circle, the way you would normally think of a pie chart. Unfortunately, there is no way to explode just one slice at a time, which is a common way to present pie charts. In general, you will probably want to use `pieslicestyle="solid"`.

Table 20.4 `<cfchartseries>` Formatting Options

ATTRIBUTE	DESCRIPTION
`seriescolor`	A color to use for the main element of the data series.
`serieslabel`	A label or title for the data series.
`paintstyle`	A style to use when filling in solid areas on the chart for this series. The default is `plain`, which uses solid colors. You can also provide `raise`, which gives each area a raised, buttonlike appearance; `shade`, which shades each area with a gradient fill, or `light`, which is a lighter version of `shade`.
`colorlist`	Relevant for pie charts only. A comma-separated list of colors to use for the slices of the pie. The first slice will have the first color in the list, the second slice will have the second color, and so on.
`markerstyle`	Relevant only for `line`, `curve`, and `scatter` charts. The look of the marker that appears at each data point. Can be set to `rectangle` (the default), `triangle`, `diamond`, `circle`, `letter`, `mcross`, `snow`, or `rcross`.

Listing 16.4 and Figure 16.4 (below) show how some of these formatting attributes can be combined to improve the appearance of the bar charts you have seen so far.

Controlling Grid Lines and Axis Labels

One of the most important aspects of nearly any chart are the numbers and labels that surround the actual graphic on the x- and y-axes. ColdFusion provides you with a number of options for controlling the *scale* of each axis (that is, the distance between the highest and lowest values that could be plotted on the chart), and for controlling how many different numbers are actually displayed along the axes.

Table 20.5 shows the `<cfchart>` attributes related to grid lines and axis labels.

Table 20.5 `<cfchart>` Options for Grid Lines and Labels

ATTRIBUTE	DESCRIPTION
`scalefrom`	The lowest number to show on the y-axis. For instance, if you want one of the budget chart examples shown previously to start at $20,000 instead of $0, you can do so with `scalefrom="20000"`.
`scaleto`	The highest number to show on the y-axis. So, if the highest budget shown in the budget chart examples is $750,000, providing `scaleto="1000000"` will cause the scale to go all the way up to 1 million, even though there aren't any data points that go up that high. The result is extra "empty space" above the highest value, giving the viewer the sense that the values plotted in the chart could have been higher than they actually are.

Table 20.3 (CONTINUED)

ATTRIBUTE	DESCRIPTION
`gridlines`	The number of grid lines to show for the data axis (generally the y-axis). This also affects the number of labeled tick marks along the axis. If you don't provide a value, ColdFusion attempts to use a sensible default value based on the size of the graph. For instance, in Figure 25.2 there are ten grid lines and tick marks (one for `0`, one for `83,300`, and so on), which seems about right.
`showygridlines`	Whether to display grid lines for the y-axis. On most types of charts, these grid lines generally make it easier to understand what the value is for each piece of data. These grid lines are shown in Figure 25.1 (the horizontal lines) and Figure 25.2 (the vertical lines). The default is `Yes`.
`showxgridlines`	Whether to display grid lines for the x-axis. The default is `No`.
`sortxaxis`	Sorts the data in the x-axis (that is, the labels) alphabetically. In general, I recommend that you use `order by` to reorder the records within a normal `<cfquery>` tag, before your code gets to the `<cfchart>` tag; that approach will be much more flexible (see the "Sorting the Data First" section earlier in this chapter).
`labelformat`	The format for the labels along the y-axis (in our examples so far, the labels that show the increasing amounts of money). You can set this to `number` (the default), `currency` (which on English systems adds a dollar sign [$]), `percent` (which multiplies by 100 and adds a percent sign [%]), or `date` (appropriate only if the data you are plotting are dates).

NOTE

You can't adjust the scale in such a way that it would obscure or chop off any of the actual data being shown in the chart. If your `scalefrom` value is higher than the lowest data point on the graph, ColdFusion will use the data point's value instead. For instance, if the lowest budget being plotted in one of the budget chart examples is $34,000 and you provide `scalefrom="50000"`, ColdFusion will start the scale at $34,000. The inverse is also true; if you provide a `scaleto` value that is lower than the highest data point, that point's value will be used instead.

NOTE

When providing hexadecimal color values, the traditional number sign (`#`) is optional. If you provide it, though, you must escape the # by doubling it, so ColdFusion doesn't think you are trying to reference a variable. In other words, you could provide `backgroundcolor="99DDDD"` or `backgroundcolor="##99DDDD"` as you prefer, but not `backgroundcolor= "#99DDDD"`.

Advanced Charting

Beyond basic charts and formatting (explicit and via skins), ColdFusion supports advanced graphing and charting options that are all exposed via tags.

Using Multiple Data Series

To use multiple data series in a single chart, simply include multiple <cfchartseries> tags. The additional <cfchartseries> tags can each display different columns from the same query, or they can display information from different queries or data sources altogether, as seen in this example:

```
<!--- This defines the size and appearance of the chart --->
<cfchart chartwidth="750"
         chartheight="450"
         yaxistitle="Budget"
         seriesplacement="cluster">

 <!--- Budget chart --->
 <cfchartseries type="horizontalbar"
                seriescolor="99ff99"
                serieslabel="Amount Budgeted:"
                query="chartquery"
                valuecolumn="amountbudgeted"
                itemcolumn="movietitle">

 <!--- Expenses chart --->
 <cfchartseries type="horizontalbar"
                seriescolor="ff4444"
                serieslabel="Actual Expenses:"
                query="chartquery"
                valuecolumn="expensetotal"
                itemcolumn="movietitle"
                paintstyle="light">

</cfchart>
```

This example defined to series of the same type, but types can be mixed as needed.

> **NOTE**
> You can't combine pie charts with other types of charts. Any `<cfchartseries>` tags that try to mix pie charts with other types will be ignored.

Drilling Down from Charts

The `<cfchart>` tag supports a `URL` attribute that you can use to create *clickable* charts, where the user is able to click the various data points in the chart to link to a different page (possibly another chart, creating a drill-down effect).

To create a clickable chart, simply add a `URL` attribute to the `<cfchart>` tag. When the user clicks one of the data points in the chart (the slices of a pie chart, the bars in a bar chart, the points in a line graph, and so on), he will be sent to the `URL` you specify. So, if you want the browser to navigate to a ColdFusion page called `details.cfm` when a chart is clicked, you would use `url="details.cfm"`. You can use any type of relative or absolute URL that would be acceptable to use in a normal HTML link.

In order to make the detail page dynamic, though, it will need to know which data point the user clicked. To make this possible, ColdFusion allows you to pass the actual data that the user is clicking as URL variables. To do so, include any of the special values shown in Table 20.6 in the `url` attribute. ColdFusion will create a dynamic URL for each data point by replacing these special values with the actual data for that data point.

Table 20.6 Special Values for Passing in `<cfchart>` URLs

VARIABLE	DESCRIPTION
`$value$`	The value of the selected row (that is, the value in the `valuecolumn` attribute of the `<cfchartseries>` tag for the data point that was clicked). This is typically the value that you are most interested in passing in the url.
`$itemlabel$`	The label of the selected row (that is, the value in the `itemcolumn` for the data point that was clicked).
`$serieslabel$`	The series label (that is, the value of the `serieslabel` attribute of the `<cfchartseries>` tag). It is usually necessary to include this value in the URL only if you have multiple `<cfchartseries>` tags in your chart; this value becomes the way that the target page knows which series the user clicked.

> **NOTE**
> Note the use of **$** to delimit variables.

These values will be passed to the target page as URL parameters, which can then be used to display additional data or perform any needed processing.

➜ URL parameters were covered in Chapter 8, "URL Variables."

Plotting Individual Points with <cfchartdata>

The most common way to provide the actual data to a <cfchartseries> tag is to specify a query attribute, then tell ColdFusion which columns of the query to look in by specifying itemcolumn and valuecolumn attributes.

It is also possible to omit the query, itemcolumn, and valuecolumn attributes and instead plot the data points individually using the <cfchartdata> tag, nested within your <cfchartseries>. The <cfchartdata> approach can come in handy if you want to permanently hard-code certain data points onto your charts, if you need to format your data in a special way, or if you come across any other situation in which you can't extract the desired data from a query in a completely straightforward manner.

Table 20.7 shows the syntax for the <cfchartdata> tag.

Table 20.7 <cfchartdata> Syntax

ATTRIBUTE	DESCRIPTION
item	The item associated with the data point you are plotting, such as a film title, a category of purchases, or a period of time—in other words, the information you would normally supply to the itemcolumn attribute of the <cfchartseries> tag.
value	The value of the data point (a number). This is what you would normally supply to the valuecolumn attribute of <cfchartseries>.

> **TIP**
> It is also possible to mix query driven series and explicit data points if needed.

Summary

The <cfchart> family of tags provide access to sophisticated graphing functionality, allowing for a variety of chart types (in Flash, JPEG or PNG formats) to be embedded in pages.

Sample Questions

1. Which are valid chart types?

   A. `gantt`

   B. `curve`

   C. `step`

   D. `bell`

2. What formats are supported by `<cfchart>`?

   A. JPEG

   B. Flash

   C. FlashPaper

   D. GIF

   E. PDF

   F. PNG

3. Which is the valid `<cfchart>` `url` attribute?

   A. `url="details.cfm?value=#value#"`

   B. `url="details.cfm?value=$value$"`

   C. `url="details.cfm?value=value"`

   D. `url="details.cfm?value={value}"`

PART 5

Advanced ColdFusion

IN THIS PART

CHAPTER 21 Scripting

IN THIS CHAPTER

<cfscript>

Although ColdFusion Markup Language (CFML) is a complete language for building ColdFusion templates, you can use an alternative syntax known as ColdFusion Script (`<cfscript>`). A ColdFusion Script block is surrounded with opening and closing `<cfscript>` tags as follows:

```
<cfscript>
// scripting will go here
// (note the different comment syntax)
</cfscript>
```

Benefits of <cfscript>

Scripting offers a few advantages over using CFML tags. First, scripting is more concise for some operations. A `<cfscript>` block begins and ends with a CFML tag, but no tags are needed within the block itself. Second, scripting resembles JavaScript and could be easier for developers familiar with traditional development languages to relate to. Finally, scripting provides an easy way to work with the parameters and methods of external objects (including Java, COM, or CORBA).

Drawbacks of <cfscript>

Although scripting is well suited for many tasks, it doesn't include all of ColdFusion functionality. Some of the strongest features—such as query services, HTTP, FTP, email, and LDAP—are not available within a `<cfscript>` block. In fact, only the following features are available to the ColdFusion scriptwriter:

- Variable assignment

- Looping
- Conditional statements
- Object invocation (including ColdFusion Components)
- Try/catch handling
- User-defined function creation

Anything beyond this list requires the use of ColdFusion's tag-based syntax.

> **NOTE**
> Although many of ColdFusion's services are not available through scripting, you can work with the data that these services return. For example, a query may return ten rows of data. Although the query couldn't be launched through scripting, the ten rows of data are exposed with no contingencies.

The biggest limitation of `<cfscript>` is that it cannot access CFML tags, so no `<cfquery>` or `<cfmail>` tags are available. However, `<cfscript>` code can access any functions and expressions, including user-defined functions.

Variable Assignment

In CFML, you assign variables by using the `<cfset>` tag. In a `<cfscript>` block, you use a simple assignment statement followed by a semicolon, as follows:

```
<cfscript>
 // simple variable assignments
 x=1;
 y=2;
</cfscript>
```

> **NOTE**
> As with CFML tags, `<cfscript>` code is not case sensitive. Every statement in a script block is followed by a semicolon, much like in Java or JavaScript. Comments in a script block are preceded by `//`.

As with the `<cfset>` tag, temporary variables are not needed in a ColdFusion script block. For example, you can use a structure or array function without the need for an equals sign (=):

```
<cfscript>
 MyStruct = StructNew();
 StructInsert(MyStruct,"new key","new value");
</cfscript>
```

Conditional Processing

Conditional processing with `<cfscript>` is similar to its function in both Java and JavaScript. Much like with CFML syntax, a conditional statement can be constructed in two ways: using either `if` or `switch/case`.

`if` Examples

A sample `if` statement appears as follows:

```
<cfscript>
 x = 1;
 if(x is 1)
 WriteOutput("In Spanish, the number one is 'uno.'<br>");
 //above line above will run if x is 1
 WriteOutput("Thanks for using our Spanish number converter.<br>");
 // above line will always run
</cfscript>
```

The preceding statement evaluates `x` in the `if` statement and prints `"In Spanish, the number one is 'uno.'"` to the browser. Note that no semicolon follows the `if` statement. There is also no such thing as an `endif` statement. All conditional processing statements run the next line if the expression is true. Therefore, the line that sends the Spanish output to the browser runs only if `x` is `1`. The second printed statement, however, always runs.

To add statements to the conditional so that more than one line relies on `x` equaling `1`, you must use curly braces like this:

```
<cfscript>
 x = 1;
 if(x is 1) { //note the curly braces start here
 WriteOutput("In Spanish, the number one is 'uno'.<br>");
 WriteOutput("Uno happens to mean 'one' in Italian as well.<br>");
 //both of these lines will run if x is 1
 } // the curly braces end
 WriteOutput("<br>thanks for using our Spanish number converter.");
 // this line will ALWAYS run whether x is 1 or not
</cfscript>
```

Predictably, `else` and `elseif` statements are similar to the preceding example, as you can see in the following code. Using curly braces is recommended to keep things in order, but it is not required:

```
<cfscript>
 x = 1;
 if(x is 1)
 {
 WriteOutput("In Spanish, the number one is 'uno'.<br>");
 WriteOutput("Uno happens to mean 'one' in Italian as well.<br>");
 }
```

```
 else if (x IS 2)
 WriteOutput("In Spanish, the number two is 'dos'.<br>");
 //no curly braces needed, but use to better organize code
 else
 // the line below runs only if x is neither 1 nor 2;
 WriteOutput("I don't know what that number is in Spanish.<br>");
 // the line below ALWAYS runs whether x is 1, 2, or something else
 WriteOutput("<br>thanks for using our Spanish number converter.");
</cfscript>
```

NOTE

You should notice a few things about the script blocks used so far. First, all conditional statements use the same operators as CFML. It is illegal to use = or <, but legal to use the operators `is` or `lt`.

Second, `<cfscript>` cannot have a `<cfoutput>` block inside it and is therefore incapable of outputting to the browser. To accomplish this task, you can use the `WriteOutput()` function.

Finally, although `<cfoutput>` is not allowed within a script block, it is completely legal outside a block, as is any other CFML tag. By nesting a `<cfscript>` tag inside a `<cfoutput>` or `<cfloop>` tag, you can loop over the script statement.

➜ Conditional operators were covered in Chapter 3, "Conditional Processing." `<cfloop>` was covered in Chapter 4, "Looping," and `<cfoutput>` looping techniques were discussed in Chapter 7, "Using Databases."

`switch/case` Examples

A `switch/case` in ColdFusion script is accomplished a bit differently than in CFML. Again, because you cannot use any tags in a `<cfscript>` block, you can turn to the following example in lieu of `<cfswitch>`:

```
<cfscript>
 x = 1;
 switch(x) {
 case 1: {
 WriteOutput("In Spanish, the number one is 'uno'.");
 WriteOutput("Uno happens to mean 'one' in Italian as well.");
 break;
 }
 case 2: {
 WriteOutput("In Spanish the number two is 'dos'.");
 break;
 }
 default: { WriteOutput("I don't know that number.");}
}
</cfscript>
```

> **TIP**
>
> An important difference between the preceding example and the normal use of a `<cfswitch>` tag involves the `break` statements needed within each `case`. If you do not place the `break` statements in each `case` block, the default always runs in addition to the true `case` expression. You can use a missing `break` tag to your advantage if more than one case tag is to be observed. For instance, within the `case 1` statement, you could set `x = 2`. If `case 1` doesn't have any break statements, the new value of `x` would lead to both `case 1` and `case 2` running.
>
> Because ColdFusion runs from top to bottom, having a `case 2` with `x` set back to `1` would not cause `case 1` to run over again.

Looping

A loop construct usually consists of the same three elements. First, an expression takes place when the loop begins. Second, a condition is tested for each iteration and signals when the loop will conclude. Finally, an expression takes place when the loop ends. You create these three elements in various ways, using the `<cfloop>` tag depending on the type of loop you require. In a `<cfscript>` block, the loop elements also vary depending on type. The different types of loops available to `<cfscript>` are described in the following sections.

`for` Loop

A `for` loop is one of the most common loop constructs. In a `for` loop, as shown in the following code, the loop iterates as long as the condition remains true:

```
<cfscript>
// the first loop element (index=1) runs BEFORE the loop
// the element (index LT 10) is the condition
// the last element (index = index+1) will run AFTER each iteration
for(index=1; index LT 10; index = index + 1)
// note there is no semicolon
//after the loop declaration above
{
 // curly braces encircle the code that will loop
 WriteOutput(index);
}
WriteOutput("loop is done!");
// the above will output after the loop is finished.
</cfscript>
```

The preceding code outputs the numbers `1` through `9`. The condition in the loop (`index LT 10`) must be true while the loop iterates. As soon as `index` is `10`, the loop terminates.

`while` Loop

`while` loops do not carry instance variables, such as `index` seen in the `for` loop example. Rather, they simply break out of the loop when a condition is met, as shown in this example:

```
<cfscript>
a = 1;

while (a LT 10)
{
 WriteOutput(a);
 a = a +1;
}
</cfscript>
```

`do-while` Loop

The difference between a `while` loop and a `do-while` loop is that the condition is tested after each iteration, rather than before:

```
<cfscript>
a=1;
do
{
 WriteOutput(a);
 a = a +1;
}
while (a LT 10);
</cfscript>
```

`for-in` Statement

A `for-in` statement is used exclusively with structures. The expression tested in a `for-in` loop checks to see whether a specific key is inside a structure:

```
<cfscript>
myStruct = structNew();
x=1;
mystruct[x]=0;
// x must be a variable for the 'FOR' statement to work
for (x in myStruct)
{
 WriteOutput("this will run because x is 1 and 1 is a key of
myStruct.");
}
</cfscript>
```

NOTE

In both conditional and loop constructs, the `break` and `continue` statements serve important roles. The `break` statement exits the entire loop or conditional statement. The `continue` statement, to be used in loops only, iterates the loop from the beginning and runs any post-loop expressions, as in this example:

```
for (index=1; index LT 10; index = index + 1)
{
 if(index IS 5) continue;
 WriteOutput(index);
}
// this will count from 1 to 9 but SKIP 5!
```

Invoking Objects

`CreateObject()` is a functional equivalent of the `<cfobject>` tag. As such, it is a way to call ColdFusion Components, CORBA, COM, Java Classes, and Enterprise Java Beans (EJB) from ColdFusion and is well suited for ColdFusion's scripting environment.

➜ The `<cfobject>` tag will be covered in Chapter 33, "Java, COM, and CORBA."

Let's take Java into consideration as our example. An object in Java is created when the `CreateObject()` function is called and the first argument is passed as `"JAVA"` with a second argument as the class name. This loads the class into memory but does not call the constructor methods of the class. A *constructor method* is the section of Java that registers an instance of the object and appropriates memory for all its properties and methods. Because you can have more than one constructor method, you must either call the default constructor or initialize one directly. You call a specific constructor by referencing the object name and calling a special method known as `init`.

The following example calls a Java object called `BankAccount`.

```
<cfscript>
// load the object into memory
BankAcc = CreateObject("java","BankAccount");

// now initialize (call the constructor) of BankAccount
BankAcc.init("John Doe","Checking Account Deposit","$50");

// now call some other method of the object
BankAcc.SendMailer("Welcome New Customer Mailer");

// Set properties of the bank account
if (customerCode is "no risk")
 BankAcc.overdraftProtection = "True";
</cfscript>
```

Based on the preceding code, the Java class is called and invoked from a ColdFusion script block. Parameters and methods of the object can be accessed using the object name returned by the `CreateObject()` function.

Because ColdFusion Components (CFC) may be accessed as objects using the `CreateObject()` function, CFCs are accessible within `<cfscript>` code.

➜ ColdFusion Components are covered in Chapter 31, "ColdFusion Components."

> **TIP**
>
> CFC code can invoke any tag, so it is indeed possible to use tags within `<cfscript>`, albeit indirectly, via CFCs.

Creating Functions

User-defined functions may be created in a `<cfscript>` block using the `function` keyword. Functions created this way may be invoked both in `<cfscript>` blocks and in regular CFML.

➜ User-defined functions are described in detail in Chapter 30, "User-Defined Functions."

Error Handling

`<cfscript>` code can include structured error handling using `try/catch` handling (whose function is similar to that of the ColdFusion `<cftry>` and `<cfcatch>` tags).

➜ `Try/catch` handling is covered in Chapter 26, "Error Handling."

Summary

ColdFusion scripting is an alternative to using CFML and offers a subset of CFML's functionality. `<cfscript>` code cannot execute CFML tags, and so you cannot use ColdFusion scripting to run queries or speak with external processes other than Java, COM, or CORBA objects. Instead, you use the scripting language primarily for variable assignments, looping, and conditional statements.

Sample Questions

1. Which of the following cannot be achieved in a `<cfscript>` block? *(Select all that apply.)*

   A. Variable assignments

   B. Looping

   C. ColdFusion Component invocation

   D. HTTP requests

   E. CORBA object invocation

   F. Custom tag execution

2. Choose the statements that are true.

   A. There are more operators (such as `++` and `&&`) in scripting than in CFML.

   B. Scripting is capable of doing everything CFML does.

   C. `switch` and `case` are available only in `<cfscript>` blocks.

   D. Scripting allows for `do-while` looping.

3. What is the output of the following code?

```
<cfscript>
x=1;
switch(x){
 case 1: {x=2; WriteOutput("World");}
 case 2: {x=1; WriteOutput("Hello");}
}
</cfscript>
```

   A. `Hello World`

   B. `World Hello World`

   C. `World`

   D. `World Hello`

CHAPTER 22

Dynamic Functions

IN THIS CHAPTER

Using Dynamic Functions

ColdFusion features three dynamic functions, which are designed to facilitate the run-time creation and evaluation of expressions (and thus are *dynamic*). Using a dynamic expression to access or assign variables, it is possible to replace multiple lines of `<cfif>` and `<cfset>` statements with a single line of code. The dynamic functions are `IIf()`, `DE()`, and `Evaluate()`. All of these functions will be covered in the next few pages.

➜ Refer to Chapter 2, "Working with Variables and Expressions," and Chapter 3, "Conditional Processing," for the CFML tag equivalents of the `<cfscript>` discussed here.

NOTE

There is one additional dynamic function, named `SetVariable()`, which can be used to set variables where the variable name itself is variable. This function is not covered here, as the need for it has been eliminated by enhancements to the core language and tags.

CAUTION

Dynamic functions take longer to parse and optimize than other functions do. Be aware that your performance will suffer when you use these functions.

IIf()

The name of the `IIf()` function is derived from the programming concept *immediate if*. The function is used as a powerful replacement for a `<cfif>` `<cfelse>` statement. The syntax of the `IIf()` function is as follows:

```
IIf(condition, string expression1, string expression2)
```

All three of these arguments are composed of ColdFusion expressions. The condition is the expression that will be tested. If the condition is `TRUE`, then `string expression1` is returned; if it is `FALSE`, then `string expression2` is returned. Because `IIf()` returns something based on a Boolean operator (`TRUE` or `FALSE`), it is to be used in place of a simple `IF/ELSE` statement. Yet, because an `IIf()` occupies one line of code, it is much more concise than an `IF/ELSE` statement. Take the following examples:

Example 1: IF/ELSE

```
<cfif DayOfWeek(Now()) IS 1>
 <!--- we are closed on Sunday --->
 <cfset bClosed=1>
<cfelse>
 <!--- we are open all other days --->
 <cfset bClosed=0>
</cfif>
```

Example 2: IIf()

```
<cfset IIf(DayOfWeek(Now()) IS 1,"bClosed=1","bClosed=0")>
<!--- same as example 1, but on one line! --->
```

TIP

Although Example 2 is a true expression, there are times when a developer might want to return something printable. To return the string without evaluating it as an expression, single quotes can be used as follows:

```
<cfset IIf(DayOfWeek(Now()) IS 1,"bClosed=1","bClosed=0")>
<cfoutput>
 #IIf(bClosed,"'We are closed!'","'We are open!'")#
</cfoutput>
<!--- The expressions will be returned without being evaluated --->
```

Note that the `DE()` function could also be used instead of the single-quote method. The `DE()` function will be explained in the next subsection.

It is important to understand that `IIf()` returns the result of the expression it has evaluated. Example 2's first use of `IIf()` might not appear to return anything at all, but it does. Setting a variable in ColdFusion returns the value of the variable itself. Therefore, the code in example 2 will return the number `1` if it is Sunday, and the number `0` if it is not.

DE()

The `DE()` function (which stands for *delay evaluation*) is mostly used within other dynamic functions such as `IIf()`. As you saw in the last subsection, there are times when control is needed over expression evaluation. If a certain function takes an expression as an argument, it will return the result of the expression after ColdFusion has processed it. If, however, the developer intends to return the expression itself, without evaluation, the `DE()` function will prevent ColdFusion from conducting this evaluation. This is useful for a handful of reasons, the most obvious being the printing of a certain string within an `IIf()`:

```
<cfset IIf(DayOfWeek(Now()) IS 1,"bClosed=1","bClosed=0")>
<cfoutput>
 #IIf(bClosed,DE("We are closed!"),DE("We are open!"))#
</cfoutput>
```

This example shows that `DE()` can be used just as the single quotes were used in the previous subsection: to escape evaluation and return the string. But the `DE()` function does more than return literals. Imagine if an expression was contained within a variable. A hypothetical example of this might be a text box in which a user could type an expression, such as 2+2. The developer could check to make sure that the expression did not contain a divide-by-zero command, and then return a result. To better understand this example, look at the following code:

```
<cfset FORM.expression="2/0">
<!--- pretend that the user typed in the above and submitted the form-
--->
<cfoutput>
#IIf(FORM.expression CONTAINS "/0",
     DE(FORM.expression),
     FORM.expression)#
</cfoutput>
```

The above code will print `"2/0"` as output. But if `FORM.expression` does not contain a command to divide by zero (division by zero is illegal), the output would be the result of the expression. For instance, `2+2` would result in `4`.

Evaluate()

The `Evaluate()` function is used to return the result of an expression. Here is a simple example of the `Evaluate()` function:

```
<cfset FORM.expression="2+2">
<cfset result=Evaluate(FORM.expression)>
<cfoutput>
 #FORM.expression# equals #result#
</cfoutput>
<!--- this will print "2+2 equals 4" --->
```

Multiple expressions can be passed to the `Evaluate()` function as arguments. Remember that when ColdFusion processes multiple expressions, it always returns the rightmost one.

TIP

An interesting way of using the `Evaluate()` function is to piece together expressions through concatenation. For example, you could allow users to create ColdFusion variables on their own and decide if they were to be structures or arrays. This could be done by piecing together the correct function names and keys/indexes based on what the user selected in a form. Look at the following example:

```
<cfparam name="FORM.createArray" default="1">
<cfparam name="FORM.createStructure" default="0">
<cfparam name="FORM.variableName" default="myVar">
<cfset function1="ArrayNew">
<cfset function2="StructNew">
<!--- did the user want to create an array? --->
<cfif FORM.CreateArray IS 1>
 <cfset Evaluate("FORM.variableName = " & function1 & "(1)")>
<cfelseif FORM.CreateStructure IS 1>
 <cfset Evaluate("FORM.variableName = " & function2 & "()")>
</cfif>
```

This logic actually creates a new array or structure by piecing together the correct combination of characters. If the user wants to create an array, you need to do an `ArrayNew(1)`, and if you need to create a structure, you need to issue a `StructNew()`. These are accomplished by using string expressions and concatenation within the `evaluate` argument.

`Evaluate()` is not needed for simple expressions. For example, to display the sum of two variables, the calculation could be performed directly inline like this:

```
<cfoutput>#var1+var2#</cfoutput>
```

Summary

Using dynamic functions (`IIf()`, `DE()`, and `Evaluate()`) makes it possible to write powerful and highly reusable code in small, easy-to-manage code blocks.

Sample Questions

1. Choose all the statements that are true.

   A. The `DE()` function is always used to display output.

   B. The `DE()` function stops ColdFusion from processing expressions.

   C. `DE()` and `IIf()` can be used together.

   D. The letters in `DE()` stand for *do evaluation*.

2. What will be the output of the following code?

   ```
   <cfoutput>#IIf(1 is 1,"Evaluate(1,2,3)","'Hello'")#</cfoutput>
   ```

   A. `1`

   B. `2`

   C. `3`

   D. `Hello`

3. What does the following code do?

   ```
   <cfset x="Array">
   <cfset Evaluate("p = " & x & "New(1)")>
   ```

   A. Creates an array named `x`.

   B. Creates an array named `p`.

   C. The code does not work.

   D. None of the above.

4. In the code below, what does z equal?

   ```
   <cfset x="y">
   <cfset y="x">
   <cfset z = IIf(x is y,DE(x),x)>
   ```

   A. `x`

   B. `y`

   C. `null`

   D. None of the above

CHAPTER 23

Stored Procedures

IN THIS CHAPTER

Using Stored Procedures

Stored procedures are sequences of precompiled SQL statements stored in a database. These SQL statements are later referenced by name and executed at run time. Because stored procedures are precompiled, they run considerably faster than SQL, which is sent from a client application. They are sent via `<cfquery>`.

In addition to being faster, stored procedures are also more secure than normal SQL statements. Stored procedures can execute SQL on a table that a user does not have access to, and a database administrator can create procedures that hide certain columns of data or do calculations before data is returned.

Stored procedures can be built to accept and return parameters to a ColdFusion template. This means that a query can be dynamic. A stored procedure can also return record sets to ColdFusion in the form of an array or a query.

ColdFusion provides two distinct interfaces for stored procedures, by way of the `<cfstoredproc>` and `<cfquery>` tags.

➜ The `<cfquery>` tag was introduced in Chapter 7, "Using Databases."

NOTE

Most of the major database vendors offer stored procedure support, with different advantages and disadvantages. Stored procedure syntax is different in each type of database; many similarities exist between Microsoft SQL Server and Sybase because those databases were initially the same product. The following stored procedure code, written in Transact-SQL, will run in either Sybase or Microsoft SQL Server:

```
Create Procedure spCheckInventory @status varchar(50)
As
declare @ret int
SELECT @ret = ProductRequestedID,productName
FROM Inventory
WHERE Status = @status
return (isNull(@ret,0))
```

The preceding statement needs to be executed only once. From that point on, the stored procedure will be called through the following SQL statement:

```
EXECUTE spCheckInventory 'in stock'
```

<cfquery> **Versus** <cfstoredproc>

To execute a stored procedure, you can use either the `<cfquery>` or `<cfstoredproc>` tag. Each has its own advantages and disadvantages.

`<cfquery>` is the simpler of the two, while `<cfstoredproc>` is more powerful and provides access to otherwise inaccessible features. For example, stored procedures can return record sets to the ColdFusion template more efficiently through the `<cfstoredproc>` tag. This tag also provides support for multiple record sets returned from a stored procedure, meaning that you can create more than one record set from the same procedure. Finally, some variables, such as the status code that is created when the tag is called, are not available through a `<cfquery>`.

Using <cfquery>

The SQL for running a stored procedure operates by referencing the stored procedure's name after the `EXEC` statement, followed by parameters. The following example shows how ColdFusion would execute a stored procedure through the use of the `<cfquery>` tag:

```
<cfquery name="CheckInventory" datasource="dsn">
 EXEC spCheckInventory
 @Status = 'in stock'
</cfquery>
<!--- see what the status is and tell the user --->
<cfif CheckInventory.ret>
 That item is in inventory!
<cfelse>
 Sorry, out of stock!
</cfif>
```

This method of calling stored procedures is perfectly valid and usable, yet the `<cfstoredproc>` tag has a few advantages, which will be discussed in the next section.

> **NOTE**
> With some DBMSs, the use of the keyword `EXEC` in the above code example is optional. And yet other DBMSs do not allow `EXEC` based execution at all.

Using <cfstoredproc>

`<cfstoredproc>` can be used to execute existing stored procedures. The tag cannot, however, be used to create stored procedures—something `<cfquery>` can do.

`<cfstoredproc>` has two child tags that are used to pass parameters into the stored procedure and to receive data back. Parameters are sent to the stored procedure by the `<cfprocparam>` tag and can be received by either `<cfprocparam>` or `<cfprocresult>`. The most efficient way to receive record sets from a stored procedure is to use the `<cfprocresult>` tag because it returns data as a record set.

<cfprocparam>

Most stored procedures depend on parameters that are sent from the client application. For each parameter, a `<cfprocparam>` tag is used. You must know each parameter's data type as it is declared in the stored procedure. This data type is passed as the required attribute `cfsqltype` of the `<cfprocparam>` tag. Valid types are:

- `CF_SQL_BIGINT`
- `CF_SQL_BIT`
- `CF_SQL_BLOB`
- `CF_SQL_CHAR`
- `CF_SQL_CLOB`
- `CF_SQL_DATE`
- `CF_SQL_DECIMAL`
- `CF_SQL_DOUBLE`
- `CF_SQL_FLOAT`
- `CF_SQL_IDSTAMP`
- `CF_SQL_INTEGER`

- CF_SQL_LONGVARCHAR
- CF_SQL_MONEY
- CF_SQL_MONEY4
- CF_SQL_NUMERIC
- CF_SQL_REAL
- CF_SQL_REFCURSOR
- CF_SQL_SMALLINT
- CF_SQL_TIME
- CF_SQL_TIMESTAMP
- CF_SQL_TINYINT
- CF_SQL_VARCHAR

Be careful to correctly match the type to the actual data type defined in the stored procedure itself.

Another required attribute of `<cfprocparam>` is the `type` attribute. It has three different values, as shown in Table 23.1, which affect other attributes in various ways.

Table 23.1 Options for the `type` Attribute of `<cfprocparam>`

VALUE	DESCRIPTION
`in`	The parameter is expected by the stored procedure, and you are passing the parameter.
`out`	A result is expected from the stored procedure, and the `<cfprocparam>` tag will be used to create a variable of a specific name to accept this returned data.
`inout`	The names of the parameters sent and received are exactly the same. If they were not, you would have used a `<cfprocparam>` for the `IN` parameter and a second `<cfprocparam>` for the `out` parameter.

The `<cfprocparam>` tag's `VALUE` attribute is used only when sending parameters into the stored procedure using `type="in"`. This process is pretty intuitive. Alternatively, the `variable` attribute works only when it's getting parameters out of a stored procedure using `out`, and represents the ColdFusion variable name holding the returned data. Finally, the `dbvarname` attribute passes the correct name of the stored procedure's variable, such as `@RET` in the stored procedure example at the beginning of this chapter.

TIP

At first glance, the `<cfprocparam>` tag appears to be the best way to get data in and out of a stored procedure. In reality, it is rarely used to get data out of a stored procedure. The tag was once the only solution available for Oracle developers, since the `<cfprocresult>` tag was not available. But because `<cfprocresult>` now works with Oracle, using it to attack most requirements is more efficient. This tag is covered in the next section.

NOTE

When more than one record sets is sent back from a `<cfprocresult>` tag, it is exposed as an array.

<cfprocresult>

The `<cfprocresult>` tag is the final piece of the stored procedure puzzle. When a stored procedure is executed, a record set may be returned to ColdFusion. The only required attribute of the tag is `name`, which creates the record set variable in ColdFusion. The following example shows the tag in action:

```
<cfstoredproc procedure="CheckInventory"
              datasource="dsn">
<!--- send the parameter --->
<cfprocparam type="IN"
             cfsqltype="CF_SQL_CHAR"
             value="in stock"
             dbvarname="@param1">
  <!--- get the result back --->
  <cfprocresult name="qItemsInStock">
  <!--- Note that cfstoredproc has an END tag! --->
</cfstoredproc>
<!--- here is what is in inventory --->
<cfoutput query="qItemsInStock">
 #productName#<br>
</cfoutput>
```

Multiple Record Sets

A very useful feature of stored procedures is their capability to return multiple record sets to the client. ColdFusion supports this capability by giving different numbers to the `<cfprocresult>` tag to identify each given record set.

For this purpose, the `resultset` attribute is used. Each result set must be addressed specifically by its number, or it will not be exposed. If, for example, a stored procedure returns ten record sets and the `resultset` attribute is not specified, only the first record set is returned. To take the example further, if the `resultset` attribute is set to `"10"`, only the last record set is returned. Now consider the following example:

```
<!--- checkInventory returns multiple record sets --->
<cfstoredproc procedure="CheckInventory"
              datasource="mySqlServer">
  <!--- send the parameter --->
  <cfprocparam type="IN"
               cfsqltype="CF_SQL_CHAR"
               value="in stock"
               dbvarname="@param1">
  <!--- get the FIRST result back --->
  <cfprocresult name="MoreThan100InStock">
  <!--- get the SECOND result back --->
  <cfprocresult name="LessThan100InStock"
                resultset="2">
</cfstoredproc>
<!--- here is what is in inventory --->
<cfoutput query="MoreThan100InStock">
 #productName#<br>
</cfoutput>
<cfoutput query="LessThan100InStock">
 #productName#<br>
</cfoutput>
```

> **NOTE**
>
> Another optional attribute of the `<cfprocresult>` tag is `maxrows`. This attribute limits the number of rows that come back from the stored procedure, functioning in exactly the same way as the identically named `<cfquery>` attribute does.

Summary

Stored procedures are precompiled SQL statements that are stored in a database and executed at run time. Each database has its own stored procedure syntax that can be sent from ColdFusion using a `<cfquery>`. A more powerful interface for stored procedures is the `<cfstoredproc>` tag. This tag has an end tag and takes two possible nested tags: `<cfprocparam>` and `<cfprocresult>`. `<cfprocparam>` can send and receive parameters, whereas `<cfprocresult>` was built to expose result sets as ColdFusion record sets.

Sample Questions

1. Why are stored procedures better than views or queries? *(Choose all that apply)*

   A. They execute faster.

   B. They are more secure.

   C. They are easier to create.

   D. They are more powerful.

   E. They work with all databases.

2. When should the `type` attribute of the `<cfprocparam>` tag be set to `inout`?

   A. A parameter needs to be sent back from a stored procedure only.

   B. A parameter is sent to a stored procedure and a different parameter is returned.

   C. A parameter of the same name is sent and received from the stored procedure.

   D. A stored procedure optionally accepts parameters.

3. `<cfprocresult>` returns what type of data?

   A. Structure of arrays

   B. Queries

   C. Arrays

   D. Simple data

CHAPTER 24 Transactions

IN THIS CHAPTER

Using Transactions

Transactions are a mechanism by which to group sets of SQL statements for execution. The primary reasons to group statements are:

- To ensure that the entire set of statements runs (or none at all)
- To prevent other statements from being executed at inopportune times

Relational databases are used by millions of people every day. Many of these people are actually using the same databases simultaneously. Transactions can prevent multiple users from editing the same data at the same time. They also allow a series of queries to succeed in bulk or not at all. If transactions were not possible, databases would be useless in multi-user environments.

As an example, say that a college student runs out of money and asks his mother for a wire transfer. His mother goes to the bank, fills out the transfer form, and hands it to the teller. The teller withdraws $100 from the woman's account, and in the same transaction deposits the money into her son's account at his local bank a few hundred miles away. Because these two actions take place within a single database transaction, the withdrawal will be canceled if the deposit fails. Therefore, even though the withdrawal is immediate, it is not "committed" to the database until the deposit succeeds a few moments later at the remote bank.

This idea of binding all actions in one transaction means that no money would be withdrawn from the woman's account unless her son's bank successfully took the deposit. In addition, a transaction will lock the woman's bank account until it is finished. If she went to another teller, for instance, she would be prevented from withdrawing more money than her eventual balance would reflect.

Two concepts are critical to understanding transactions and can be translated into features offered by the major database vendors. These concepts are *locking* and *isolation*.

Locking

Locking is a simple idea that is exposed through complex algorithms in each database engine. Fortunately, for our purposes as ColdFusion developers, we need concern ourselves only with the simple ideas of *exclusive* and *shared* locking.

In the wire transfer example, the bank's database system might give exclusive privileges to the transaction so that no other reads could take place. If the woman conducting the wire transfer went to another teller to ask for her current balance, the second teller would inform her that the balance could not be calculated because a pending transaction was in progress. This means that the wire transfer placed an exclusive lock on the information being changed. If, on the other hand, a shared lock had been placed on the account, the teller would be able to provide a balance. A shared lock would allow the woman to see the balance but make no updates to it.

> **NOTE**
>
> Although an explanation of shared and exclusive locks is important, it does not follow that ColdFusion can declare locks on the database. Usually, locking is handled by the database on its own. In addition, databases can escalate a lock from record to table to database, depending on how much data is being modified. ColdFusion has no bearing on these affairs. Yet ColdFusion does have the capability to change isolation levels, which affects the lock type. Isolation levels are covered next.

Isolation

Isolation levels are the only means by which ColdFusion can recommend lock types to the relational database. Isolation levels were created to increase performance by giving the database a plan for locking records before the transaction executes.

Four isolation levels are supported by relational databases, and thus all are supported by ColdFusion's transaction tags. These levels are listed below.

> **NOTE**
>
> The isolation levels described here affect performance. They are listed from worst performance (`serializable`) to best (`read_uncommitted`).

➜ Other performance considerations related to ColdFusion's use of databases are explored in Chapter 48, "Improving Performance."

serializable

`serializable` is the highest isolation level provided by a database and is also the default. `serializable` isolation is equivalent to an exclusive lock. No data can be read by other transactions until the transaction that owns the lock is finished. This makes `serializable` the most reliable isolation level.

repeatable_read

`repeatable_read` is the second-highest isolation level. A repeatable read is similar to the `serializable` level, except that other SQL statements can insert data during the transaction. This can change the results of a transaction if the transaction repeats a query that yields the newly inserted data. If you know ahead of time that inserted data will not affect the transaction, using `repeatable_read` is preferred to using a `serializable` isolation level for performance reasons.

read_committed

The third-highest level of isolation, `read_committed`, means that locks will be shared for both inserts and updates across transactions. So a transaction could read some data once and, before finishing, read for a second time the data that had changed since the original read. Note that the other transactions (the ones updating) must be finished for the read to be different. A successfully finished transaction is said to have been *committed*.

read_uncommitted

The final level of isolation, providing the best performance of the four, is `read_uncommitted`. This isolation level is the most dangerous to use, because *dirty reads* are very likely. A dirty read occurs when a certain transaction reads data that has not been committed. If this isolation level was employed in the wire transfer example, the woman could be the victim of some erroneous accounting. Say that the bank were to run its interest rate calculations on her account after her withdrawal of $100. Now imagine if her son's bank went offline and was not able to accept the deposit. Because the entire transaction would fail, her interest rate would be calculated incorrectly. In the same way, a `read_uncommitted` isolation level allows inserts and updates to be read regardless of whether a transaction has finished.

<cftransaction>

Transactions and isolation levels are implemented using the `<cftransaction>` tag. This tag has a matching end tag and encloses all ColdFusion queries and logic pertinent to a given transaction. If no isolation levels are sent, the default is `serializable`.

The following example demonstrates the wire transfer example. Notice that this example uses custom tag <cfx_sendwire> to send information to the son's bank. This tag does not really exist but is used to demonstrate the concept. This nonexistent tag returns the variable wireResult equal to 1 or 0 based on successful wire transfers:

```
<cftransaction>
  <!--- remove $100 from the woman's account --->
  <cfquery datasource="AccountDB">
  UPDATE Account
  SET Balance = Balance - 100
  WHERE AccountID = 4334044033
  </cfquery>

  <!--- enter the woman's name in the wire transfer log --->
  <cfquery datasource="TransferLog">
  INSERT INTO transferLog
  (accountID,Time,BankID,wiredAmount,recipientAccountID)
  VALUES (4334044033,getDate(),3344212,100,4403343402)
  </cfquery>

  <!---
  call C++ wire transfer library to send data to other bank
  --->
  <cfx_sendwire bankid="3344212"
                amount="100"
                accountid ="4403343402">
  <cfif wireResult is 0>
    <cfabort>
  </cfif>
  <!---
  if aborted transaction won't finish--updates/inserts cancel
  --->
</cftransaction>
```

<cftransaction> has no required attributes. The isolation attribute can be set to read_uncommitted, read_committed, repeatable_read, and serializable. The default isolation is serializable.

Controlling Commits

So far, we reviewed an example in which <cftransaction> took no attributes. We briefly explained isolation levels. The only other attribute for <cftransaction> is action, which controls what is and is not committed to a database.

commit

When a transaction is finished, and the ColdFusion server finds the closing tag of <cftransaction>, all updates made to the database are subsequently committed. This means that the status of the updates is changed from questionable to certain, and the locks are released.

If, however, a commit within a given transaction makes sense before the transaction is complete, a nested `<cftransaction>` tag can be used with an `action` of `commit`. Turning back to the wire transfer example, say that the woman decided to give wire transfers to all her children instead of just one. In this new situation, the bank considers this a single transaction and thus locks any databases once. But each successful deposit can force a `COMMIT` to the database and allow other transactions to read more accurate balance information. The new example looks like this:

```
<cftransaction>
  <!--- here is a list of all her children's bank IDs ---->
  <cfset bankIDList="234234234,2345234,6456456456,34534345">
  <!--- here is a list of all her children's account numbers --->
  <cfset AccountIDList="34234234,234562345,6123563,635789345">

  <!--- four accounts... loop four times --->
  <cfloop from=1 TO=4 index="i">
    <!--- remove $100 from the woman's account --->
    <cfquery datasource="AccountDB">
    UPDATE Account
    SET Balance = Balance - 100
    WHERE AccountID = 4334044033
    </cfquery>

    <!--- call the wire transfer tag (sends data to bank #2) --->
    <cfx_sendwire bnkid="#listGetAt(bankIDList,i)#"
                  amount="100"
                  accountid ="#listGetAt(AccountIDList,i)#">
    <cfif wireResult is 0>
      <cfabort>
    </cfif>
    <cftransaction action="COMMIT"/>
     <!--- commit each deposit when it completes --->
  </cfloop>

  <!--- enter the woman's name in the wire transfer log --->
  <cfquery datasource="TransferLog">
  INSERT INTO transferLog
    (accountID,Time,BankIDList,wiredAmount,recipientAccountIDList)
  VALUES (4334044033,getDate(),'#bankIDList#',100,'#accountIDList#')
  </cfquery>

</cftransaction>
```

NOTE

The statement `<cftransaction action="commit"/>` may look strange because of the forward slash at the end. This slash is XML syntax and is used here in lieu of an end tag. Because this specific example of `<cftransaction>` doesn't have an end tag, you must signify the end tag with the forward slash or as `<cftransaction action="commit"><cftransaction/>` (with nothing between the two tags). This is both legal and supported.

rollback

Another `action` type in addition to `commit` is `rollback`. Rolling back is a way of telling the transaction to purposely fail. In database vernacular, these two are the only options for any transaction. Either a transaction commits the new changes, or it rolls back to the original state of the database.

For our example, using `rollback` is a better solution than using `<cfabort>`. If you look at the sample code so far, it will abort in the event of a deposit failure at one of the children's banks. This is not the best scenario because each deposit is contingent on the success of the previous one. Instead of using `<cfabort>`, you can use `<cftransaction action="rollback"/>` (paying attention to the XML syntax as explained in the preceding Note):

```
<cftransaction>
  <!--- here is a list of all her children's bank IDs ---->
  <cfset bankIDList="234234234,2345234,6456456456,34534345">
  <!--- here is a list of all her children's account numbers --->
  <cfset AccountIDList="34234234,234562345,6123563,635789345">

  <!--- four accounts... loop four times --->
  <cfloop from=1 TO=4 index="i">
    <!--- remove $100 from the woman's account --->
    <cfquery datasource="AccountDB">
    UPDATE Account
    SET Balance = Balance - 100
    WHERE AccountID = 4334044033
    </cfquery>

    <!--- call the wire transfer tag (sends data to bank #2) --->
    <cfx_sendwire bnkid="#listGetAt(bankIDList,i)#"
                  amount="100"
                  accountid ="#listGetAt(AccountIDList,i)#">
    <cfif wireResult is 0>
      <cftransaction action="rollback"/>
    </cfif>
    <!--- commit each deposit when it completes --->
    <cftransaction action="commit"/>
  </cfloop>

  <!--- enter the woman's name in the wire transfer log --->
  <cfquery datasource="TransferLog">
  INSERT INTO TransferLog
     (accountID,Time,BankIDList,wiredAmount,recipientAccountIDList)
  VALUES (4334044033,getDate(),'#bankIDList#',100,'#accountIDList#')
  </cfquery>

</cftransaction>
```

> **NOTE**
>
> The third and last option for the `action` attribute is `begin`. It indicates that a transaction is starting and is the default value.

> **NOTE**
>
> Some operations may require transactions that span requests. Unfortunately, the nature of the Web and the way in which ColdFusion uses it makes this impossible. All transactions must start and end on the same page.

> **TIP**
>
> A popular technique of database administrators is to build transactions into stored procedures instead of using the `<cftransaction>` tag. As was discussed in Chapter 23, stored procedures are precompiled and thus run faster than passing SQL from ColdFusion. In addition, multiple transactions can be placed within a single stored procedure, allowing transactions to complete regardless of the ColdFusion server's availability. Finally, some databases, such as Microsoft's SQL Server, offer robust features wherein a transaction can spawn remote procedures on other databases.

→ Calling stored procedures via CFML was covered in Chapter 23, "Stored Procedures."

Summary

Transactions are an integral part of any relational database. You control transactions through a ColdFusion application by using the `<cftransaction>` tag. This tag has no required attributes but controls isolation levels through the `isolation` attribute, and can conditionally commit or roll back parts of a transaction through the `action` attribute. Transactions cannot be spanned across pages.

Sample Questions

1. Which of the following statements are true?

   A. The `<cftransaction>` tag can control isolation levels.

   B. Isolation levels affect performance.

   C. Isolation levels affect locking.

   D. ColdFusion enforces isolation when a database does not.

2. What is the primary purpose of `<cftransaction>`?

   A. To commit all inserts to the database

   B. To make sure dirty reads do not take place

   C. To support `commit` and `rollback` features of a relational database system

   D. To supplement the `<cflock>` tag in locking database records

3. What is wrong with the following code?

```
<cftransaction>
 <cfquery datasource....> ... </cfquery>
 <cftransaction action="commit">
</cftransaction>
```

   A. Commits must be performed in a `<cfif>` block.

   B. Inner `<cftransaction>` is not terminated.

   C. Transaction tags can't be nested.

   D. Queries must be performed after commits are executed.

4. Which isolation level is the least efficient?

   A. `serializable`

   B. `repeatable_read`

   C. `read_uncommitted`

   D. `read_committed`

CHAPTER 25 Debugging

IN THIS CHAPTER

ColdFusion Debugging

Development tools such as ColdFusion offer a number of helpful utilities that help to solve and avert problems. These problems, or *bugs*, are systematically isolated in a process known as *debugging*. Debugging tools look into an application's circuitry. If a template fails or takes an inordinate amount of time to execute, the developer needs to look under the hood and see what is misfiring.

Error messages alone do not yield enough information to solve a problem. Error messages are normally used as a starting point in a debugging strategy.

> **TIP**
>
> As a rule, you should solve problems as soon as they occur. No matter how mundane an issue might seem, the ramifications and complexities grow exponentially if a problem is not fixed immediately after it is discovered.

Debugging utilities provide information about performance and inconsistent behavior, but they are most critical in isolating exceptions. *Exceptions* are events that stop ColdFusion from processing any template. Common exceptions include dividing by zero and placing an equal sign (=) in a `<cfif>` clause instead of an `IS` or `EQ`.

➜ Exceptions that usually cause errors can be handled in alternative ways. This is known as exception handling and is covered in Chapter 26, "Error Handling."

Debugging must be enabled server-wide before any debugging information is exposed. Debugging is enabled and disabled via an option in ColdFusion Administrator.

Accessing Debugging Information

ColdFusion's debugging information can be accessed in three ways:

- Debugging output can be generated along with Web pages and can be appended to the bottom of the generated page (called *classic* format) or displayed in a separate window, which may be docked if needed. You can switch between classic and dockable views in ColdFusion Administrator's Debugging Settings screen.
- Debugging information can also be displayed within the Macromedia Dreamweaver development environment's Results window.
- Debugging information is also available programmatically at run time by way of exposed application services.

Exposed Information

Every time a ColdFusion template runs, information is made available to the developer. You can expose most of this information by toggling certain debug settings in ColdFusion Administrator. The debug settings provide a list of categories, each representing a type of debugging that can be performed. The variations in the way debugging information is exposed depend on the category. The following sections cover each category of information and how it is exposed.

Report Execution Times

An important part of debugging is locating poorly performing code. This option reports the individual execution time for all modules, includes, and components so as to isolate problem spots. In addition, you may specify an *ideal* response time; any items that exceed that time will be flagged as such.

General Debug Information

Information about a request, including specifics about the browser and server, can be extremely useful when debugging.

Database Activity

Debugging database-related problems requires knowing what SQL statements were submitted (after any dynamic processing) and what was returned. This option displays the record count, SQL, and execution time for each database query.

> **TIP**
>
> ColdFusion Administrator does not need to be used in order to show query information on a page. ColdFusion supports an alternative method that involves placing the word `debug` inside a `<cfquery>` tag, as follows:
>
> ```
> <cfquery name="query" datasource="dsn" debug>
> ```
>
> By placing this toggle inside the `<cfquery>` tag, debug information is automatically printed to the page, regardless of the debug settings in Administrator.

Exception Information

Enable this option to display all gathered exception information (details about what occurred) in the debug output.

Tracing Information

Developers can use the `<cftrace>` tag to embed custom debug output within their code. The following snippet displays the contents of the `SESSION.loggedin` variable along with descriptive text:

```
<cftrace var="SESSION.loggedin"
        text="Login process complete">
```

Turn on this option to display developer-provided debug output.

Timer Information

Enable this option to turn on support for the `<cftimer>` tag which can be embedded in pages to perform code performance analysis.

Flash Form Compile Errors and Messages

When developing applications using Flash Forms, enable this option to see Flash compiler messages.

➜ Flash Forms are covered in detail in Chapter 16, "Flash Forms."

Variables

When you turn on the Variables debug option, a list of variables is generated along with the debug output. Up to nine variable types may be displayed, each of which may be enabled or disabled explicitly:

- `APPLICATION`
- `CGI`

- `CLIENT`
- `COOKIE`
- `FORM`
- `REQUEST`
- `SERVER`
- `SESSION`
- `URL`

Other variables—for example, local variables—are not displayed automatically. These may be output manually if need be, using the `<cftrace>`, `<cfdump>`, or manual debugging techniques described below.

Enable Robust Exception Information

As a rule, your users should never see error messages. ColdFusion provides error-handling features to allow the developer to control error handling and error display.

However, error screens sometimes may be generated; when this occurs, the developer can determine what information should be shared. Enable this option to include the following:

- Actual template path
- Template URL
- Code line number and code snippet
- SQL statements
- Data source names
- Java stack trace

> **TIP**
>
> This option generally should not be enabled on production sites, as the information exposed could be of interest to hackers.

Enable Performance Monitoring and Enable `cfstat`

Performance monitoring is a handy tool for tracking the efficiency of a ColdFusion application under load. It can be helpful when you're deciding whether additional hardware should be used, or whether you need to replace code or components.

A utility named `cfstat` is provided with ColdFusion as an interface for performance data. In addition, users of Windows NT, 2000, and XP can use the Windows Performance Monitor to access this information. To enable performance monitoring, check the Enable Performance Monitoring option; to enable `cfstat`, check the Enable `cfstat` option.

Performance can be monitored in real time through the use of the ColdFusion function `GetMetricData()`. The function takes one argument, which is the name of the performance-monitoring system that the operating system uses. In Windows, the argument is `PERF_MONITOR`; in Unix, it's `cfstat`. The function returns a structure with a number of keys. The keys of this structure match the data exposed through the visual and textual performance-monitoring features:

```
<cfset stDebug=GetMetricData("PERF_MONITOR")>
<cfloop collection="#stDebug#" ITEM="i">
 <cfoutput>The debug info for #i# is #stDebug[i]#</cfoutput><br>
</cfloop>
<!--- the above will output debug info on a Windows system --->
```

The data exposed through performance monitoring, including the key names returned through `GetMetricData()`, is shown in Table 25.1.

Table 25.1 Data Returned Through ColdFusion Performance Monitoring

KEY	DESCRIPTION
avgDBTime	Average database transaction time
avgQueueTime	Average queue time
avgReqTime	Average request time
bytesIn	Incoming bytes per second
bytesOut	Outgoing bytes per second
dbHits	Database hits per second
InstanceName	Instance name of the ColdFusion service
pageHits	Page hits per second
reqQueued	Number of queued requests
reqRunning	Number of running requests
reqTimedOut	Number of timed requests

Access to Debug Information

Debugging information should not be made available to all users. ColdFusion allows you to restrict access to debug information by the IP address that the requests are coming from. The allowed IP addresses are specified in the Debugging IP Settings screen in ColdFusion Administrator.

If no IP addresses are listed, debugging information will be published to all clients. This is generally not what you'd want, so make sure that at least the `localhost` address (`127.0.0.1`) is always listed.

Manual Debugging

Manual debugging is the process of exposing information by way of ColdFusion Markup Language (CFML) tags in order to trace errors or strange behavior. The debugging instructions or output are embedded right inside your code.

The first thing to do before placing these tags in a ColdFusion template is to critically read the error messages returned in a browser. They tell you where the problem occurred by line number and by template. Sometimes, syntax errors can cause ColdFusion to return incorrect line numbers, but usually the problem is somewhere near the line number specified.

The following represents a manual debug page:

```
<cfset X="1,2,3,4,5,a,7">
<cfloop list="#X#" index="i">
 <!--- manually debug for i --->
 <cfif not isNumeric(i)>
 <cfoutput>i equals: #i# at loop num:#ListFind(X,i)#</cfoutput>
 <cfabort>
 </cfif>
 <cfset Y=i+3>
 <!--- I keep getting an error above that 'i' is not numeric --->
</cfloop>
```

This code shows how you could use a combination of `<cfoutput>`, functions, and `<cfabort>` to figure out why a problem was occurring.

Using `GetTickCount()`

A useful debugging technique is to use the `GetTickCount()` function to ascertain how long it is taking a template or code block to execute. `GetTickCount()` must be called twice, with the first result subtracted from the second. This way, you can calculate the total number of milliseconds that has elapsed:

```
<cfset start=GetTickCount()>
<cfloop from="1"
        to="30000"
        index="i">
  <!--- I wonder how long this will take? --->
</cfloop>
<cfset end=GetTickCount()>
<cfoutput>
<!--- here is how long this took: --->
Total milliseconds elapsed: #end-start#
</cfoutput>
```

Some language elements important to debugging are:

- `<cfabort>`, used to stop processing
- `<cfdump>`, used to dump the contents of variables
- `IsDebugMode()`, which allows for code to be executed only when debugging
- All of the `Is` functions used in decision checks

Using `<cftimer>`

`<cftimer>` cam also be used to perform code timing execution tests. To use `<cftimer>`, wrap code to be tested within `<cftimer>` tags, and name the timer block. ColdFusion will display the execution time in several formats:

- In the debug output
- In HTML comments at the code location
- In the page output at the code location
- Within outlines surrounding the code

Here is an example:

```
<cftimer label="myloop">
<cfloop from="1"
        to="30000"
        index="i">
  <!--- I wonder how long this will take? --->
</cfloop>
</cftimer>
```

> **NOTE**
> To display `<cftimer>` output you must enable support for the tag in the ColdFusion Administrator.

Using Log Files

Log files let a developer audit events. If an exception occurs, it is written to the ColdFusion log file when the error is returned to the user. Along with the error itself, other information is stored in the log file, such as the user's browser type and originating IP address.

In addition to ColdFusion error logs, other types of log files are available to the developer. The log files are named and described in Table 25.2.

Table 25.2 ColdFusion Log Files

LOG FILE NAME	DESCRIPTION
`application.log`	Logs problems reported to the user, including all run-time errors
`car.log`	Logs problems with site archive and restore operations
`customtag.log`	Logs problems with custom tags
`exceptions.log`	Logs stack traces occurring in the server
`executive.lo`	Logs problems with the ColdFusion service, including unexpected service restarts
`mail.log`	Logs problems with an SMTP mail server
`mailsent.log`	Logs messages sent by ColdFusion
`scheduler.log`	Logs scheduled events and problems with them
`server.log`	Logs slow-running pages; similar to `webserver.log` but with less intelligible diagnostic information than is intended for the Macromedia technical support team

Managing Log Files

You can manage log files from the Log Files screen in ColdFusion Administrator. Active logs are listed in the Available Log Files table and can be managed directly through the Web-based interface controls in the following ways:

- Log entries can be searched and viewed in report, concise, or raw formats, in descending order. The Filter tool provides options to restrict the report by date range, entry type, and keywords.
- The entire log can be downloaded for offline processing.
- Logs can be archived or stored. Archived logs are simply renamed and saved to the log directory as `logname.nnn`, where `nnn` starts at `001`.
- Active logs can be deleted from the server.

The Logging Settings screen is used to specify the log file directory, set the maximum log file size, and configure other logging options.

<cflog>

ColdFusion lets developers generate their own log information. `<cflog>` can be used to record entries in the existing set of ColdFusion logs or in completely new logs that have the same format as the existing ones.

For example, a syndication service might be scheduled to retrieve information from a remote site and store it within the local application. `scheduler.log` records the success or failure of the ColdFusion template's execution, but it doesn't record any detail about what actually occurred during syndication. If there were a run-time error, you would have to crawl through `application.log` looking for an answer. `<cflog>` could be used to create a special `syndication.log` file to record information about the agent's activity.

```
<!--- retrieve wddx news data from moreover --->
<cftry>
  <cfhttp url="http://p.moreover.com/
                 cgilocal/page?c=Australia%20news&o=wddx"
          method="GET"
          resolveurl="false"
          timeout="1"
          throwonerror="Yes">
  </cfhttp>

  <cfcatch type="COM.ALLAIRE.COLDFUSION.HTTPFAILURE">
    <cfdump var="#cfcatch#">
    <cflog text="Agent unable to connect to server."
           file="syndication"
           type="Warning">
    <cfabort>
  </cfcatch>
  <cfcatch type="COM.ALLAIRE.COLDFUSION.HTTPCONNECTIONTIMEOUT">
    <cflog text="Agent timed out connecting to server."
           file="syndication"
           type="Warning">
    <cfabort>
  </cfcatch>
  <cfcatch type="Any">
    <cflog text="Agent failed - unknown error."
           file="syndication"
           type="Warning">
    <cfabort>
  </cfcatch>
</cftry>

<!--- agent successful --->
<cflog text="Agent shaken but not stirred."
       file="syndication">
```

➜ HTTP agents are discussed in Chapter 43, "Other Internet Protocols."

Summary

Debugging is a primary component of any application development process. ColdFusion offers a variety of utilities to debug applications, including visual debugging tools, the exposure of variables, and programmatic functions and tags. Manual debugging offers the most flexibility and control—and certain features, such as performance monitoring, can allow for greater insight into a ColdFusion environment's overall strengths and weaknesses. Macromedia offers a wealth of log information that is stored in specific directories and is accessible with any text editor. ColdFusion provides tools for detailed custom logging as well.

Sample Questions

1. What types of variables are exposed through server-side debug options?

   A. CGI

   B. ARGUMENTS

   C. REQUEST

   D. SESSION

   E. VARIABLES

2. What would you use to time the execution of specific lines of code?

   A. <cflog>

   B. <cftimer>

   C. GetTickCount()

   D. Debug()

3. From which of the following can ColdFusion debugging output be accessed?

   A. ColdFusion Administrator

   B. Dreamweaver

   C. cfstat

   D. Web browser

CHAPTER 26

Error Handling

IN THIS CHAPTER

Understanding ColdFusion Error Handling

By default, when an error occurs, ColdFusion displays diagnostic information to the user, and an entry is made in one of the ColdFusion logs. Not only does this make for a poor user experience, but it also means that the error was not trapped and dealt with in a better manner.

Several ColdFusion tools are available to handle errors in a better way. We'll discuss `<cferror>`, `onError()`, then `<cftry>`.

<cferror type="request">

When an error occurs, diagnostic information is displayed using a default page that looks nothing like the rest of the application. Using `<CFERROR>` allows you to decide the following:

- What parts, if any, of the error message are shown to the user
- The look and feel of the page

The attributes of the `<cferror>` tag are listed in Table 26.1.

Table 26.1 `<cferror>` Tag Attributes

ATTRIBUTE	DESCRIPTION
`exception`	To be discussed later in the chapter.
`mailto`	An optional attribute that sends an email address to the template specified.

Table 26.1 (continued)

ATTRIBUTE	DESCRIPTION
`template`	The template to be displayed instead of the default error diagnostic page.
`type`	The type of error to catch. For now, consider `Request` and `Validation`.

The first type of error we'll cover is `Request`. It traps any error unless it is a server-side validation error. The ideal location for a `<cferror>` tag is in the `Application.cfm` file. If you don't place the `<cferror>` tag in `Application.cfm`, you'd have to place the tag on every page in your application.

➜ You can find further information about server-side form field validation errors in Chapter 9, "`FORM` Variables," and more on the `Application` files in Chapter 6, "The Application Framework."

Consider the following `<cferror>` tag placed in an `Application.cfm` file:

```
<cferror type="Request"
         template="ErrorTemplate.cfm">
```

Any errors that occur in a ColdFusion template call for `ErrorTemplate.cfm` to be processed. This includes ColdFusion syntax errors, which cause parsing errors, as well as errors that occur during template execution. For instance, a `<cfquery>` tag without a `datasource` attribute causes the error template to be called, because that is a syntax error. By the same token, a `<cfquery>` tag with a `datasource` attribute that points to a nonexistent data source also calls the error template.

What should be on the error template? That is your decision. Most likely, you will want it to look like the rest of your site. You may also choose to have some information about the error, and error variables can help you do that.

The error variables available are listed in Table 26.2.

Table 26.2 Error Variables for Type Request

VARIABLE	DESCRIPTION
`Error.Browser`	Browser that was running when the error occurred.
`Error.DateTime`	Date and time when the error occurred.
`Error.Diagnostics`	Detailed error diagnostics from the ColdFusion server.
`Error.GeneratedContent`	The failed request's generated content.
`Error.HTTPReferer`	Page from which the client accessed the link to the page where the error occurred. This will be an empty string if there is no referrer.

Table 26.2 (continued)

VARIABLE	DESCRIPTION
`Error.MailTo`	Email address of the administrator who should be notified (corresponds to the value set in the `mailto` attribute of `<cferror>`).
`Error.QueryString`	URL query string of the client's request. It is equal to the empty string if there is not a referrer.
`Error.RemoteAddress`	IP address of the remote client.
`Error.Template`	Page being executed when the error occurred.

You can use these variables only on the error template page. They act like regular ColdFusion variables in that they must have number signs (#) around them. But unlike other ColdFusion variables, they need not be surrounded with a `<cfoutput>` block. In fact, when the type is `Request` or `Validation`, no ColdFusion tags on the page specified in the `TEMPLATE` attribute are executed.

NOTE

There is a very good reason that no ColdFusion tags can be used on the error template when the type is **`Request`** or **`Validation`**. Consider what would happen if the error template itself had a syntax error. It would call the error template again, which would have an error, and call the error template again, which would have an error, and so on.

To avoid the chance of having an infinite loop, you cannot use ColdFusion tags on the error template when the type is **`Request`** or **`Validation`**. Even if you use some ColdFusion tags on the page, they are ignored.

<cferror type="validation">

As you learned earlier, when the type is `Request`, it traps all errors except server-side validation errors. Those are trapped when the type is `Validation`.

On a form, you can use two `<input>` tags as follows:

```
<input type="text"
       name="TheNumber">
<input type="hidden"
       name="TheNumber_integer"
       value="This is my error message">
```

You can use a `<cferror>` tag in the `Application.cfm`, like this:

```
<cferror type="validation"
         template="DisplayErrorValidation.cfm">
```

When you use the tags shown here, if the user fills the text box with a string, an error of type `Validation` will occur and the `DisplayErrorValidation.cfm` template will be called. The same rules apply to building this error template as to building the Request template, except that the `CFERROR` variables you can use on a validation error template are different. They are listed in Table 26.3.

Table 26.3 Error Variables for Type Validation

VARIABLE	DESCRIPTION
`Error.InvalidFields`	Unordered list of validation errors that occurred
`Error.ValidationFooter`	Text for the footer of a validation message
`Error.ValidationHeader`	Text for the header of a validation message

NOTE

`Error.ValidationHeader` is the following text: "Form Entries Incomplete or Invalid. One or more problems exist with the data you have entered."

`Error.ValidationFooter` is the following text: "Use the Back button on your web browser to return to the previous page and correct the listed problems."

`Error.InvalidFields` is a bulleted list of the default error messages, or the message in the `VALUE` attribute of the hidden form tag, if used.

`onError()`

`Application.cfc` is used to define code that is executed when specific events occur. The `onEvent` method is called when an error occurs, much like `<cferror type="request">`.

➜ `Application.cfc` is explained in Chapter 6, "The Application Framework."

When an error occurs, ColdFusion executes the onError method, passing to it two required arguments as listed in Table 26.4.

Table 26.4 onError Arguments

ARGUMENT	DESCRIPTION
`Exception`	An exception structure, containing the error variables listed in Table 26.2 previously.
`EventName`	The name of the event handler that generated the exception (this will be a blank string if an error occurred during page processing).

Exception Handling

<cferror> traps both parsing and run-time errors. Errors that occur when the template is executed are also called *exceptions*. Exceptions include any event that disrupts the normal flow of instructions in a ColdFusion page when it is being executed. Exceptions can be more intelligently handled than what you've seen so far using <cferror>.

<cftry>/<cfcatch>

When you use the <cftry>/<cfcatch> tag set, exceptions can be caught and then acted upon programmatically. For instance, instead of throwing an error when attempting to write a duplicate indexed value to a database, ColdFusion can catch the error, then inform the user of the problem and ask him to change the offending data.

The general format of catching an exception in ColdFusion is as follows:

```
<cftry>
  Possible error producing code
<cfcatch type="ExceptionType">
  Code to run if error is caught
</cfcatch>
...additional <cfcatch></cfcatch> blocks...
</cftry>
```

> **CAUTION**
>
> It is important to understand that <cftry>/<cfcatch> does not catch syntax errors like <cferror> does. For instance, using a <cftry> block around a <cfquery> tag without a `datasource` attribute does nothing, because the syntax of the <cfquery> is not correct and the page cannot be parsed correctly. If, on the other hand, the `datasource` attribute is there but the listed data source does not exist, the <cftry> block catches that exception.

The following is a simple <cftry>/<cfcatch> example. It assumes that a personalized header is included. If for some reason the personalized header is not available, a standard header is displayed.

```
<cftry>
  <cfinclude template="#Personalized#.cfm">
  <cfcatch type="MissingInclude">
    <cfinclude template="StandardHeader.cfm">
  </cfcatch>
</cftry>
```

The `type` attribute in the <cfcatch> tag is the exception type. Table 26.5 lists the possible exception types and the situations in which they are used.

Table 26.5 Exception Types

EXCEPTION TYPE	DESCRIPTION
`Any`	All exceptions are caught.
`Application`	Custom exception types using `<cfthrow>` without specifying a custom type.
`Custom Type`	Custom exception types using `<cfthrow>` and specifying a custom type fail.
`Database`	Database operations fail.
`Expression`	Expression evaluation fails.
`Lock`	Locking operations fail.
`MissingInclude`	Included files cannot be found.
`Object`	Code using `<cfobject>` fails.
`Template`	General application page errors are returned.
`SearchEngine`	Verity search engine exceptions are returned.
`Security`	Code using ColdFusion security fails.

`<cfcatch>` Variables

When an error is caught, you should attempt to "fix" it in the `<cfcatch>` block—that is, programmatically supply a solution to the problem. This task is made easier by the variables available in the scope of the `<cfcatch>` block. A set of variables is defined for all exception types. Other variables exist only for certain exception types. Those variables that are defined for all exception types are listed in Table 26.6.

Table 26.6 Variables Defined for All Exception Types

VARIABLE	DESCRIPTION
`Detail`	A message from the CFML interpreter. Here, you can see which tag threw the exception.
`Message`	The exceptions message.
`Type`	The exception type as specified in `<cfcatch>`.

`<cfthrow>`

In some cases, it is advantageous to centralize exception handling. For instance, you might have a page that calls a number of custom tags. Rather than deal with exceptions in detail on every custom tag, you could simply throw the error back to the calling page in all cases and deal with the exceptions in detail there.

To do so, you can use the <cfthrow> tag, which is a useful tool. The attributes available when using <cfthrow> are listed in Table 26.7.

Table 26.7 <cfthrow> Tag Attributes

ATTRIBUTE	DESCRIPTION
detail	Detailed information you select.
errorcode	An error code you select.
extendedinfo	Extended information you select.
message	A message you select.
object	Java object to which to throw the exception to.
type	The custom exception type you name. This attribute is optional.

For an example of <cfthrow>, consider a custom tag that checks inventory against the quantity ordered, as shown in the following code. If the inventory is less than the quantity ordered, an exception is raised.

```
<cfif Ordered GTE Inventory>
  <cfthrow type="Reorder"
           message="Reorder product #ProdName#"
           extendedinfo="#Now()#"
</cfif>
```

This code uses a custom exception type named `Reorder`. You also can see that the `message` and `extendedinfo` attributes pass back to the calling page the name of the product to reorder and the time stamp indicating when the exception was thrown.

If the name of the custom tag with this code were called `PlaceOrder.cfm`, you could call it in a <cftry> block as follows:

```
<cftry>
  <cf_PlaceOrder>
  <cfcatch type="Reorder">
    <cfoutput>
    #CFCATCH.Message#.
    The alert occurred at #CFCATCH.ExtendedInfo#.
    </cfoutput>
  </cfcatch>
</cftry>
```

NOTE

If the `type` attribute were not used in <cfthrow>, you could have caught the exception by using `type="Application"` in <cfcatch>. The purpose of the `Application` type is to catch exceptions from <cfthrow> when a type is not specified.

<cfthrow> can also be used to throw exceptions to a Java object. If object is used, no other <cfthrow> attributes are used.

<cfrethrow>

In some cases, you might want to throw the exact error that occurred. For instance, suppose a database error occurs on a custom tag, and you want to throw that exact error to the calling page and deal with it in that location. The <cfrethrow> tag does this job. Using this tag saves you from having to build a custom type and supply the appropriate values for the message, detail, errorcode, and extendedinfo attributes. Assume the following code is in a custom tag called MyInsert.cfm:

```
<cftry>
  Some database action performed here, for example an insert
  <cfcatch type="Database">
    <cfrethrow>
  </cfcatch>
</cftry>
```

You then can handle the call to the custom tag like this:

```
<cftry>
  <CF_MyInsert>
    <cfcatch type="Database">
      Database error occurred!
      <cfoutput>The error code is #CFCATCH.SQLState#</cfoutput>
   </cfcatch>
</cftry>
```

This code shows that the exact error originally thrown on the custom tag (in this example, of type Database) can be caught on the calling page.

Exceptions in <cfscript>

Code written in <cfscript> can also implement exception handling via the try and catch keywords. <cfscript> does not support throw and rethrow.

As with <cftry>, every try must have a matching catch. Within the catch code, a variable named exceptionvariable contains the information exposed by CFCATCH.type, explained previously.

<cferror> and Exceptions

Earlier in the chapter, you learned about <cferror> with the type attribute equal to Request and Validation. Now that you've learned about exceptions, you can extend the use of <cferror>.

<cferror type="exception">

The `<cferror>` tag directs program execution to a designated error template when the type is `Request` or `Validation`. The information from the error template is displayed, and program processing ends. The same is true when the type is `Exception`, except that on the error template, you have access to the full set of ColdFusion tags, as well as the `<cferror>` variables as needed.

If you do not specify an exception type using the `exception` attribute, the default is `Any`, so any exception that occurs is directed to the error template. You can also use multiple `<cferror>` tags in `Application.cfm` as follows:

```
<cferror type="Exception"
         template="ExpressionTemplate.cfm"
         exception="Expression">
<cferror type="Exception"
         template="DatabaseTemplate.cfm"
         exception="Database">
```

This code directs exceptions of type `Expression` to one template, and of type `Database` to another.

> **TIP**
>
> You might think that you don't need `<cferror>` with type `Request` if you are using type `Exception`. This is not true. The Request template is used if an exception occurs on the template specified with the type equal to `Exception`.

<cferror> and <cftry> Together

If you use a `<cftry>/<cfcatch>` block to catch an exception, the `<cferror>` tag does *not* do its job and fails to redirect processing to the error template. The `<cftry>/<cfcatch>` block makes it seem that an exception did not occur. In essence, the `<cftry>` "overrides" the `<cferror>`.

Sitewide Error Handler

In the Settings area of ColdFusion Administrator, you can find an option to provide a path for the sitewide error handler. This is a global way to specify `<cferror type="Exception">`. The template specified in ColdFusion Administrator becomes the template where processing is directed if an exception occurs.

> **NOTE**
>
> On the template specified as the sitewide error handler, you can use ColdFusion tags. You also have access to the `error` variables.
>
> If a `<cferror>` or onError is used, it overrides the setting from ColdFusion Administrator.

Summary

ColdFusion has a rich environment to catch syntax errors and exceptions that occur when a template is being parsed or processed. `<cferror>` with the `type` attribute set equal to `Request` or `Validation` redirects processing to a template where you cannot use other ColdFusion tags. If the type is set to `Exception`, processing is redirected to a template where you can use ColdFusion tags.

Rather than redirect processing to an error template, you might want to catch the error and deal with it programmatically. You can do so by using the `<cftry>`/`<cfcatch>` tag set.

Sample Questions

1. Which of the following `<cferror>` types is used to check form input?

   A. `Form`

   B. `Validation`

   C. `Exception`

   D. `Error`

2. `<cfthrow>` is used with no `type` attribute. What type of exception should you use to catch it?

   A. `Expression`

   B. `Any`

   C. `Database`

   D. `Application`

3. Which error-handling options are available in CFML but not `<cfscript>`?

   A. `try`

   B. `catch`

   C. `throw`

   D. `rethrow`

CHAPTER 27 Application Security

IN THIS CHAPTER

Understanding ColdFusion Security

ColdFusion provides a framework on which to implement application security. ColdFusion does not provide a complete out-of-the-box solution for application security, as that would be too limited and not flexible enough to handle all the needs of numerous developers building very different applications. Rather, the framework provides the essential building blocks with which to create a robust and flexible role-based security system.

> **NOTE**
> Do not confuse application security with development security. ColdFusion provides administrators with the ability to secure entire applications so that developers and users on shared boxes do not step on each other's virtual feet. This is achieved using server sandboxes and is not the subject covered in this chapter. Application security is implemented within specific applications to grant or deny access and to implement access control (whereby users have access only to what they are supposed to).

Application Security Fundamentals

ColdFusion application security is designed to let you easily do the following:

- Require a login to access an application
- Allow *anything* to be used to validate users (databases, LDAP directories, NT domains, Web server authentication, and more), not tying security to any specific authentication implementation

- Implement access control based on user roles (group or affiliations)
- Automatically time out logins when appropriate (or terminate them when a browser is closed)

The application security framework makes use of several important terms, which are listed in Table 27.1.

Table 27.1 Application Security Terms

TERM	DESCRIPTION
Authentication	The act of validating that users are who they say they are, based on some user input or provided credentials.
Authorization	The act of determining what a user has the rights to do once she has been authenticated. This usually occurs by determining what role a user belongs to.
Role	A logical group that has rights to specific data or features. Users belong to roles, and roles are granted access as needed—access is never granted to users directly.

Implementing Application Security

Application security is implemented using three CFML tags:

- `<cflogin>`
- `<cfloginuser>`
- `<cflogout>`

The `<cflogin>` Tag

When you implement application security, your application must have code that determines whether a user is logged in and responds or takes action as necessary. Rather than check this manually, you can use the `<cflogin>` tag to define a block of code that is executed *only* if no user is logged in.

To secure applications safely, the security code must always be executed; as such, it should be placed in an `Application` file.

→ `Application.cfm` and `Application.cfc` were covered in Chapter 6, "The Application Framework."

The following snippet shows the code that would be executed based on whether a user is logged in:

```
<cflogin>
  Any code here will be executed only if not logged in
```

```
</cflogin>
Any code here will be executed for all requests
```

The <cflogin> tag itself does not log users in or out; it simply marks a block of code that will be executed if no user is logged in (or if a user's login has timed out). Within <cflogin> you can place any code needed, including redirecting to login forms.

The <cfloginuser> Tag

To log a user in to the security system, use the <cfloginuser> tag. <cfloginuser> does not perform authentication; your code should do that using whatever code is necessary (<cfquery> to authenticate against a database, <cfldap> to authenticate against an LDAP server, <cfntauthenticate> to authenticate against NT domains and Active Directory, <cfinvoke> to authenticate with a component or Web Service, and so on). Once your code has determined that a user has been authenticated correctly, use the <cfloginuser> tag to pass the user information (name, password, and role) to the security framework.

The basic code flow is like this:

```
<cflogin>
  ... Authentication code goes here ...
  ... Code to find roles goes here ...
  <cfloginuser name="#FORM.login#"
               password="#FORM.password#"
               roles="#roles#">
</cflogin>
```

It is also possible to rely on the Web server to perform the authentication, in which case the ColdFusion cflogin structure will be populated with login information automatically. The following snippet logs a user in to the application using Web server-provided information (roles will not be returned by the Web server):

```
<cflogin>
  ... Code to find roles goes here ...
  <cfloginuser name="#CFLOGIN.name#"
               password="#CFLOGIN.password#"
               roles="#roles#">
</cflogin>
```

NOTE

To force the Web server to generate a login dialog (so that you do not have to create one manually), use the following code:

```
<cfsetting enablecfoutputonly="yes"
           showdebugoutput="no">
<cfheader statuscode="401">
<cfheader name="WWW-Authenticate"
          value="Basic realm=""MyRealm""">
<cfoutput>Authorization failed</cfoutput>
```

Replace the realm name with one of your own, and customize the failure message if needed.

ColdFusion detects the presence of two special form fields, `j_username` and `j_password`. If these are present (the names used in your own login form), ColdFusion will use them automatically and will populate `CFLOGIN` with them.

Once a user has been logged in, you can use `<cffunction>` and `IsUserInRole()` to implement access control as described below.

The `<cflogout>` Tag

User logins time out automatically. To force an immediate logout (perhaps in response to a user clicking a Logout option), use the `<cflogout>` tag.

Using Application Security

`<cflogin>` and related tags are responsible for logging users in to and out of applications. It is up to the developer to implement access control based on role affiliation.

Explicit Access Control

To determine whether a logged-in user occupies a specific role, use the `IsUserInRole()` function. `IsUserInRole()` takes the name of a role as an argument and returns `TRUE` or `FALSE`.

The following example displays a series of menu options, one of which is available only to administrators:

```
<li><a href="browse.cfm">Browse</a></li>
<li><a href="add.cfm">Add</a></li>
<cfif IsUserInRole("admin")>
  <li><a HREF="approve.cfm">Approve</a></li>
</cfif>
<li><a href="/login/logout.cfm">Logout</a></li>
```

> **NOTE**
> It is dangerous to merely restrict access by hiding menu options; the code that the menu actually calls must be protected too.

`GetAuthUser()` can be used at any time to determine the name of the authenticated user (the name that was passed to `<cfloginuser>`). This can be used for additional processing if needed.

Component Based Access Control

ColdFusion Components are reusable application components used within ColdFusion applications. ColdFusion Components are files containing sets of related functions (known as *methods*), which are defined using the `<cffunction>` tag.

For greater security and access control when building sophisticated applications, individual components' methods may be secured by listing the ROLES that have rights to them. The `<cffunction>` `roles` attribute takes a list of roles into which an authenticated user must have been authorized in order to be able to execute the method.

➜ ColdFusion Components are covered in Chapter 31, "ColdFusion Components."

Advanced Security Options

In addition to the basic (and not so basic) functionality described thus far, the security framework features some more advanced options that may be used as needed.

Setting the Time-out

The default login time-out is 30 minutes (1800 seconds). To change this value, pass a new time-out (in seconds) to the `idletimeout` attribute in the `<cflogin>` tag.

Securing Parts of an Application

By default, security is tied to the ColdFusion application. Any code in the same application (sharing the same application `name`) shares the same security system. This behavior can be changed by specifying a name to the `<cflogin>` `applicationtoken` attribute. Security will then be shared only by code using the same `applicationtoken`.

A single application can have multiple `applicationtoken` values for different sections, allowing various sections to be secured in different ways. In addition, a number of applications can share security if needed.

Restricting Clients Based on Domain

The `<cflogin>`-based security system will allow logins from any host as long as the user can be authenticated. To restrict access to specific hosts, specify the domain in the `<cflogin>` `cookiedomain` attribute. For example, the following allows logins only from hosts in the domain `forta.com`:

```
<cflogin cookiedomain="forta.com">
```

> **NOTE**
>
> `cookiedomain` can also be used to specify subdomains and even specific hosts if needed.

Cookieless Security

`<cflogin>` depends on HTTP cookies. If cookies cannot be used, logins may still occur, lasting only for the duration of the single request. This may be desirable if credentials are passed back on each request, or if you are building a single-request system (for example, a Web Service).

→ Web Services are covered in Chapter 32, "Web Services."

If cookies are not being used, `<cfloginuser>` should be used without the `<cflogin>` tag.

Summary

ColdFusion provides a framework for implementing security-based access control using `<cflogin>` and related tags. The security framework relies on external authentication and can interact with databases, LDAP servers, NT domains and Active Directory, and more. Security is role based, and access is granted to roles. Roles may be used for controlling access to specific code as well as to component methods.

Sample Questions

1. Where should `<cflogin>` be used?

   A. In a `<cfapplication>` tag

   B. In `Application.cfm`

   C. In `index.cfm`

   D. In `OnRequestEnd.cfm`

   E. In `Application.cfc`

2. When is a user logged out of an application? *(select two)*

   A. When the time-out is reached

   B. When the next user logs in

   C. When the browser is closed

   D. When her password changes

3. Which HTTP status code should be used to force a browser login form to be displayed?

   A. `200`

   B. `401`

   C. `404`

   D. `500`

PART 6 Extending ColdFusion

IN THIS PART

CHAPTER 28
Custom Tags

IN THIS CHAPTER

What Is a Custom Tag?

ColdFusion comes with a great number of useful tags. Using them in combination lets you create powerful Web applications. ColdFusion Custom Tags take your productivity even further by allowing you to create your own reusable, modular, and maintainable tags.

At their simplest, Custom Tags are just regular ColdFusion templates acting like little self-contained programs that perform tasks. You can think of them as extensions of regular ColdFusion tags and functions, except that you get to code them to do whatever you want!

➜ More advanced forms of custom functionality are discussed in Chapter 24, "Advanced Custom Tags."

Why Use Custom Tags?

The three main reasons for using Custom Tags are

- Reusability
- Maintainability
- Hiding complexity

These three reasons are related, the latter two being by-products of the first.

Two of the most important tags that you learn as a beginning ColdFusion developer are `<cfquery>` and `<cfoutput>`.

➜ `<cfquery>` is introduced in Chapter 7, "Using Databases," and `<cfoutput>` is introduced in Chapter 2, "Working with Variables and Expressions."

The following example shows how those two tags might be used together to query the database for information and then display the results in an HTML table.

```
<!--- first, query the database --->
<cfquery name="GetEmployees" datasource="dsn">
SELECT FirstName, LastName, Phone, Email
FROM Employees
</cfquery>

<!--- second, display the table caption --->
<h1>All Company Employees</h1>
<!--- then display the query results in a table --->
<table border="1">
 <tr>
  <th>First Name</th>
  <th>Last Name</th>
  <th>Phone Number</th>
  <th>Email Address</th>
 </tr>
 <cfoutput query="GetEmployees">
  <tr>
   <td>#FirstName#</td>
   <td>#LastName#</td>
   <td>#Phone#</td>
   <td>#Email#</td>
  </tr>
 </cfoutput>
</table>
```

You have probably used similar code a thousand times in your ColdFusion applications, which makes it a good candidate for a Custom Tag. Instead of typing all that code every time, you could call this functionality by just typing one tag:

```
<cf_queryprinttable datasource="HR"
 TABLENAME="Employees"
 columnnames="FirstName, LastName, Phone, Email"
 columnheaders="First Name, Last Name, Phone Number, Email Address"
 caption="All Company Employees">
```

This Custom Tag will use the attributes passed to it to generate the same results the preceding example did, but this tag is more flexible because you can reuse the code by merely passing it different values through the attributes each time you need the functionality.

Every programmer has looked at code that he or she built a year previously and cringes. As you develop your skills, you find better and more efficient ways of coding, and you'll want to return to your old code and improve it. If you do not use Custom Tags, you will have to hunt through all your code to find and update the multiple places where you embedded code for one piece of functionality. That could take weeks or even months, depending on the complexity of your application. However, if you used Custom Tags, you can open one template with the functionality code, and update it—and then all the applications that use it will immediately benefit from the change.

> **NOTE**
>
> Custom Tag execution may be slightly slower than that of ColdFusion Components or User Defined Functions. As such, they should not be used for all reuse, but for the right situations they are invaluable.

If you work as part of a team of developers, Custom Tags can have an additional benefit. Teams often consist of people with different skill sets and a varying degree of proficiency even within the same skill set. In a situation like this, it is often beneficial to have senior developers create Custom Tags, which junior developers can then use to perform common functions.

A senior developer can even encode the Custom Tag template so that the complexity of the code does not confuse junior developers.

→ Template encoding is discussed in Chapter 1, "Web Technology and Terminology."

Simple Custom Tags

In our earlier example, the Custom Tag we discussed used attributes. We'll go into more detail about attributes in the next section. However, the simplest form of Custom Tag takes no attributes at all. Such tags simply perform one task.

Despite their one-track nature, simple Custom Tags can be quite powerful. Consider the Custom Tag `<CF_EmbedFields>`. This tag takes no attributes, but is indispensable when working with multiple form pages.

> **TIP**
>
> `<CF_EmbedFields>`, along with the other Custom Tags mentioned in this chapter, can be found on the Macromedia Developer's Exchange at `http://devex.macromedia.com/developer/gallery/index.cfm`.

`URL` and `FORM` variables allow developers to pass information from one page to another, but if information must persist across multiple pages, most developers use `APPLICATION`, `SERVER`, `SESSION`, `COOKIE`, or `CLIENT` variables.

→ `FORM` and `ACTION` pages are discussed in Chapter 9, "`FORM` Variables." `SESSION`, `COOKIE`, and `CLIENT` variables are introduced in Chapter 11, "Session State Management."

The complexity of persistent variables, however, is sometimes overkill for simple problems. For instance, if you have a wizard that takes users through multiple forms, you don't necessarily want to maintain that information in `SESSION` variables.

The Custom Tag <CF_EmbedFields> forces FORM variables to be passed from one form page to another by embedding the results of one submission as hidden form fields in the next form.

The following code makes up the functionality of <CF_EmbedFields>:

```
<!--- Check that FieldNames exists --->
<cfif IsDefined("FORM.FieldNames")>
 <!--- Create empty list of processed variables --->
 <cfset fieldnames_processed="">
 <!--- Loop through fieldnames --->
 <cfloop index="form_element" list="#FORM.FieldNames#">
  <!--- Try to find current element in list --->
  <cfif ListFind(fieldnames_processed, form_element) IS 0>
   <!--- Make fully qualified copy of it
   (to prevent accessing
    the wrong field type) --->
   <cfset form_element_qualified="form." & form_element>
   <!--- Output it as a hidden field --->
   <cfoutput>
    <input type="hidden"
           name="#form_element#"
           value="#Evaluate(FORM_element_qualified)#">
   </cfoutput>
   <!--- And add it to the processed list --->
   <cfset fieldnames_processed=
          ListAppend(fieldnames_processed, form_element)>
  </cfif>
 </cfloop>
</cfif>
```

This code evaluates the special FORM variable FORM.FieldNames, which is a list of all the names of the FORM variables being passed from a FORM.

➜ FORM variables, specifically the special variable FORM.FieldNames, are discussed in Chapter 9, "FORM Variables." Lists are discussed in Chapter 13, "Lists."

As the code loops over the FORM.FieldNames list, it generates one HTML hidden form field for each field that was passed from the previous form. Using this Custom Tag, you can easily continue to pass information from page to page, essentially maintaining state, without worrying about the complexities of using a database or session state variables.

<CF_EmbedFields> is a simple Custom Tag in that it takes no arguments and returns no data.

Calling Custom Tags

Creating a Custom Tag is the easy part. Like any other ColdFusion template, a simple Custom Tag is merely a bunch of CFML code saved into a file with a .cfm extension.

Custom Tags are really defined by how they are accessed. Most ColdFusion pages are run when the Web server passes them to the ColdFusion application server. Custom Tags are run when they are called from within another ColdFusion template.

> **NOTE**
>
> In Chapter 5, "Redirects and Reuse," you were introduced to the `<cfinclude>` tag. This tag calls another page to be run. However, it should not be confused with a Custom Tag.

Simple Syntax (`cf_`)

After you've created a file that you will use as a Custom Tag, you need a way of calling that page to run. There are a number of ways to do this.

The easiest method is to use simple syntax. If you have a Custom Tag template that you have named `customtag.cfm`, you can simply call it by typing `<cf_customtag>`. Notice that the filename is prefixed with `<cf_` and that the `.cfm` extension is dropped.

When using simple syntax, ColdFusion automatically looks for the Custom Tag in the same directory as the calling template. If it doesn't find the Custom Tag there, it searches a special directory that is created by ColdFusion upon installation (on Windows machines this is usually `c:\cfusionmx7\customtags\`).

> **TIP**
>
> ColdFusion always looks for Custom Tags in the current directory before it searches the **`CustomTags`** directories. By default the Custom Tags directory are under the ColdFusion root directory, but additional Custom Tag directories may be added using the ColdFusion Administrator.

`<cfmodule>`

You can also call a Custom Tag using the built-in ColdFusion tag `<cfmodule>`. `<cfmodule>` lets you use two separate methods to call the Custom Tag.

The first method works only if the Custom Tag is in the special directory `c:\cfusionmx7\customtags\`. The syntax is as follows:

```
<cfmodule name="Developers.Emily.Header">
```

The value `Developers.Emily.Header` calls the `header.cfm` Custom Tag in a directory called `Emily`, which is in a directory called `Developers`. `Developers` is a subdirectory of the Custom Tags directory.

TIP

If you're in a hosted environment, your ISP might allow you access to your own directory inside `c:\cfusionmx7\customtags\`. The ColdFusion application server recursively searches through the `CustomTags` directory and all its subdirectories until it locates the Custom Tag in question. This can be a problem if two users being hosted on the same server have given identical names to their Custom Tags. For instance, `header.cfm` is a common Custom Tag name. If one person has her Custom Tag template in `c:\cfusionmx7\customtags\Developers\Emily\header.cfm` and another has his Custom Tag template in `c:\cfusionmx7\customtags\Developers\Matt\header.cfm`, there will be a problem when calling this Custom Tag using simple syntax like `<cf_Header>`. When Matt calls `<cf_Header>` from within his own application, he will always run the `header.cfm` Custom Tag in the `Emily` directory. This will be the first file by that name that ColdFusion encounters, because it recursively searches alphabetically through the subdirectories of `c:\cfusionmx7\customtags\`. Using `<cfmodule>` with the NAME attribute enables you to explicitly specify which Custom Tag in `c:\cfusionmx7\customtags\` will run.

`<cfmodule>` gives us an even more flexible means of calling a Custom Tag. So far, we have been restricted to putting our Custom Tags in the same directory as the calling page, or in the `c:\cfusionmx7\customtags\` directory. Using the `template` attribute of `<cfmodule>`, you can place a Custom Tag anywhere and call it using either a relative path or a ColdFusion mapping.

```
<!--- using a relative path --->
<cfmodule template="../customtags/header.cfm">
<!--- using a ColdFusion mapping --->
<cfmodule template="/customtags/header.cfm">
```

➜ ColdFusion mappings were introduced in Chapter 5, "Redirects and Reuse."

Attributes

Custom Tags should be built with flexibility. Essentially this means that the more attributes the tag takes, the more flexible and reusable it will be.

Earlier in the chapter, we discussed the sample Custom Tag used to query the database and output the data in an HTML table:

```
<cf_queryprinttable datasource="dsn"
 tablename="Employees"
 columnnames="FirstName, LastName, Phone, Email"
 columnheaders="First Name, Last Name, Phone Number, Email Address"
 caption="All Company Employees">
```

The attributes we list here could be considered the absolute minimum needed to make the Custom Tag run properly. However, we could easily enhance the Custom Tag by adding more attributes for formatting issues:

```
<cf_queryprinttable datasource="dsn"
 tablename="Employees"
```

```
columnnames="FirstName, LastName, Phone, Email"
columnheaders="First Name, Last Name, Phone Number, Email Address"
caption="All Company Employees"
width="80%"
cellpadding="3"
cellspacing="0"
border="0"
headerbgcolor="blue"
databgcolor="yellow">
```

To make the query in the Custom Tag recognize the attributes, use the following:

```
<cfquery name="MyQueryName"
         datasource="#ATTRIBUTES.datasource#">
SELECT #ATTRIBUTES.ColumnNames#
FROM #ATTRIBUTES.Tablename#
</cfquery>
```

> **CAUTION**
>
> The `ATTRIBUTES.` prefix is required when referencing values passed into a Custom Tag using attributes.

Notice that the only value that is hard-coded in the preceding query is the query name itself. Because the name of the query is being used only to output the values within the Custom Tag, it is not necessary for us to change it. Similarly, the rest of the code that displays the caption and the HTML table will also reference these attributes.

For this Custom Tag to work at all, we have to make sure that certain attributes are passed. `datasource`, `tablename`, `columnnames`, `columnheaders`, and `caption` are all required for the Custom Tag to function even on the most limited basis. You don't want the code to break in the event one of the attributes is not assigned, so you should implement some validation at the beginning of your Custom Tag to display an error message if a required attribute is missing. Such code might look like this:

```
<cfif NOT IsDefined("ATTRIBUTES.datasource")>
 <cfabort showerror="The datasource attribute is required.">
</cfif>
```

→ To perform validation, review Chapter 3, "Conditional Processing," and the discussion about custom validation in Chapter 9, "`FORM` Variables."

> **NOTE**
>
> The code uses `<cfabort>`, which will stop ColdFusion dead in its tracks. As soon as ColdFusion encounters this tag, it stops whatever it was doing. There might be instances in which this immediate halt is unnecessary or too abrupt. In these instances, consider using `<cfexit>` instead. This tag will stop the processing of the Custom Tag but will not hinder ColdFusion from finishing the processing of the calling page. Used outside of a Custom Tag, `<cfexit>` acts just like `<cfabort>`.

Now, after we've validated that all of the required tags are passed, we need to address the issue of the optional attributes. `cellpadding`, `cellspacing`, `border`, `headerbgcolor`, and `databgcolor` are all optional attributes that affect only the display of the HTML table. If they are used, the table should take on the declared physical characteristics. However, if they are not used, the Custom Tag should revert to default values for those attributes.

To set default values, you use the `<cfparam>` tag as follows:

```
<cfparam name="ATTRIBUTES.border" default="0">
```

➜ `<cfparam>` was introduced in Chapter 2, "Working with Variables and Expressions."

Notice that the value of the `NAME` attribute is `ATTRIBUTES.border`—with the `ATTRIBUTES.` scope prefix. This simply states that you are creating a default value specifically for the `border` attribute.

CALLER **Scope**

The relationship between a regular template file and a Custom Tag can often be one-sided, meaning that the template passes information to the Custom Tag but not vice versa. There are instances, however, when the Custom Tag should pass data back to the calling template.

A login script for security can be wrapped into a Custom Tag. This script will take the user name and password passed into it, along with attributes that declare which data source and table to authenticate against, and pass back a flag that declares whether the user has logged in successfully.

Most often in a scenario like this, the name of the flag being returned to the calling page is determined by the person who created the login Custom Tag. If you're working in a team environment, this is not always ideal because your team has most likely created coding standards for the naming of variables. Therefore, it would be better if you could tell the Custom Tag what you would like to name the variable being returned, as in the following Custom Tag call:

```
<cf_loginscript username="#FORM.UserName#"
 psswd="#FORM.PSSWD#"
 datasource="dsn"
 tablename="Users"
 loginflag="LoginFlag">
```

The preceding code declares that the `username` and `password` are being passed from a form submission and that the `loginflag` returned should be named `LoginFlag`.

To create a local variable from within a Custom Tag, you simply type the following code, just as you would for any local variable:

```
<cfset LoginFlag="1">
```

➜ Local variables are introduced in Chapter 2, "Working with Variables and Expressions."

To create this variable in the calling page, you must prefix it with `CALLER`:

```
<cfset caller.LoginFlag="1">
```

`CALLER` tells ColdFusion to let this variable escape the protection of the Custom Tag and make it available to the calling page. This code is perfectly legal, but it is also dangerous: Hard-coding variable names is never a good idea.

To dynamically name and create the variable, you could use this:

```
<cfset "Caller.#ATTRIBUTES.LoginFlag#"="1">
```

Because we declared that `ATTRIBUTES.LoginFlag` will have a value of `LoginFlag`, the variable is ultimately named `CALLER.LoginFlag`, and because of the `Caller.` prefix, it will be exposed to the calling page.

> **TIP**
>
> As a rule, Custom Tags should never arbitrarily create variables in the `CALLER` scope. Always allow caller code to specify the name of the variable to be created so that Custom Tag code does not inadvertently overwrite other variables.

Summary

Custom Tags allow you and your development team to create modular code with an incredible degree of maintainability. Custom Tags can be written with or without attributes, and can be invoked in a number of ways. Within the Custom Tag, you should perform validation on the attributes and set default values for them as necessary. Custom Tags can also return data to calling pages (via the `CALLER` scope); this capability must be used with care.

Sample Questions

1. Which code would you use to create a variable in a Custom Tag that could be passed back into the calling page?

   A. `<cfset FirstName="Emily">`

   B. `<cfset Caller.FirstName="Emily">`

   C. `<cfset SetVariable(FirstName, "Emily")>`

   D. `<cfset ExposeVariable(FirstName, "Emily")>`

2. Assuming a default installation on a Windows machine, which file could be executed if <cf_mytag> were used in your code? *(select two)*

   A. C:\cfusionmx7\MyTag.cfm

   B. MyTag.cfm in the current directory

   C. C:\cfusionmx7\customtags\MyTag.cfm

   D. c:\customtags\MyTag.cfm

3. What is the best way to set default values for optional Custom Tag attributes?

   A. <cfparam name="ATTRIBUTES.MyAttribute" default="MyValue">

   B. <cfset MyAttribute="MyValue">

   C. <input type="hidden" name="MyAttribute" value="MyValue">

   D. <cf_mycustomtag myattribute="MyValue>

CHAPTER 29 Advanced Custom Tags

IN THIS CHAPTER

What Are Advanced Custom Tags?

The last chapter reviewed how you can create and use Custom Tags to improve the maintainability of your code and increase your overall productivity. All of that will remain true during our discussion of advanced Custom Tags in this chapter.

The main reason to implement advanced Custom Tags is to increase functionality. The main programmatic difference between regular Custom Tags and advanced ones is that the latter utilize the ability to nest Custom Tags within each other. The nested Custom Tag architecture actually increases the power of Custom Tags because it allows them to interact with each other to better perform tasks.

To find good reasons for using nested Custom Tags, you don't have to look any further than the ColdFusion language itself. `<cfhttp>`, `<cfquery>`, `<cfreport>`, and `<cfmail>` all use nested tags, called `<cfhttpparam>`, `<cfqueryparam>`, `<cfreportparam>`, and `<cfmailparam>`, respectively.

→ `<cfhttp>` and `<cfhttpparam>` are discussed in Chapter 43, "Other Internet Protocols." `<cfquery>` is discussed in Chapter 7, "Using Databases," and `<cfqueryparam>` is discussed in Chapter 47, "Advanced Database Features." `<cfmail>` and `<cfmailparam>` are both introduced in Chapter 41, "Email Integration." `<cfreport>` and `<cfreportparam>` are both introduced in Chapter 19, "Reporting."

In each of these cases, the *base* or *parent* tag is completely functional on its own, but by adding the use of a *subtag* or *child* tag, the tag becomes even more powerful.

For instance, `<cfhttp>` by itself lets you create an HTTP call inside your ColdFusion template. By adding `<cfhttpparam>`, however, you can not only grab another Web page, but also post variables to it.

Alone, <cfquery> connects you to a data source. By adding <cfqueryparam>, you can perform data validation on the variables being passed to the SQL statement and declare the variable's data type.

<cfmail> also offers increased functionality through the use of its child tags. By itself, <cfmail> sends plain-text or HTML mail through an SMTP server. However, when you use <cfmailparam> in conjunction with <cfmail>, you can send one or more attachments with the email message.

Tag Pairs

Let's say you have a Custom Tag called <cf_PrintDate> that contains only the following code:

```
<cfoutput>
Today's Date: #DateFormat(Now(), "mm/dd/yyyy")#
</cfoutput>
```

When you run this Custom Tag, you will find that it simply displays a formatted date. Here is a calling code snippet:

```
<cf_printdate>
</cf_printdate>
```

The preceding code actually calls the Custom Tag two times—if you were to execute it you would see the date displayed twice on the screen. This is because regardless of whether the call to the Custom Tag references a start or an end tag, it will always run the Custom Tag.

> **NOTE**
>
> If you use <cfmodule> to call the Custom Tag, you can also use it as an end tag, like this: </cfmodule>.

➜ <cfmodule> was first introduced in Chapter 28, "Custom Tags."

However, it is not useful to run the same code when we call the start and end tags. Typically, when the start tag is run, the Custom Tag's environment is created—meaning that the necessary default variables and validation are performed here. The actual functionality of the Custom Tag is usually run when the end tag is accessed.

ThisTag Scope

Nested Custom Tags have some degree of intelligence about their own state. You can use the ThisTag scope to access the information, or tag instance data, that the tags know about themselves.

ThisTag is a structure. It can be used to store your own data (so that the data persists for the duration of the tag processing), and it also contains several default members.

➜ Structures were covered in Chapter 15, "Structures."

ThisTag.ExecutionMode

ThisTag.ExecutionMode is a variable that tells us whether we're in the start, inactive, or end mode of a tag pair set. start mode refers to the start tag, end mode refers to the end tag, and inactive mode refers to any code or text that is run between the two tags.

Within our Custom Tag, we can specify what part of the program we would like to run in start or end mode. We simply evaluate which mode ColdFusion is currently processing, and instruct the program to react accordingly. The following code shows how we determine the value of ThisTag.ExecutionMode:

```
<cfswitch expression="#ThisTag.ExecutionMode#">
<cfcase value="start">
 <!--- in start mode, initialize variables --->
 <cfparam name="Attributes.FirstName" value="Emily">
</cfcase>
<cfcase value="end">
 <!--- in end mode, perform the processing --->
 <cfoutput>#ATTRIBUTES.FirstName#</cfoutput>
</cfswitch>
```

➜ <cfswitch> and <cfcase> were introduced in Chapter 3, "Conditional Processing."

When ColdFusion runs the start tag, ThisTag.ExecutionMode will evaluate to start and only the <CFPARAM> tag will be run. When ColdFusion runs the end tag, ThisTag.ExecutionMode will evaluate to end and the value of ATTRIBUTES.FirstName will be evaluated and printed.

> **TIP**
> Generally, start mode is used for initialization, end mode for actual processing.

ThisTag.HasEndTag

ThisTag.HasEndTag is a variable that holds instance data about whether a particular start tag has an associated end tag. This value is used for validation purposes; some Custom Tags should not be processed without an end tag present. Analyze the following code:

```
<cfif NOT ThisTag.HasEndTag>
 This Custom Tag requires an end tag.
 <cfexit>
</cfif>
```

➜ <cfif> was introduced in Chapter 3, "Conditional Processing." <cfexit> was introduced in Chapter 28, "Custom Tags."

Because `ThisTag.HasEndTag` has either a `yes` or `no` value, it can be directly evaluated to a true or false statement by using the `<cfif>` tag. In the preceding code, if `ThisTag.HasEndTag` is not true, an error will be printed and the Custom Tag will be aborted. The usual place for this logic to occur is within the `start` case of the `ThisTag.ExecutionMode` evaluation.

ThisTag.GeneratedContent

Any text that ColdFusion types or generates during the inactive mode of `ThisTag.ExecutionMode` (in other words, between the start and the end Custom Tags) can be accessed by evaluating the variable `ThisTag.GeneratedContent`.

This is used primarily to access or change information between the start and end tags. For example, consider the following snippet:

```
<cf_applyformat format="alert">
#message#
</cf_applyformat>
```

`<cf_applyformat>` treats text based on a specified format. Here the `alert` format is used, and the text to be formatted for display is a ColdFusion variable named `message` (it may be a database column too). `<cf_applyformat>` needs to access whatever data is in `message` and then update it with the formatted data. It can do this by both reading and writing `ThisTag.GeneratedContent`.

Tag Families

In the earlier example, you saw how introducing an end tag can improve the functionality of your Custom Tags. In this section, the power of Custom Tags is increased even further with the introduction of child tags to the scenario.

Almost every Web site has some sort of menu system that helps visitors navigate the site. We will use a nested menu system to discuss the use of nested Custom Tags.

> **TIP**
>
> Custom Tags can be nested more than one level deep. You can nest Custom Tags within Custom Tags as far as you desire. However, for performance reasons, it is recommended that you do not nest deeper than a few levels.

In the following code, we call two Custom Tags multiple times to create a menu structure:

```
<cf_menu text="Products"
         url="products.cfm">
  <cf_menuitem text="ColdFusion"
               url="productinfo.cfm?prod_ID=4">
  <cf_menuitem text="JRun"
               url="productinfo.cfm?prod_ID=5">
  <cf_menuitem text="Flash"
               url="productinfo.cfm?prod_ID=8">
</cf_menu>
<cf_menu text="Support"
         url="help.cfm">
  <cf_menuitem text="Knowledge Base"
               url="helptools.cfm?tool_ID=1">
  <cf_menuitem text="Developer's Exchange"
               url="helptools.cfm?tool_ID=2">
</cf_menu>
<cf_menu text="About Macromedia"
         url="about.cfm">
```

The `<cf_menu>` tag will display the main sections of the Web site, whereas the `<cf_menuitem>` tags will display specific pages within the section. Note, however, that `<cf_menu>` does not have to contain child tags, and can stand alone as a top-level menu item if necessary.

Custom Tag Functions

Two functions are used with Custom Tags to extend the intelligence of instance data and facilitate the transfer of data in a nested Custom Tag architecture.

GetBaseTagList()

When working with nested Custom Tags, we need a method of validation that helps us ensure that the tags are nested properly. The function `GetBaseTagList()` will be used for just this purpose. Review the following code:

```
<cfset ParentTag=GetBaseTagList()>
<cfif NOT ListFindNoCase(ParentTag, "cf_menu")>
  This child tag must be embedded
  within a parent tag called <cf_menu>
  <cfabort>
</cfif>
```

We place this code within the child tag `<cf_menuitem>`. `GetBaseTagList()` returns a list comprising the names of all tags surrounding, and including, the child tag. With that list, you can use the string function `ListFindNoCase()` to check whether the parent tag is one of the tags surrounding the child tag. If the parent tag `<CF_menu>` does not surround the child tag, an error message will be displayed.

CAUTION

GetBaseTagList() can help you validate to ensure that your child tag is in fact embedded inside the correct parent tag. However, if you have multiple levels of nesting, you will have to do further parsing to ensure that the tags are nested in the correct order.

GetBaseTagData()

To create the most reusable and flexible Custom Tags, it's a good idea to make sure that a child tag can react differently to commands within the parent tag. In our example, the parent tag <cf_menu> has an attribute called containsitems. If the value of this attribute is set to yes, the child tags will be displayed below the parent tag. If the value of this attribute is set to no, child tags will not be displayed, even if child tags are listed.

For the child tags to react appropriately, they must know whether the parent tag has declared containsitems as yes or no. We will use the function GetBaseTagData() within the child tag to grab this data from the parent tag. Evaluate the following code:

```
<cfset GetParentTagVars=GetBaseTagData("cf_menu")>
<cfset ParentTagContainsItems=
       stGetParentTagVars.ATTRIBUTES.ContainsItems>
```

In the first <cfset> statement, all the variables in the parent tag <cf_menu> are pulled into the child tag as a structure and placed within a new structure called stGetParentTagVars.

➜ Structures are discussed in Chapter 15, "Structures."

In the second <cfset> statement, we access the containsitems attribute from directly within the stGetParentVars structure. After we have this value, we can easily use it within conditional statements to force different behavior from the child tag.

<cfassociate>

We have just discussed how to pass variables from the parent tag to the child tag. Now we have to reverse our track and discuss a way to pass child data back to parent data.

We will accomplish this task by using a ColdFusion tag called <cfassociate>. This tag grabs all attributes passed to a child tag and organizes them as structures. In our previous example, one of the declared child tags was as follows:

```
<cf_menuitem text="ColdFusion"
             url="productinfo.cfm?prod_ID=4">
```

If we converted the attributes of this child tag into a structure, they might be represented in this manner:

```
Menu Item #1
text="ColdFusion"
url="productinfo.cfm?prod_ID=4"
```

If we represented the next two child tags' attributes in the same manner, we would have this:

```
menu Item #2
text="JRun"
url="productinfo.cfm?prod_ID=5"
```

and this:

```
Menu Item #3
text="Flash"
url="productinfo.cfm?prod_ID=8"
```

From what you know about structures and arrays, you should be able to see immediately that when you organize data in this manner, the data can be stored as an array of structures.

➜ Lists, arrays, and structures are discussed in Chapters 13, 14, and 15, respectively.

That is exactly what `<cfassociate>` does—converts every child tag's attribute set into a structure, which is then placed into an array. The syntax for the tag is:

```
<cfassociate basetag="cf_menu"
             datacollection="MenuItemData">
```

The first attribute, `basetag`, declares the parent tag to which you will be passing all the child tag data. The `datacollection` attribute is what you use to name the array of structures that holds the child tag data.

> **NOTE**
> If you do not explicitly name the array of structures using the **`datacollection`** attribute, ColdFusion refers to it by default as **`AssocAttribs`**.

Once all the data is passed back to the parent tag, the variable is referred to as part of the `ThisTag` scope. In our example, we would refer to the array of structures in the parent tag as `ThisTag.MenuItemData`. You would use your knowledge of arrays and structures to access the data being held within this variable.

> **NOTE**
> The array of structures is passed back to the **`end`** mode of the parent tag set.

Summary

Custom Tags can be simple tags, as reviewed in the previous chapter, or as complex and sophisticated as needed. Custom Tags may be made up of tag pairs or entire tag families (using nested parent and child tags). The key to working with tag pairs and tag families is to understand the lifetime of a tag and its use of the ThisTag scope. A set of CFML tags and functions are used specifically for creating and working with advanced Custom Tags.

Sample Questions

1. Which variable of the ThisTag scope declares whether the tag is in start or end mode?

   A. ThisTag.GeneratedContent

   B. ThisTag.StartOrEnd

   C. ThisTag.HasEndTag

   D. ThisTag.ExecutionMode

2. In which ExecutionMode should most Custom Tag processing typically occur?

   A. start

   B. end

   C. inactive

3. The <cfassociate> tag is used with nested Custom Tags to do what?

   A. Pass generated content to the Custom Tag's end mode

   B. Pass data from the start mode to the end mode

   C. Pass a child tag's data back to the parent tag

   D. Pass a parent tag's data to the child tag

CHAPTER 30

User-Defined Functions

IN THIS CHAPTER

Understanding User-Defined Functions

ColdFusion Markup Language (CFML) is made up of tags and functions. The prior two chapters reviewed the ability to create your own tags; this chapter reviews creating your own functions.

User-defined functions (UDFs) are just that: functions you create for use in your own applications. UDFs are similar to custom tags in that they allow developers to encapsulate tried-and-true functionality for the reuse of code throughout and between ColdFusion applications.

➜ Visit `http://www.cflib.org` to browse and download the most extensive public UDF libraries.

Unlike Custom Tags, which are created using tags, UDFs can be created using tags and `<cfscript>`. Any CFML code can use UDFs, regardless of how they are written. The big difference between tag- and `<cfscript>`-based UDFs is what they can do (`<cfscript>` is limited in that it cannot execute tags).

NOTE

The only advantage of `<cfscript>`-based tags is that they are sometimes easier to port to and from other languages (like JavaScript and ActionScript).

Tag-Based UDFs

Tag-based UDFs are created using three tags:

- `<cffunction>`, which defines the function
- `<cfargument>`, which defines any function arguments
- `<cfreturn>`, which defines the function return value

Creating UDFs

UDFs are created using the `<cffunction>` tag; the function itself is placed between `<cffunction>` and `</cffunction>`.

Here is a simple example:

```
<cffunction name="Tomorrow" returntype="date">
  <cfreturn DateAdd("d", 1, Now())>
</cffunction>
```

`Tomorrow()` returns tomorrow's date (calculated by adding `1` day to today's date). The function is named using `<cffunction>`, and a return data type is defined. `<cfreturn>` returns the result.

Processing Arguments

Functions can accept arguments (parameters). When creating UDFs, you should use `<CFARGUMENT>` tags to enumerate every argument. Each argument should be named, and its type should be specified, so that ColdFusion can validate passed values automatically. In addition, if needed, arguments can be flagged as required—again, so that ColdFusion can perform automatic validation.

Here is an example:

```
<cffunction name="Cube" returntype="numeric">
  <cfargument name="num"
              type="numeric"
              required="yes">
  <cfreturn num*num*num>
</cffunction>
```

`Cube()` returns the cube of a passed number. It takes a required argument (the number to be cubed) and returns the cube value.

`<cfargument>` takes an optional `default` value to be used if an argument is not specified. An example of this follows in the next section.

Local Variables

Within UDFs, it may be necessary to create variables for data storage. It is legal to do the following within a UDF:

```
<cfset x=1>
```

The above code works, but the variable that it creates will be in the calling page, not local to the UDF. So, if a variable named `x` already existed, the above code would overwrite it.

To create local variables (that is, local to the UDF), use the `VAR` prefix like this:

```
<cfset var x=1>
```

This way, references to `x` will refer to the local `x`, not the `x` in the caller code.

> **NOTE**
> To access variables in the caller code, use the `VARIABLES` prefix. Failure to do so will cause the local variable to be used (if it exists).

Here is a complete example:

```
<!--- Is the browser IE? --->
<cffunction name="IsIE" returntype="boolean">
  <!--- If no browser id passed, use current --->
  <cfargument name="browser"
              default="#CGI.HTTP_USER_AGENT#">

  <!--- Init variable --->
  <cfset var result="No">

  <!--- Look for IE identifier --->
  <cfif FindNoCase("MSIE", browser)>
    <!--- Yep, got it --->
    <cfset result="Yes">
  </cfif>

  <!--- Return result --->
  <cfreturn result>

</cffunction>
```

`IsIE()` checks to see whether a specified browser is Microsoft Internet Explorer. It takes a browser ID string as a parameter, defaulting to the current browser by inspecting `CGI.HTTP_USER_AGENT`. A local variable named `result` is created (the `VAR` keyword ensures that it is local to the UDF) and is initialized to `"no"`. If the text `MSIE` is found in the browser ID, `result` is set to `"yes"`, then `result` is returned.

> **NOTE**
>
> Incidentally, to create an `IsMozilla()` function like the `IsIE()` used here, just modify the `<cfif>` to check the following:
>
> ```
> <cfif FindNoCase("mozilla", browser)
>       and not FindNoCase("MSIE", browser)>
> ```

<cfscript>-Based UDFs

`<cfscript>`-based UDFs are defined using the `function` keyword; return values are specified using `return`.

➜ `<cfscript>` was reviewed in Chapter 21, "Scripting."

Creating UDFs

UDFs are created using `function` within a `<cfscript>` block. Here is the `<cfscript>` equivalent of the `Tomorrow()` function seen previously:

```
<cfscript>
function Tomorrow()
{
 return DateAdd("d", 1, Now());
}
</cfscript>
```

Again, `Tomorrow()` returns tomorrow's date (calculated by adding `1` day to today's date). The function is named using scripting syntax, just as it would be done in JavaScript, and the return value is specified using `return`.

Processing Arguments

`<CFSCRIPT>`-based UDFs can also accept arguments, but with a very important limitation. When you create UDFs in `<cfscript>`, arguments are enumerated in the function definition. But there is no way to specify a data type—regardless of whether the argument is required—or specify the default values if needed. You'll need to do that processing yourself. Here is the `Cube()` example in `<cfscript>`:

```
<cfscript>
function Cube(num)
{
 // return the cube
 return num*num*num;
}
</cfscript>
```

`Cube()` returns the cube of a passed number. From a required argument (the number to be cubed) it returns the cube value. What makes the argument required is the fact that it is enumerated in the function declaration. In `<cfscript>`-based UDFs, all listed arguments are required.

Local Variables

Local variables can be created in `<cfscript>`-based UDFs too. To create a local variable, simply place `var` in front of the variable definition, like this:

```
var result="no";
```

Using UDFs

You can use a UDF in all the same places you'd use a built-in function. The following code displays today's and tomorrow's dates using a mixture of built-in functions and UDFs (the function we created previously):

```
<cfoutput>
Today is: #DateFormat(Now())#<br>
Tomorrow is: #DateFormat(Tomorrow())#<br>
</cfoutput>
```

Advanced UDF Use

The basic UDF syntax and use described thus far is typical of most UDFs that will be created. ColdFusion also supports some advanced UDF features that are worth reviewing.

Variable Parameter Lists

UDFs can access arguments that are not explicitly named. This is primarily of value in `<cfscript>`-based UDFs, as it is the only way to support optional arguments, but it can be used in tag-based UDFs too.

All UDF arguments, regardless of whether they are enumerated explicitly, are stored in an array named `arguments`. As such, `arguments[1]` always refers to the first passed argument, `arguments[2]` to the second, and so on.

An example of using arguments this way is to create a `<cfscript>`-based UDF that adds specified values. Consider the following UDF:

```
<cfscript>
function Sum()
{
 return ArraySum(arguments);
}
</cfscript>
```

`Sum()` simply returns the sum of any values in the `arguments` array using the `ArraySum()` function. To add two numbers, you could use the following:

```
<cfoutput>
#Sum(2, 3)#
</cfoutput>
```

But because the UDF is not explicitly expecting two arguments, the following two calls will also work:

```
<cfoutput>
#Sum(2)#
#Sum(2, 3, 4, 7)#
</cfoutput>
```

Scoping UDFs

UDFs are visible only when they are defined inside the calling page or included with `<cfinclude>`. You can, however, place UDFs within shared-scoped variables. After the UDF definition, you can copy the UDF into a shared scope simply by using the scope prefix:

```
<cfscript>
function functionName()
{
... function definition ...
}
</cfscript>

<cfset REQUEST.functionName=functionName>
```

In this example, the function is put into the `REQUEST` scope. This means that any custom tags within the calling page will also have access to this UDF.

You also can create UDFs by using other shared scopes, such as `SERVER` and `APPLICATION`, if needed.

UDFs as Parameters

Because UDFs can be stored in variables, they also can be passed as parameters. This is used primarily in the creation of callback functions, where the name of a function is passed to a second function so that the first may make calls to the second when needed.

To pass a UDF as a parameter, simply specify its name (without parentheses) like this:

```
#BuildMenu(menu, MenuFormat)#
```

Here, `BuildMenu()` is a UDF, `menu` is menu text to be processed, and `MenuFormat` is a second UDF that is being passed to `BuildMenu()`.

Code that is expecting UDFs as parameters can use the following two functions to check that they are what is expected:

- `IsCustomFunction()` checks whether a specified function is actually a UDF.
- `GetMetaData()` returns details about a function (the parameters it is defined to expect, what it returns, and so on) and can be used to check that a passed function is defined as intended.

Organizing UDFs

You can define a function in the following places:

- On the page where it is called, as long as it's declared before it's used
- On a page where the UDF is included by using a `<cfinclude>` tag

Creating a function within one application page might be useful if you want the code to be organized and readable. It is accessible only from the page on which it is declared, and it must be declared before it is used.

You can create many functions within one CFML page. Therefore, you can create a library of functions that can be used throughout an application or within a subset of application pages. It is useful to group commonly used functions into separate files to be included when needed.

Summary

The ability to create user-defined functions is an important part of any programming language, and CFML provides two ways to create UDFs. Tag-based UDFs are more powerful than `<cfscript>`-based UDFs, and they do more of the work for you by, for example, simplifying data validation. `<cfscript>`-based UDFs are advantageous when porting function code between languages. UDFs may process required and optional arguments, may be stored in scopes, and may even be passed as parameters to other functions.

Sample Questions

1. Which of the following arrays contains information passed into a UDF?

   A. `Attributes`

   B. `Arguments`

   C. `Parameters`

   D. `Var`

2. Which of the following keywords creates protected variables within a UDF?

   A. `var`

   B. `set`

   C. `return`

   D. `variable`

3. What are the advantages of tag-based UDFs over `<cfscript>`-based UDFs? *(select two)*

   A. Execution speed

   B. Automatic argument and type checking

   C. Ability to be used as tag attributes

   D. Ability to access any CFML language elements

   E. Ability to be passed as a parameter to another UDF

CHAPTER 31

ColdFusion Components

IN THIS CHAPTER

Understanding ColdFusion Components

ColdFusion Components are essential building blocks used in creating tiered, structured, and scalable applications. ColdFusion Components combine the power of objects with the simplicity of CFML.

Unlike Custom Tags, which are primarily used to encapsulate processing, and UI abstractions, ColdFusion Components are designed to black-box processing, transactions, back-end integration, and the like.

Code within ColdFusion Components can call any other CFML tags and functions, and has complete access to databases, external systems, Internet protocols, underlying Java, transactions, and more.

Creating ColdFusion Components

ColdFusion Components (often referred to as CFCs) are plain text files, just like any other ColdFusion files. They may be created manually or by using the interactive screens in Dreamweaver MX.

File Naming

ColdFusion Components are special files and are named using an extension of `.cfc`. This extension distinguishes ColdFusion Components from other ColdFusion files (which have a `.cfm` extension).

File Location

Unlike Custom Tags, which have a specific storage location on the server, CFCs can be in any directory under the Web root. CFCs that are used throughout an application can be stored in directories designated for just that purpose; more focused or specific CFCs can be stored in the directory in which they are to be used.

➜ Custom Tags were covered in Chapter 28, "Custom Tags," and Chapter 29, "Advanced Custom Tags."

CFC Tags

CFCs are created using a series of CFML tags as described below.

> **NOTE**
> ColdFusion Components are created using the same tags used to create User Defined Functions.

The `<cfcomponent>` Tag

ColdFusion Components are defined using a pair of `<cfcomponent>` tags. `<cfcomponent>` must be the first tag in a `.cfc` file, and `</cfcomponent>` must be the last. All component code must be placed in between those tags, like this:

```
<cfcomponent>
 ...
</cfcomponent>
```

`<cfcomponent>` supports the use of two optional attributes, as listed in Table 31.1:

Table 31.1 `<cfcomponent>` Attributes

ATTRIBUTE	DESCRIPTION
`extends`	Specifies the name of a component to be inherited (reviewed later in this chapter).
`output`	Turns on or off output display: if `yes`, component output is permitted; if `no`, then it is not.

> **TIP**
> As a general rule, CFCs should never generate output, so `output="no"` is recommended.

The <cffunction> Tag

Within the <cfcomponent> and </cfcomponent> tags, the individual functions are defined using pairs of <cffunction> tags. A CFC must contain one or more functions. Functions are declared like this:

```
<cfcomponent>
 <cffunction name="Get">
 ...
 </cffunction>
 <cffunction name="Set">
 ...
 </cffunction>
</cfcomponent>
```

Every function must be named using a name attribute, as seen in the above code snippet. <cffunction> attributes are shown in Table 31.2:

Table 31.2 <cffunction> Attributes

ATTRIBUTE	DESCRIPTION
access	The access level, used to control access based on the origin of a request (as described later in this chapter). Valid values are package, private, public, and remote.
name	The function name, which must be unique within the CFC.
output	Turns on or off output display: if yes, function output is permitted; if no, then it is not.
returntype	The data type returned by the function; it must be one of the types listed below (default is any).
roles	List of roles that can invoke this function (described later in this chapter).

CFC functions usually return results. The data type of the result can be specified in the returntype attribute, and must be one of the following values:

- any
- array
- binary
- boolean
- date
- guid
- numeric
- query

- `string`
- `struct`
- `uuid`
- `variableName`
- `void`
- `xml`
- a component name

TIP

It is recommended that the `returntype` always be specified.

NOTE

CFC functions are sometimes referred to as "methods."

The `<cfargument>` Tag

CFC functions can accept parameters (or arguments). Each function parameter is defined using a `<cfargument>` tag, like this:

```
<cfcomponent>
  <cffunction name="Get">
  <cfargument name="id">
  ...
  </cffunction>
</cfcomponent>
```

Every argument must be named using a `name` attribute, as seen in the above code snippet. The complete list of `<cfargument>` attributes is shown in Table 31.3:

Table 31.3 `<cfargument>` Attributes

ATTRIBUTE	DESCRIPTION
`default`	The default value, used if argument is not specified.
`name`	The required argument name, must be unique within the function.
`required`	Flag indicating whether or not an argument is required.
`type`	Optional argument data type, used to perform type validation. It must be one of the types listed below.

Arguments can accept any type of data, but to perform data validation, `type` may be used to specify one of the following data types:

- `any`
- `array`
- `binary`
- `boolean`
- `date`
- `guid`
- `numeric`
- `query`
- `string`
- `struct`
- `uuid`
- `variableName`
- `xml`
- a component name

> **TIP**
>
> It is recommended that the `type` always be specified.

Within CFC code, arguments are accessed by their names (with or without a prefix), so the argument specified in the code snippet above could be accessed as `#id#` or `#ARGUMENTS.id#`. In addition, `ARGUMENTS` can be accessed as an array, so `id` (being the first argument) can be accessed as `#arguments[1]#`.

Arguments must be specified before any function processing. If `<cfargument>` is used after any other tag, an error will be thrown.

> **NOTE**
>
> The order of `<cfargument>` tags is unimportant if CFCs are invoked using tags. But if they are invoked using functions, or as Web Services, then order is very important. As such, order arguments appropriately (required ones first, group related arguments) to ensure that your CFC will be usable in as many scenarios as possible.

The <cfreturn> Tag

CFC functions return data via the <cfreturn> tag. <cfreturn> takes the value to be returned as an attribute, as seen here:

```
<cfcomponent>
  <cffunction name="Get">
   <cfargument name="id">
   <cfset result="">
   ...
   <cfreturn result>
  </cffunction>
</cfcomponent>
```

Generally each function should have a single <cfreturn> (just one exit point),and it should be the last line of code in the function.

> **TIP**
>
> Functions can return a single result only; to return multiple values, use a complex data type (like a structure or an array or a query).

Invoking ColdFusion Components

ColdFusion Components may be invoked in several different ways: using tags, functions, or URLs. The syntax for each is obviously different, but all forms of invocation expose the same functionality.

When CFCs are used, they are referred to by the paths to them. Paths are specified using dot notation, as seen here:

```
users.user
```

The above refers to a `user.cfc` in the `users` directory under the Web root.

> **NOTE**
>
> If no path is specified, than the invocation will refer to a `.cfc` file in the current directory.

Using <cfinvoke>

The <cfinvoke> tag is used to invoke a CFC and execute a specific method. The `COMPONENT` may be the path to a CFC or a previously instantiated object (see "Using <cfobject>" below). <cfinvoke> requires that the `component` be specified as an argument, as seen here:

```
<cfinvoke component="user"
          method="Get"
          id="#id#"
          returnvariable="user_id">
```

In this example a component named `user.cfc` (in the current directory, as no path is provided) is being loaded, and the `Get` method (function) is being invoked. An argument named `id` is being passed, as is the optional name of the variable to contain the return value.

Arguments may also be passed using the `<cfinvokeargument>` tag. The following snippet is functionally equivalent to the previous example:

```
<cfinvoke component="user"
          method="Get"
          returnvariable="user_id">
  <cfinvokeargument name="id"
                    value="#id#">
</cfinvoke>
```

Another way to pass arguments to a CFC method is to create a structure containing `name=value` pairs (one per argument), and then pass that structure to the `<cfinvoke>` `argumentcollection` attribute, as seen here:

```
<!--- Create arguments structure --->
<cfset args=StructNew()>
<!--- Populate it --->
<cfset args.id=id>
<!--- Invoke CFC method --->
<cfinvoke component="user"
          method="Get"
          argumentcollection="#args#"
          returnvariable="user_id">
```

Functionally, all three forms of `<cfinvoke>` accomplish the exact same thing, but the choice of which to use is up to you.

> **TIP**
>
> One benefit of using `<cfinvokeargument>` or `argumentcollection` is that those syntaxes are better suited for programmatically or conditionally appending arguments.

Using `<cfobject>`

CFCs can be used as objects. Doing so requires that CFC be instantiated as an object, using the `<cfobject>` tag. The following example demonstrates this technique:

```
<!--- Load CFC as an object --->
<cfobject component="user"
          name="userObj">
<!--- Invoke method --->
<cfinvoke component="#userObj#"
          method="Get"
          id="#id#"
          returnvariable="user_id">
```

As seen here, `<cfobject>` loads a CFC as an object, and then `<cfinvoke>` can be used to invoke methods within that object. There are several important advantages to this form of invocation:

- Multiple methods in a CFC can be invoked without reloading the component.
- Data can persist in a component between method invocations.
- Components can be loaded into specific scopes (described later in this chapter).

Once loaded, CFCs can be used in any expressions. For example, as seen here:

```
<cfoutput>
#userObj.Display(100)#
</cfoutput>
```

Using CreateObject()

`CreateObject()` is a functional equivalent of the `<cfobject>` tag. `CreateObject()` can be used to instantiate CFCs just like `<cfobject>` can, but there is one notable difference: As a function, `CreateObject()` can be used in a `<cfscript>` block (whereas `<cfobject>` cannot).

The following snippet is the `CreateObject()` version of the previous example:

```
<cfscript>
// Load CFC as an object
userObj=CreateObject("component", "user");
// Invoke method
user_id=userObj.Get(id);
</cfscript>
```

`CreateObject()` supports several object types, and so the first argument must specify the type (here it is `"component"`). `CreateObject()` returns an instance of an object that can then be used to invoke methods.

➜ `<cfscript>` was reviewed in Chapter 21, "Scripting."

This form of CFC invocation will be most useful to developers who have worked with objects in other languages, as the syntax will be familiar to them.

URL Invocation

CFCs can also be invoked on the command line directly; every CFC has a URL that points to it. When invoking CFCs via URLs, the method and any arguments are passed as URL parameters, as seen here:

```
http://localhost/users/user.cfc?method=get&id=1
```

This form of invocation is used by both Web Services and Flash Remoting.

➔ Web Services are covered in Chapter 32, "Web Services." Flash Remoting is covered in Chapter 36, "Flash Remoting."

Advanced ColdFusion Component Use

In addition to the basic functionality reviewed thus far, advanced CFC features are also available.

Scopes

All the invocation examples reviewed thus far instantiate CFCs without specifying a scope. In other words, they used the default `VARIABLES` scope (just as `<cfset>` would if no scope is specified). CFCs can also be loaded into these other scopes so as to make them persist:

- `REQUEST`
- `SESSION`
- `APPLICATION`
- `SERVER`

> **NOTE**
> CFCs cannot be loaded into the `CLIENT` scope, as `CLIENT` does not support complex data types.

The advantages of persistent CFCs are that they need not be reloaded, and that they can contain data and state within themselves that persists in between requests.

Loading a CFC into a shared scope requires that it be loaded as an object (using `<cfobject>` or `CreateObject()` as reviewed above). The example below uses `<cfobject>` to load a CFC into a users `SESSION` scope:

```
<!--- Load CFC as an object --->
<cfobject component="user"
          name="SESSION.userObj">
<!--- Invoke method --->
<cfinvoke component="#SESSION.userObj#"
          method="Get"
          id="#id#"
          returnvariable="user_id">
```

Using code like this, each user (each `SESSION`) can have its own instance of a component.

> **TIP**
> Generally CFCs should not access specific scopes (like `SESSION`). Rather, the CFC itself should be instantiated in a scope whenever possible.

The THIS Scope

Within a CFC there is a special scope named `THIS`. `THIS` persists for as long as the CFC persists—if loaded as an object, then `THIS` will persist for as long as the object persists; if loaded with a simple `<cfinvoke>`, then `THIS` will persist for a single request only.

To set a variable in THIS, simply use the THIS prefix:

```
<cfset THIS.user=StructNew()>
<cfset THIS.user.NameFirst="Ben">
<cfset THIS.user.NameLast="Forta">
```

`THIS` is automatically available to all functions in a component, so a data set in one function (or in the constructor, as seen below) can be accessed in other functions.

> **NOTE**
>
> Each instance of a CFC has its own `THIS` scope, so if a CFC is loaded into a users `SESSION`, each user will have a separate `THIS`.

The VARIABLES Scope

CFML is not an object-oriented language, but CFCs do share traits with objects, and do support some object-type features. But unlike objects in typical object oriented languages, `THIS` within the CFC is not private. That is to say that code that instantiates a CFC as an object can access CFC `THIS` scope members.

To keep CFC internal data private, use the `VARIABLES` scope inside of the CFC instead of `THIS`.

Constructors

In object-oriented development, constructors are specials functions that are automatically executed when an object is instantiated. Constructors are often used for initialization, validation, and error-checking. In CFCs, constructors are supported as follows: any code within a `<cfcomponent>` but not within a `<cffunction>`, is constructor code. Consider the following example:

```
<cfcomponent>
  <cfset THIS.user=StructNew()>

  <cffunction name="Get">
    <cfargument name="id">
    <cfset result="">
    ...
    <cfreturn result>
  </cffunction>
</cfcomponent>
```

The above snippet is a CFC with a single method named `Get`. The `<cfset>` statement (second line) is constructor code, which will be executed automatically when the CFC is instantiated. So when will the constructor code be executed? That depends:

- If a `<cfinvoke>` is used to load and invoke a method, then the constructor will be executed before the method code is executed.
- If `<cfobject>` (or `CreateObject()`) is used to load the CFC as an object, then the constructor code is executed at instantiation time, before any method is invoked.

Constructor code may be used to store data in `THIS` or `VARIABLES`, which makes it available to all CFC methods.

> **NOTE**
> *Destructors* are not supported by CFCs.

Inheritance

Inheritance is another object oriented feature that has made its way into CFML. Inheritance allows code to be reused by basing a CFC on another CFC. For example, the `user.cfc` snippet used throughout this chapter contains methods for interacting with users. If an additional CFC was needed for a special class of user, an administrator, the new CFC could be based on the old one by simply using the following syntax:

```
<!--- admin.cfc file --->
<cfcomponent extends="user">
...
</cfcomponent>
```

Using the above syntax, the methods and functionality defined in `user.cfc` would also be available to `admin.cfc` (but not vice-versa). This way the base CFC can be extended.

A single CFC can be extended multiple times (multiple CFCs can extend it). In addition, nested inheritance is supported—so the `admin.cfc` created above could be extended (another CFC could extend it).

> **NOTE**
> Multiple inheritance is not supported.

Securing ColdFusion Components

By default, ColdFusion Components are as secure as any other ColdFusion files—they can be accessed only by ColdFusion, only locally (not by remote servers), and also to all application users (assuming the application is written to allow that). However, it is possible to control access to CFC methods in two ways: by *where* the request is coming from, and by *who* the request is coming from.

> **NOTE**
> CFCs are protected at the method level (each `<cffunction>` individually), not at the CFC level.

Controlling Access

The `<cffunction>` `access` attribute defines the access level for a method. Valid access levels are listed in Table 31.4:

Table 31.4 Method `access` Levels

LEVEL	DESCRIPTION
`package`	Available to other methods within the CFC, as well as any code in the same directory.
`private`	Available only within the CFC itself.
`public`	Available to the entire ColdFusion server.
`remote`	Available locally and externally (other hosts and servers).

If unauthorized access is attempted, an error will be thrown.

The default `access` level is `public`. To allow CFCs to be accessed remotely (as Web Services or via Flash Remoting), `access="remote"` must be specified.

Using `access` it is possible to restrict or grant access to specific methods based on where the request is coming from.

User Security

In addition to securing methods based on the point of origin of a request, it is also possible to grant or deny access based on who the current user is logged in as. The `<cffunction>` `roles` attribute takes a comma-delimited list (either hard-coded or a variable) that contains the roles that a request must already have been authenticated as so as to gain access.

The security and `ROLES` are based on the security framework exposed via `<CFLOGIN>` and related tags. If unauthorized access is attempted an error will be thrown.

→ See Chapter 27, "Application Security," for details on the security framework and <cflogin>.

Using `roles` it is possible to restrict or grant access to specific methods based on who the requester has been authenticated as.

Documenting ColdFusion Components

ColdFusion Components can be "introspected," meaning that they can be instructed to describe themselves. This documentation is made available in three ways:

- Formatted HTML documentation access by invoking the CFC via a URL, with no passed parameters (no query string)
- From within Dreamweaver MX
- Via WSDL (described in Chapter 32, "Web Services")

Via the tags used to create CFCs, ColdFusion can document method names, return code, arguments, inheritance, and more. All this is done automatically by ColdFusion, with no extra work from the developer.

However, to better document CFCs, ColdFusion allows developers to embed documentation information directly within CFCs. This documentation is ignored during regular processing, and is only used when documentation is generated. Additional documentation is specified using the optional `hint` attribute in the `<cfcomponent>`, `<cffunction>`, and `<cfargument>` tags.

The following snippet demonstrates the use of `hint`:

```
<cfcomponent hint="All sorts of user processing">
  <cffunction name="Get"
              hint="Get user details">
    <cfargument name="id"
                hint="User ID">
    <cfset result="">
    ...
    <cfreturn result>
  </cffunction>
</cfcomponent>
```

> **TIP**
>
> It's a good idea to use `hint` for every tag to improve the quality of your documentation. The extra effort is well worth it.

Summary

ColdFusion Components are object-type building blocks used to create reusable, scalable, tiered, and structured code. CFCs are created using a set of special tags and are saved in `.cfc` files. CFCs may be invoked in several ways: invoking them as objects allows them to be loaded into persistent scopes. CFCs support inheritance and constructors, and they have an internal scope that persists as long as the CFC persists. CFCs can be secured on a per-method basis, and they can self-document and be introspected.

Sample Questions

1. What are valid reasons to use CFCs? *(select three)*

   A. Reuse

   B. Access to underlying Java

   C. Tiered development

   D. Accessible outside of ColdFusion

   E. Error handling

2. What is wrong with the following code?

   ```
   <cfobject component="emps" name="empObj">
   <cfinvoke component="empObj" method="Get">
   ```

   A. Missing path in `<cfobject>`

   B. `component` in `<cfinvoke>` is not a valid object

   C. `<cfobject>` is missing a `method` attribute

   D. Missing `returnvariable` attribute

3. Which of the following `<cffunction>` arguments is required?

   A. `access`

   B. `name`

   C. `output`

   D. `returntype`

4. Which `<cffunction>` argument is used to enable methods to be accessed outside of local ColdFusion?

   A. `access`

   B. `name`

   C. `output`

   D. `roles`

5. Using `<cfobject>` or `CreateObject()`, which scopes can components be instantiated in? *(select four)*

   A. `CLIENT`

   B. `COOKIE`

   C. `REQUEST`

   D. `SERVER`

   E. `SESSION`

   F. `URL`

   G. `VARIABLES`

CHAPTER 32
Web Services

IN THIS CHAPTER

Understanding Web Services

Web Services is the term used to describe a set of technologies that facilitate distributed computing. Using Web Services, it is possible to create applications that invoke remote code —optionally passing structured data and obtaining results back.

Web Services are gaining popularity because:

- They are supported by all major industry hardware and software vendors.
- They are built on readily available open and nonproprietary technologies.
- They are highly portable, allowing applications to be shared despite differences in hardware, platforms, and operating systems.
- The technology is inexpensive.

ColdFusion fully supports Web Services—both consuming (using) Web Services hosted locally or elsewhere and creating Web Services for use by other servers and applications.

The Technology

Web Services are built on top of several important technologies and protocols:

- XML
- HTTP
- SOAP (Simple Object Access Protocol)
- UDDI (Universal Description, Discovery, and Integration)

WSDL

Web Services are documented via an XML format named WSDL (Web Services Description Language). Every Web Service has a corresponding WSDL that describes what methods the Web Service exposes, what arguments those methods expect, what they return, the URL to each, and so on.

Consuming Web Services requires the URL to the Web Service WSDL, as well as knowledge about the Web Services' methods (information gleaned from the WSDL).

Creating Web Services requires that a WSDL document be created to describe the Web Service, and that the URL to it is made available.

Consuming Web Services

ColdFusion consumes Web Services via the `<cfinvoke>` tag (the same tag used to invoke ColdFusion Components). When invoking Web Services, the `webservice` attribute is used (instead of the `COMPONENT` attribute—the two are mutually exclusive).

➜ `<cfinvoke>` and ColdFusion Components were reviewed in Chapter 31, "ColdFusion Components."

The following complete application demonstrates the consumption of a Web Service. It displays a form prompting for text (in English) and a target language, and then translates that text via the BableFish Web Service and displays the translation:

```
<!--- Was a form submitted? --->
<cfif IsDefined("FORM.string")>

  <!--- Yes, invoke service --->
  <cfinvoke webservice="
http://www.xmethods.com/sd/BabelFishService.wsdl"
            method="babelFish"
            returnvariable="aString">
    <cfinvokeargument name="translationmode"
                      value="#FORM.lang#"/>
    <cfinvokeargument name="sourcedata"
                      value="#FORM.string#"/>
  </cfinvoke>

  <!--- Display results --->
  <cfoutput>
  <strong>Text:</strong> #FORM.string#<br>
  <strong>Translation:</strong> #astring#<P>
  </cfoutput>

</cfif>

<!--- Form --->
<cfoutput>
```

```
Enter some text and select the language
you'd like it translated into.<P>
<form action="#CGI.SCRIPT_NAME#"
       method="post">
Text: <input type="text" name="string">
<select name="lang">
  <option value="en_fr">French</option>
  <option value="en_es">Spanish</option>
  <option value="en_de">German</option>
  <option value="en_it">Italian</option>
  <option value="en_pt">Portuguese</option>
</select>
<br>
<input type="submit" value="Translate">
</form>
</cfoutput>
```

This code is both a form and its action, and so the form submits to itself (using `CGI.SCRIPT_NAME` as the `action`). The form submits two fields: `string` is the string to be translated and `lang` is the target language. A `<cfif>` statement checks to see if a form has been submitted (it would not have been on the first call); if it has, `<cfinvoke>` is used to invoke the translation Web Service. The `webservice` itself is identified by the URL to its WSDL; the `method` specifies the Web Service method to be invoked; and `returnvariable` is the name of the variable that contains the result. The two parameters are passed to `<cfinvokeargument>` tags (although they could have just as easily been `name=value` pairs in the `<cfinvoke>` itself).

If the text `Hello, my name is Ben` is entered, and the target language is French, the output would be `bonjour, mon nom est Ben`.

ColdFusion handles any conversion between data types automatically. Web Services may return text, numbers, arrays, structures, and more, and ColdFusion automatically converts the results to native data types that can be used just like any other ColdFusion variables.

NOTE

All SOAP and XML processing is handled internally by ColdFusion, so there is no need to interact with Web Services' SOAP and XML directly.

TIP

As easy as ColdFusion makes using Web Services, Dreamweaver makes it even easier. Dreamweaver can process WSDL content natively so as to construct a tree-control- type menu of available methods. By specifying the URL to the WSDL in the Application panel's Component tab, Dreamweaver will display Web Service details and allow Web Service invocation by simply dragging methods into your code.

Proxy Server Considerations

As should be apparent from the example, ColdFusion connects to remote servers to invoke Web Service methods. If a proxy server is used you must provide relevant information to `<cfinvoke>` (using the `proxyserver`, `proxyport`, `proxyuser`, and `proxypassword` attributes).

Working With SOAP Headers

ColdFusion deliberately conceals the inner workings of SOAP so as to simply Web Service invocation. However, when greater control is needed, the following functions may be used:

- `AddSOAPRequestHeader()` adds headers to a SOAP request before the request is made.
- `GetSOAPResponseHeader()` provides access to SOAP headers after the request is processed.

These functions cannot be used if simple `<cfinvoke>` invocation is used, and require an object type invocation via `<cfobject>` or `CreateObject()`.

Creating Web Services

In addition to supporting the consumption of Web Services, ColdFusion also allows developers to create their own Web Services for consumption by ColdFusion, .NET, Java, and more. Web Services are created using ColdFusion Components.

➜ ColdFusion Components were reviewed in Chapter 31, "ColdFusion Components."

ColdFusion Components are automatically ready to be used as Web Services, but for security reasons code is not accessible as a Web Service unless specifically enabled. To make a CFC method accessible as a Web Service, simply set `access="remote"`, as seen here:

```
<!--- User component --->
<cfcomponent>

  <!--- List users method --->
  <cffunction name="List"
              access="remote"
              returntype="query">

    <!--- Get users --->
    <cfquery name="users"
             datasource="exampleapps">
    SELECT EmployeeID AS UserID, FirstName, LastName
```

```
    FROM tblEmployees
    ORDER BY LastName, FirstName
    </cfquery>

    <cfreturn users>
   </cffunction>

</cfcomponent>
```

The List method in this component returns a query (obtained by using a `<cfquery>` tag), and because `access="remote"`, the method will be accessible as a Web Service.

> **NOTE**
>
> The `<cffunction> returntype` attribute is optional in ColdFusion Components, but it is required if the method is used as a Web Service.

ColdFusion also automatically generates the required WSDL on demand. The WSDL URL for any ColdFusion Component is the URL to the CFC appended with `?wsdl`. For example, the WSDL for the ColdFusion Tip-of-the-Day Web Service at www.forta.com is:

```
http://www.forta.com/cf/tips/syndicate.cfc?wsdl
```

> **TIP**
>
> ColdFusion Components can be invoked as CFCs or as Web Services, but for performance reasons, CFC invocation is preferred.

Working With SOAP Headers

Within CFCs, the following functions may be used to access SOAP headers (that is, headers within a received request):

- `AddSOAPResponseHeader()` adds headers to a SOAP response before it is returned.
- `GetSOAPRequest()` provides access to the complete SOAP request.
- `GetSOAPRequestHeader()` provides access to received SOAP headers.
- `IsSOAPRequest()` can be used to determine whether or not a CFC method was invoked as a Web Services method (as opposed to a direct CFC invocation or a Flash Remoting invocation).

Summary

Web Services facilitate the creation and use of distributed applications. ColdFusion can consume Web Services via the `<cfinvoke>` tag, and Web Services can be created using ColdFusion Components.

Sample Questions

1. Which protocols are Web Services built on? *(select two)*

   A. MIME

   B. POP

   C. SOAP

   D. XML

   E. LDAP

   F. RSS

2. Which tag is used to invoke Web Services?

   A. `<cfhttp>`

   B. `<cfinvoke>`

   C. `<cfobject>`

   D. `<cfxml>`

3. Which `<cffunction>` attributes are required for a function to be accessible as a Web Service? *(select three)*

   A. `access`

   B. `name`

   C. `output`

   D. `returntype`

   E. `roles`

CHAPTER 33
Java, COM, & CORBA

IN THIS CHAPTER

Extending CF with Other Technologies

ColdFusion comes with built-in support for integration with databases, email systems, Internet protocols, and more. In addition, ColdFusion can be extended using Custom Tags, User-Defined Functions (UDFs), and ColdFusion Components.

→ Custom Tags were reviewed in Chapters 28 and 29, UDFs in Chapter 30, and CFCs in Chapter 31.

Custom Tags, UDFs, and CFCs are used to encapsulate and reuse ColdFusion functionality. For most applications this is all the extensibility ever needed, but occasionally it may be necessary to interact with external systems, and so ColdFusion provides several ways to accomplish this:

- Access to Java
- Access to COM
- Access to CORBA
- Ability to write CFX extensions in Java and C++

Using Java

ColdFusion runs on underlying Java technology, and so support for Java is native to ColdFusion. ColdFusion allows access to Java objects, APIs, EJBs, and more, and also provides special support for JSP Tag Libraries.

Using Java Objects

Java objects, API, beans, and EJBs, are all accessed via the `<cfobject>` tag. In this example the ColdFusion internal Java factory object is used to obtain a list of defined datasources:

```
<!--- Get "factory" --->
<cfobject action="CREATE"
          type="JAVA"
          class="coldfusion.server.ServiceFactory"
          name="factory">
<!--- Get datasource service --->
<cfset dsService=factory.getDataSourceService()>
<!--- Get data sources --->
<cfset dsFull=dsService.getDatasources()>
<!--- Extract names into an array --->
<cfset dsNames=StructKeyArray(dsFull)>

<!--- List names --->
<ul>
<cfloop index="i" from="1" TO="#ArrayLen(dsNames)#">
  <cfoutput>
  <li>#dsNames[i]#</li>
  </cfoutput>
</cfloop>
</ul>
```

The function equivalent to `<cfobject>`, `CreateObject()`, can also be used to invoke Java objects.

Using JSP Tag Libraries

JSP (Java Server Pages) features the ability to create reusable tags (similar to Custom Tags in ColdFusion. JSP Tag Libraries are accessible from within CFML code by importing the Tag Libraries using `<cfimport>`, as seen here:

```
<!--- Load JSP tag library --->
<cfimport taglib="/WEB-INF/lib/davisor2d.jar"
 prefix="2d">

<!--- Create image --->
<2d:imageSubmit bgPaint="image-images/#image#"
                text="#text#"
                textAlign="#align#"
                paint="#textcolor#"
                vpadding="#padding#"
                hpadding="#padding#"
                fontface="#fontface#"
                font="#fontsize#"
                scope="session" />
```

This example imports a graphics Tag Library and invokes a method named `imageSubmit`, which builds an image based on passed text, colors, font information, and more.

`<cfimport>` takes the Tag Library to load as the `taglib` value, and loads the Tag Library into a namespace specified by `prefix`. The namespace is then used to invoke specific methods, as in `2d:imageSubmit`, which invokes the `imageSubmit` method in the `2d` namespace.

Casting Variables

ColdFusion is a typeless language, and Java is hard-typed. Therefore, you might need to cast ColdFusion's string variable into a hard-typed Java variable. One reason for this would be for calling an overloaded method because its arguments can take more than one data type.

To cast a ColdFusion variable into a Java variable, you use the `JavaCast()` function, which takes two arguments:

- `type` is the data type to which to convert the ColdFusion variable, before passing it to the Java method. The data types are `boolean`, `double`, `float`, `int`, `long`, `null`, and `string`.
- `variable` is a ColdFusion variable that holds a scalar or string type (must be `""` if `type` is `null`).

This function should be used only for scalar and string arguments.

You use this function inside the `<cfobject>` tag before you call the Java method to which you want to pass the value. If the method takes more than one overloaded argument, then you must call `JavaCast()` for each overloaded argument.

You cannot use `JavaCast()` to cast between complex objects or to cast to a superclass. You should use the result of this function only on calls to Java objects. Because there is no one-to-one correspondence between internally stored ColdFusion types and Java scalar types, some conversions cannot be performed.

Using COM

The Component Object Model (COM) is a Microsoft specification that enables you to implement component modules in a program. COM objects can be written in many languages; as long as each language understands COM, it can understand any COM object, even if it is written in another language.

The fact that COM objects can be written in many languages gives them an immediate advantage over the CFX custom tags. Whereas CFX custom tags are written specifically for use in the ColdFusion environment, COM objects can be used across many applications.

> **NOTE**
> COM is only supported on Windows platforms.

> **TIP**
>
> Before you call a COM object from within ColdFusion code, you must first register it with the system. Most objects come with instructions on how to do this.

To call a COM object in ColdFusion, type the following:

```
<cfobject type="COM"
          class="Macromedia.Comex.1"
          name="objCompany"
          action="Create">
```

This example creates a `Company` object and then populates it with properties such as the following:

```
<cfset objCompany.company_name="Macromedia">
<cfset objCompany.for_profit="1">
<cfset objCompany.revenues="85000323.56">
```

The following code then creates a department and populates it with an array of employees:

```
<cfset objDoc=objCompany.CreateDepartment('Documentation')>
<cfset doc_employees=ArrayNew(1)>
<cfset doc_employees[1]="MetMaker, Baldy">
<cfset doc_employees[2]="HealthFood, Donuts">
<cfset doc_employees[3]="Mellow, Fellow">
<cfset objDoc.AddEmployees(doc_employees)>
```

➜ Arrays are discussed in Chapter 14, "Arrays."

The information that you have entered into the object can be used within a ColdFusion page as follows:

```
<cfoutput>
 Company Name: #objCompany.company_name#<br>
 For Profit: #objCompany.for_profit#<br>
 Revenues: #objCompany.revenues#<br>
 Departments: #objCompany.department_count#<br>
</cfoutput>

<cfset Revenue=objCompany.revenue>
<cfset Revenue.Q1="22124345.83">
<cfset Revenue.Q2="18536444.02">
```

This code first assigns the `objCompany.revenue` object to the ColdFusion local variable `Revenue`, and then assigns quarterly earnings to it.

> **NOTE**
>
> As ColdFusion runs on underlying Java technology and in a JVM (Java Virtual Machine), support for COM is never native, even on Windows. Rather, the COM requests are handled by an external interface to which requests are routed. This has performance implications, and so the use of Java extensions is preferable.

Using CORBA

The *Common Object Request Broker Architecture* (CORBA) is another distributed object technology. This technology is spearheaded by the *Object Management Group* (OMG) and is more of a community standard than is COM.

However, unlike many community standards, CORBA is a pretty expensive choice for implementing objects. Most ColdFusion developers do not use CORBA as a way to extend ColdFusion. However, for organizations that have already made an investment in CORBA, ColdFusion provides an easy way to extend and interact with that technology.

If you need to use ColdFusion with CORBA, you can interact with the CORBA objects by using `<cfobject>`, like this:

```
<cfobject action="connect"
          class="c:\cfo_account.ior2"
          name="objAccount"
          type="CORBA"
          context="IOR">
```

This code is a simple banking example. After you tell ColdFusion which CORBA server to access, as in the previous code, and what to name the object to reference, you can set and retrieve attributes, as follows:

```
<!--- setting an attribute --->
<cfset objAccount.long_attrib="43453">
<!--- retrieving an attribute --->
<cfset balance=objAccount.balance()>
```

Because you've written the account balance attribute into a ColdFusion local variable, you can use the results of the CORBA statement in any way that you want.

➜ Local variables are introduced in Chapter 2, "Working with Variables and Expressions."

Using CFX

The CFX interface was the original ColdFusion extensibility interface (it was introduced in ColdFusion 2). It is fast and powerful, and allows for tags to be written in Java or in C/C++. That's the good news.

The bad news is that CFX tags are limited—they have access to only a few ColdFusion data types (essentially whatever existed back in ColdFusion 2 days).

CFX tags are executables that must be registered in the ColdFusion Administrator so as to bind an alias with the name of the actual executable. Using the CFX interface, it is possible to write extensions that cannot be written using other interfaces.

For example, the following code snippet uses a C++ CFX named <cfx_zip> to unzip a ZIP file and save the contents into a specified directory:

```
<!--- Unzip C:\FILES\FIGURES.ZIP into C:\SALES --->
<cfx_zip action="UNZIP"
         destination="C:\SALES"
         zipfile="C:\FILES\FIGURES.ZIP">
```

ColdFusion comes with headers and includes files and sample code that should be used when creating CFX tags.

Summary

ColdFusion has built in support for most day-to-day operations. When needed, ColdFusion extensibility options can be used to access the worlds of Java, COM, and CORBA. In addition, extensions can be written in C++ or Java via the CFX interface.

Sample Questions

1. What is the preferred extensibility interface for ColdFusion (as of ColdFusion MX)?

   A. Java

   B. COM

   C. CFX

   D. CORBA

2. What tag would you use to access a JSP Tag Library?

   A. `<cfobject>`

   B. `<cfmodule>`

   C. `<cfinvoke>`

   D. `<cfimport>`

3. What CFML language element can be used to invoke a Java object? *(select two)*

   A. `<cfobject>`

   B. `JavaCast()`

   C. `CreateObject()`

   D. `<cfjava>`

CHAPTER 34
XML

IN THIS CHAPTER

Understanding XML

XML is a meta-language—a language used to describe languages. An XML language describes data, and XML documents contain data according to the description. XML gives you a way to store and share data in a highly shareable and reusable format, readable and writable by both human and machine.

An XML document actually is less a document than a string of text—a string containing data and tags as delimiters. XML documents may indeed be actual documents, but they may also be stored in databases, transmitted in email messages, transmitted via HTTP, and more.

Creating XML documents involves embedding the appropriate XML tags and data as per the language requirements (so that they are *well formed*). Reading XML documents involves traversing the tag structure and extracting the data as needed.

XML in ColdFusion

ColdFusion has built-in support for reading, writing, and manipulating XML data. Low-level functions allow for a more granular level of access, while higher-level functions and tags abstract and simplify common operations.

XML Documents vs. XML Document Objects

An XML document is simply a big string. While this makes moving and storing the XML data easy, it presents problems when it comes to extracting and working with specific elements. An easier way to work with XML is by treating it as a tree: a hierarchical view of the data. In ColdFusion, this hierarchical view is the document object—essentially a big nested ColdFusion structure. The structure contains all the XML document's data stored in arrays and structures that are given the names of the XML tags. This form of representation makes working with XML data very easy indeed.

> **NOTE**
> The document object is a structure that contains other arrays and structures. As such, the standard array and structure functions may be used to manipulate XML data.

Reading an XML Document

Reading an XML document is simply a matter of reading the data, perhaps using a `<cffile>` or some other tag. Once the raw XML content is available, you can create an XML Document Object using the `XMLParse()` function, as seen here:

```
<!--- Read XML file --->
<cffile action="read"
        file="menu.xml"
        variable="menu_data">

<!--- Parse it --->
<cfset menu=XMLParse(menu_data)>
```

In this example, an XML file containing menu data is read using `<cffile>`. `XMLParse()` then creates an XML Document Object representation of the data.

> **TIP**
> To see the XML Document Object in all its glory, dump it using `<cfdump>`.

Validating an XML Document

The format of data within an XML document is defined as an XML schema or DTD (Document Type Definition). XML documents may be well formed but still invalid if they do not comply with a set of rules.

To check that an XML document conforms to all specified rules (likely including names of elements, data types, required flags, and more), use the `XMLValidate()` function, as follows:

```
<!--- Read XML file --->
<cffile action="read"
        file="menu.xml"
        variable="menu_data">

<!--- If valid --->
```

```
<cfif XMLValidate(menu_data, schema)>
  ...
</cfif>
```

Validation can also be performed while parsing XML data using `XMLParse()` (seen previously) by passing optional validator details.

Creating an XML Document

In addition to being able to create XML Document Objects from existing XML data, ColdFusion can also create new, empty XML Document Objects that may be populated as needed. There are two ways to programmatically create an XML Document Object: using a tag or using a function.

<cfxml>

The `<cfxml>` function creates a new XML Document Object. `<cfxml>` requires that a variable name be provided for the new object. An optional flag can be used to specify whether the document elements and attributes should be case- sensitive (the default is `no`).

The following example creates a new XML Document Object named `users`:

```
<cfxml variable="users">
```

XMLNew()

`XMLNew()` is a function that is equivalent to `<cfxml>`, and it may be used wherever expressions are used, as well as in a `<cfscript>` block. `XMLNew()` does not take the name of a variable like `<cfxml>` does (since it returns the object); however, it does take the same optional case-sensitive flag. Here is the same example using `XMLNew()`:

```
<cfset users=XMLNew()>
```

and using `<cfscript>`:

```
<cfscript>
users=XMLNew();
</cfscript>
```

➜ `<cfscript>` was reviewed in Chapter 21, "Scripting."

Writing XML

The XML Document Object is perfect for manipulating data within ColdFusion, but outside of ColdFusion it is useless. Because XML data must be shared in its text form, XML Document Objects must be converted back to their text forms when work on them is complete.

The `ToString()` function handles several forms of data conversions (all to string format), including XML. To convert the previously created XML Document Object to a string, you could use the following code:

```
<cfset users_string=ToString(users)>
```

Working with XML

XML data in XML Document Object form can be accessed and manipulated just like any other ColdFusion structures can. For example, consider the following XML menu code:

```
<menu name="Menu">
 <item>
 <text>Home</text>
 <link>/index.cfm</link>
 </item>
 <menu name="Products">
 <item>
 <text>ColdFusion</text>
 <link>/products/cf.cfm</link>
 </item>
 <item>
 <text>Flash</text>
 <link>/products/flash.cfm</link>
 </item>
 </menu>
 <item>
 <text>Search</text>
 <link>/search.cfm</link>
 </item>
 <item>
 <text>Login</text>
 <link>/logout.cfm</link>
 </item>
</menu>
```

Once this menu data has been read (perhaps using code as shown above) and parsed with `XMLParse()`, the structure `menu` would be accessible just like any other ColdFusion structure would be. For example, to access the first set of child tags (the first menu item), you could use the following code:

```
#menu.menu.xmlchildren[1]#
```

`menu.menu.xmlchildren` is an array of menu items, with each array element a structure containing the menu item text and link, an array of any submenus, and so on. It is this open-ended structure, so typical of XML, that makes ColdFusion's XML Document Object so invaluable.

Here is another example, this time populating an XML Document Object with the results of a database query:

```
<!--- Create XML object --->
<cfxml variable="UserRecs">
```

```
<UserRecs>
<!--- Loop through users --->
<cfoutput query="users">
<!--- Write user --->
<user>
<UserID>#UserID#</UserID>
<FName>#FName#</FName>
<LName>#LName#</LName>
</user>
</cfoutput>
</UserRecs>
</cfxml>
```

In this example, the tags and data are automatically converted into the appropriate XML Document Object elements in a `<cfoutput>` loop.

Writing specific cells is just as simple and can be performed using `<cfset>`, as seen here:

```
<cfset menu.menu.xmlchildren[1].xmlchildren[1].xmltext="Homepage">
```

In this example, a specific element in the menu structure is being set (`Home` is being changed to `Homepage`).

Advanced XML

In addition to the basic reading and writing of XML data, ColdFusion also supports XSL styles, XPath searches, and low-level access to XML data when needed.

Applying XSL Stylesheets

XSL (Extensible Stylesheet Language) is used to define formatting and output instructions to be applied to XML. ColdFusion itself does not create or manage XSL style sheets, but it does provide a function that may be used to apply style sheets—returning the transformed data.

The process of applying style sheets is known as XSLT (Extensible Stylesheet Language Transformation) and is performed using the `XMLTransform()` function, like this:

```
<cffile action="read"
        file="C:\cfusionmx7\wwwroot\xsl\standard.xsl"
        variable="xslDoc">
<cfoutput>
#XMLTransform(users, xslDoc)#
</cfoutput>
```

Here an XSL style sheet is read using `<cffile>` and then used in an `XMLTransform()`.

> **NOTE**
>
> `XMLTransform()` can take an XML Document Object and an XML document (in string form) as its first argument.

Performing Searches

Extracting data from an XML document is not difficult, but searching for data can be. As XML documents are made up of both data and tags, it can be tricky to search for specific data or tags or at specific nesting levels. XPath is a searching language not unlike what Regular Expressions are for text—an XPath search involves creating a search pattern and then using it to extract data from an XML document.

XPath is supported in ColdFusion by the `XMLSearch()` function, which takes a search pattern and an XML Document Object to be searched. A simple example is seen here:

```
<cfset results=XMLSearch(users, "user/UserID")>
<cfoutput>
Found #ArrayLen(results)# matches
</cfoutput>
```

This example searches for `user` elements containing a `UserID` element and returns an array of matches.

> **NOTE**
>
> XPath is defined by the W3; details are at `http://www.w3.org/TR/xpath`.

Other XML Functions

In addition to the XML functions used thus far, ColdFusion provides several other XML functions that may be used as needed:

- `IsXML()` is used to test whether or not a string is well formed XML.
- `IsXMLAttribute()` is used to test whether or not a parameter is a valid node attribute.
- `IsXMLDoc()` is used to test whether a variable contains a valid XML Document Object.
- `IsXMLElem()` is used to test whether or not a parameter is a valid object element.
- `IsXMLNode()` is used to test whether or not a parameter is a valid object node.
- `IsXMLNode()` is used to test whether or not a parameter is the root of an XML object.

- `XMLChildPos()` is used to locate specific child elements.
- `XMLElemNew()` is used to add an element to an XML Document Objects.
- `XMLGetNodeType()` is used to determine the type of an XML document object.
- `XMLFormat()` is used to escape text so as to make it safe for inserting within an XML document.

Summary

XML documents are an important way to share and store data. You can use ColdFusion tags and functions to read and write XML, as well as to perform searches, apply XSL transformations, and more. ColdFusion uses a structure to contain hierarchical representations of XML that simplify data access and manipulation.

Sample Questions

1. Which of the following CFML language elements create XML Document Objects? *(select two)*

   A. `<cfxml>`

   B. `XMLParse()`

   C. `XMLSearch()`

   D. `XMLFormat()`

2. Which function is used to convert an XML Document Object to its string representation?

   A. `XMLFormat()`

   B. `XMLParse()`

   C. `ToXML()`

   D. `ToString()`

3. Which of the following statements are true? *(select two)*

   A. XML documents may be case-sensitive.

   B. XML documents are in a binary format.

   C. XML documents contain page-formatting information.

   D. XML documents must be well formed.

CHAPTER 35 WDDX

IN THIS CHAPTER

XML and WDDX

XML is used to describe data. For XML to work, both sender and recipient must agree on an XML language, and all data must be well formed according to that language. WDDX is Macromedia's contribution to the XML community. It is an open-source XML DTD (Document Type Definition) that defines generic data types such as strings, arrays, structures, and recordsets. WDDX is an XML language that defines data—not any specific implementation, but raw data itself. This can make data sharing via XML quick and painless (it doesn't require that an XML language be agreed upon).

➜ XML was reviewed in Chapter 34, "XML."

The following example shows a two-dimensional array:

```
<cfscript>
 products=ArrayNew(2);
 products[1][1]="33-2112";
 products[1][2]="10";
 products[1][3]="S";
 products[2][1]="29-3564";
 products[2][2]="8";
 products[2][3]="M";
 products[3][1]="21-1153";
 products[3][2]="10";
 products[3][3]="L";
</cfscript>
```

If you then convert this data into WDDX, you see the following:

```
<wddxPacket version='1.0'><header/><data><array length='3'>
<array length='3'><string>33-2112</string><string>10</string>
<string>S</string></array><array length='3'>
<string>29-3564</string><string>8</string><string>M</string>
</array><array length='3'><string>21-1153</string><string>10</string>
<string>L</string></array></array></data></wddxPacket
```

> **NOTE**
> Converting data into a WDDX packet is called serialization; converting it from WDDX back to native data is called deserialization.

Notice that the packet doesn't give the data a name as it did in the earlier example (like `SKU` or `Quantity`); rather, it defines the data generically as strings and arrays.

If you pass this packet to an ASP program or Perl script that understands the WDDX DTD, those programs will convert the data back into variables that are understood by their own systems.

The real power of WDDX is that it allows you to use a simplified implementation of XML without having to worry about learning XML or DTDs. The WDDX DTD is interpreted either by ColdFusion or by the other system that understands WDDX. The user never has to get his hands dirty.

> **NOTE**
> To learn more about WDDX, go to `http://www.openwddx.org/`.

<cfwddx>

To turn the preceding code example into a WDDX packet, you can use a tag called `<cfwddx>`, like this:

```
<cfwddx action="CFML2WDDX"
        input="#products#"
        output="NewPacket">
```

> **CAUTION**
> Note the pound signs (#) around the value for the `input` attribute. If you forget them, ColdFusion thinks you are trying to serialize the literal string `products`.

Table 35.1 lists the attributes of the `<cfwddx>` tag.

Table 35.1 `<cfwddx>` Attributes

ATTRIBUTE	DESCRIPTION
`action`	Tells ColdFusion what action to take on the variable
`input`	Tells ColdFusion which variable to serialize
`output`	Names the variable into which ColdFusion will place the packet
`toplevelvariable`	If you are using WDDX to create JavaScript, this is the name of the JavaScript variable being created

Table 35.2 lists the possible values for the action attribute.

Table 35.2 Values for the action Attribute

VALUE	DESCRIPTION
`cfml2wddx`	Serializes ColdFusion data into a WDDX packet
`wddx2cfml`	Deserializes the ColdFusion data from a WDDX packet to ColdFusion data
`wddx2js`	Deserializes a WDDX packet into native JavaScript
`cfml2js`	Turns ColdFusion data directly into JavaScript data using WDDX as a bridge

> **NOTE**
> JavaScript and ColdFusion are only two of the languages that understand WDDX. Some others are PHP, Perl, ASP, Python, and Java.

If you have a query record set called `GetStates` and want to serialize it into a WDDX packet, you can type:

```
<cfwddx action="CFML2WDDX"
        input="#GetStates#">
```

Because the preceding `<cfwddx>` code doesn't have an `output` attribute, the data is output directly to the page itself rather than being put into a variable.

> **CAUTION**
>
> WDDX packets don't like special characters such as < or > outside the XML tags. When you're developing applications, you probably have the ColdFusion debugging settings turned on in ColdFusion Administrator. The debugging is displayed at the bottom of your HTML page using HTML code. This means that when your WDDX packet is written to the page, it becomes corrupted by the extra HTML debugging information.
>
> To deal with this problem, always place the tag `<cfsetting showdebugoutput="No">` at the top of your page. It suppresses debugging on the page.

> **TIP**
>
> Two ColdFusion functions that are helpful for creating valid WDDX packets are `XMLFormat()` and `IsWDDX()`. The former converts special characters in data to an acceptable XML format. The latter verifies that the WDDX packet is valid.

Using WDDX with Other Technologies

The most important point to remember about serializing and deserializing a WDDX packet is that what you put in is what you get out. So if your ColdFusion application takes a query record set and turns it into a WDDX packet, then passes it on to an ASP program, that program ends up with a record set as well.

WDDX is a powerful tool when used for syndication purposes. When you're sharing data between two Web sites, getting the data in just the right format can be difficult if both sites use different programming languages. Now, with WDDX, if both programs understand the WDDX DTD, they have a translator that allows them to transfer data seamlessly.

Summary

XML facilitates data sharing between diverse and disparate applications and services. WDDX provides some of the core benefits of XML without requiring the learning and understanding of XML itself—and on all major platforms (including ColdFusion).

Sample Questions

1. Which of the following is *not* a valid `action` attribute for the `<cfwddx>` tag?

   A. `CFML2ASP`

   B. `CFML2JS`

   C. `WDDX2CFML`

   D. `CFML2WDDX`

2. Which of the following options would you use to convert a ColdFusion two-dimensional array called `names` into a WDDX packet and write the results to the page?

   A.
   ```
   <cfwddx action="CFML2WDDX"
       input="#names#">
   ```

   B.
   ```
   <cfwddx action="CFML2PAGE"
       input="#names#">
   ```

   C.
   ```
   <cfwddx action="CFML2WDDX"
       input="#names#"
       writetopage="Yes">
   ```

   D.
   ```
   <cfwddx action="CFML2WDDX"
       input="#names#"
       output="This.Page">
   ```

CHAPTER 36

Flash Remoting

IN THIS CHAPTER

Understanding Flash Remoting

Macromedia Flash is Macromedia's rich-client technology, used to build applications that run within a Flash player on PCs, PDAs, game consoles, interactive TVs, mobile devices, and more. Some of the benefits of Flash as a user-interface technology are:

- Portability
- Ready availability
- Consistency of output
- Extensive UI control
- Light weight

Macromedia Flash is often used as a client-only technology, but in truth Flash is very capable at functioning as a client in a client/server world. Flash Remoting is a technology that allows a client's Flash to interact with server-side processing, so that data may be passed back and forth between Flash and

- ColdFusion
- Java
- .NET

NOTE

Flash Remoting is a standard feature included with ColdFusion (and JRun), but must be purchases for other Java servers and for .NET.

Using Flash Remoting

Using Flash Remoting involves the following steps:

1. Plan the application, separating client and server processing as needed.
2. Write the server-side code.
3. Create the Flash application using Flash.
4. Embed ActionScript code in the Flash application to invoke the server-side code via Flash Remoting.
5. Pass requests to the server as needed and process any returned results.

Obviously, using Flash Remoting requires a basic understanding of Flash and ActionScript.

> **NOTE**
> Flash movie and animation features–for example, use of the timeline–are not required to leverage Flash Remoting.

Within ColdFusion, you have three ways to respond to Flash Remoting requests:

- ColdFusion Components
- Straight `.cfm` calls
- Server-side ActionScript

Each of these is reviewed below.

Using ColdFusion Components

ColdFusion Components (CFCs) are used to encapsulate back-end processing. CFCs can be used by ColdFusion, by Flash Remoting, and as Web Services.

➜ CFCs were reviewed in Chapter 31, "ColdFusion Components."

ColdFusion Components contain methods (or functions). By default, methods are available only to ColdFusion. To make CFC methods available to the outside world (including to client-side Flash), you must set the `access` level to `remote`, as seen here:

```
<cfcomponent>

  <cffunction name="GetEmployees"
              access="remote"
              output="no"
              returntype="query">
```

```
        <cfquery name="Employees"
                 datasource="exampleApps">
        SELECT *
        FROM tblEmployees
        ORDER BY LastName, FirstName
        </cfquery>

      <cfreturn Employees>

    </cfcomponent>
```

The above code defines a CFC containing a single method; `GetEmployees` returns a list of employees from a database. This code could be used in ColdFusion applications, and because `access="remote"`, it can also be invoked by client-side ActionScript.

To invoke this code from within Flash, ActionScript code is used. Here is a code snippet:

```
#include "NetServices.as"

var gwURL="http://localhost:8500/flashservices/gateway";
NetServices.setDefaultGatewayURL(gwURL);
gw=NetServices.createGatewayConnection();

employeeService=gw.getService("hr.employees", this);
employeeService.getEmployees();
```

This script includes the Flash Remoting client-side code, then defines a connection to the ColdFusion server. `/flashservices/gateway` is a virtual path to the Flash Remoting engine in ColdFusion.

Once the gateway connection has been established, access to specific CFCs can be defined. In this example, `employeeService` is being bound to `hr.employees`, the `employees.cfc` (the above ColdFusion Component) in the `hr` directory.

The final line of code then executes the `getEmployees()` method in `employeeService`, the method defined above. `getEmployees()` expects no arguments; had this not been the case, arguments could have been provided as function parameters.

All of this happens without a client-side refresh; data is sent back and forth on demand and can be processed as needed.

> **NOTE**
>
> As `getEmployees()` returns a result, Flash will expect a function named `getEmployees_Result()` to receive the returned data. If the function is not present, a notification to that effect will be displayed in the output box (when in the Flash development environment).

Using CFML

ColdFusion Components are ideal for creating applications where the client and server are explicitly separated, as seen above. However, when needed, Flash Remoting can also be used to directly access any `.cfm` file in much the same way as described above.

Consider the following ActionScript code:

```
#include "NetServices.as"
var gwURL="http://localhost:8500/flashservices/gateway";
NetServices.setDefaultGatewayUrl(gwURL);
gw = NetServices.createGatewayConnection();

hrService = gatewayConnection.getService("hr", this);
hrService.List();
```

The ActionScript looks much like the ActionScript used to interact with a CFC. However, in this example the service being connected to is `hr`, the directory (as opposed to a specific CFC). The `hrService.List()` invocation is executing `list.cfm` in the `hr` directory.

Unlike ColdFusion Components, straight CFML files do not have a structured way to accept and return data. To this end, ColdFusion provides a special interface to Flash within `.cfm` files via the `FLASH` scope (which will be present only if a `.cfm` file is invoked via Flash Remoting). Table 36.1 lists the members of the `FLASH` scope.

Table 36.1 The FLASH Scope

ELEMENT	DESCRIPTION
`pagesize`	The number of records at a time to be returned to Flash. This allows for data to be displayed or used before it has all been transmitted. The default is `10`.
`params`	Provides access to passed arguments (parameters). Data is in an array (either indexed or associative) and can be accessed using array or structure functions.
`result`	Data to be returned to Flash.

➜ Arrays and structures were covered in Chapters 14 and 15, "Arrays" and "Structures," respectively.

Data returned by Flash Remoting is automatically converted to appropriate client-side data types. For example, ColdFusion queries are returned as ActionScript RecordSets, and structures are returned as named arrays.

> **NOTE**
> Only data stored in `FLASH.result` is sent back to Flash on the client.

> **TIP**
>
> The downside of using `.cfm` files instead of `.cfc` files for Flash Remoting is that the CFML code must be Flash-specific, and will not be portable. As a general rule, interaction via ColdFusion Components is preferred.

Using Server-Side ActionScript

CFCs or straight CFML are ColdFusion developers' primary interfaces to Flash Remoting. For Flash developers who may be familiar with ActionScript but not CFML, Flash Remoting also allows very basic access to the ColdFusion world via server-side ActionScript—ActionScript source code that ColdFusion processes on the server.

The following is a code snippet that is functionally equivalent to the `GetEmployees` CFC method seen previously:

```
function basicQuery()
{
 employees=CF.query(
   {datasource:"exampleapps",
    sql:"SELECT *
         FROM tblEmployees
         ORDER BY LastName, FirstName"
   });
 return employees;
}
```

Assuming that this code was saved as `list.asr` in the `hr` directory, the ActionScript invocation code used to invoke a CFML page could be used here.

> **NOTE**
>
> Server-side ActionScript does not fully expose CFML and ColdFusion. In fact, all it exposes are database queries (equivalent to `<cfquery>`, as seen here) and server-side HTTP requests (equivalent to `<cfhttp>`).

Using DataGlue

Once data has been received inside of Flash, it must be processed, usually by looping through results and associating them with UI elements. To simplify this process, Flash includes a function library called DataGlue (which, as its name suggests, is used to bind data with objects).

To use DataGlue, the `DataGlue.as` file must be included in the ActionScript code, like this:

```
#include "DataGlue.as"
```

`DataGlue.as` defines a collection of functions that may used as needed. The following example is the result-processing function that the CFC invocation described earlier in this chapter may use—it receives data from the `GetEmployees()` method, which it uses to populate a combo box:

```
function getEmployees_Result(result) {
DataGlue.bindFormatStrings(employee_cb,
 result,
 "#lastname#, #firstname#",
 "#employeeid#");
}
```

> **NOTE**
>
> DataGlue is not always needed; some Flash UI components (for example, the DataGrid) can accept RecordSets directly.

Debugging

Flash features its own debugger as well as a NetConnection Debugger—kind of a sniffer window that reports on the requests and results that are sent back and forth between Flash on the client and Flash Remoting on the server. To use NetConnection Debugger, you must use the following `#include` statement in the ActionScript code:

```
#include "NetDebug.as"
```

NetConnection Debugger can also display any and all ColdFusion debugging information if debugging is enabled on the server.

➜ Debugging was reviewed in Chapter 20, "Debugging."

Summary

Macromedia Flash is a powerful client-side UI technology, and Flash Remoting gives that client the ability to interact with server-side processing. ColdFusion can be accessed via Flash Remoting using CFCs, straight CFML, or server-side ActionScript. Flash provides functions to simplify working with data returned from Flash Remoting, and a debugger that can publish ColdFusion debugging output.

Sample Questions

1. Which of the following can be invoked directly via Flash Remoting?

   A. Custom Tags

   B. ColdFusion Components

   C. User-defined functions

2. Which scope is used to access data submitted via Flash Remoting? *(select two)*

   A. `ARGUMENTS`

   B. `ATTRIBUTES`

   C. `FLASH`

   D. `URL`

3. Why are CFCs the preferred method for utilizing Flash Remoting? *(select two)*

   A. Separation of presentation and content

   B. Performance

   C. Simplified integration

   D. Access to all CFML

   E. Portability

CHAPTER 37

Event Gateways

IN THIS CHAPTER

Understanding Event Gateways

Event gateways are connectors, bridges between ColdFusion and other systems and technologies. Whereas out of the box ColdFusion can respond to HTTP requests (via Web Server connectors) and can talk to a variety of back-end technologies (databases, LDAP, Web Services, and more), event gateways allow ColdFusion to respond to and interact with just about anything.

> **NOTE**
> Event gateways are supported in ColdFusion Enterprise and ColdFusion Developer Edition, but not in ColdFusion Standard.

Gateway Internals

A thorough understanding of event gateway processing is required to effectively leverage this powerful technology.

The Event Gateway Service

ColdFusion includes an event gateway service, a process that may be started or stopped from within the ColdFusion Administrator. The gateway service queues and processes all gateway requests, and must be running for any gateways to be used.

> **NOTE**
> ColdFusion *remembers* the gateway service setting, and will automatically restart it upon server restart if needed.

All gateway requests are routed by ColdFusion to the event gateway service. The service queues requests until a thread is available, and then hands it off for execution within a thread. If the queue is full, requests will not be executed and an exception will be thrown.

> **TIP**
>
> The default request queue size is `25000` and the default number of available threads for event gateway processing is `10`. These values can be changed using the ColdFusion Administrator.

Gateway Types

Gateways themselves are written in Java, and must be registered with ColdFusion as a *gateway type* before use. Registration maps a *gateway type name* to a Java class file (the actual gateway). The ColdFusion Administrator providers an interface for registering and managing gateway types.

The Java classes are generally not tied to any specific ColdFusion code or implementation. Rather, they are tied to specific back-ends or technologies and provide hooks that ColdFusion code can tie in to. For example, a gateway to an ERP system would need to be intimately tied to that system, exposing functionality that ColdFusion code could then connect to.

> **NOTE**
>
> The Java code for a stubbed gateway is included with ColdFusion, as is code for several complete working examples. These can be used as starting point for your own gateways.

ColdFusion ships with a set of gateways already installed and registered ready for you to use:

- **CFML** provides access to asynchronous ColdFusion processing.
- **Directory Watcher** allows developers to write code that will be automatically executed when changes are made to a watched directory (file added, file changed, file deleted).
- **JMS** provides access Java Message Service queuing.
- **SAMETIME** provides Lotus Sametime integration.
- **SMS** enables communication between ColdFusion and SMS clients and devices.
- **Socket** allows ColdFusion to respond to activity on watched sockets.
- **XMPP** provides access to instant messaging via XMPP.

Gateway Instances

Gateway instances are specific uses of gateways, a Java gateway type and an associated ColdFusion Component. Gateway instances are also registered in the ColdFusion Administrator, and there is no limit to the number of gateway instances that may be defined nor the number of instances of any gateway type.

> **NOTE**
> Gateway instances are bound to ColdFusion Components, and not to `.cfm` files.

Back to the ERP example, if three different ColdFusion applications (doing very different things) all had to interact with the ERP system, there would likely be three gateway instances defined (each with a different CFC tied to the same Java class).

> **NOTE**
> Gateway instances can also point to optional configuration files, plain text files that contain gateway settings. This allows for the same gateway to be used with different options or settings defined.

When gateway instances are defined, a startup mode is specified:

- `Automatic` starts gateway instances automatically upon server start-up.
- `Manual` makes the gateway instance usable, but it will need to be manually started to be used.
- `Disabled` prevents a gateway instance from being used.

> **TIP**
> The Gateway Instance screen in the ColdFusion Administrator displays two counters for each gateway, in is the number of inbound requests and out is the number of outbound requests. This activity indicator is a useful debugging tool.

Initiators And Responders

Event gateway activity falls into one of two categories (and specific gateway types support either or both, depending on what the gateway does).

- Initiator gateways are those where ColdFusion (or CFML code) trigger execution. For example, a ColdFusion event gateway instance may initiate a JMS transaction by placing an item on an outbound JMS queue. Or a ColdFusion event gateway instance my send an IM or SMS message to inform a user that an error has occurred.

- Responder gateways are those where ColdFusion event gateway execution is triggered by an external event. For example. A file uploaded to a watch folder could trigger CFML code to be executed via a directory watcher gateway. Or an IM or SMS message from a user may cause ColdFusion to execute a database query the results of which are sent back via a return message.

In the examples listed here, the directory watcher gateway instance is a responder, the JMS gateway instance is an initiator, and the IM and SMS gateways are both initiators and responders.

Using Gateways

More often than note, ColdFusion developers will not be writing brand new gateway types (although they definitely can do so). The majority of the work required of ColdFusion developers is the ColdFusion integration piece. Going back to a previous examples, to send a JMS message a ColdFusion developer must write code to make that action occur. Similarly, if a directory watcher gateway detects that a file has been added to a directory it sends a message to ColdFusion code that a ColdFusion developer must write, code that will do something with that new file.

Initiators

Initiating an event gateway request in ColdFusion requires the use of a single function named `SendGatewayMessage()`. This function requires two parameters be passed to it, as listed in Table 37.1.

Table 37.1 SendGatewayMessage() Parameters

PARAMETER	DESCRIPTION
`gateway`	The id of a registered (and running) gateway instance.
`data`	A structure to be passed to the gateway instance, the contents of the structure being specific to gateway type being used.

The following example send text to be logged to an asynchronous CFML gateway named `logger`:

```
<cfset props=StructNew()>
<cfset prop.message="Text to be logged goes here">
<cfset SendGatewayMessage("logger", props)>
```

Here a single field is being set in the passed structure, some gateway types may require far more information. For example, to send an IM message you'd need to specify the recipient name as well as the message to be sent. `SendGatewayMessage()`

instructs the event gateway service to send a request to `logger` passing the props structure to it..

The request will thus be routed to a ColdFusion Component that may look like this:

```
<cfcomponent>
<cffunction name="onIncomingMessage"
            output="no">
    <cfargument name="CFEvent"
                type="struct"
                required="yes">
      <cflog text="#CFEvent.Data.message#"
          file="mylog.log"
          type="info"
          thread="yes"
          date="yes"
          time="yes"
          application="yes">
  </cffunction>
</cfcomponent>
```

The default name for the CFC entry-point method is `onIncomingMessage`. This method is invoked by the event gateway service in response to the `SendGatewayMessage()` function. The method accepts a single argument, a structure that will contain the fields listed in Table 37.2.

Table 37.2 CFEvent Fields

FIELD	DESCRIPTION
`CFCMethod`	CFC method to be invoked (usually `onIncomingMessage`).
`CFCPath`	Location of associated CFC file.
`CFCTimeout`	Timeout interval in seconds.
`Data`	A structure containing the event data.
`GatewayID`	The id of the gateway that sent the event or will handle the outbound event.
`GatewayType`	The gateway type.
`OriginatorID`	Originator ID identifying message sender.

> **NOTE**
> Not all gateway types populate all of these fields listed in Table 37.2

In the example above the CFC code uses just one `CFEvent` field, `data`, to obtain the text to be logged.

Responders

Gateway responders obviously do not rely on CFML code to invoke them. A gateway type that acts as a responder (like the directory watcher) sends a message to the event gateway service when an event occurs (directory content changes, for example).

This executes the same CFC method seen previously, passing the `CFEvent` structure defined in Table 37.2.

If a gateway needs to respond to multiple events, two options are available:

- Use a single CFC method (probably `onIncomingMessage`) and pass a flag in the `CFEvent` data field defining the event type. The CFC CFML code can then check this flag and respond to different event appropriately.
- Alternatively, a different CFC method could be defined for each event, in which case the configuration file must define the CFC method name to be invoked for each event. (Incidentally, this is how the directory watcher gateway works, executing a different CFC method for file added, file changed, and file deleted).

The SMS Gateway

One gateway type deserving special mention is the SMS gateway. SMS is used to send text messages between devices (usually phones and PDAs), and can also be used to send messages between applications and devices. Creating SMS applications requires:

- Access to the SMS world.
- An SMS account.
- Devices that can send and receive SMS messages.
- Application code that can interact with SMS.

To deploy a production SMS application you will need SMS access and an SMS account. But for development, ColdFusion comes with everything you need:

- An SMS server that simulates the SMS world on your server, allowing messages to be sent back and forth between applications and "devices".
- An SMS gateway that can connect ColdFusion to the SMS world.
- A preconfigured gateway instance connected to the local SMS server.
- A Java applet device emulator that can be used to simulate one or more devices (communicating with each other and with ColdFusion code).

The techniques used to send and receive SMS messages are no different from what was described previously. All that will differ is the gateway instance name and the `CFEvent` contents.

Summary

Event gateways are used to connect ColdFusion to all sorts of systems and technologies. The event gateway server manages event gateway requests, and passes them to gateway instances for processing by ColdFusion Component methods. Both initiator and responder gateways are supported, and a series of example gateway (including an SMS gateway and supporting tools) are included with ColdFusion.

Sample Questions

1. What function is used to initiate an event gateway request?

   A. `CreateObject()`

   B. `OnIncomingMessage()`

   C. `SendGatewayMessage()`

   D. `SetGatewayMessage()`

2. Which gateway types can be used to perform asynchronous processing?

   A. JMS

   B. CFML

   C. Directory Watcher

   D. XMPP

3. What is required for a gateway instance definition?

   A. Gateway type

   B. Event gateway service

   C. `SendGatewayMessage()` function

   D. Configuration file

   E. CFC file

PART 7

Services and Protocols

CHAPTER 38

Full-Text Searching

IN THIS CHAPTER

Understanding Full-Text Searching

Full-text searching is the performing of sophisticated searches on blocks of text. Unlike database indexing, which usually sorts data alphabetically, full-text searching accesses its indexed data in many different ways—substring searches, proximity searches, relevancy searches, and more.

To facilitate full-text searching, ColdFusion includes with a custom implementation of the Verity K2 Server. This integrated Java based engine allows developers to perform full-text searches on database queries and file libraries. Verity generates a read-optimized set of indexes called a *collection*, and it provides search tools to retrieve result sets ranked by relevancy. Verity runs as a separate service or daemon that must be installed and running to be used.

> **NOTE**
> Verity, Inc., offers a range of enterprise-level search and indexing products. The ColdFusion Verity implementation is a customized version of one of its core products. See `http://www.verity.com` for more details.

A Verity collection is a group of files and associated metadata that is optimized for searching. Collections include various word indexes, an internal- documents table that contains document field information, and pointers to the actual files for file and path indexes. ColdFusion provides a number of Verity functions with which to create, maintain, and optimize collections. This maintenance can be performed through ColdFusion Administrator or with the `<cfcollection>` and `<cfindex>` tags.

Searching a Verity collection is fast and leverages the search-command vocabulary of the Verity engine. Users can perform sophisticated searches by using `<cfsearch>`, which handles boolean operators, wildcards, and other advanced search options.

> **NOTE**
> Verity can index and search most popular office file types, including text, HTML, XML, RTF, Adobe PDF, Microsoft Word, WordPerfect, Excel, and PowerPoint.

Verity Collections

A Verity collection is a read-optimized, logical database made up of a number of physical files stored on a Web server's hard drive. When a collection is created, the physical files and directories that make up the Verity collection are written to the server.

The collection's logical name is associated with its physical file structure on disk. The logical name also is used when referring to collections by way of the `<cfindex>` and `<cfsearch>` tags' `collection` attribute.

Creating and Indexing Collections

A Verity collection can be created in a number of ways: through ColdFusion Administrator, the `<cfcollection>` tag, or some other third-party Verity tool. The initialization of the collection effectively sets up the directory structure and records a logical name for the collection. The following code snippet builds a collection programmatically using the `<CFCOLLECTION>` tag:

```
<cfcollection action="create"
              collection="SnailsAndPuppyDogTails"
              path="c:\cfusionmx7\verity\collections"
              language="English">
```

The default directory location for all collections is `verity\collections` under the ColdFusion root. The contents of these directories is managed and maintained by ColdFusion and Verity, and can for the most part be ignored. Once a collection is created, ColdFusion access to it is via this name (in much the same way that data sources are used to access databases).

`<cfcollection>` also can be used to map an alias to an existing Verity collection that was created by a tool other than ColdFusion. The `action`, `collection`, and `path` attributes are required. The path must point to a valid Verity collection; mapping does not validate the path.

> **NOTE**
> Deleting a mapped collection unregisters the alias; the base collection is not deleted.

Maintaining Collections

A collection starts its life empty and must be populated by way of `<cfindex>`. You can use `<cfindex>` to create both file- and query-based indexes. The collection simply needs to know where to find the body of words on which the engine is to search, and what information will make up the result key to be returned on a successful match. Additional attributes are available for filtering and providing result summaries, among other features.

A file library containing a mixture of file types could be indexed by using the following:

```
<cfindex action="update"
         collection="SnailsAndPuppyDogTails"
         key="c:\filestore\whatboyslike"
         type="PATH"
         extensions=".doc, .xls, .ppt, .pdf"
         RECURSE="Yes">
```

The `key` attribute for `type="PATH"` is a directory on the server. Each record in the index uses the filename as the key value. The `extensions` attribute lets you restrict the file types to be indexed in the specified directory. `recurse="YES"` instructs ColdFusion to work recursively through all subdirectories in the branch of the nominated root directory.

A database query with large text fields could be indexed efficiently using the following:

```
<cfquery name="GirlsLike" datasource="dsn">
SELECT *
FROM AllThingsNice
</cfquery>

<cfindex action="update"
         collection="SugarAndSpice"
         key="Things_ID"
         type="CUSTOM"
         title="Sugar"
         query="GirlsLike"
         body="Spice"
         custom1="AllThings"
         custom2="">
```

In this example, `key`, `title`, `body`, and `custom1` are all fields in the collection index that are mapped to a specific column in the query object. `key` is the unique identifier for the record (the primary key, in this instance); `title` is a descriptive name, which is not unique; `body` refers to the document to be searched; and `custom1` and `custom2` are developer-definable fields that are returned with the search results. In effect, any query object can be used to populate a `custom` index, including queries generated from `<cfpop>`, `<cfldap>`, and `<cfquery>`.

As application data changes, the Verity collection must be updated in order to synchronize with the information kept in the database or file store. `<cfindex>`, with both `update` and `delete` actions, can be used to update collections one record at a time. This type of action might be coupled with data changes in the application to ensure that the Verity collection is always up to date:

```
<!--- updating a document in a file store index --->
<cfindex action="update"
         collection="SnailsAndPuppyDogTails"
         key="c:\filestore\whatboyslike\escargot.doc"
         type="file">
<!--- deleting a single record from query-based index --->
<cfindex action="delete"
         collection="SugarAndSpice"
         key="1234">
```

The entire index could be purged and made ready for repopulation or, alternatively, cleared and repopulated by using the `refresh` action. However, these options are not always suitable for regular update procedures and might be very time-consuming on large data stores.

> **TIP**
>
> On a high-traffic site, you might need to schedule downtime for the search interface while the collection is maintained. If you choose to maintain the collection after every data change in the application, the collection might not be available for searching during frequent or prolonged update periods.

From time to time, the Verity collection can become corrupted. If this happens, you can repair the collection by using `<cfcollection>`:

```
<cfcollection action="repair"
              collection="SugarAndSpice">
```

In some instances, you might need to delete the collection entirely and reindex.

Optimizing Collections

Verity collections require regular optimization, depending on the frequency of updates to the collection. Rather than performing a complete reindex each time the collection is updated, Verity adds additional files to the collection. This is a faster update mechanism, but it eventually leads to fragmentation of the collection. When a search is performed, each file in the collection is checked for a match. The more files or fragmentation present in an index, the slower the search. Optimization compacts and aggregates the Verity metadata files, which significantly improves the overall performance of the search engine.

Collections can be optimized through ColdFusion Administrator, or programmatically by using the `<cfcollection>` tag:

```
<cfcollection action="optimize"
              collection="SugarAndSpice">
```

> **TIP**
>
> Every update leads to further fragmentation of the Verity collection. Fragmented collections take up significantly more disk space and can eventually slow the collection to the point of being unsearchable.
>
> One method of minimizing fragmentation is to reduce the number of transactions being performed on the collection. Rather than updating the collection every time you update your data, you should consider periodic updates that bulk all your data changes into a single submission.
>
> In any event, be sure to optimize regularly!

Indexing XML Documents

Verity can index XML documents. The documents need to have the `.xml` extension in order for Verity's universal XML filter to process them. XML documents with any extension can be indexed into an XML-only collection by modifying Verity's Style files. The Style files can be used to modify the XML filter to correctly reflect specific XML Schemas. Style files contain configuration parameters and can be modified with a standard text editor.

Creating a Search Interface

The `<cfsearch>` tag is used to query Verity collections. Typically, an application has a form that collects search parameters from the user; this form is submitted to an application page that invokes the `<cfsearch>` tag. `<cfsearch>` generates a query object containing records from the specified collection that match the keywords of the `criteria` attribute. The following snippet performs a search and returns a query named `SearchResults`:

```
<cfsearch collection="SnailsAndPuppyDogTails"
          name="SearchResults"
          type="SIMPLE"
          criteria="#FORM.keywords#">
```

There are two search types: simple and explicit. The `criteria` attribute of a simple search is commonly just a list of keywords. In an explicit search, `criteria` can refine the results with any number of Verity operators and modifiers, but each must be explicitly invoked.

NOTE

If you search for an all-uppercase or all-lowercase string, the search is not case-sensitive:

```
criteria="COLDFUSION"
criteria="coldfusion"
```

If you search for a mixed-case string, the search is case-sensitive:

```
criteria="ColdFusion"
```

A simple query expression is simple only in that you, the developer, do not need to identify any special Verity operators. You can enter multiple words separated by commas, in which case the comma is treated like a logical `or`. If you omit the commas, the query expression is treated as a phrase. Wildcards can be specified for pattern matching. In addition, the `simple` search `type` packs a very powerful combination of the Verity engine `stem` operator and the `many` modifier.

A `stem` search automatically includes words that are derived from the ones listed in `criteria`. For example, a word such as *view* returns records that contain *view*, *viewing*, *views*, and so on.

The `many` modifier ranks search results according to a relevancy score. Relevancy is based on the density of the search term in the searched data. The more often a word appears in a document, the higher the document's score. Furthermore, if a keyword has the same frequency in two documents, the smaller document is given a higher relevancy. For example, a 500-page report that mentions the word *corruption* ten times is ranked with less significance than a 5-page document that also has ten instances of *corruption*.

An explicit query expression can include any of the Verity operators and modifiers. However, they all must be explicitly specified. You might consider assembling an explicit search expression programmatically from an advanced search form, or simply letting power users submit their own expressions.

The query object generated by `<cfsearch>` can be processed as usual with `<cfoutput>` to build a table of results. The available query results are listed in Table 38.1. Optionally, a status structure can also be returned providing additional information as listed in Table 38.2.

➜ Dynamic URL parameters are covered in Chapter 8, "URL Variables."

Table 38.1 `<cfsearch>` result Variables

RESULT	DESCRIPTION
`author`	Extracted from document (including Microsoft Office documents and PDF files) if available.
`category`	A list of associated categories, if present.
`categoryTree`	A hierarchal category tree, if categories are present.
`columnlist`	The list of column names for the result set.
`context`	A context summary highlighting the matched text (if `contextpassages` specified).
`currentrow`	The current row being processed by a loop, such as `<cfoutput>`.
`custom1`	The value of the column indicated in the `custom1` attribute of the `<cfindex>` tag (`custom`).
`custom2`	The value of the column indicated in the `custom2` attribute of the `<cfindex>` tag (`custom`).
`custom3`	The value of the column indicated in the `custom3` attribute of the `<cfindex>` tag (`custom`).
`custom4`	The value of the column indicated in the `custom4` attribute of the `<cfindex>` tag (`custom`).
`key`	The full filename of the document in a `file` or `path` collection type, or the value of the query column indicated in the `key` attribute of `custom` index.
`rank`	Rank within search results.
`recordcount`	The number of records in the result set.
`recordssearched`	The total number of records searched.
`score`	The relevancy score that Verity dynamically calculates based on the search `criteria`.
`size`	Number of bytes in matching document.
`summary`	The automatic summary that `<cfindex>` generates. The default selects the best three matching sentences, up to a maximum of 500 characters.
`title`	The value of the title of an `HTML`, `PDF`, or Microsoft Office document (`file` or `path`), or the value of the column indicated in the `TITLE` attribute (`custom`).
`type`	The MIME type of the matching document.
`url`	The `url` indicated in the `<cfindex>` tag used to populate the collection, plus the filename for the document matched.

Table 38.2 `<cfsearch>` status Variables

STATUS	DESCRIPTION
`found`	The number of documents that matches the search.
`keywords`	A structure containing alternate suggested keywords.
`keywordScore`	Same structure as `keywords`, but contains score values.
`searched`	The total number of records searched.
`suggestedQuery`	Alternate query suggestion that may return better results (for example, due to misspellings).
`time`	Search processing time (in milliseconds).

For query-based collections, **the primary key is usually returned in** `key` and can be used in a `where` clause to return the complete record. File-based collections use a combination of the `url` or `key` columns, depending on how the collection was originally populated. For example, if the `urlpath` attribute of `<cfindex>` was used, you would use this:

```
<!--- query the collection --->
<cfsearch collection="SnailsAndPuppyDogTails"
          name="SearchResults"
          type="SIMPLE"
          criteria="#FORM.keywords#">
<!--- format and output the results --->
<table>
<tr>
 <td>Score</td>
 <td>Document</td>
</tr>
<cfoutput query="SearchResults">
<tr>
 <td>#Score#</td>
 <td><A HREF="#URL#">#Title#</a><br>#Summary#</td>
</tr>
</cfoutput>
</table>
```

NOTE

External Verity collections (that is, collections not created in ColdFusion) can be referenced by using the `external="YES"` attribute of the `<cfindex>` and `<cfsearch>` tags. The collection name in the `COLLECTION` attribute should be set to that of the directory path where the collection resides on the hard drive.

The two fields you can reference in an external collection are `key` and `score`. These are the only fields common to all Verity collections, regardless of the interface through which the collection is created. This means you do not have access to `url`, `title`, `summary`, or the `custom` fields. Likewise, custom fields (that is, non-ColdFusion fields) in external collections cannot be referenced.

> **TIP**
>
> The `<cfsearch>` result set is limited to 64 Kbytes. Using broad search terms, coupled with a large enough collection, users might hit the limit and get an error message. The easiest way to handle the problem is to catch and trap the error and instruct the user to furnish more specific search criteria.

→ Error trapping is discussed in Chapter 26, "Error Handling."

→ Full-text searching can also be performed in SQL databases, by using the `LIKE` operator. SQL searches and pattern matching are covered in Chapter 44, "Basic SQL."

Summary

ColdFusion integration of the Verity search engine lets developers implement powerful full-text searching. Collections can be indexes of all kinds of document types, and they also can represent the contents of a database query.

`<cfcollection>` is used for basic collection maintenance, from creating to optimizing the data. `<cfindex>` is responsible for populating and updating Verity collections. `<cfsearch>` enables users to run complex searches across single or multiple collections.

Sample Questions

1. Which Verity features are inherent in a `simple` query expression?

   A. `stem` operator

   B. `many` modifier

   C. `near` operator

   D. Wildcards

2. Which tag is used to optimize a Verity collection?

   A. `<cfcollection>`

   B. `<cfindex>`

   C. `<cfoptimize>`

   D. `<cffile>`

CHAPTER 39
System Integration

IN THIS CHAPTER

Server File Management

ColdFusion provides comprehensive server-side file and directory management through a series of tags: `<cffile>`, `<cfcontent>`, and `<cfdirectory>`. `<cffile>` is responsible for creating and manipulating files; `<cfcontent>` is used primarily for delivering files of different MIME types from the server to users; and `<cfdirectory>` handles directory listings and management. Together they provide a set of tools with which you can build complex file-management applications that can be operated from a Web browser.

> **NOTE**
>
> As a server-side technology, ColdFusion does not allow the manipulation of files residing on the client's machine. Client-side file manipulation through a Web browser is heavily restricted, for obvious security reasons. For a user on a standard Web browser, the developer can do little more than ask for the file she would like to upload. Client-side file manipulation can be done only through client-side Java applets, ActiveX controls, or similar embedded executables within the Web browser itself. The user must authorize these programs to have additional privileges on his machine.

Working with Files

`<cffile>` is a very flexible tag, with features to upload, read, write, append, copy, move, and delete files on the ColdFusion server. The syntax of `<cffile>` is very intuitive and straightforward, but several attributes and their uses deserve some explanation.

For example, to copy a file from one location to another on the server, you would use the following syntax:

```
<cffile action="COPY"
        source="C:\x\sweet.txt"
        destination="C:\temp\supersweet.txt"
        attributes="ReadOnly,Archive"
        mode="755">
```

`attributes` is a comma-separated list of file settings such as `ReadOnly` and `Archived`. Not specifying `attributes` leaves the file with the original settings.

`mode` is a Unix-only setting that defines permissions for a file. Valid entries correspond to the octal (not symbolic) values of the Unix `chmod` command. Permissions are assigned for owner, group, and other, in sequence. For example, `MODE="755"` gives `rwxr-xr-x` permissions (owner=read/write/execute, group=read/execute, other=read/execute). `mode` is ignored by Windows.

> **CAUTION**
>
> You should be careful when implementing access to `<cffile>` in your application. There are obvious security ramifications in allowing users to perform file management operations on the server. The ColdFusion Administrator application can specifically lock down `<cffile>` so that the tag cannot be used on the server at all.

A file can be read into memory as a variable using `<cffile>` with the `read` action. This variable can be processed like any other variable. The line-feed and carriage-return characters (ASCII 10 and 13 respectively) are frequently used as delimiters for each line of the file. These are referenced in ColdFusion using `Chr(10)` and `Chr(13)`, as shown here:

```
<!--- read the file into a variable --->
<cffile action="READ"
        file="c:filesdaemonite.txt"
         variable="FileText">
<!-- converting file into a more manageable array format -->
<cfset aFile=ArrayNew(1)>
<cfloop list="#FileText#" index="i" delimiters="#Chr(10)##Chr(13)#">
 <cfset tmp=ArrayAppend(aFile, i)>
</cfloop>
```

The act of writing and appending to files is essential for generating static HTML content, log files, and other text files on the server. `<cffile>` with `action="Write"` creates a file and populates it with the contents of the `output` attribute. Appending additional lines of information is easy when you use `action="Append"`. The

ADDNEWLINE attribute, as shown in the following example, even provides a new line, making it ideal for logging:

```
<cffile action="WRITE"
        file="c:\files\helloboys.txt"
        output="hello cruel world!"
        addnewline="Yes">
```

> **TIP**
>
> <cffile> is fairly cumbersome in its approach to writing when the `output` string value is multilined or contains characters that are text delimiters. A clever approach to this problem is to use the <cfsavecontent> tag to capture a long, complex text string as a variable:
>
> ```
> <!--- custom tag to capture long string --->
> <cfsavecontent variable="myTextString">
>  Wherever there is a "Crazy Date"
>  Or a "Dutch Wink" or three
>  You are bound to find plenty of haught
>  And a battered-sav to see!
> </cfsavecontent>
> <cffile action="WRITE"
>         file="c:\files\helloboys.txt"
>         output="#myTextString#"
>         addnewline="Yes">
> ```

> **TIP**
>
> ColdFusion offers a variety of useful functions for working with the server's file system. You often have to work with absolute paths, and several functions are designed to help you determine appropriate pathnames. Some useful functions include the following: `FileExists()`, `ExpandPath()`, `GetCurrentTemplatePath()`, and `GetTemplatePath()`.

<cffile> can read binary files, such as an image or an executable, into a binary object variable in memory like this:

```
<cffile action="ReadBinary"
        file="c:\images\logo.gif"
        variable="logo">
```

The returned variable can be used anywhere in your code like a normal variable. Typically, it is used in conjunction with one of the Web protocols, such as HTTP (using <cfhttp>) or SMTP (using <cfmail>), or for writing to a database (using <cfquery>). The variable is converted to ASCII using base 64 (with the `ToBase64()` function) and can be handled like any other string variable.

→ HTTP and FTP protocols will be covered in Chapter 43, "Other Internet Protocols." SMTP and <CFMAIL> will be discussed in Chapter 41, "Email Integration."

Uploading Files to the Server

Uploading files through a Web browser is a part of the HTTP protocol. The HTML interface and form post have nothing to do with ColdFusion per se. However, ColdFusion and `<cffile>` kick in when the form post reaches the Web server, and the uploaded file needs to be saved to the server file system.

> **CAUTION**
> Different Web browsers have varying degrees of support for the HTTP protocol. Be sure to check that your application's target audience is using a browser that fully supports file uploads.

The standard HTML form needs an additional attribute and input field in order for file uploads to work, as in this example:

```
<form action="upload.cfm"
      method="post"
      enctype="multipart/form-data">
File to upload:<br>
<input type="file" name="uploadfile" size="30"><br>
<input type="submit" value="Upload that file!">
</form>
```

The `enctype` attribute specifies the media type used to encode the form data. The default `enctype` is the MIME type `"application/x-www-form-urlencoded"`, and it's such a mouthful that nobody bothers to specify it in a standard form. However, for a file upload, the media type is different, so you must nominate the appropriate MIME type, `"multipart/form-data"`, in the `enctype` attribute so that the upload will work.

The `<input type="file">` form field is used exclusively for uploading files. It provides a Browse button that activates an operating system–specific dialog box for selecting a single file. You can upload multiple files at once, but each file must have its own form field of `type="file"`, and each form field requires a unique name.

The action page for the upload form contains a `<cffile>` tag with `action="Upload"`. The `filefield` attribute corresponds to the specific form field name in the form post for the file you are saving to the server. If multiple files are being uploaded in a single form post, you need a separate `<cffile>` for each uploaded file, as shown here:

```
<!--- sample upload.cfm file --->
<cffile action="UPLOAD"
        filefield="UploadFile"
        destination="c:\temp"
        nameconflict="OVERWRITE"
        accept="image/gif, image/jpg">
```

If the file upload is successful, ColdFusion writes the file to the server and generates a structure of the file's details. The structure is stored in the `CFFILE` scope and can be accessed using `CFFILE.variablename`.

> **TIP**
>
> `CFFILE` is the default return structure name, unless an alternate name is specified in the **`result`** attribute.

You can use the `nameconflict` attribute to nominate how filename clashes will be handled. The default is `Error`, but you can make more interesting choices:

- **`Error` (default).** The file is not saved, and ColdFusion aborts and returns a run-time error.
- **`Skip`.** The file is not saved, and no error is thrown. This value is designed for custom error handling based on values in the file-upload status parameters.
- **`Overwrite`.** This value replaces an existing file of the same name in the `<cffile>` destination.
- **`MakeUnique`.** If a name conflict occurs in the destination directory, a unique filename is automatically generated for the uploaded file. This name is available in the `CFFILE.ServerFile` variable.

When you are managing a file library, you often might want to restrict the uploaded files to a specific set of MIME types. For example, if you are managing an image library, you may want to restrict uploaded files to those of type .gif or .jpg. The `accept` attribute takes a comma-separated list of valid MIME types as a value and prevents nonconforming MIME types from being uploaded.

> **TIP**
>
> Don't wait for the file to upload before telling your users that they have accidentally (or otherwise) uploaded a file whose MIME type is restricted. You can warn them straightaway with some client-side scripting.
>
> Using JavaScript and the document object model of your Web browser, you can examine the string that contains the path and filename that a user is trying to upload (look for something like **`document.formName.uploadFieldName.value`**). Simply parse this string to make sure the file extension has a match within a predetermined list of valid file extensions.
>
> Although the file extension doesn't actually confirm the file's MIME type, it's likely to catch nearly all your problems. More often than not, the file extension corresponds to a specific MIME type for that file.

You can use `CFFILE.FileSize` to reject a file if it is larger than a predetermined size. Unfortunately, you cannot easily determine the file size prior to uploading. If a user uploads a file that exceeds your file size restriction, he will likely have to wait until the whole file is uploaded before you give him the bad news.

> **TIP**
>
> File size is listed in bytes. To format the value in the more familiar kilobytes, use the following:
>
> `#Numberformat(CFFILE.FileSize/1024)# KB.`

> **TIP**
>
> When a file is uploading via HTTP through a Web browser form post, no feedback is provided on progress. In other words, during the upload the user has no idea how long it has left to go.
>
> You should always provide a detailed explanation to the user that the file may take some time to upload. Give an estimate of upload time based on file size and common connection speeds. If you have a file size restriction, always inform the user before she starts uploading her file!

Delivering Files from the Server

To deliver a file in a simple Web application, you need only a correctly qualified URL to initiate a download using HTTP. Here's an example:

```
<A HREF="http://www.forta.com/sales/leads.xls">Download Leads</A>
```

In more sophisticated applications, you might need to dynamically deliver a file based on a reference in a database. This problem is further complicated by the need to deliver files from an area of the directory tree that is not mapped by the Web server. In other words, the files may not be directly accessible using a URL in the Web browser. This is an absolute requirement for a secure file store, where the application needs to authenticate a user before granting access to the file store.

You can choose from three strategies for delivering files securely:

- Deliver an existing file from the file system.
- Create a file on the fly and deliver.
- Create a temporary file, deliver, and clean up by deleting the temporary file.

The `<cfcontent>` tag specifies a MIME type header to be sent to the browser so that the file will be interpreted as something other than a normal Web page. For example, you may be delivering a comma-separated value (CSV) file or Word document. The output can be generated on the fly, or you can specify an existing file to be delivered from anywhere on the server's file system. `<cfcontent>` also provides the option of deleting the file being delivered, which is perfect for cleaning up temporary files:

```
<!--- for example, delivering a Word document --->
<cfcontent type="application/msword"
           file="C:\FileStore\CALENDAR.DOC"
           deletefile="No">
```

The strategy that you choose for file delivery will largely depend on the type of application you are building. However, all three methods run afoul of the same problem: specifying the filename of the delivered file.

Imagine that you have access to a human resources database. You need to extract a listing of employees for a specific department and deliver it as a CSV file for use in a spreadsheet program. You can build a code template called `employee_list.cfm` that queries the database using a URL parameter called `URL.DID`, then generates the appropriate CSV file:

```
<!--- employee_list.cfm --->
<cfquery name="GetEmp" datasource="dsn">
SELECT *
FROM Employees
WHERE Department_ID = #Val(URL.DID)#
</cfquery>

<cfcontent type="application/unknown">"ID","LName","FName","Email"
<cfoutput query="GetEmp">#EmpID#,"#LastName#","#FirstName#","#Email#"
</cfoutput>
```

TIP

By specifying a MIME type of `"unknown"`, you guarantee that the Web browser will attempt to save the file to disk rather than spawn an application the Web browser believes is appropriate.

The Web browser calls a URL that ends with the filename `employee_list.cfm`, as you can see in this example:

```
http://www.forta.com/hr/employee_list.cfm?did=123
```

The Web browser attempts to save a file called `employee_list.cfm`. If you want to save a file as something like `emplist.csv`, you have to trick the Web browser into seeing a different filename, like this:

```
http://www.forta.com/hr/employee_list.cfm/emplist.csv?did=123
```

Note that you specify the URL parameter as usual at the end of the URL itself. The Web browser picks up the last filename specified and uses it as the filename to save as.

Alternatively, you could try using the `"Content-Disposition"` HTTP header as follows to specify the filename for the user:

```
<cfheader name="Content-Disposition" value="inline;
         filename=emplist.csv">
```

```
<cfcontent type="application/unknown">"ID","LName","FName","Email"
<cfoutput query="GetEmp">#EmpID#,"#LastName#","#FirstName#","#Email#"
</cfoutput>
```

➜ <CFHEADER> and <CFCONTENT> were discussed in Chapter 5, "Redirects and Reuse."

CAUTION

`<cfcontent>` can deliver any file from the server via the Web browser. Furthermore, the tag can be programmed to delete any file on the server. For these reasons, you must carefully consider the use of `<cfcontent>`. The tag can be locked down in ColdFusion Administrator to prevent any use by developers whatsoever.

Working with Directories

The `<cfdirectory>` `list` action returns a query object of files and directories from the specified `directory` attribute. The remaining actions of `<cfdirectory>` can be used to create, delete, and rename directories on the server. These actions, as shown in the following example, are straightforward in their implementation, and combined they can build quite elegant systems for managing directories on the server:

```
<cfdirectory action="LIST"
             directory="C:\Inetpub\wwwroot\cftrain"
             name="dir"
             sort="DESC">
```

TIP

Two ColdFusion functions useful for working with directories are `DirectoryExists()` and `GetDirectoryFromPath()`.

TIP

Universal Naming Convention (UNC) paths on Windows and Novell Netware are possible in ColdFusion but require a few extra steps. When you install ColdFusion, the application server services, by default, start under the standard `system` account. This account normally has no network privileges, so network resources are unavailable to ColdFusion. If you modify the service to start under a specific named account, such as `cfuser`, it is possible to grant specific network privileges for that account and thereby grant ColdFusion access to network resources.

The following code snippets use functions on the UNC path for the computer `elfsbane`, the file share `cdrive`, and the directory `files`:

```
#DirectoryExists("\\elfsbane\cdrive\files")#
#FileExists("\\elfsbane\cdrive\files\test.txt")#
```

CAUTION

<cfdirectory> gives developers access to the entire directory structure of the server. This potential security risk can be prevented by blocking the use of the tag through ColdFusion Administrator.

Registry Integration

Windows uses a database called the Registry to maintain system information about users, hardware, and installed software.

NOTE

Registry use and the <cfregistry> tag are supported only on the Windows platform.

The Registry stores information through a hierarchy of keys and values:

- Keys can contain values or other keys.
- A key and any keys or values below it are known as a *Registry branch*.
- Values are split into two components: the value name and the value data.

CAUTION

The Registry contains system-critical information. Editing the Registry incorrectly may severely damage your system. At the very least, you should back up the Registry data on the server before tinkering. For obvious reasons, you can restrict developer access to <cfregistry> through ColdFusion Administrator.

You can use <cfregistry> to query the Registry; it returns a standard query object of keys and values. Use the `action` attribute with `get` to retrieve one entry or with `getall`, as shown here, to retrieve multiple keys and values from the Registry:

```
<!--- Grabbing data from the Registry --->
<cfregistry action="GetAll"
            branch="HKEY_LOCAL_MACHINE\Software\Macromedia"
            type="Any"
            name="reg">

<table border="1">
<tr>
 <th>Entry</th>
 <th>Type</th>
 <th>Value</th>
</tr>
<cfoutput query="reg">
```

```
<tr>
 <td>#Entry#</td>
 <td>#Type#</td>
 <td>#Value#</td>
</tr>
</cfoutput>
</table>
```

> **TIP**
>
> In the `<cfregistry>` result set, if `#Type#` is a key, then `#Value#` is an empty string. When you specify `TYPE="Any"`, `GetAll` returns any binary Registry values. However, the binary value's `#Type#` variable contains `unsupported`, and `#Value#` is blank.

The `<cfregistry>` tag allows you to add, edit, and delete Registry values. You can use the `set` action to add or update Registry keys and value data. `<cfregistry>` simply creates the key or value if it does not already exist. You need to specify attributes for `branch`, the `entry` to set, the value's `type` of data, and the value data itself. You can also use `<cfregistry>` with the `delete` action to delete Registry keys and values.

Executing from the Command Line

`<cfexecute>` lets you execute any process on the server machine. The process is effectively invoked from the command line, spawning a separate thread. This powerful tag provides your ColdFusion code with access to a wealth of system applications, from Perl and shell scripts to Windows executables and batch files.

You can pass `<cfexecute>` a series of command-line `ARGUMENTS` as either a string or an array:

```
<cfexecute name="c:\perl\bin\perl.exe"
           arguments='-e print "hello world!";'
           timeout="20">
</cfexecute>
```

> **NOTE**
>
> In Perl, `-e` allows a line of code to be executed from the command line.

> **NOTE**
>
> On Windows systems, you must specify the extension–for example, `.exe`–as part of the application's name. The application's full pathname is also required.

The output of the external program is directed to the specified `outputfile`, as shown in the following example. Alternatively, if no file is nominated, the output is written back to the page from which it was called.

```
<cfscript>
 aArgs=ArrayNew(1);
 aArgs[1]="/all";
</cfscript>

<cfexecute name="C:\WinNT\System32\ipconfig.exe"
           arguments="#aArgs[1]#"
           outputfile="c:\x\ipsettings.txt"
           timeout="500">
```

The `timeout` indicates how long in seconds the ColdFusion executing thread will wait for the spawned process to finish. Using the default `timeout` of `0` forces the ColdFusion thread to spawn a process and immediately return without waiting for the process to terminate. The file is effectively executed asynchronously from the ongoing processing of the calling application page.

> **NOTE**
>
> The effective user of the ColdFusion executing thread must have permissions to execute the program on the server. If not, a security exception is thrown.

Summary

ColdFusion provides comprehensive server-side file management using `<cffile>`, `<cfcontent>`, and `<cfdirectory>`. Standard file operations such as move, copy, and delete can be performed using `<cffile>`. `<cffile>` can create or write new files and append to existing ones. The `<cffile>` tag reads string and binary files into ColdFusion variables. `<cffile>` is required to write uploaded files to disk at the end of an HTTP post. `<cfcontent>` can deliver files of different MIME types from the server to the user's Web browser. `<cfdirectory>` manipulates and reads directory listings on the server.

`<cfregistry>` gives you complete access to the Registry system information repository. `<cfexecute>` allows programmers to spawn processes from the command line of the server.

Sample Questions

1. Access to which of the following tags can be restricted in ColdFusion Administrator? *(select four)*

   A. `<cffile>`

   B. `<cfcontent>`

   C. `<cfdirectory>`

   D. `<cfregistry>`

   E. `<cfquery>`

   F. `<cfparam>`

2. Which tag would you use to obtain the size of a file?

   A. `<cffile>`

   B. `<cfcontent>`

   C. `<cfdirectory>`

   D. `<cfsize>`

3. Which value of the `enctype` attribute of `<form>` is required to enable file uploads from the browser?

   A. `enctype="text/plain"`

   B. `enctype="multipart/form-data"`

   C. `enctype="application/x-www-form-urlencoded"`

   D. `enctype` is *not* a required attribute.

CHAPTER 40

Scheduling and Event Execution

IN THIS CHAPTER

Scheduling Events in ColdFusion

The ColdFusion server maintains a list of events or tasks that can be scheduled to run periodically. Scheduling events in ColdFusion is similar to using the Unix operating system's `cron` table or Windows' `AT` command. Each event corresponds to a ColdFusion template file that gets executed according to the parameters set in the schedule.

The execution mechanism in ColdFusion is restricted to HTTP calls. A `<cfhttp>` agent calls the scheduled template and runs the file at the designated time. Any template that can be run by a Web browser can be executed using the scheduler, thereby covering just about everything you might want ColdFusion to achieve.

➜ `<cfhttp>` and HTTP agents are covered in Chapter 42, "Other Internet Protocols."

Scheduling a Task

You can schedule individual tasks by using the Web-based ColdFusion Administrator application, or programmatically by using the `<cfschedule>` tag. Schedule information is loaded into the ColdFusion server memory. The active schedule list is also reloaded when the ColdFusion service is cycled.

ColdFusion Administrator provides an easy-to-use interface for maintaining, creating, and deleting schedules through a Web browser. All the features of scheduling are available through a series of form inputs, including a very convenient list of currently active schedules. However, you need access to Administrator to view these options. Access may not be available in many hosting environments, especially those maintained by ISPs and commercial ColdFusion hosting partners.

`<cfschedule>` provides you with access to all the features of ColdFusion Administrator. You can update, run, or delete individual schedules according to the chosen

ACTION. The tag attributes are intuitive and correspond directly to the form fields in Administrator. However, you cannot use `<cfschedule>` to display a listing of currently active schedules.

For example, the Crazy Date schedule that follows should run for three years, firing off every day and running the `tasks/partydate.cfm` application page with a timeout of `300` seconds:

```
<!--- Set up the Crazy Date schedule --->
<cfschedule action="UPDATE"
            task="crazy date"
            operation="HTTPRequest"
            url="http://127.0.0.1/tasks/partydate.cfm"
            startdate="12/12/00"
            starttime="03:45 AM"
            enddate="12/12/03"
            interval="Daily"
            requesttimeout="300">
```

The scheduler's refresh interval defaults to 15 minutes and can be modified through ColdFusion Administrator. This interval determines how often the scheduler checks the saved scheduled task list for new tasks. Valid intervals are:

- once
- daily
- weekly
- monthly
- Number of seconds (the minimum is `60`)

Upon refresh, the scheduler updates the active task list as required. The list is then regularly inspected to determine which tasks are ready to be run.

CAUTION

Scheduled events correspond to an application page that must necessarily reside on a mapped area of the Web server. The schedule agent uses `<cfhttp>` to execute the task pages on the Web server, just like any other pages in the Web application.

The agent is not sophisticated enough to log in to an application with session management, so the application page is essentially exposed to anyone with a Web browser. Depending on the type of task you are scheduling, it may not be appropriate for everybody using a browser to be able to execute the event page.

A good practice is to secure a nominated "tasks" directory to allow only the local ColdFusion server access to run pages. Using the Web server security for virtual directories, you can restrict access to the Web server's own IP address or `127.0.0.1` for the tasks directory. Alternatively, you can include code like the following at the beginning of the event application page to check the HTTP agent for appropriate `CGI` variables:

```
<cfif CGI.remote_host NEQ "127.0.0.1">
 <cfabort showerror="Go away, bad person!">
</cfif>
```

Publishing to Static Pages

ColdFusion applications serve dynamic content, which is generated upon each request. Sometimes it may be preferable to save static versions of the content, the advantage being that they'll perform better, but the cost is that they won't always be up to date.

You can use scheduled events to publish static Web pages. Normally, a scheduled event is executed, performs some task, and doesn't bother about output to the screen because no one is there to see it work. However, `<cfschedule>` can be instructed to save the results of the event page output and write them to the file system, as follows:

```
<!--- Publish static HTML for the wind section --->
<cfschedule action="update"
            task="Orchestral"
            operation="HTTPRequest"
            url="http://127.0.0.1/tasks/flautist.cfm"
            startdate="8/7/99"
            starttime="01:30 AM"
            interval="3600"
            resolveurl="Yes"
            publish="Yes"
            file="theflute.htm"
            path="c:\inetpub\wwwroot\windup"
            requesttimeout="600">
```

Setting `publish="Yes"`, with appropriate directory `path` and `file` attributes, directs the scheduled event to save the resulting output of its application template to disk. `resolveurl` behaves similarly to the attribute in `<cfhttp>`. For example, publishing using a scheduled task is ideal for building long-running reports that can be executed during quiet server periods. In addition, dynamic content that is updated infrequently can be published periodically using `<cfschedule>` to save hits on the database.

➜ `<cfhttp>` and HTTP agents will be covered in Chapter 43, "Other Internet Protocols."

Running a Scheduled Event

Scheduled events usually run when they are scheduled to, as you'd expect. If need be, ColdFusion allows you to trigger a scheduled event so that it runs on demand. To execute a scheduled event, use `action="run"`, as seen here:

```
<!--- Run now --->
<cfschedule action="run"
            task="Orchestral">
```

Deleting a Scheduled Event

Scheduled tasks may be deleted by using ColdFusion Administrator, or with `<cfschedule>` and `action="delete"`, as seen here:

```
<!--- delete it --->
<cfschedule action="delete"
            task="orchestral">
```

Logging Scheduled Events

The scheduled event's task name, time stamp, and success or failure status are written to log files for future reference.

For example, a log entry for the `Orchestral` task mentioned earlier might reveal the following:

```
"Information","TID=960","12/04/00","03:30:00","Scheduled action
Orchestral, template http://127.0.0.1/tasks/flautist.cfm submitted
successfully."
```

Unfortunately, the log is not terribly informative about telling you whether the event was executed successfully. If a task failed and generated a ColdFusion run-time error, you would expect to see the details of the error indicated in the ColdFusion `application.log`.

Alternative Scheduling Options

Most operating systems have mechanisms for scheduling the periodic execution of tasks. You can execute ColdFusion from the command line by calling the server executable and passing the location of the template to be executed.

Windows use the `at` command. `at` can be used to list existing commands in the schedule or to schedule commands and programs to run on a computer at a specified time and date. The Windows `Schedule` service must be running to use `at`.

Unix uses a handy little utility called `Cron`, which is controlled by a set of files called `crontabs`. A master file is stored in the `/etc/crontab` directory, along with `crontab` files for individual users in `/var/spool/cron/`.

`crontab filename` will install the file you specify as a new `crontab`. The `crontab` command has some other switches that list, edit, and remove `crontabs`, but the basic syntax is all you need. If you want to edit the `crontab`, you simply reinstall the file with a new `crontab` command.

> **NOTE**
>
> For more information, run `man cron` and `man crontab` for your particular flavor of Unix.

Summary

The schedule event subsystem of ColdFusion is ideal for periodic, asynchronous execution of CFML templates. You can schedule tasks over the Web by using ColdFusion Administrator, or programmatically by using the `<cfschedule>` tag. You also can direct scheduled tasks to publish their output to files such as static Web pages. Event execution timings are managed by the ColdFusion server and have their own log file for recording success or failure.

Sample Questions

1. How does the ColdFusion scheduler execute code in a specified template?

   A. Using an HTTP call

   B. Using `cron` or `at` processes, depending on the operating system

   C. Using command-line arguments

   D. None of the above

2. Which are valid `<cfschedule> ACTION` values? *(select three)*

   A. `add`

   B. `update`

   C. `delete`

   D. `run`

3. Which of the following are valid scheduler intervals?

   A. `hourly`

   B. `weekly`

   C. `90`

   D. `15`

CHAPTER 41

Email Integration

IN THIS CHAPTER

Sending Mail with ColdFusion

ColdFusion provides out-of-the-box support for sending email through Simple Mail Transfer Protocol (SMTP) mail servers with the `<cfmail>` tag. The ColdFusion Application Server does not ship with its own built-in SMTP mail server. To provide messaging services for your application, you must have access to a separate SMTP server (the same is true for POP mail, described later in this chapter).

Sending Simple Text Email

`<cfmail>`'s behavior is similar to that of `<cfoutput>`. Whereas `<cfoutput>` sends information back to the Web browser, `<cfmail>` outputs the same information to an email message. The additional attributes of `<cfmail>` correspond to those fields required to correctly format an email message.

`<cfmail>` can contain CFML, and it resolves variables just like `<cfoutput>`. However, although `<cfmail>` accepts a `query` attribute, its behavior depends on how the query is used. This issue is discussed in detail later in this chapter.

You can specify multiple recipients by providing a comma-separated list of qualified email addresses, as follows:

```
<cfmail to="john@doe.com,jane@doe.com"
        from="pal@yourfriend.com"
        subject="Hope you're feeling better!"
        cc="buddy@myfriend.com"
        bcc="agent@watchingyou.com">
```

```
<cfif recipient is "alive">
Hey, get well soon ... hope I'm not too late.
</cfif>
This message was sent #DateFormat(Now())#.
</cfmail>
```

➜ Lists were covered in Chapter 13, "Lists."

You can specify a default SMTP mail server in ColdFusion Administrator. Alternatively, you can specify SMTP settings in the `<cfmail>` tag itself, which will override the default settings. If no SMTP server is specified, a standard ColdFusion run-time error occurs.

TIP

Text inside an email message is not like text on a Web page. White space can be very important in an email message, and every space, tab, and return affects the formatting. So you need to be careful how you format ColdFusion code within the `<cfmail>` tag.

Long lines of text without line breaks may cause some email clients to display the message improperly. It is good practice to force text wrapping in your message by starting a new line at the end of every 65 characters or so. Several third-party Custom Tags are available to help implement text wrapping.

CAUTION

If you place a single period (`.`) on its own line in the body of a generated email message, some SMTP servers see it as a command to end the message and may truncate your text at that point.

Sending HTML Email

You can use `<cfmail>` to send HTML mail by setting the appropriate attribute, as shown in the following example:

```
<cfmail from="newsletter@funstuff.com"
        to="geoff@hottermail.com"
        subject="This Month in Fun Stuff!"
        type="HTML">
<h1>November Fun Stuff</h1>
<p>Jump for joy fun stuff brings you <strong>plenty</strong> of
things to keep you <font color="red">amused</font> for hours.</p>
</cfmail>
```

The `type` attribute sets headers for the receiving email client; these headers serve as instructions that the email message contains embedded HTML to be rendered. Images in the HTML are typically referenced with absolute URLs to servers online and are not included in the HTML message itself.

> **CAUTION**
>
> Not all email clients can handle HTML mail. Indeed, even among those clients that can, some users may have set their preferences to view email as text rather than HTML. HTML mail in a text email client is difficult to read.
>
> If you reference images in your message, the recipient must be online to be able to see them. Otherwise, all she'll see are a series of broken images. References to images should consist of complete (absolute) URLs, not relative URLs.

Query-Driven Email

Just like `<cfoutput>`, `<cfmail>` can loop over a query object, as shown here, resolving each record in the query into an individual and personalized email:

```
<cfmail query="GetCustomers"
        from="service@forta.com"
        to="#EMail#"
        subject="Registration Verification">
Dear #FirstName#,
We'd like to verify ... blah ... blah ...
</cfmail>
```

You can use the `GROUP` attribute in a fashion similar to that of `GROUP` in `<CFOUTPUT>`. You also can group sets of records to send a series of individual email messages, each with the records of a particular group category.

Using a nested set of `<cfoutput>` tags has a slightly different effect than you might expect. The code behaves as though you are using `group`, except that all the records belong to a single group category. The text within the nested `<cfoutput>` tag is repeated for every row in the nominated query, as shown in the following example, while the text surrounding it serves as the header and footer for a single email message:

```
<cfmail query="ProductRequests"
        from="webmaster@forta.com"
        to="marketing@forta.com"
        subject="MegaDeveloper Status Report">
Here is a list of people who have inquired about
MegaDeveloper over the last seven days:
<cfoutput>
#FirstName# #LastName# (#Company#) - #EMailAddress#
</cfoutput>
Regards,
The WebMaster
webmaster@mega.com
</cfmail>
```

Sending File Attachments

`<cfmailparam>` is a subtag of `<cfmail>`. To send MIME-encoded file attachments, you can use it as follows:

```
<cfmail from="field@forta.com"
        to="sales@forta.com"
        subject="Monthly Reports">
<cfmailparam file="c:\reports\jan.xls">
<cfmailparam file="c:\reports\feb.xls">
Here is a copy of the sales numbers.
Regards
</cfmail>
```

The `file` attribute must specify an absolute path on the ColdFusion server to the file being attached. You can specify multiple files by using multiple `<cfmailparam>` tags.

A common misconception is that users can combine an email form and a file attachment in their Web applications. The file must be on the ColdFusion server, not the client's workstation, in order for the mail attachment to work. Web-based mail clients use a two-step process for attachments: uploading the files to the server, then sending and attaching the files to the email.

➜ Chapter 39, "System Integration," discussed uploading files to the server.

> **NOTE**
> In earlier versions of ColdFusion, the `mimeattach` attribute was used to specify a single file attachment only. This attribute has been superseded by the `<cfmailparam>` tag, but the server continues to be backward-compatible.

Inline Attachments

Attachments can also be used within the message body. For example, an HTML e-mail message may refer to an image that is included with the message as an attachment (instead of needing a URL back to a server). To do this use `<cfmailparam>` and specify `disposition="inline"` and a `contentid`. That `contentid` can then be used within the message body, like this:

```
<cfmail from="ben@forta.com"
        to="kids@forta.com"
        subject="Hi there">
        type="html">
<cfmailparam file="c:\images\ben.gif"
             disposition="inline"
             contentid="ben">
<img src="cid:ben">
</cfmail>
```

Additional Mail Headers

You can set additional mail headers—beyond those that you can specify directly from the <CFMAIL> attributes—by using <cfmailparam> as follows:

```
<cfmail from="orders@forta.com"
        to="list@forta.com"
        subject="Shipping!">
<cfmailparam name="Reply-To"
             value="feedback@forta.com">
The new CF Certification Study Guide is shipping!
</cfmail>
```

Retrieving POP Mail

Post Office Protocol (POP) is a very common store-and-forward email standard used by Internet service providers and corporate administrators alike.

<cfpop> contacts a qualified POP email account and retrieves the message file as a ColdFusion query object for use in your application. In effect, <cfpop>'s behavior is similar to that of <CFQUERY>, except that it retrieves information from a POP server rather than a SQL database.

ColdFusion does not ship with a built-in POP server. You must have a valid POP account on an external POP server. For each retrieval, the <cfpop> tag, shown here, requires the server and user account details specified:

```
<cfpop action="getheaderonly"
       name="GetHeaders"
       server="mail.forta.com"
       username="lalalalala"
       password="dumdeedum">
```

> **NOTE**
> Unlike with `<cfmail>`, the `server` attribute `<cfpop>` is required; there is no server default.

<cfpop> can perform a variety of actions on the POP server; these actions are specifically designed to leverage the POP mail standard:

- `getheaderonly` Retrieves only message headers
- `getall` Retrieves an entire message body
- `getall` Retrieves file attachments when `ATTACHMENTPATH` is specified
- `delete` Deletes messages on the server

The two retrieval actions, `getheaderonly` and `getall`, are provided to maximize performance. Header information is generally small in size and quick to retrieve. The size of the full message, including the body and any attached files, is impossible to predict because the information is not available in the `getheaderonly` query, so the message body and files are generally retrieved one at a time.

> **NOTE**
> Building a Web-based POP interface is a relatively straightforward matter. The application involves retrieving the message headers from the server, and providing a drill-down to individual messages with the option to retrieve files and the capability to delete unwanted messages from the server. ColdFusion can also use a POP account as a drop box for collecting email messages and processing their contents autonomously. For example, you could schedule a process to poll the POP account periodically, collect the mail, and update a database.

POP Dates

The date field in the `<CFPOP>` query object is in a specific POP date format and needs to be processed before it can be manipulated like a standard date. The `ParseDateTime()` function accepts an argument for converting POP date/time objects into Greenwich mean time:

```
#ParseDateTime(queryname.date, "POP")#
```

File Attachments

File attachments are returned with the `GETALL` action only if the `ATTACHMENTPATH` attribute is set to a valid directory path on the ColdFusion server, as follows:

```
<cfpop action="getall"
       name="GetMail"
       messagenumber="1"
       attachmentpath="c:mailattach"
       generateuniquefilenames="Yes"
       server="mail.forta.com"
       username="lalalalala"
       password="dumdeedum">
```

In this instance, two additional columns are returned:

- `attachments` A tab-separated list of the source attachment names
- `attachmentfiles` A tab-separated list of the actual temporary filenames written to the server

In the event that there are no attachments, both of these columns are returned as empty strings. By setting the `generateduniquefilenames` attribute of `<cfpop>` to `"Yes"`, you can avoid duplicate filenames when saving attachments to the ColdFusion server.

You can then use `<cffile>` to move temporary files to a more permanent storage area on the server.

Attachments need to end up with their original names, but POP is an open and portable protocol available on many different operating systems. Unfortunately, not all operating systems that support POP (servers and clients) support the same filenames. For example, if you send a file named `super green price list.xls` from Windows 2000 to someone on a DOS box, you'll have problems. DOS supports only filenames in the 8.3 format. Or perhaps you need to send two files whose names are exactly the same, except for the letter casing, from a Unix box (which differentiates filenames by case) to an NT box (which does not).

To solve this problem, POP keeps two pieces of information for each file: the original source filename and the name of the actual attached file, which can be different. The physical attachments are named by their alternative names when they are retrieved from the POP server; those names are safe. `<cfpop>` returns those filenames in two tab-separated lists, `attachments` and `attachmentfiles`, respectively.

➜ File manipulation on the ColdFusion server was covered in Chapter 39, "System Integration." Lists were discussed in Chapter 13, "Lists."

Deleting Mail

Deleting messages from a POP server is different from deleting records from a database. Each message on the POP server is uniquely identified by a `MESSAGENUMBER`. For example, starting with the oldest message, you have `1, 2, 3`, and so on up to the total number of messages in the mailbox. However, this unique assignment is only temporary.

Message numbers are reassigned at the end of every `<CFPOP>` delete action. If three messages are retrieved from a POP mail server, the message numbers returned are `1, 2,` and `3`. If message `2` is deleted, message `1` remains `1` and message `3` is assigned as message number `2`. Therefore, unlike a typical database primary key, the `messagenumber` key is reassigned depending on what is present in the message queue.

Troubleshooting ColdFusion Mail

To understand where to look when things go wrong with mail services, we need to inspect what ColdFusion does when it sends email.

The `<cfmail>` command generates a mail spool file containing information about the server to use, recipients, sender, and so on, and places it in the `cfusionmx7\mail\spool` directory. A special low-level thread sweeps the `spool` directory every 15 seconds, sending any spool files to the SMTP server specified in the mail headers.

> **NOTE**
> A mail spool file is a simple text file specifically formatted for an SMTP server. It starts with a series of mail headers and finishes with the body of the mail message.

If the specified SMTP server refuses to send the message, or if ColdFusion is unable to contact the SMTP server, an error is logged, and the spool file is moved to the `cfusionmx7\mail\undelivr` directory.

You can set mail error-logging options in ColdFusion Administrator. Your SMTP server's log may be another place to look for enlightenment.

> **CAUTION**
> SMTP servers have a multitude of configuration options. A common cause of undelivered mail is anti-relay measures on the SMTP server. This can prevent unauthorized senders from using the mail server at all. Depending on your environment, you might need to ensure that the ColdFusion server is authorized to use the SMTP server and that the sender field has a correctly formatted email address, among other things.
>
> The ColdFusion log files and your SMTP server's transaction log are good places to look when email inexplicably appears in the `undelivr` directory.

Undelivered mail can be reprocessed by simply moving the spool file from `cfusionmx7\mail\undelivr` back to `cfusionmx7\mail\spool`. This procedure can be done programmatically through ColdFusion or manually by an administrator. You can automate this by scheduling a process to scan the `undelivr` directory and move any files back to the `spool` directory. However, malformed spool files or files with incorrect header information (such as a bad email address) may be in the `undelivr` directory for a very good reason—that is, they are undeliverable!

➜ Scheduling periodic processes was covered in Chapter 40, "Scheduling and Event Execution."

> **CAUTION**
> The message numbers returned by `<cfpop>` are relative to the position of the email messages in the POP message queue. Message numbers should not be stored as unique identifiers because they change whenever email is deleted from the mailbox queue. They should be used immediately because of the transient nature of POP mail storage.

Summary

ColdFusion offers comprehensive email integration with both SMTP and POP servers. Text and HTML mail messages can be sent. Query-driven mail can be generated and personalized to combine database content with the mail output. POP accounts can be queried for stored email and associated MIME file attachments. Overall, the depth of support provided lets you generate sophisticated Web applications that seamlessly leverage the Internet's most ubiquitous information system—email.

Sample Questions

1. <cfmailparam> is used to perform which of the following? (select two)

   A. Generate HTML email

   B. Send attachments

   C. Set mail headers

   D. Retry undelivered mail

2. ColdFusion supports which of the following mail protocols?

   A. SMTP

   B. POP

   C. IMAP

   D. MIME attachments

3. Which character should never appear alone on a line in a generated email message?

   A. #

   B. <

   C. >

   D. .

4. Which are valid <cfpop> actions?

   A. getheaderonly

   B. getattachments

   C. getall

   D. delete

CHAPTER 42
LDAP

IN THIS CHAPTER

Understanding LDAP

Lightweight Directory Access Protocol (LDAP) was conceived as a simplified interface to X.500 directories. Today, LDAP is an interface to all sorts of proprietary directory services, including Microsoft Exchange and Novell, and is a directory server protocol in its own right.

LDAP is a protocol that allows organizations to store and access directory-style information. For example, developers can build a central store of contact lists, user authentication, and security policies. This repository might form the basis of a single login for a myriad of different services, such as Novell's NDS, Lotus Notes, Windows Active Directory, and more. Because LDAP is an Internet standard, client programs and applications can be built to common specifications to hook into the directory's information repository. `<cfldap>` is the tag in ColdFusion that lets developers communicate with any LDAP interface.

A directory is similar to a database but contains more descriptive, attribute-based information. The information in a directory is generally read much more often than it is written. As a result, directories don't normally implement the complicated transaction schemes that regular databases use for high-volume, complex updates. LDAP updates typically are simple all-or-nothing changes. Directories are tuned to give quick response to high-volume lookup and search operations.

The LDAP directory data model is based on collections of attributes called *entries*. The unique reference to an entry is called a *distinguished name (DN)*. Each of the entry's attributes has a type and one or more values. The types are typically mnemonic strings, such as `"cn"` for common name and `"mail"` for email address. The values depend on the type of attribute it is. For example, a mail attribute might contain the value `"ben@forta.com"`.

LDAP directory entries are arranged in a treelike structure. Entries representing countries appear at the top of the tree. Below them are entries representing organizations. Further down the branch, you might find entries representing people, organizational units, printers, documents, and just about anything else you can think of.

Through the use of a special LDAP attribute called an `objectclass`, you can control which attributes are required and allowed in an entry. The values of the `objectclass` attribute determine the directory schema rules to which the entry must adhere.

An entry is referenced by its distinguished name, which is constructed by concatenating the name of the entry itself (called the *relative distinguished name*, or *RDN*) and the names of its ancestor entries.

Connecting to LDAP

LDAP defines directory operations for adding or deleting an entry, modifying an existing entry, and changing the name of an entry. However, LDAP is used primarily to search for information in the directory. The LDAP search operation allows a section of the directory to be searched for entries that match criteria specified by a search filter. From a programming perspective, LDAP is just another client/server data management system.

For example, the following code would extract employee data from an LDAP directory:

```
<cfldap action="QUERY"
        name="emp"
        attributes="cn,o,l,c,mail,telephonenumber"
        start="o=forta, c=US"
        sort="cn ASC"
        server="ldap.forta.com">

<!--- Display employees --->
<cfoutput>
There were #emp.RecordCount# employees found.
</cfoutput>
<table>
 <tr>
 <th>Name</TH>
 <th>Organization</th>
 <th>Location</th>
 <th>EMail</th>
 <th>Phone</th>
 </tr>
 <cfoutput query="emp">
 <tr>
 <td>#cn#</td>
 <td>#o#</td>
 <td>#l#, #c#</td>
 <td><a href="mailto:#mail#">#mail#</a></td>
```

```
    <td>#telephonenumber#</td>
    </tr>
    </cfoutput>
  </table>
```

The ATTRIBUTES parameter dictates which entities—or in a database sense, which columns—the search returns. START nominates the branch in the directory hierarchy at which the search should start. We are sorting by common name in ascending order. Matching information is returned as a query object specified by the NAME attribute. See Table 42.1 for more <cfldap> attributes.

➜ Displaying query objects with <cfoutput> is discussed in Chapter 7, "Using Databases."

Table 42.1 <cfldap> Attributes and Their Use

VARIABLE NAMES	DESCRIPTION
action	Must be add, modify, modifydn, delete, or query.
attributes	Comma-delimited list of attributes to be returned in the QUERY or updated on the directory.
delimiter	Delimiter used in multiple name-value pairs.
dn	Distinguished name (DN) is the directory key for the entity being updated.
filter	The filter attribute is more akin to the search criteria of a query rather than an actual filter. No filter returns all entries.
filterfile	An absolute file path or filename in cfusionldap that conforms to the LDAP filter file format (as defined in RFC 1558).
maxrows	The maximum number of rows returned. May be superseded by a maxrows setting on the LDAP directory itself.
modifytype	Specifies how to process a value in a multivalue list. May be ADD, DELETE, or REPLACE.
name	The name of the query object returned by <cfldap>.
password	Login password needed for authenticated directory access. This is typically required to perform updates on the directory.
rebind	Specifies whether referral callback is used. If not, referred connections are anonymous.
referral	Number of hops used for referral (if rebind is used).
scope	The depth to which the search will run in the directory hierarchy. Defaults to ONELEVEL.
secure	Provides security options for encrypting the transmission of data to and from the LDAP server.
separator	Delimiter used in multivalue attributes; the default is a comma.

Table 42.1 (CONTINUED)

VARIABLE NAMES	DESCRIPTION
`server/port`	Required to locate the `LDAP` server. `server` can be a qualified domain name or an IP address. `PORT` defaults to `389`.
`sort`	An attribute listed in `ATTRIBUTES`. `sort` can be either ascending (`ASC`) or descending (`DESC`). This attribute may not be supported on all servers.
`sortcontrol`	Enter `NOCASE` for non-case-sensitive sorting.
`start`	Specifies the DN of the entry branch from which to start the search.
`startrow`	Start row of a query; useful for building a Next/Previous-style results page. Defaults to `1`.
`timeout`	Operational time-out. Defaults to 60 seconds.
`username`	Login user name needed for authenticated directory access. This is typically required to perform updates on the directory.

LDAP offers a collection of `filter` operators. These can be used to apply Boolean and wildcard searches on the directory entries. For example, restricting a search to an organization name of `Forta` and a country of `US` could be done using the following line:

```
filter=(&(o=Forta)(c=US))
```

`<cfldap>` provides actions for updating LDAP directories. Typically a `username` and `password` with appropriate permissions are required to perform additions or modifications to the directory. For modifications or deletions, you will need to know the distinguished name, which acts like a database primary key. Lastly, the `attributes` parameter is used to specify a list of LDAP attributes to be updated or added to the hierarchy:

```
<cfldap action="add"
        dn="cn=Ben Forta, ou=Development, o=forta.com"
        attributes="objectclass=top, person, organizationalPerson;
        mail=ben@forta.com;
        telephonenumber=555-5555;
        ou=Development"
        modifytype="REPLACE"
        server="ldap.forta.com"
        username="cn=admin, ou=IT, o=forta.com"
        password="tralala">
```

In this example, a `DN` for an administrator, `admin`, is used as the `username`; the particular record being updated is specified in the `DN` attribute; and the `attributes` list the values for updating an entry for `Ben Forta`.

> **NOTE**
>
> If a single attribute value contains a comma, you must escape it by adding an extra comma.

Summary

LDAP is a directory protocol used as an interface to many disparate directory vendors. It allows a common coding interface for developers to access directory information. LDAP is similar to other data management systems, such as databases, and is read-optimized for fast, high-volume lookup searches. ColdFusion uses the `<cfldap>` tag to provide query and update actions on LDAP-compliant servers.

Sample Questions

1. What does LDAP use as a unique reference or primary key in the directory hierarchy?

   A. `UUID` (Universally Unique Identifier)

   B. `DN` (distinguished name)

   C. `RDN` (relative distinguished name)

   D. `objectclass`

2. Which `<cfldap>` attribute is used to specify the distinguished name of the entry for a directory branch within which a search is performed?

   A. `start`

   B. `startrow`

   C. `dn`

   D. `scope`

3. In LDAP, the distinguished name is what? *(select two)*

   A. A unique reference to an attribute in the directory

   B. A concatenation of an `RDN` and its ancestor attributes

   C. The name of an entry in the directory

   D. The `objectclass` definition

CHAPTER 43
Other Internet Protocols

IN THIS CHAPTER

Using HTTP Agents

HTTP agents provide developers with the opportunity to leverage other Web servers as an information resource. ColdFusion uses `<CFHTTP>` to connect to and retrieve content from remote servers. The agent (your ColdFusion code) behaves just like a Web browser, retrieving the entire contents of the designated URL's page. Combined with other ColdFusion technologies, HTTP agents form the basic transport for content and application syndication services. HTTP agents fall into two camps: unilateral and cooperative.

Unilateral agents retrieve the contents of a Web page without any type of cooperation with the remote information resource. The developer has to determine flexible methodologies for coping with the returned data to accommodate potential changes in the structure of the information returned. For example, when syndicating headlines from the home page of a news portal, the portal owner might change the layout of his Web site from time to time. Consequently, unilateral agents are generally more complex to code, can break easily, and are prone to copyright infringements.

Cooperative agents are those that work in concert with a back-end page or robot on the remote server. A back-end page is not designed to be seen by a user with a Web browser; rather, it is coded specifically to respond to an HTTP agent. As a result, cooperative agents are generally very easy to put together and do not break often. On the other hand, a back-end page can be fairly complex depending on the level of functionality being delivered to the incoming agent: for example, a news portal delivering an XML news feed to syndicate partners.

Creating HTTP Agents

The `<cfhttp>` tag spawns an external agent that goes to a specified URL and retrieves the page's contents via HTTP. The agent is sophisticated and remarkably simple to implement:

```
<cfhttp url="http://www.forta.com/"
        method="GET"
        resolveurl="true">
</cfhttp>

<cfoutput>
#CFHTTP.FileContent#
</cfoutput>
```

In this example, `<cfhttp>` is sending an agent to retrieve and then display the `forta.com` home page. The entire contents of the page are returned as the variable `CFHTTP.FileContent`. The `method="get"` attribute is used to retrieve any text or binary file from the URL.

When a file is brought back from a remote server, any relative links to images, other Web pages, and so on will no longer be valid. `resolveurl` determines whether to resolve URLs found in `CFHTTP.FileContent` to absolute addresses. Absolute links will then point to the correct remote address.

When a Web browser accesses a Web server, it indicates the browser's type and version. The `useragent` attribute can be used to nominate the agent or browser of your choice. The default is `"ColdFusion"`.

> **TIP**
>
> Web sites often use routines to detect the type of browser the user is operating. This information is then used to deliver a different client-side experience depending on the browser detected. To ensure that your HTTP agent returns the Web page you expect, make sure that the `USERAGENT` attribute is set to an actual Web browser type.
>
> You can determine a Web browser's user agent value by browsing a ColdFusion server while debugging is turned on. Check the `CGI` variables for `HTTP_USER_AGENT`.

➜ ColdFusion debugging is covered in Chapter 25, "Debugging."

The `<cfhttp>` agent has the same issues as any other Web browser does. If your server is located in a network that must use a proxy server to reach the Web, you will need to specify a proxy using the appropriate attributes for the `<cfhttp>` agent as well.

> **TIP**
>
> <cfhttp> is not clever enough to tell the proxy server to bypass the cache. Therefore, depending on how your proxy server has been configured, a <cfhttp> agent might continue to retrieve the cached version of a Web page even though the actual page has long since been modified.
>
> You can often trick the proxy server's cache by adding a different URL parameter onto the end of the remote address each time you request a page. A URL-encoded time stamp works well.
>
> ```
> <cfset timestamp=URLEncodedFormat(Now())>
> <cfhttp url="http://www.forta.com/index.cfm?#timestamp#"
>         method="GET">
> ```

<cfhttp> returns a number of useful variables in addition to CFHTTP.FileContent. These are listed in Table 43.1.

Table 43.1 <cfhttp> Return Variables

VARIABLE NAMES	DESCRIPTION
CFHTTP.CharSet	Returns the character set of a retrieved URL
CFHTTP.FileContent	Returns the entire contents of the remote file for text and MIME files
CFHTTP.Header	Returns the entire response header in its raw-text format as a simple variable
CFHTTP.MimeType	Returns the MIME type of the file—for example, "text/html"
CFHTTP.ResponseHeader	Returns the entire response header in a structure. If there are multiple instances of a header key—multiple cookies, for example—the values are placed in an array within the ResponseHeader structure.
CFHTTP.StatusCode	Returns the HTTP error code and associated error string—for example, "200 Success"

<cfhttp> can send variables to a URL ahead of its retrieval of the Web page. This is what you would expect given that a standard Web browser can submit form variables, cookies, and URL parameters to the Web server. By submitting variables to the Web server directly, you can activate a form's action pages and other dynamic content, effectively bypassing the user interface that a normal Web user would navigate.

To submit variables, you must change to method="POST" and specify the variables to send using a series of <cfhttpparam> tags nested between <cfhttp> and </cfhttp>.

For example, when submitting text-searching variables to a search page, you can use the following code:

```
<cfhttp url="http://www.forta.com/cf/tips/browse.cfm"
        method="POST"
        resolveurl="yes">
  <cfhttpparam type="FORMFIELD"
               name="search"
               value="XML">
</cfhttp>
```

`<cfhttpparam>` can be used to specify any combination of the following variable types:

- BODY
- CGI
- COOKIE
- FILE
- FORMFIELD
- HEADER
- URL
- XML

> **TIP**
>
> If using `type="file"`, the `mimetype` should be specified too.

`<cfhttp>` can also be used to retrieve a file and save it directly to disk. This is particularly useful if you are grabbing binary files such as images, but it works equally well with Web pages and other text files. You need to specify the `PATH` where the file is to be saved. If you don't specify a `FILE` attribute, the original filename will be used.

```
<cfhttp url="http://www.forta.com/images/0321125169_m.gif"
        method="GET"
        path="C:\images"
        file="0321125169_m.gif"
        resolveurl="false"
        throwonerror="yes">
```

Remote Data File Queries

`<cfhttp>` can be used to retrieve a remote data file and dynamically generate a query object. `<cfhttp>` sends out an agent to retrieve the file and then parses the data according to the `delimiter` attribute. `textqualifier` indicates the character at the start and finish of a column. The `columns` attribute can dictate column headings; otherwise, the very first record is used for column names.

```
<cfhttp url="http://www.forta.com/sales/jan.txt"
        method="GET"
        name="sales"
        columns="isbn,quantity"
        textqualifier=""""""
        delimiter=","
        resolveurl="false"></cfhttp>
<cfoutput query="sales">
#isbn#: #quantity#<br>
</cfoutput>
```

NOTE

To specify quotation marks as a `textqualifier`, you need to escape each quotation mark with yet another quotation mark!

```
textqualifier=""""""
```

There are six quotation marks in this example: two to define the value of the attribute and two for each quotation mark in the value.

Secure HTTP

`<cfhttp>` supports secure connections between ColdFusion (the client) and remote HTTP servers. To use secure connections, simply use `https` instead of `http` as the protocol in the URL. `<cfhttp>` will then automatically use port `443`; you may override this if needed.

Handling Proxy Servers

If your ColdFusion server accesses the outside world via a proxy server, `<cfhttp>` calls will fail unless ColdFusion itself routes HTTP requests via the proxy server. `<cfhttp>` supports the use of proxy servers but does not autodetect them. To use a proxy server, you must pass its host name or IP address to the `PROXYSERVER` attribute.

Troubleshooting HTTP Agents

`<cfhttp>` spawns an additional process that sends out an HTTP agent. The calling application page waits until the agent has traveled onto the network and returned before it continues processing. The agent's activity on the Web is largely beyond the developer's control. Any number of issues, from network congestion to the remote host's simply being unavailable, can cause the agent to fail.

If the agent fails or takes an inordinate amount of time to complete its mission, it might jeopardize the processing of the calling page. It is a good idea to set a `timeout` attribute for the agent so that you can code appropriate error handling to deal with long-running agents. Set `throwonerror="Yes"` to raise a standard exception should `<cfhttp>` time out—or alternatively, check the `CFHTTP.Status` variable.

> **NOTE**
> `TIMEOUT` is not supported if running a JVM's prior to version 1.4.

➜ Trapping errors is covered in Chapter 26, "Error Handling."

On occasion, the remote host might respond with an error. In other words, the remote host is available on the network, but the Web service has failed for some reason. You can test the `CFHTTP.Status` variable to detect whether things have gone wrong and respond accordingly.

> **NOTE**
> A successful HTTP agent will return a `STATUSCODE` of `"200 Success"` or `"200 OK"`.

Page Scraping

A *page scrape* involves capturing an HTML page from another Web server and then processing the page for information. For instance, you might be interested in harvesting a list of contacts from an affiliate's Web site and displaying them on your own. However, you might want to get rid of the header and footer displayed on the affiliate's site and substitute your own.

Excising a particular piece of content from a Web site is done using string parsing. Typically this is achieved by locating a region on the page above and below the desired content. A region is identified as a constant string (such as a heading or a comment), or a pattern that can be reliably matched using a regular expression. Using string functions, you then remove all the text above and below the content you want in the `CFHTTP.FileContent` variable.

This form of syndication can be useful when you are dealing with a partner who has a basic Internet site. As long as the structure of the page (that is, the regions you are matching) does not change, you can syndicate content from the Web page with little or no input from the partner. However, because pages do change, relying on specific content in a specific format presents a high risk of error. Web Services are a far safer way to implement syndication and data sharing.

➜ Web Services were reviewed in Chapter 32, "Web Services."

FTP Agents

<cfftp> allows developers to implement File Transfer Protocol operations from the ColdFusion server to an FTP server. The <cfftp> tag governs all the actions you require to connect to and perform file actions on the FTP server.

> **NOTE**
>
> The <cfftp> tag is specifically for transferring files between a ColdFusion server and an FTP server. <cfftp> is unable to move files between a ColdFusion server and a browser (client). Use <cffile> with action="upload" to copy files from the client to a ColdFusion server; use <cfcontent> to move and copy files from a ColdFusion server to the browser.

➜ <cffile> and <cfcontent> are covered in Chapter 39, "System Integration."

First you need to establish, or "open," a connection with the FTP server. After a connection is made, the details (server, user name, password, and so on) can be cached by <cfftp>, so you need only refer to the name of the connection for subsequent actions on the server for that FTP session. If the FTP session times out or your connection is closed for whatever reason, you will need to reopen the connection.

```
<cfftp action="OPEN"
       server="ftp.forta.com"
       username="grover"
       password="elmo"
       stoponerror="Yes"
       connection="xfer">
```

After a connection has been made, the other ACTION attribute values can be used to perform operations on the FTP server. Generally the ACTION performs some task and returns a variable, CFFTP.ReturnValue. The value of this variable depends on the task being performed. For example, for an ACTION="ExistsFile" operation to test whether a file exists on the FTP server, CFFTP.ReturnValue will be either YES or NO. The exception to this is ACTION="ListDir", which instead generates a query object containing a directory listing of the specified directory.

```
<cfftp action="LISTDIR"
       stoponerror="Yes"
       name="sales_files"
       directory="/"
       connection="xfer">

<cfoutput query="sales_files">
# Name#: #URL#<br>
</cfoutput>
```

On the FTP server, you must navigate to the directory you want before performing a file operation. For example, you might log in to a home directory on the FTP server, but then need to change the directory to `/pub/uploads` before being able to upload a file. You cannot nominate the directory and file in a single operation. FTP uses a slightly different vocabulary than you might be used to. `PUT` is used for uploading a file to the FTP site, and `GET` is used for retrieving files.

```
<!--- check to see if the directory is there --->
<cfftp action="EXISTSDIR"
       stoponerror="No"
       directory="/pub/uploads"
       connection="xfer">
<cfif CFFTP.returnvalue IS "NO">
 <cfabort showerror="Uploads directory does not exist!">
</cfif>

<!--- change directory --->
<cfftp action="CHANGEDIR"
       stoponerror="No"
       directory="/pub/uploads"
       connection="xfer">

<!--- upload file to the current directory --->
<cfftp action="PUTFILE"
       stoponerror="No"
       localfile="c:salesjul.xls"
       remotefile="jul.xls"
       transfermode="AUTO"
       connection="xfer">
```

NOTE

When your application is finished with the FTP connection, it is polite to close the FTP session by using `action="CLOSE"`. If you neglect to close the session, it will remain open until the connection times out. This would be considered particularly poor etiquette if a connection time limit existed on the FTP server you were contacting.

CAUTION

Use of `<cfftp>` on the ColdFusion server can be blocked using basic security under ColdFusion Administrator. There are obvious security issues when allowing developers to move any file off the server to any remote FTP server.

Summary

ColdFusion provides HTTP agent technology through the use of `<cfhttp>`. `<cfhttp>` can be used to retrieve Web pages and files from remote Web servers and build query objects from remote data files. Cooperative agent technology can provide highly sophisticated content and application syndication services. Using HTTP agents provides a powerful platform for utilizing the Web as an information resource for your applications. FTP remains one of the primary Internet services for transferring files. `<cfftp>` allows you as a developer to integrate FTP communication between servers from within your applications.

Sample Questions

1. `<cfhttp>` with `method="GET"` can send what type of parameters to the remote URL?

   A. `FORM` variables

   B. `COOKIE` variables

   C. `URL` parameters

   D. `FILE` uploads

2. What tags would be needed to upload a file from a client's browser to the ColdFusion server and then syndicate the file to a remote FTP site?

   A. `<cffile>` and `<cfcontent>`

   B. `<cffile>` and `<cfftp>`

   C. `<cfcontent>` and `<cfftp>`

   D. `<cffile>` only

3. Which `<CFHTTP>` variable would you inspect to learn information about the remote Web server?

   A. `MimeType`

   B. `FileContent`

   C. `Header`

   D. `StatusCode`

PART 8
Databases

IN THIS PART

CHAPTER 44
Basic SQL

IN THIS CHAPTER

Database Basics

The term "database" is used in many different ways, but for our purposes (and indeed, from SQL's perspective), a database is a collection of data stored in some organized fashion.

Databases contain tables, and data itself is stored in *tables* (not in databases). A table is a structured container that can store data of a specific type. A table might contain a list of customers, a product catalog, or any other list of information.

Tables are made up of *columns*. A column contains a particular piece of information within a table. Each column in a database has an associated data type. A data type defines what type of data the column can contain. For example, if the column were to contain a number (perhaps the number of items in an order), the data type would be a numeric data type. If the column were to contain dates, text, notes, currency amounts, and so on, the appropriate data type would be used to specify this fact.

Data in a table is stored in *rows*. Each record saved is stored in its own row. If you envision a table as a spreadsheet-style grid, the vertical columns in the grid are the table columns, and the horizontal rows are the table rows.

Every row in a table should have some column (or set of columns) that uniquely identifies it. A table containing customers might use a customer number column, a table containing orders might use the order ID, and an employee list table might use an employee ID or the employee Social Security number column. This column (or set of columns) that uniquely identifies each row in a table is called a *primary key*. You use the primary key to refer to a single row. Without a primary key, updating or deleting specific rows in a table becomes extremely difficult.

> **TIP**
>
> Although primary keys are not actually required, most database designers ensure that every table they create has a primary key so that future data manipulation is possible and manageable.

Any column in a table can be established as the primary key, as long as it meets the following conditions:

- No two rows can have the same primary key value.
- Every row must have a primary key value (a column cannot allow `NULL` values).
- The column containing primary key values can never be modified or updated.
- Primary key values can never be reused (if a row is deleted from the table, its primary key cannot be assigned to any new rows).

The `SELECT` Statement

`SELECT` is the most frequently used SQL statement. It retrieves data from one or more tables. At a minimum, `SELECT` takes two clauses: the data to be retrieved and the location to retrieve it from.

> **NOTE**
>
> Technically, `SELECT` statements don't even need table names. It is perfectly valid (although uncommon) to do something like this:
>
> ```
> SELECT 100 AS id
> ```
>
> This statement returns a single row with a single column–data is not retrieved from any table at all.

In practice, however, most basic `SELECT` statements are made up of four parts that must appear in this order:

- The data to retrieve
- The location to retrieve it from
- Filtering conditions (to restrict the data being retrieved)
- Sort order (to specify how returned data is sorted)

Specifying the Data to Retrieve

You specify the data to be retrieved by listing the required table column names as the first clause (right after the keyword `SELECT`). At least one column must be specified.

> **NOTE**
> The maximum number of columns (or the width of a retrieved row) that may be retrieved varies from one DBMS (Database Management System) to the next. There is no standard size or limitation.

The following example retrieves a single column (named `product_id`) from a table (named `products`):

```
SELECT product_id
FROM products
```

To retrieve multiple columns, you must separate the column names with commas:

```
SELECT product_id, product_name
FROM products
```

> **NOTE**
> To retrieve unique values, use the `DISTINCT` keyword before the column name.

You also can retrieve all columns without listing them individually. You do so by using the wildcard character `*` as follows:

```
SELECT *
FROM products
```

> **TIP**
> For performance reasons, it is generally not a good idea to use `SELECT *` (unless you actually need every column). As a rule, retrieve just what you need and nothing more.

You can also rename columns when retrieving them by assigning aliases to them. You do so by using the `AS` keyword, which lets you specify an alternative name for a column, as follows:

```
SELECT product_id AS id, product_name AS name
FROM products
```

In this example, the returned columns are `id` and `name`, even though the actual table names are `product_id` and `product_name`.

> **TIP**
>
> You most often use aliases when working with aggregate functions (covered in Chapter 46, "Aggregates"), but another important use allows you to rename illegally named columns. For example, some databases allow you to include spaces and special characters (such as the # sign or plus and minus signs) in column names, and these characters could render the column names unusable in other applications (such as ColdFusion). Using aliases, you can rename the columns, giving them safe (and legal) names when they are retrieved.

Specifying the Table

The table name is always specified using the `FROM` keyword, as follows:

```
SELECT product_id, product_name
FROM products
```

Data can be retrieved from multiple tables, in which case commas must separate the table names. You usually do so only in *join* operations.

➜ Joins are covered in Chapter 45, "Joins."

> **NOTE**
>
> Some databases require that table names be fully qualified (with a prefix that indicates the table owner and database).

Filtering

Retrieved data is filtered using the `WHERE` clause, which must contain one or more filter conditions using supported operators. Table 44.1 lists the operators supported by most SQL implementations.

Table 44.1 `WHERE` Clause Operators

OPERATOR	DESCRIPTION
`=`	Equality
`<>`	Non-equality
`<`	Less than
`<=`	Less than or equal to
`>`	Greater than
`>=`	Greater than or equal to
`IN`	One of a set of
`LIKE`	Wildcard match

Table 44.1 (continued)

OPERATOR	DESCRIPTION
`BETWEEN`	Between two specified values
`IS NULL`	Is a `NULL` value
`AND`	Combine clauses
`OR`	Or clauses
`NOT`	Negate clauses

The basic mathematical type operators are used as follows:

```
SELECT product_id, product_name
FROM products
WHERE product_id=1
```

You use the `IN` operator to specify multiple values, which must be separated by commas and enclosed within parentheses:

```
SELECT product_id, product_name
FROM products
WHERE product_id IN (1,3,7,18,45)
```

TIP

You can use lists and the list functions to pass values to the `IN` operator. See Chapter 13, "Lists," for more information.

You use the `LIKE` operator for wildcard searches. The SQL specification supports three wildcards, as shown in Table 44.2 (although some databases do not support them all).

Table 44.2 Wildcard Operators

OPERATOR	DESCRIPTION
`%`	Match zero or more characters
`_`	Match a single character
`[]`	Match one of a set of characters

You use wildcard searches to search for patterns within column text. The following example finds all products beginning with the letter `s`:

```
SELECT product_id, product_name
FROM products
WHERE product_name LIKE 's%'
```

Wildcards can be used anywhere within a string, not just at the beginning. The following example finds all products that contain the text `widget`:

```
SELECT product_id, product_name
FROM products
WHERE product_name LIKE '%widget%'
```

> **TIP**
>
> Wildcard matches are generally the slowest form of filter. This is particularly true of wildcards used in the start of a search pattern. And as such, they should not be overused unnecessarily.

You can combine searches by using the `AND` and `OR` operators. The following example finds all products with the text `widget` in the name and a cost of $5 or more:

```
SELECT product_id, product_name
FROM products
WHERE product_name LIKE '%widget%' AND product_price >= 5
```

> **CAUTION**
>
> When using multiple search conditions (using `AND` and `OR`), you should use parentheses to group clauses appropriately. They prevent ambiguity and prevent clauses from being evaluated in an unexpected order.

To negate a condition, you use the `NOT` operator before the condition as follows:

```
SELECT product_id, product_name
FROM products
WHERE NOT product_id IN (1,3,7,18,45)
```

Sorting

Retrieved data can be sorted using the `ORDER BY` clause. Data can be sorted in one or more columns .If more than one column is specified, data is sorted by the first column and then by the second, if multiple rows have the same first column value, and so on.

The following example retrieves all products and sorts them by name:

```
SELECT product_id, product_name
FROM products
ORDER BY product_name
```

Data is sorted in ascending or descending order, which you specify by using the `ASC` or `DESC` keywords, respectively. If neither keyword is provided, `ASC` is assumed by default.

The `INSERT` Statement

The `INSERT` statement inserts one or more rows into a table. `INSERT` always takes the name of the table into which data is to be inserted, as well as the appropriate columns and values. The columns are listed as comma delimited in parentheses after the table name, and the values for each column are listed comma delimited in parentheses after the `VALUES` keyword.

> **NOTE**
>
> Data cannot be inserted into more than one table in a single operation. The same is true for `UPDATE` and `DELETE` operations.

The following example inserts a new row into a `products` table:

```
INSERT INTO products(product_name, product_price)
VALUES('Super deluxe widget', 299)
```

> **CAUTION**
>
> Unlike ColdFusion, SQL is not typeless. Strings must be enclosed within quotation marks, and numbers must not be.

You cannot use `INSERT` to insert multiple rows unless the data is the result of a `SELECT` operation (known as an `INSERT SELECT`). The following example inserts all the data from one table into another:

```
INSERT INTO products(product_name, product_price)
SELECT product_name, product_price
FROM new_prods
```

> **TIP**
>
> ColdFusion developers often use `INSERT SELECT` as a way to insert multiple user selections. They do so by passing the user selections (usually from form fields) to an `IN` clause in the `SELECT` statement so that it selects only the user-selected data.

The `UPDATE` Statement

The `UPDATE` statement updates data in one or more rows. `UPDATE` takes the name of the table to be updated, as well as the rows to be affected, and the new values.

The following example updates a single row in a table:

```
UPDATE products
SET product_price=49.99
WHERE product_id=235
```

The `WHERE` clause restricts the rows being updated, and without it, all rows are updated. The following example increases the price of all products by `10`:

```
UPDATE products
SET product_price=product_price+10
```

To update multiple columns, you must separate each column=value pair with a comma.

> **CAUTION**
> Care must be taken to ensure that a `WHERE` clause is specified where needed (usually it will be). If you want to update a single row, the `WHERE` clause should always filter by the primary key.

The `DELETE` Statement

The `DELETE` statement deletes one or more rows from a table. `DELETE` takes the name of the table to be processed, as well as the rows to be affected.

The following example deletes a single row from a table:

```
DELETE FROM products
WHERE product_id=235
```

The `WHERE` clause restricts the rows being deleted, and without it, all rows are deleted.

> **CAUTION**
> Care must be taken to ensure that a `WHERE` clause is specified where needed (usually it will be). If you want to delete a single row, the `WHERE` clause should always filter by the primary key.

Summary

The basic SQL statements are `SELECT`, `INSERT`, `UPDATE`, and `DELETE`. These four statements, combined with features and functions to be reviewed in the next few chapters, account for the majority of SQL written by ColdFusion developers.

Sample Questions

1. Which of these keywords are used in `SELECT` statements?

   A. `SET`

   B. `ORDER BY`

   C. `RETRIEVE`

   D. `WHERE`

2. Which of the following wildcard searches are valid for use in `WHERE` clauses?

   A. `LIKE 'widget'`

   B. `LIKE NOT '%widget%'`

   C. `LIKE 100%`

   D. `LIKE '%a%b%c%d%e%'`

3. To delete data from specific columns in a row, which statement should you use?

   A. `DELETE`

   B. `UPDATE`

   C. `NULL`

4. Which of the following statements about primary keys is true?

   A. Primary keys are required.

   B. Primary keys may be made up of multiple columns.

   C. Primary keys may be updated.

   D. Primary keys are always numbers.

CHAPTER 45
Joins

IN THIS CHAPTER

Understanding Relational Database Design

You use SQL *joins* to perform operations and extract data from relational databases. As such, an understanding of relational database design is a prerequisite to successfully using joins.

Relational databases are sets of tables that each store parts of a complete data set; these parts relate to each other, and thus are termed "relational". The underlying principle here is that data should be organized so that it never has to be repeated (stored more than once), while at the same time keeping it in small, manageable sets.

> **NOTE**
>
> Databases that are not relational are often referred to as being "flat."

Some examples will help you understand this concept:

- A list of employees could be stored in a flat table—one big (and wide) table with employee and department information in each row. But employees are members of departments, and many employees share the same department information. Relational database design would then dictate that the data be broken into three tables—an employee table, a department table, and a third table that connects the two by storing the primary keys of employees and departments to relate them to each other.

- An orders database is another classic example of data that should be stored relationally. Customer information is not tied to a specific order (a customer may have many orders), order items are not tied to a specific order (an order may have multiple order items), and products are not tied to specific orders (a single product could be part of many orders). Relational design might require a table for products, a table for customers, a table for orders (which relates to the customers table), and a table for order items (which relates to both the orders and products tables).

When you're planning relational databases, there is no real right or wrong design, and there is always more than one way to lay out the tables. The following are some of the issues that you need to consider when planning relational table design:

- **Data access.** The less relational the data is, the harder it will be to extract required data filtered or ordered as needed.
- **Maintainability.** Relational databases can be maintained far more easily, but special attention has to be paid to the links between tables so as not to break them.
- **Storage.** A well-designed relational database can use disk space far more efficiently.
- **Performance.** Relational databases can perform far quicker than flat databases, if the design is well thought out and implemented.

NOTE

Primary keys, which were introduced in Chapter 44, "Basic SQL," are columns within tables that uniquely identify every row within those tables. Primary keys are an important part of relational database design because they are the values that connect tables to each other.

NOTE

A full discussion of relational database design is beyond the scope of this chapter and book. For an explanation of relational databases from a ColdFusion perspective, see ColdFusion MX 7 Web Application Construction Kit (ISBN: 0-321-22367-5).

Another important type of key used in relational databases is the foreign key. It is a column within a table whose value is that of another table's primary key. For example, an orders table might use the order number as a primary key, in which case the order number stored in the related order items table is a foreign key. Unlike primary keys, foreign keys need not be unique, and they can be updated as needed. Like primary keys, they always have values (and should not be `NULL`).

Understanding Joins

Data broken up across relational databases has all the advantages listed previously. It also has a disadvantage in that retrieving the data is more complex. To retrieve a list of customers with matching orders information, you might have to retrieve data from two tables. And to retrieve a list of employees with the department data, you might have to retrieve the information from three tables.

If you want to retrieve data from multiple tables (within a single operation, or with a single `SELECT` statement), the tables must be joined (and thus the term "joins").

> **NOTE**
>
> Joins are logical entities, that is, data is not actually stored in any joined format, and joins do not exist or persist. Data is joined as needed, while a SQL statement is being executed.

Basic Join Syntax

You join tables by using the SQL `SELECT` statement to specify all the tables to be joined. For example, the following code snippet retrieves every customer and order joined into a single resultset:

```
SELECT customers.customer_name, customers.customer_id,
 orders.order_id, orders.order_date
FROM customers, orders
```

In this example, `customers` and `orders` are both tables, and both are listed in the `FROM` clause. The database processes this SQL statement and returns data from both tables.

> **TIP**
>
> When retrieving columns from multiple tables, you need to provide the fully qualified table column name in the format `table.column` if any column appears in more than one table. Many developers find that using this fully qualified format prevents ambiguity, so they always use it for all SQL statements.

But how does the database engine know which rows in the `orders` table to relate to rows in the `customers` table? The answer is that it does not; the join condition must be specified, or all rows will be joined to each other. So if you had 100 customers and 200 orders, the preceding SQL statement would return 20,000 rows (100 times 200) instead of 200. This kind of output is known as a *Cartesian product* or a *cross join*, and is seldom the desired output.

> **NOTE**
>
> Although join syntax is, for the most part, consistent across database implementations, some subtle differences can have an impact on your `SELECT` statements. Refer to your database's documentation for more information.

To properly join tables, you must explicitly provide the join condition. You can choose from two primary forms of syntax for doing so:

- Most databases allow you to join data in the `WHERE` clause, specifying the columns in each table that must be matched.
- ANSI SQL syntax requires that you specify joins in the `FROM` clause using the `JOIN` keyword.

The following example retrieves customers and orders (the same SQL statement used previously) joined using a `WHERE` clause:

```
SELECT customers.customer_name, customers.customer_id,
 orders.order_id, orders.order_date
FROM customers, orders
WHERE customers.customer_id=orders.customer_id
```

The condition provided in the `WHERE` clause instructs the database to join the tables by a common column—in this case, `customer_id`—which is the primary key of table `customers` and a foreign key in table `orders`.

> **TIP**
>
> You can join tables by using any comparison operators (not just =), and you can use multiple comparison operators (using **AND**, for example) too.

The following is the ANSI SQL version of this same statement:

```
SELECT customers.customer_name, customers.customer_id,
 orders.order_id, orders.order_date
FROM customers JOIN orders
 ON (customers.customer_id=orders.customer_id)
```

Using ANSI SQL syntax, you specify the join condition itself by using the `ON` keyword immediately after the names of the tables being joined.

> **NOTE**
>
> The number of tables that you can join in a single `SELECT` statement varies from one database to the next. SQL Server, for example, allows you to join 256 tables, whereas Oracle has no limit. Consult your database documentation for more information.

Inner Joins

The most commonly used join is the inner join (the type of join used in the previous sections). Inner joins use a join condition (including a comparison operator) to match rows from both tables using values in common columns. In other words, the join condition must match rows in both tables, and values that appear in one table but not in the other are not retrieved.

Using ANSI SQL, you can specify the join type in front of the `JOIN` keyword as follows:

```
SELECT customers.customer_name, customers.customer_id,
 orders.order_id, orders.order_date
FROM customers INNER JOIN orders
 ON (customers.customer_id=orders.customer_id)
```

> **TIP**
>
> If no join type is specified, `INNER` is assumed by default.

> **NOTE**
>
> There are actually two forms of `INNER JOIN`. The syntax shown here (testing for equality between two tables) is known as an equi-join. Another (lesser used) form of `INNER JOIN` is the natural join in which repeated values are eliminated from the resultset.

> **NOTE**
>
> Although ANSI SQL requires that you specify joins in the `FROM` clause, an exception is made for inner joins. It is the only form of join that ANSI SQL allows you to specify in the `WHERE` clause.

Outer Joins

Outer joins join tables while including rows that do not have corresponding (related) rows in the other tables. For example, to retrieve all customers (including those with no orders), you could use an outer join. The outer join assigns `NULL` values to all columns that are empty (because they have no matching row).

Three forms of outer joins are supported:

- `LEFT OUTER JOIN` (or `LEFT JOIN`) retrieves all rows from the left table (the left of the `JOIN` clause) and only related rows from the right table.
- `RIGHT OUTER JOIN` (or `RIGHT JOIN`) retrieves all rows from the right table (the right of the `JOIN` clause) and only related rows from the left table.
- `FULL OUTER JOIN` (or `FULL JOIN`) retrieves all rows from both tables and assigns `NULL` values to the columns for all rows that do not have a match in the other table.

The following example uses the ANSI SQL syntax to retrieve all customers (including those who don't have orders):

```
SELECT customers.customer_name, customers.customer_id,
 orders.order_id, orders.order_date
FROM customers LEFT OUTER JOIN orders
 ON (customers.customer_id=orders.customer_id)
```

In this example, the columns `order_id` and `order_date` contain `NULL` for all customers with no orders.

The following `SELECT` statement uses a `WHERE` clause join:

```
SELECT customers.customer_name, customers.customer_id,
 orders.order_id, orders.order_date
FROM customers, orders
WHERE customers.customer_id*=orders.customer_id
```

Here, `*=` creates the join. Because the `*` is on the left of the equal sign, all rows from the left table are retrieved (just like the `LEFT OUTER JOIN`). To retrieve all rows from the right table, you could use `=*` instead.

TIP

The only difference between `LEFT OUTER JOIN` and `RIGHT OUTER JOIN` is the order of the tables (which table is on which side of the `JOIN` keyword). You can change join types by simply switching the positions of the table names within the `SELECT` statement.

TIP

Regardless of the join type you're using, you can filter the data being retrieved by using additional conditions (known as predicates) in the `ON` clause.

Self-Joins

Tables can be joined to themselves to perform filtering based on data derived from the same table. This is known as a *self-join*. Self-joins do not require a special join syntax, so you can use all the standard join types and syntax. What makes a join a self-join is that the same table name is used twice, and this use obviously presents a syntax difficulty because SQL does not allow names to be duplicated within a `SELECT` statement.

To create self-joins, you must assign *aliases* to tables, temporary names used in the SQL statement in lieu of the real names. You specify table aliases after the table names as follows:

```
SELECT customers.customer_name
FROM customers c1 INNER JOIN customers c2
 ON (c1.customer_city=c2.customer_city)
WHERE c1.customer_state='CA'
```

In this example, the `customers` table is self-joined, so each occurrence of the table is given a unique alias (here, `c1` and `c2`) in the `FROM` clause. Once assigned, aliases are used like any other table names.

Summary

Relational database design is an important part of application design in general, and one that has a significant impact on everything from application performance to data manageability to resource usage to SQL complexity. Relational data is joined for retrieval, and several join types are supported (the most common being the `INNER JOIN`). Tables are usually joined by their primary and foreign keys.

Sample Questions

1. Which statement is used to join tables?

   A. `SELECT`

   B. `INSERT`

   C. `UPDATE`

   D. `DELETE`

2. What kind of join is being used in this statement?

   ```
   SELECT customers.customer_name, customers.customer_id,
    orders.order_id, orders.order_date
   FROM customers, orders
   WHERE customers.customer_id=*orders.customer_id
   ```

   A. `Inner`

   B. `Equi`

   C. `Right outer`

   D. `Full outer`

3. Which of these keywords are used in `JOIN` statements?

   A. `INNER`

   B. `SELF`

   C. `LEFT`

   D. `FULL`

CHAPTER 46 Aggregates

IN THIS CHAPTER

Understanding Aggregate Functions

Although you usually access a database to retrieve stored data, you often need to access calculations performed against data (and not the data itself). The SQL aggregate functions are a set of special functions that perform mathematical calculations against data, returning the results of those calculations to the calling application.

The SQL aggregate functions are both powerful and flexible, and can be used in conjunction with tables, joins, and any other database features.

> **TIP**
>
> Many database developers find using the aggregate functions troublesome and even complex at times. So instead of using them, they retrieve large amounts of data and then programmatically perform the calculations themselves. This practice should be avoided at all costs. First, the database engine can process these calculations far quicker than any client application can. And second, sending unneeded data across a connection from a database server to a client host can have a significant effect on network traffic and performance.

Using Aggregate Functions

The following five primary aggregate functions are supported by most major databases:

- `AVG` calculates the average value of a numeric column.
- `COUNT` obtains the number of rows that match a specific condition.
- `MAX` obtains the greatest value in a numeric column.

- `MIN` obtains the smallest value in a numeric column.
- `SUM` obtains the total of all values in a numeric column.

You can use these functions in two locations within `SELECT` statements:

- The `SELECT` list (the list of columns being selected)
- The `HAVING` clause (discussed later in this chapter)

The following example retrieves the cost of the most expensive product in a `products` table:

```
SELECT MAX(product_price) AS expensive
FROM products
```

Here, the `MAX` function is assigned to an alias using `AS` so that it can use the value.

➜ The use of aliases within `SELECT` statements was discussed previously in Chapter 44, "Basic SQL."

Multiple aggregate functions can be used within a single `SELECT` statement. This next example retrieves both the most and least expensive items in a `products` table:

```
SELECT MAX(product_price) AS expensive, MIN(product_price) AS cheap
FROM products
```

> **NOTE**
>
> Some databases extend the standard set of aggregate functions with additional proprietary functions. Examples are SQL Server's `STDEV` (statistical standard deviation) and `VAR` (statistical variance of all values) functions. If your database supports these functions, you can use them in the same way you use the standard functions. The only downside is that the SQL code is not portable to other databases.

Handling `NULL` Values

With the exception of `COUNT`, aggregate functions ignore `NULL` values. So returning the `MIN` of a column returns the actual value (and not `NULL`). `COUNT` obtains the number of rows that match a condition and as such can (optionally) include rows with `NULL` values. You determine whether or not to include `NULL` values by specifying (or not specifying) a column to count.

This first example counts the number of rows in a `products` table:

```
SELECT COUNT(*) AS num_products
FROM products
```

This next example counts only the rows that have a product description (not `NULL` in the `prod_desc` column):

```
SELECT COUNT(prod_desc) AS num_products
FROM products
```

As you can see, if * is used, all rows are counted. If a column name is specified, only rows that do not have a NULL value in that column are counted.

Another important distinction between COUNT and the other aggregate functions is the returned value. With the exception of COUNT, the aggregate functions return NULL if no rows are processed (for example, the SUM of no rows). COUNT, however, returns 0 if no rows are processed (or if no rows match selection criteria).

Processing Distinct Values

By default, the aggregate functions perform calculations on all rows. To calculate only unique values, you can use the DISTINCT keyword. This example counts the number of unique products in a table:

```
SELECT COUNT(DISTINCT prod_name) AS num_prods
FROM products
```

> **TIP**
>
> The opposite of DISTINCT is ALL, which you can use when all rows are to be processed. But because that is the default behavior, if neither ALL nor DISTINCT is specified, most developers ignore that keyword.

> **NOTE**
>
> You can use DISTINCT with AVG, COUNT, and SUM, but not with MAX and MIN. Obviously, if you want to know the greatest or smallest values in a column, DISTINCT would have no relevance.

Grouping Results

Thus far, we have reviewed the basic use of aggregate functions, applying them to entire tables. Aggregate functions can also be used to perform analysis on groups of data. For example, instead of counting all the employees in a company, a function can count them by department. Or instead of returning the highest priced item in a table, a function can return the highest priced item in each category. This type of calculation involves grouping , or specifying how data is to be grouped). When grouped, the aggregate functions return multiple rows—one per group.

You accomplish grouping by using the GROUP BY keyword. GROUP BY takes one or more columns to be grouped (comma delimited if more than one is specified)—columns that must be specified in the SELECT list.

The following example returns a list of department IDs and the number of employees in each department:

```
SELECT department_id, COUNT(*) AS num_employees
FROM employees
GROUP BY department_id
```

Joined tables can be grouped in the same way. This next example joins two tables (using a WHERE clause) to return a list of department names and the number of employees in each department:

```
SELECT department_name, COUNT(*) AS num_employees
FROM employees, departments
WHERE employees.department_id=departments.department_id
GROUP BY department_name
```

➜ Joins and join clauses were covered in Chapter 45, "Joins."

> **NOTE**
> If a SELECT statement includes a WHERE clause, you must use GROUP BY after it. Similarly, if you use an ORDER BY clause, you must use GROUP BY before it.

GROUP BY does not sort data, and although grouped columns may be sorted in ascending order, this order must never be assumed. The only guaranteed safe way to sort grouped data is to use the ORDER BY clause.

Filtering Results

Aggregated data can be filtered in two ways to allow you complete flexibility within SELECT statements:

- You can use the WHERE clause to filter rows before they are grouped. Rows excluded by the WHERE condition are not included in aggregate calculations and processing. WHERE conditions can be used regardless of whether grouping is used and can reference any valid expression.
- You can use the HAVING clause to filter entire groups. This condition is applied after groups have been processed to eliminate aggregate values that do not match a specific condition. HAVING can be used only in conjunction with grouping and can reference any items in the select list.

➜ The WHERE clause was reviewed in Chapter 44, "Basic SQL."

The following example returns the number of employees in each department, including only employees residing in the specified country:

```
SELECT department_name, COUNT(*) AS num_employees
FROM employees, departments
WHERE employees.department_id=departments.department_id
 AND employees.country='USA'
GROUP BY department_name
ORDER BY department_name
```

This next example returns the number of employees in each department that has 100 or more employees:

```
SELECT department_name, COUNT(*) AS num_employees
FROM employees, departments
WHERE employees.department_id=departments.department_id
GROUP BY department_name
HAVING COUNT(*) >= 100
ORDER BY department_name
```

> **NOTE**
> You can use both `WHERE` and `HAVING` in the same `SELECT` statement if necessary. `WHERE` must always be the first clause after the tables (specified in the `FROM` clause).

Summary

The SQL aggregate functions perform calculations on data, returning the calculation results instead of the data itself. The standard aggregate functions are `AVG`, `COUNT`, `MAX`, `MIN`, and `SUM`. Aggregate calculations can filter data as needed using combinations of `WHERE` and `HAVING`, and data can be grouped using `GROUP BY`.

Sample Questions

1. Which `SELECT` clause must be used in order to obtain counts or other aggregates for different rows (as opposed to for all rows)?

   A. `ORDER BY`

   B. `GROUP BY`

   C. `HAVING`

   D. `WHERE`

2. What is wrong with the following SQL statement?

```
SELECT product_name, COUNT(*)
FROM products
GROUP BY product_name
HAVING MAX(prod_price) > 10
```

   A. It doesn't have a `WHERE` clause.

   B. The `ORDER BY` clause is missing.

   C. The alias is missing.

   D. The `HAVING` clause does not match the `SELECT` list.

3. Which of the following are valid aggregate functions?

   A. `AVERAGE`

   B. `COUNT`

   C. `TOTAL`

   D. `MIN`

CHAPTER 47 Advanced Database Features

IN THIS CHAPTER

Constraints

Relational databases require that information be broken into multiple tables, each storing related data. Keys are used to create references from one table to the other (and thus the term *referential integrity*), so as to be able to join tables.

➜ Relational databases and joins were discussed in Chapter 45, "Joins."

For relational database designs to work properly, you need a way to ensure that only valid data is inserted into tables. For example, if an `Orders` table stored order information and `OrderItems` stored order details, you'd want to ensure that any order IDs referenced in `OrderItems` exist in `Orders`. Similarly, any customers referred to in `Orders` would have to be present in the `Customers` table.

Although you could perform checks yourself before inserting new rows (do a `SELECT` on another table to make sure that the values are valid and present), that is generally a practice to avoid because:

- If database integrity rules are enforced at the client level, every client will have to enforce those rules—and inevitably some clients won't.
- You'd also have to enforce the rules on `UPDATE` and `DELETE` operations.
- Performing client-side checks is a time-consuming process; having the DBMS do the checks for you is far more efficient.

DBMSs enforce referential integrity by imposing constraints on database tables. Most constraints are defined in table definitions by using a `CREATE TABLE` or `ALTER TABLE` statement.

> **TIP**
>
> Constraints force databases to throw errors (rejecting SQL statements) when they are violated. Within ColdFusion, these errors can be trapped using `<cftry>` and `<cfcatch>` (covered in Chapter 26, "Error Handling").

> **CAUTION**
>
> There are several different types of constraints, and each DBMS provides its own level of support for them. Refer to your DBMSs documentation before proceeding.

Unique Constraints

Unique constraints are used to ensure that all data in a column (or set of columns) is unique. This is similar to primary keys, but there are some important distinctions:

- A table may contain multiple unique constraints, but only one primary key is allowed per table.
- Unique constraint columns may contain `NULL` values.
- Unique constraint columns may be modified or updated.
- Unique constraint column values may never be reused.
- Unlike primary keys, unique constraints may not be used to define foreign keys.

➔ Primary keys were discussed in Chapter 44, "Basic SQL."

An example of using unique constraints might be an employees table. Every employee has a unique Social Security number, but you would not want to use that for the primary key because it is too long (and you might not want that information to be easily available). So every employee would have a unique employee ID (a primary key) in addition to his Social Security number.

Because the employee ID is a primary key, you can be sure that it'll be unique. But you also might want the DBMS to ensure that Social Security numbers are unique too (to make sure that someone does not make a typo and reuse someone else's number). You could do this by defining a `UNIQUE` constraint on the Social Security number column.

The syntax for unique constraints is similar to that for other constraints: either the `UNIQUE` keyword is defined in the table definition or a separate `CONSTRAINT` is used.

Check Constraints

Check constraints are used to ensure that data in a column (or set of columns) meets a set of criteria that you specify. Common uses of this are:

- Checking minimum or maximum values—for example, preventing an order of `0` items (even though `0` is a valid number).
- Specifying ranges—for example, making sure that a ship date is greater than or equal to today's date but not greater than a year from now.
- Allowing only specific values—for example, allowing only `M` or `F` in a gender field.

In other words, a datatype restricts the type of data that may be stored in a column. Check constraints place further restrictions within that datatype.

The following example creates a table named `OrderItems` and applies a check constraint to it to ensure that all items have a quantity of greater than `0`:

```
CREATE TABLE OrderItems
(
 order_num INTEGER NOT NULL,
 order_item INTEGER NOT NULL,
 prod_id CHAR(10) NOT NULL,
 quantity INTEGER NOT NULL CHECK (quantity > 0),
 item_price MONEY NOT NULL
);
```

To check that a column named `gender` contained only `M` or `F`, you could do the following:

```
CONSTRAINT CHECK (gender LIKE '[MF]')
```

> **TIP**
>
> Some DBMSs enable you to define your own datatypes. These are essentially simple datatypes with check constraints (or other constraints) defined. So, for example, you could define your own datatype called `gender` that would be a single-character text datatype with a check constraint that restricted its value to `M` or `F` (and perhaps `NULL` is unknown).
>
> The advantage of custom datatypes is that the constraints are applied only once (in the datatype definition), and they are automatically applied each time the datatype is used. Check your DBMS's documentation to determine whether user-defined datatypes are supported.

Understanding Indexes

The best way to understand indexes is to envision the index at the back of a book (this book, for example).

Suppose that you wanted to find all occurrences of the word "datatype" in this book. The simple way to do this would be to turn to page one and scan every line of every page looking for matches. Although that would work, it is obviously not a workable solution. Scanning a few pages of text might be doable, but scanning an entire book is not. As the amount of text to be searched increases, so does the time it takes to pinpoint the desired data.

And so books have indexes. An index is an alphabetical list of words with references to their locations in the book. To search for "datatype," you would find that word in the index to determine what pages it appears on. You could then turn to those specific pages to find your matches.

So what is it that makes an index work? Simply, the fact that it is sorted correctly. The difficulty in finding words in a book is not the amount of content that needs to be searched; rather, it is the fact that the content is not sorted by word. If the content were sorted like a dictionary, an index would not be needed (which is why dictionaries don't have indexes).

Database indexes work in much the same way. Primary key data is always sorted—that's just something the DBMS does for you. So retrieving specific rows by primary key is always a fast and efficient operation.

But searching for values in other columns is usually not as efficient. For example, what if you wanted to retrieve all customers who lived in a specific state? Because the table is not sorted by state, the DBMS would have to read every row in the table (starting at the very first row) looking for matches—just as you would have to do if you were trying to find words in a book without using an index.

The solution is to use an index. You may define an index on one or more columns so that the DBMS keeps a sorted list of the contents for its own use. After an index is defined, the DBMS uses it in much the same way that you would use a book index. It searches the sorted index to find the location of any matches and then retrieves those specific rows.

But before you rush off to create dozens of indexes, bear in the mind the following:

- Indexes improve performance of retrieval operations, but they degrade the performance of data insertion, modification, and deletion. This is because when those operations are executed, the DBMS has to dynamically update the index.
- Index data can take up lots of storage space.
- Not all data is suitable for indexing. Data that is not sufficiently unique (a state, for example) will not benefit as much from indexing as data that has more possible values (first name or last name, for example).

- Indexes are used for data filtering and for data sorting, so if you frequently sort data in a specific order, that order might be a candidate for indexing.
- Multiple columns may be defined in an index (for example, State plus City), in which case that index will be of use only when data is sorted in that order. If you wanted to sort by City, that index would not be of any use.

There is no hard and fast rule as to what should be indexed and when. Most DBMSes provide utilities that you can use to determine the effectiveness of indexes, and you should use these regularly.

Indexes are created with the `CREATE INDEX` statement (the syntax of which varies dramatically from one DBMS to another). The following statement creates a simple index on a `Products` table's product name column:

```
CREATE INDEX prod_name_ind
ON PRODUCTS (prod_name)
```

Every index must be uniquely named. Here the name `prod_name_ind` is defined after the keywords `CREATE INDEX`. `ON` is used to specify the table being indexed, and the columns to include in the index (just one in this example) are specified in parentheses after the table name.

> **TIP**
> Index effectiveness changes as table data is added or changed. Many database administrators find that what was once an ideal set of indexes might not be so ideal after several months of data manipulation. As such, it is a good idea to revisit indexes on a regular basis to fine-tune them as needed.

> **NOTE**
> Index use is essentially transparent to ColdFusion development.

Stored Procedures

Stored procedures are SQL statements that are stored on the DBMS server itself. Instead of entering SQL directly, you can call the stored procedure by name to execute the stored SQL.

Stored procedures are invaluable for several reasons:

- Stored procedures execute more quickly than straight SQL statements because the code saved on the server is already parsed and ready for use.
- Stored procedures may contain multiple SQL operations, which enables you to call a single command and execute a set of statements (without having to specify them individually).

- Depending on the DBMS being used, stored procedures might be able to return multiple result sets as well as output parameters.
- Stored procedures can be used to hide complex data structures, so users can call the procedures and pass them values as needed, and the procedures can internally manipulate tables as required.
- Stored procedures can be used to secure underlying data. Users might not be given access to underlying tables (to prevent abuse or misuse); instead, they communicate with a stored procedure that in turn interacts with the underlying tables.

There are lots of reasons to use stored procedures, which are created using the SQL `CREATE PROCEDURE` statement (which varies dramatically from one database to the next).

➜ For information about invoking stored procedures from within your ColdFusion code, see Chapter 23, "Stored Procedures."

Triggers

Triggers are special stored procedures that are executed automatically when specific database activity occurs. Triggers may be associated with `INSERT`, `UPDATE`, and `DELETE` operations on specific tables (or any combination thereof).

Unlike stored procedures (which are simply stored SQL statements), triggers are tied to individual tables. A trigger associated with `INSERT` operations on an `Orders` table will be executed only when a row is inserted into that `Orders` table. Similarly, a trigger on `INSERT` and `UPDATE` operations on a `Customers` table will be executed only when those specific operations occur on that table.

Within triggers, your code has access to the following:

- All new data in `INSERT` operations
- All new data and old data in `UPDATE` operations
- Deleted data in `DELETE` operations

Depending on the DBMS being used, triggers may be executed before or after the specified operation is performed.

Triggers have three primary uses:

- Ensuring data consistency—for example, converting all states to uppercase during `INSERT` and `UPDATE` operations
- Performing actions on other tables based on changes to a table—for example, writing an audit trail record to a log table each time a row is updated or deleted

- Performing additional validation and rolling back data if needed—for example, making sure that a customer's available credit has not been exceeded, and blocking the insertion if it has

Trigger creation syntax varies from one database to another. The following example creates a trigger that converts the `cust_state` field to uppercase on all `INSERT` and `UPDATE` operations on a `Customers` table. This is the SQL Server version:

```
CREATE TRIGGER customer_state
ON Customers
FOR INSERT UPDATE
AS
UPDATE Customers
SET cust_state = Upper(cust_state)
WHERE Customers.cust_id = inserted.cust_id
```

This is the Oracle version:

```
CREATE TRIGGER customer_state
AFTER INSERT UPDATE
FOR EACH ROW
BEGIN
 UPDATE Customers
 SET cust_state = Upper(cust_state)
 WHERE Customers.cust_id = :OLD.cust_id
END;
```

> **TIP**
>
> As a rule, constraints are processed quicker than triggers, so whenever possible use constraints instead.

Summary

Databases support a wide range of advanced features (some support more features than others). These features can and should be used to improve performance, ensure data integrity, and help protect data.

Sample Questions

1. Which of the following technologies could you use to ensure data consistency?

   A. Stored procedure

   B. Trigger

   C. Index

   D. Primary key

2. Which of the following statements are true?

   A. Stored procedures execute quicker than regular SQL statements.

   B. Stored procedures are supported by all databases.

   C. Stored procedures cannot be called from within ColdFusion code.

   D. Stored procedures can help secure your data.

3. Which of the following statements support triggers?

   A. `INSERT`

   B. `UPDATE`

   C. `DELETE`

   D. `SELECT`

4. Which of the following technologies could be used to prevent database hacking via URL tampering?

   A. Stored procedure

   B. Trigger

   C. Index

   D. Constraints

CHAPTER 48

Improving Performance

IN THIS CHAPTER

Eliminating Unnecessary Database Access

Database access (and waiting for databases) is the single biggest bottleneck in ColdFusion applications. As such, ColdFusion developers invest (or should invest) a significant amount of time into improving database access time (and even eliminating it when possible). There are lots of things that can negatively impact database performance:

- Poor database and table design
- Nonrelational tables
- Incorrect data types used
- Poorly written SQL
- Lack of indexes
- Not using stored procedures
- ... and much more

→ Stored procedures, relational databases, and SQL are covered in the previous four chapters (Chapters 44-47).

Even if all these issues were to be addressed properly, they'd still be a potential database bottleneck in that most Web-based applications have to make frequent databases requests—often for the same data over and over. This being the case, an important part of optimizing database performance is preventing unnecessary database access by saving query results for later use.

ColdFusion provides two very different ways to accomplish this, each designed for very different situations:

- Variable-based query caching
- Query result caching

Variable-Based Query Caching

Some database queries change infrequently (or never), and are thus perfect candidates for caching. Examples of these types of queries are:

- Countries
- U.S. states and Canadian provinces
- Company information (such as addresses and phone numbers)
- Product catalogs
- Employee extensions and email addresses

Variable-based query caching takes advantage of ColdFusion's support for persistent data by using the scopes designed for just that purpose. Three scopes are supported:

- Data that needs to persist for a single user can be stored in the `SESSION` scope.
- Data that needs to be available application-wide can be stored in the `APPLICATION` scope.
- Data that needs to be available across all applications on a server can be stored in the `SERVER` scope.

➜ For an explanation of how to use these persistent scopes, see Chapter 10, "`APPLICATION` and `SERVER` Variables," and Chapter 11, "Session State Management."

> **CAUTION**
> As a rule, use of the `SERVER` scope should be avoided. Most variable-based query caching belongs in the `APPLICATION` scope unless it is user-specific (in which case it belongs in the `SESSION` scope). The `SERVER` scope is shared by all applications and is therefore far more susceptible to the introduction of bugs or corruption by other developers or applications.

Storing a variable in the `APPLICATION` scope (for example) is as simple as prefixing the variable name with the scope specifier, as follows:

```
<cfset APPLICATION.dsn="my_data_source">
```

Caching queries into the APPLICATION scope is just as simple. The following example reads the list of U.S. states into a query within the APPLICATION scope (using the previously assigned APPLICATION variable as the datasource):

```
<cfquery datasource="#APPLICATION.dsn#"
         name="APPLICATION.states">
 SELECT state_name, state_abbrev
 FROM states
 ORDER BY state_name
</cfquery>
```

This query now resides within the APPLICATION scope and will persist for as long as APPLICATION variables are configured to persist. The query can be used like any other query, and must be referred to by the fully qualified name (scope plus name). The following example populates a drop-down list box with the list of states:

```
<select name="state">
 <cfoutput query="APPLICATION.states">
 <option id="#state_abbrev#">#state_name#</option>
 </cfoutput>
</select>
```

Of course, if the query is in the APPLICATION scope, then the majority of times it is used it will not need to be retrieved from the database. As such, the code that creates the query should always first check whether the query exists. The following code snippet demonstrates this process:

```
<cfif NOT IsDefined("APPLICATION.states")>
 <cfquery datasource="#APPLICATION.dsn#"
          name="APPLICATION.states">
 SELECT state_name, state_abbrev
 FROM states
 ORDER BY state_name
 </cfquery>
</cfif>
```

Using this code, the list of U.S. states can be read from the database just once (or as often as needed), and then used and reused without anyone ever having to access the database again. This can dramatically reduce redundant database access, which in turn can dramatically improve application performance.

> **TIP**
>
> The Application files are the perfect place for initializing APPLICATION scope data. See Chapter 6, "The Application Framework," for more information.

Of course, the other scopes can be used just as easily; just specify the appropriate prefix, and ColdFusion does the rest.

Variable-based query caching is not suited for queries that need to persist for short periods. Nor is it well suited for dynamic queries (for example, queries that are driven by form fields).

Query Result Caching

Variable-based query caching is ideal for queries that change infrequently, are not highly dynamic, and are of use across users or parts of applications. For all other queries, ColdFusion features another form of caching: query result caching.

This form of query caching is ideally suited for:

- Search results
- "Next N"–style interfaces
- User-specific queries

Query result caching is specified within the `<CFQUERY>` tag by using one of two optional (and mutually exclusive) attributes:

- `cachedwithin` is used to cache data for a specified interval (relative time) which is specified as a time span (using the `CreateTimeSpan()` function).
- `cachedafter` is used to cache data after a specific date (specified as absolute time) is reached.

The following example attempts to cache the results of a dynamic, form-driven `SELECT` statement:

```
<cfquery datasource="dsn"
         name="product_search"
         cachedwithin="#CreateTimeSpan(0,0,10,0)#">
 SELECT prod_id, prod_name, prod_desc
 FROM products
 WHERE prod_name LIKE '%#Trim(FORM.prod_name)#%'
 ORDER BY prod_name
</cfquery>
```

Here the `cachedwithin` attribute specifies a time span of `10` minutes (`0` days, `0` hours, `10` minutes, and `0` seconds). If the query is cached, any further queries for the same data within that interval will use the cached data automatically.

> **TIP**
>
> Most developers find that `cachedwithin` is the more useful of the two cache attributes. `cachedafter` is of use only when data is being retrieved from databases that are updated at known regular times.

But it is important to understand that `cachedwithin` (and `cachedafter`) are not instructions to cache data, they are *requests*. Data will be cached only if the administrator so allows, and if there is sufficient space in the cache. If the data can be cached, it will; if not, it won't. In fact, there is no way for developers even to know whether or not the query was cached. This is deliberate and by design, as this form of caching is designed to be as hands-off and transparent as possible.

> **NOTE**
>
> The number of queries that may be cached server-wide is specified in the ColdFusion Administrator.

Using cached queries is no different from using any queries—just refer to the query name. If a cached query can be used, it will; if not, it will not be used. The cached query will not be used if neither of the cache attributes is specified. But, if either of them is specified, and a cached query exists, ColdFusion will use it automatically.

> **NOTE**
>
> What makes a cached query unique is not the query name. In fact, a query can use a cached query even if the name is different, as long as it is the same query. So, what is it that makes a query unique? It's the combination of the following:
>
> - Datasource name
> - Datasource type (if specified)
> - SQL text (post and dynamic and programmatic processing)
> - Login information (if specified)

> **TIP**
>
> If debugging output is enabled, ColdFusion will let you know that a cached query was used (in lieu of the standard execution time output).

Using Bind Parameters

Most databases provide a mechanism to bind SQL parameters to specific datatypes. Doing so prevents the database (and database drivers) from having to perform implicit type conversions. The major benefits of parameter binding are:

- Improved performance
- Support for large columns
- From a ColdFusion perspective, preventing hacking via URL parameter manipulation

Parameter binding requires that a parameter be specified along with a datatype with which it is to be bound. The following are the names of the ColdFusion-supported types:

- CF_SQL_BIGINT
- CF_SQL_BIT
- CF_SQL_BLOB
- CF_SQL_CHAR
- CF_SQL_CLOB
- CF_SQL_DATE
- CF_SQL_DECIMAL
- CF_SQL_DOUBLE
- CF_SQL_FLOAT
- CF_SQL_IDSTAMP
- CF_SQL_INTEGER
- CF_SQL_LONGVARCHAR
- CF_SQL_MONEY
- CF_SQL_MONEY4
- CF_SQL_NUMERIC
- CF_SQL_REAL
- CF_SQL_REFCURSOR
- CF_SQL_SMALLINT
- CF_SQL_TIME
- CF_SQL_TIMESTAMP
- CF_SQL_TINYINT
- CF_SQL_VARCHAR

ColdFusion parameter binding is implemented via the `<cfqueryparam>` tag, which must be used in between `<cfquery>` and `</cfquery>` tags. The following query uses `<cfqueryparam>` to bind a URL parameter to a specific datatype (an integer):

```
<cfquery datasource="DSN"
         name="Product">
SELECT product_id, product_name
FROM products
```

```
WHERE product_id=<cfqueryparam value="#URL.product_id#"
                               cfsqltype="CF_SQL_INTEGER">
</cfquery>
```

The `<cfqueryparam>` `cfsqltype` attribute defaults to `CF_SQL_CHAR`, if not specified. Additional attributes may be used optionally to specify value lengths and ranges.

> **CAUTION**
> SQL query parameter binding is not supported by all databases and database drivers. Refer to the ColdFusion documentation to determine whether your database is supported.

> **NOTE**
> The exact syntax used by the database for query parameter binding varies dramatically from one database to the next. Fortunately, this is handled internally by the `<cfqueryparam>` tag so that you need not worry about it.

Summary

Database response and access times play a pivotal role in the performance of ColdFusion applications. Most performance issues are caused by bad SQL, poor database design, and other fundamental database-related concerns. But in addition to those, eliminating unnecessary database and network load can help application performance, and ColdFusion provides the mechanisms to accomplish this.

Sample Questions

1. Database queries can be cached into which of the following scopes?
   - **A.** `VARIABLES`
   - **B.** `CLIENT`
   - **C.** `COOKIE`
   - **D.** `APPLICATION`
   - **E.** `SERVER`
2. Which of the following statements are true?
   - **A.** Query-based caching can be disabled.
   - **B.** Variable-based caching can be disabled.
   - **C.** Query-based caching requires the use of locks.
   - **D.** Variable-based caching requires the use of locks.

3. Which `<cfquery>` attribute is used to reduce the number of round-trips to the database server during data retrieval?

   A. `cachedwithin`

   B. `cachedafter`

   C. `blockfactor`

   D. `packetsize`

4. Which of the following technologies could be used to prevent database hacking via URL tampering?

   A. Caching

   B. Trigger

   C. Index

   D. Bind parameter

PART 9

Tuning and Optimization

IN THIS PART

CHAPTER 49 Application Performance Tuning and Optimization

IN THIS CHAPTER

Employing Effective ColdFusion Coding

There are many strategies that you can employ to improve the performance of Web applications. The first step is writing code that runs efficiently. Tuning the server and caching are also effective, but they are not cure-alls for poorly written code. This chapter describes techniques you can use to increase the performance of ColdFusion applications. Remember that ColdFusion is like any other language: You can write code that is efficient and performs well, or you can write sloppy code that performs poorly.

Avoiding Nesting `<cfif>`, `<cfcase>`, and `<cfloop>`

Although nesting is sometimes critical in implementing an algorithm, nested `<cfif>`, `<cfcase>`, and `<cfloop>` tags take a toll on processing. As a rule, do not nest deeper than a few levels.

Using `<cfcase>` Versus Multiple `<cfelseif>` Tags

Rather than using a number of `<cfelseif>` tags in a conditional statement, use the `<cfswitch>/<cfcase>` tag set if possible. However, keep in mind that `<cfcase>` tests for multiple values of the same expression, while `<cfif> / <cfelseif>` tests for multiple conditions.

→ For exact syntax and more information on conditional statements, see Chapter 3, "Conditional Processing."

Optimizing Conditional Expressions in <cfif>

When evaluating expressions, it often is not necessary to use logical operators in <cfif> statements. For instance, you might use the `ListFind()` function to see whether an element appears in a list. If it does not, the function returns `0`; otherwise, it returns the index position of the element. The conditional expression can check whether the returned value is `0`, as follows:

```
<CFIF ListFind(TheList,"Testing") IS NOT 0>
```

You don't actually need to use `IS NOT 0` because the value returned by the function is inherently true or false. If the function returns any number besides `0`, the value is true, and the comparison using the operator is not necessary.

ColdFusion supports shortcut Boolean evaluations. You should take advantage of this type of evaluation when writing conditional expressions. For example, if you're checking for the existence of a variable and then for a certain value, use the `IsDefined()` function, then use a logical `AND` with the next check. If the existence test is false, ColdFusion will know that the result will be false when it sees the logical `AND`, and it stops the evaluation of the expression.

Avoiding Unnecessary Dynamic Expression Evaluation

The `Evaluate()`, `DE()`, and `IIf()` functions permit you to write highly flexible and dynamic code, but they are processing-intensive and should not be used unless they are truly needed.

➜ You can find more information about the evaluation of dynamic expressions in Chapter 22, "Dynamic Functions."

Reusing Code: <cfinclude> Versus Custom Tags And CFCs

Reusing code with <cfinclude> incurs almost no additional processing time, and the code executes quicker than Custom Tags and ColdFusion Components. For simple processing, the use of <cfinclude> may be preferable.

➜ The <cfinclude> tag is discussed in Chapter 5, "Redirects and Reuse." Custom Tags are covered in Chapter 28, "Custom Tags." ColdFusion Components are reviewed in Chapter 31, "ColdFusion Components."

Typing Variables When Performance Counts

ColdFusion is a typeless language, which can have a small impact on performance. To compensate for this, you could use the <CFPARAM> tag's `TYPE` attribute when assigning values to help performance. Consider the following:

```
<cfif TheVar IS 10>
```

If this condition existed, it would be evaluated marginally faster if TheVar were assigned a value, by using:

```
<cfparam name="TheVar" default="10" type="Numeric">
```

rather than

```
<cfset TheVar=10>
```

> **NOTE**
> As mentioned previously in this chapter, specifying type has a minimal impact on performance. The real benefit of using `<cfparam>` with the `type` attribute is error-checking.

Using Variable Prefixes

If you do not use variable prefixes, ColdFusion must scan a list of variable scopes in a predetermined order so as to find the specified variable. When you use a prefix, the variable's value can be retrieved directly, which saves processing time. However, hard-coding a specific scope can get in the way of implementing flexible code.

➜ See Chapter 2, "Working with Variables and Expressions," for a full discussion of variable prefixes.

Letting the Database Do Its Job

Databases are built and optimized to manipulate data. For instance, SQL's aggregate functions are faster at finding an average or a sum of a set of numbers than at reading the set of numbers, looping over them with a `<cfoutput query="">` tag, and doing the arithmetic in ColdFusion. Therefore, you should use your database to enforce referential integrity, apply constraints, and use triggers when one database activity needs to cause another to be performed.

In addition, avoid performing calculations or analysis in database data within ColdFusion. Wherever possible use stored procedures to achieve this. As a rule, any time data retrieved in one query is passed to a second query, that operation should be a stored procedure.

➜ Stored procedures were reviewed in Chapter 47, "Advanced Database Features."

Using `<cfcache>`

In many applications, templates are built dynamically every time a page is requested. But often a ColdFusion template stays the same every time it's requested. An example of this scenario is a home page that has no personalized content. Why should the page be built dynamically from the ColdFusion template when it rarely changes? This is a good question, and the `<cfcache>` tag can help resolve the issue.

When the `<cfcache>` tag is used on a page, it creates a separate file of the HTML code that the page generates. When the page is requested next, the tag sends the Web server the generated HTML code that was saved earlier, rather than dynamically rebuilding the page. This means that complete pages that do not change often can be cached, thus saving processing time and improving performance.

When a page is cached, it is uniquely identified by its URL. For instance, `Product.cfm`, `Product.cfm?Prod_ID=6`, and `Product.cfm?Prod_ID=11` all would be considered unique pages and cached as different pages. All of these pages would be considered good candidates for `<CFCACHE>`. But some pages are poorly suited to `<CFCACHE>`. Consider an action page based on a form that varies depending on user input in form controls. In most cases, this would be a terrible candidate for `<CFCACHE>`. The first user to fill in the form would generate output from the action page, and that output would be cached. All subsequent users, no matter how they filled in the form, would see the cached page until it timed out or was deleted.

The attributes used with `<cfcache>` are shown in Table 49.1. All are optional.

Table 49.1 `<cfcache>` Tag Attributes

ATTRIBUTE	DESCRIPTION
`action`	Specifies the action that the tag should perform. The options are `Cache` (the default), `Flush`, `ClientCache`, and `Optimal`.
`directory`	Specifies the directory from which cached files should be flushed (used with `action="Flush"`).
`expireurl`	Specifies the generated HTML files whose original files should be deleted; for instance, `expireurl="Product.cfm?*"` (used with `action="Flush"`).
`password`	Login password to be used if the page requires Web server—level authentication.
`port`	Specifies the port to be used during the communication between the tag and server. The default is `80`.
`protocol`	Specifies the protocol to be used during the communication between the tag and server. The options are `http://` (the default) and `https://`.
`timespan`	The time-out interval. Valid values are numbers and time spans.
`username`	Login user name to be used if page requires Web server—level authentication.

You can create a template as follows:

```
<cfcache>
<html>
<head>
 <title>Untitled</title>
</head>
<body>
<cfset thevar="Pass the test!">
<cfoutput>#VARIABLES.TheVar#</cfoutput>
</body>
</html>
```

A file is created and saved, and ColdFusion generates its name. The saved file looks like this:

```
<html>
<head>
 <title>Untitled</title>
</head>
<body>
Pass the test!
</body>
</html>
```

After the ColdFusion tags are processed, the HTML code is generated and then saved as a separate file. The next time a user browses this page, ColdFusion sees the `<cfcache>` tag and uses a special map file to check whether the generated code already exists.

The cached page can be timed out in a number of ways. One is to use the `TIMEOUT` attribute with the `<cfcache>` tag. The following example would time out the cache after 5 hours:

```
<cfcache action="Cache" timeout="#DateAdd("h","-5",Now() )#">
```

You also can schedule a page to run at certain intervals or dynamically by using the `Flush` value for the `action` attribute, as follows:

```
<cfcache action="Flush" expireurl="*">
```

> **CAUTION**
>
> The ColdFusion documentation is inconsistent about whether you should use attributes when `action="Flush"`. In some places, it implies that no attributes are needed, and in others, it indicates that both `EXPIREURL` and `DIRECTORY` are required. In practice, at least `EXPIREURL` must be used.

Measuring Performance

This chapter suggests a number of techniques to improve application performance, and you will come across others while learning about ColdFusion. How can you tell whether they are helping in your application? As you'll read in the following subsections, a number of ColdFusion tools are available to help with this task.

Execution Time

In ColdFusion Administrator, you can select the Report Execution Times checkbox under Debugging. This option displays the total time of page processing and execution. By recording a page's execution times, you could see whether changes to the page help improve performance.

`<cftimer>`

To determine the execution time of specific lines of code, wrap that code within `<cftimer>` tags. Results will be displayed in the debug output (default), inline, in HTML comments, or in generated page outlines (depending on the `type` specified):

```
<cftimer label="some label" type="outline">
 Code to time
</cftimer>
```

`GetTickCount()`

`<cftimer>` leverages a function named `GetTickCount()` internally, and this function may be used directly too:

```
<cfset Start=GetTickCount()>
 Code to time
<cfset End=GetTickCount()>
<cfoutput>The time to process is: #End-Start#</cfoutput>
```

Improving Perceived Response Time

After each application page, the database, and the server environment have been tuned, a page takes as long to respond as the operations it executes. Some of those operations, such as long-running database queries, require that users wait for a response. Studies indicate that the acceptable response time for users is 8 seconds. This means that users wait an average of 8 seconds without a noticeable response before they go elsewhere or click the Refresh button.

The `<CFFLUSH>` tag can help accelerate users' perceived response time. With this tag, you can flush incremental output to browsers so that users have a visual indication that their request is successful and will be completed soon.

CAUTION

Before ColdFusion can flush data, it must compile the data to return. A long-running query must complete before data can be flushed. Some queries might be too long for the `<cfflush>` tag to help with perception of performance. In those cases, it's best to give users a "please wait" dialog or message to let them know you're processing their request.

The `<cfflush>` tag takes one optional attribute, `INTERVAL`, which is the number of bytes to collect and flush to a browser at one time. You should use `INTERVAL` only when a large amount of output will be sent to the client; it is used like this:

```
<cfflush interval="integer number of bytes">
```

`interval` data will be flushed automatically whenever the specified number of bytes is in the output buffer (additional `<cfflush>` tags are not required).

TIP

You shouldn't use `interval` when generating complete HTML pages. Doing so could cause partial data to be flushed–incomplete DHTML, for example. If the user were to activate that partial code, browser errors could be thrown. You should use `interval` only when outputting raw data, such as CSV content or XML.

Using `<cfflush>`

You should use `<cfflush>` when you think you can incrementally flush large amounts of data back to the user and help with perceived response time.

Because an HTML header is the first component to be flushed, errors occur if any subsequent tags change the header information. Tags that can alter the HTML header include the following:

- `<cfcontent>`
- `<cfcookie>`
- `<cfform>`
- `<cfheader>`
- `<cfhtmlhead>`
- `<cflocation>`

All these errors, except for `<cfcookie>`, can be caught and handled with the `<cfcatch type="template">` tag. Cookie errors can be caught with `<CFCATCH type="any">`.

Summary

ColdFusion code can execute very efficiently or run very poorly, depending on how you write the code. You can use a number of techniques to write code that will perform optimally. For example, you can identify effective ColdFusion coding techniques, avoid having ColdFusion do the database's job, enforce strict attribute validation, and use <cfcache> when logical. To be sure that a particular technique has actually increased performance, you can use a number of ColdFusion tools, such as the <cftimer> tag and GetTickCount() function, to show processing time.

Sample Questions

1. When many expression values will be tested, what tag is best to use?

   A. <cfif>/<cfelseif>

   B. <cftestcase>

   C. <cfswitch>/<cfcase>

   D. <cfloop>

2. Which of the following tags reuses code most efficiently?

   A. <cfinclude>

   B. <cf_CustomTag>

   C. <cfparam>

   D. <cfmodule>

3. Which of the following tags cannot be used after a <cfflush>?

   A. <cfdump>

   B. <cfinvoke>

   C. <cfsetting>

   D. <cfform>

CHAPTER 50

Server Performance Tuning

IN THIS CHAPTER

The Operating System

An operating system is the underlying software that issues commands to the computer's hardware. It handles such functions as:

- Allocating storage space
- Scheduling tasks
- Acting as an interface to the user's computer when an application is running

Web sites are constantly putting further demands on the operating system of the server. It is therefore important to select an operating system that is flexible, can protect itself from multiple server processes competing for system resources, and is able to support essential server-side processes such as application servers and search engines. All the while, the operating system must continue to perform well.

Certainly performance is a critical factor in the selection of an operating system, but you also should consider other factors. In determining which operating system best meets your needs, you should be mindful of the following criteria:

- Scalability/flexibility. Can it scale to a platform that is capable of accommodating large traffic loads? Is it flexible enough to work with a variety of Internet services? How many CPUs can it handle?
- Network management. Can it support common IP network management applications? Does it integrate with your existing network environments and directory services?

- Application availability. Can it run the applications you run today? Are new applications being developed for it? How much do the applications that you need cost?
- Management. Does it provide flexible, accessible management utilities?
- Cost. What are the costs for related hardware, the operating system itself, and any required server software? Is the operating system so complex that it will require additional spending for specialized personnel to install and maintain the system?
- Performance. How many users can you support with a single machine? Does the operating system support symmetric multiprocessing (SMP)? Does it let you balance loads across multiple systems?
- Application development. Are the development tools you use available for the platform? Are there standard operating system services and industry-standard interfaces to support development?
- Reliability. Does it support RAID or clustering? Can you hot-swap components?

The Web Server

The difficult decision of which Web server to use is complicated by many factors. The most important considerations are which operating system you intend to use and which Web server software has the feature set and performance potential to handle your Web site's expectations and traffic load. The following factors might be important when you're selecting a Web server:

- Operating system
- Familiarity with the operating system
- Price
- Access to support and other resources
- Ability to host multiple Web sites on a single Web server
- Log reporting
- Server-side includes
- User access security
- Transaction security
- Server programming and database support

- Current equipment (hardware, network, network operating system)
- Scalability
- Application server support
- Management tools

Many factors can affect the performance of a Web server, including the following:

- The server's processor
- The type and quantity of RAM on the server
- The type of bus used for the network adapter card and the disk controller on the server
- The disk drive's operating characteristics
- LAN utilization
- WAN bandwidth
- The type of content included on Web pages (multimedia versus text)

When an Internet or intranet Web site gets extremely busy, server performance suffers. The first option to improve the situation is to add memory so that more requests can be serviced from the cache. This might not help, though, especially if the server is busy because of background or communication tasks. If that is the case, you have two options: You can purchase a more powerful server and quit using the older one, or you can add individual servers and a load balancer.

Load balancers distribute the incoming requests among a group of Web servers. Load balancing provides the opportunity to utilize your existing resources and then add servers as needed. It also adds fault tolerance: If one server goes down, the others can keep providing service. This fault-tolerance feature also provides uninterrupted service during routine maintenance in which servers need to be offline. A load balancer functions by sitting between the Internet and the Web servers, connected on one side to the Internet router, and to a hub or a switch on the other side. The load balancer uses a virtual IP address to communicate with the router. This address is what is advertised to the Internet for all Web servers, and it masks the actual IP address of the Web server, which aids security. The hub or switch connected to one side of the load balancer is the point of connectivity for all Web servers.

The Application Server

An application server provides the services that connect applications and databases, and it generally has development tools that work with it. It should provide a framework to link the Web site to existing applications and data. The application server should provide these services at the fastest speed possible.

Many criteria, including the following, should be used when selecting an application server:

- The language used and the learning curve for its use
- Database connectivity options and throughput
- Load-balancing and fail-over options
- Supported operating systems and Web servers
- Availability of development tools
- Ability to work with various industry standards
- Security options

ColdFusion can be used as an application server (via the integrated JRun), or can be used with a J2EE application server of your choice. High-end J2EE servers feature scalability and performance options that ColdFusion can leverage in that environment.

Separate Servers for Separate Tasks

Even after careful selection of the operating system and Web server, it most likely will be too much to expect one computer to handle all the tasks associated with a Web site. A single piece of hardware acting as the host for all services will shortly overwhelm its resources. To correct this problem, you should run separate servers for ColdFusion and the Web server, the database, email, and so on.

Specific Tuning Techniques (ColdFusion Administrator Settings)

After you've made decisions about the operating system and Web server, you can turn your attention to tuning the ColdFusion application server. There are a number of knobs to turn to optimize the performance of the ColdFusion server, as described in the following subsections.

Saving Class Files

ColdFusion compiles `.cfm` (and other ColdFusion) files into Java bytecode, which is read upon execution. By default code is compiled in memory and not saved to disk. However, on production systems (where code does not change) they may be a performance gain by checking the "Save class files" option.

Another important option is "Trusted Cache". If this box is checked, the ColdFusion Application Server trusts that the CFML code of the template being requested has not changed. If changes are made to templates, the changes are ignored until the Trusted Cache box is unchecked and the particular templates are browsed. After that, Trusted Cache can be turned on again.

> **TIP**
>
> If Trusted Cache is being used and a substantial number of templates are changed, every template has to be browsed before the Trusted Cache option can be turned on again. In that case, it might be easiest to cycle the ColdFusion services to clear all cached pages.

Simultaneous Requests

In ColdFusion Administrator's Server Settings group, the Settings option contains Limit Simultaneous Request to *x* Tunable. This setting determines the number of listener threads the ColdFusion Application Server sets up to receive Web server requests. When all the threads are busy, new requests are queued.

There is no rule of thumb for setting this option optimally. Only testing under load can determine the best setting for any given configuration.

> **NOTE**
>
> This option is only applicable to the standalone ColdFusion. The J2EE editions require that the underlying J2EE server be tuned to manage requests.

Server Performance Monitoring

This chapter makes several suggestions about how to improve the ColdFusion Application Server's performance. Tools are available to watch and see the effects of the changes. Using a good load-testing tool with a well-planned load-testing script is the best way to see the effects of the changes when the server is under load. It is also possible to gain a look into how the ColdFusion server is behaving by using Performance Monitor or `CFSTAT`.

Performance Monitor

Performance Monitor is built into Windows (NT, 200, XP). It looks at resource use for specific components and program processes. In ColdFusion Administrator, under Debug Settings, the Debug Options menu item lets you click a checkbox to enable performance monitoring. Applying the changes will expose ColdFusion counters to Performance Monitor.

> **CAUTION**
> Unlike some of the other settings in debugging, the ColdFusion Application Server service must be restarted in order for Performance Monitor to be able to see the ColdFusion object's counters.

Table 50.1 shows the counters available.

Table 50.1 ColdFusion Counters Available in Performance Monitor

COUNTER	DESCRIPTION
`Average DB Time (msec)`	A running average of the amount of time, in milliseconds, that an individual database operation launched by ColdFusion spent to complete.
`Average Queue Time (msec)`	A running average of the amount of time, in milliseconds, that requests spent waiting in the ColdFusion input queue before ColdFusion began to process them.
`Average Request Time (msec)`	A running average of the total amount of time, in milliseconds, that ColdFusion spent to process a request. In addition to general page-processing time, this value includes both queue time and database processing time.
`Bytes In/Sec`	The number of bytes per second that the ColdFusion Server received.
`Bytes Out/Sec`	The number of bytes per second that the ColdFusion Server returned.
`Cache Pops/Sec`	The number of times per second that a cached template had to be ejected from the template cache to make room for a new template.
`DB Hits/Sec`	The number of database operations per second that the ColdFusion Server performed.
`Page Hits/Sec`	The number of Web pages per second that the ColdFusion Server processed.
`Queued Requests`	The number of Web pages per second that the ColdFusion Server processed.
`Running Requests`	The number of requests that the ColdFusion Server is currently actively processing.
`Timed Out Requests`	The number of requests that timed out and never got to run while waiting for the ColdFusion Server to process.

The server tuning options mentioned in this chapter either directly or indirectly affect some of these counters. For example, `Cache Pops/Sec` reports the number of times a template was removed from the cache to make room for a newly parsed template. If this number is not at or near zero, the Template Cache Size setting in ColdFusion Administrator needs to be increased, and possibly more memory added in the server.

The `Running Requests` counter is never more than the Limit Simultaneous Requests To setting in ColdFusion Administrator's Server Settings.

Performance Monitor has a graphical user interface that lets you graph any of the counters and also log the counters graphically.

cfstat

Performance Monitor is available only in Windows operating systems. Even in Windows, you might want a command-line interface to see the ColdFusion Application Server's counters. `cfstat` is a command-line utility that is available for all platforms on which ColdFusion runs.

> **TIP**
>
> You can use the counters in a ColdFusion template by using the `GetMetricData("monitor_name")` function. In Windows, `monitor_name` is `PerfMonitor`; on UNIX/Linux, it is `CFStat`.

You can use two optional switches to modify `CFSTAT`'s behavior. They are listed in Table 50.2.

Table 50.2 `CFSTAT` Switches

SWITCH	DESCRIPTION
`-n`	This instructs `cfstat` not to display column headers, which is helpful if you are redirecting output to a file and don't want the column headers.
`x`	This number specifies, in seconds, how often the counters should be polled and displayed.

> **NOTE**
>
> As with Performance Monitor, the Enable Performance Monitoring option must be checked and the ColdFusion Application Server service restarted in order for `cfstat` to function.

Server Settings Summary

ColdFusion can list all server settings in a single report that can be saved or printed for later use. This is a recommended practice so that you can re-create changes later if needed.

In addition, the report indicates when changes were made. This information is invaluable when diagnosing problems that may have been caused by changes in ColdFusion Administrator.

The server report is accessible via ColdFusion Administrator's Settings Summary option.

Summary

Critical to the Web server's performance are the underlying operating system and Web server software you select. After the ColdFusion Application Server is installed and running on the system, a number of tuning options are available, including settings for code cache size, Trusted Cache, and the number of simultaneous requests. You can use Performance Monitor and `CFSTAT` to determine whether the tuning did in fact aid performance.

Sample Questions

1. Which of the following are counters for the ColdFusion object in Performance Monitor? *(select all that apply)*

   A. `Average ColdFusion Execution Time`

   B. `Average Request Time`

   C. `Average DB Time`

   D. `Average Queue Time`

2. Which counter is an indicator of sufficient memory for the cache?

   A. `Bytes In/Sec`

   B. `DB Hits/Sec`

   C. `Queued Requests`

   D. `Cache Pops/Sec`

PART 10 Appendix

IN THIS PART

APPENDIX A Answers

Chapter 1

1. A, B, and D. CGI variables are usually sent when a URL is requested, but they are not part of the URL itself.
2. B and C. All ColdFusion requests are submitted via a Web Server and thus via `http` or `https`.
3. A, C, and D. ColdFusion runs on the server, not on the client, and therefore it can access only server resources, not client-side files. As for Microsoft Word, files are accessible by ColdFusion if they reside on the server, not the client.
4. A and C. XML has nothing to do with CFML, and JavaScript is a client technology.

Chapter 2

1. A and C. `MOD` is an operator, and `LCase()` is a function.
2. B. The order of evaluation dictates that the URL appears before the others.
3. D. Although all are legal, the best use of #s, or in this case lack of #s, is shown in D.

4. A. `<cfparam>` can be used to check for the presence of variables and to verify that they are of the correct type, but `<cfparam>` supports a finite site of types. `<cfif>` provides far more flexibility in that in can do all that `<cfparam>` can do, and much more too. (Although you'll have to write more code to get the job done).

5. C. `<cfdump>` accepts an expression, not a variable name. The output would have been A if `VAR="#name#";` without the #s the output will be the string `name`. So, C is correct (although it'll probably not be what you want).

Chapter 3

1. C and E. The normal operator symbols cannot be used.

2. A, C, and D. Remember that any number except zero evaluates to true.

3. D. `<cfswitch>` takes an `expression` as an attribute. As #s were not specified, `name` would not be evaluated.

Chapter 4

1. C. Index loops can iterate only over numeric values.

2. D. Because the counter `i` is incremented and then displayed, the first value displayed is 2. The number `4` is shown because the loop does not terminate immediately when the condition is false; rather, it finishes the loop.

3. A. The variable specified in the `item` attribute takes on the keys of the structure in the loop.

4. B and D. The conditional loop has only one attribute, `condition`, and the collection loop uses `item`.

Chapter 5

1. C. `addtoken` appends client identification information within the query string of the redirected page. These may be set as cookies too, but not necessarily so.

2. B and C. <cfheader> is used on the server side to alter response headers. The response header is sent to the browser and can tell it not to cache a page.

3. B. The first character after the quotation mark is a forward slash (/), so a ColdFusion mapping is used.

4. D. reset="Yes" clears any display before the tag, so ABC is not shown.

Chapter 6

1. B. There is no onRequestNew() method, and onRequest() executes in between onRequestStart() and onRequestEnd().

2. D. Each OnRequestEnd.cfm is paired with an Application.cfm file. OnRequestEnd.cfm runs only if it is located in the same directory as the Application.cfm file that was executed.

3. A and C. onRequest() cannot be used with Web Services or Flash Remoting.

4. B. Local variables are indeed local to the CFC, but as the requested page is included using <cfinclude> that page shares the CFCs scope.

Chapter 7

1. A, and B. dbtype is an attribute of the <cfquery> tag that is used to specify the type of query, and executionTime is not in the query object (it is returned as cfquery.executionTime).

2. C. Although the <cfoutput> group attribute can be used in conjunction with SQL GROUP BY operations, <cfoutput> GROUP and GROUP BY are not related (the latter is used when performing aggregate calculations).

3. D. Query of queries requires a NAME attribute to reference the resulting query variable and dbtype="query" to instruct ColdFusion to look for table names in available query variables.

4. A, B, C, and D. Any SQL statement can be passed to the database by using `<cfquery>`, provided that the designated driver can handle it.

Chapter 8

1. C. `?` is used to separate the query string from the URL itself, and `&` separates each `name=value` pair.
2. B. While it is a good idea to `Trim()` URL variables to avoid extraneous whitespace, `URLEncodedFormat()` is the function that converts problematic characters to safe sequences.
3. C. Answer A does not specify a name for the `URL` variable. `URLVar` in answer B is not a valid prefix for `URL` variables. The proper prefix is `URL`. In answer D, the `<A>` tag's `NAME` attribute is used to name the target location for a link on a page, not to create the link.

Chapter 9

1. C. `post` is the safest `method` to use.
2. C. A select control that allows multiple options but has none selected could act like a set of checkboxes (depending on the browser used). However, this question lists a drop-down select control. A drop-down, by default, always passes a value.
3. A. `FavCountry=CAN,FRA`. Because both form controls have the same name, their values are concatenated.
4. C. Anything that is sent to the browser (as client-side and auto-generated server-side are) is inherently less secure that manual server-side validation.

Chapter 10

1. B. Unlike `APPLICATION` variables, `SERVER` variables are always available and may always be used. This cannot be prevented.
2. A. All of the other options are incorrect.

3. E. This is a trick question. There is no `onServerStart()` method, if there was that would be the place to set `SERVER` variables. And while `onApplicationStart()`, `onRequestStart()`, and `onRequest()` could indeed be used to set SERVER variables, so could any other files and code too, and there is no special reason that these should be used.

Chapter 11

1. D. `session` and `browser` are not valid settings for the `expires` attribute. `now` would expire the cookie immediately. By not setting an `expires` attribute at all, you create a browser session cookie.

2. A and D. `CLIENT` is the only variable types that is stored to disk, and J2EE session variables can be replicated between servers by the underlying J2EE server.

3. A. `CLIENT` and `COOKIE` may only store simple data.

Chapter 12

1. D. A is incorrect because `CFLOCK` requires either the `SCOPE` or the `NAME` attribute. B is incorrect because `NAME` and `SCOPE` are mutually exclusive attributes. C is incorrect because the `SCOPE` attribute must be a valid scope name, such as `APPLICATION` or `SESSION`.

2. C, D, and E. All three could be shared between requests.

3. A and B. C is incorrect because deadlocks occur only when locks are nested. D is incorrect because the `CLIENT` scope is not a variable type that requires locking.

Chapter 13

1. A and D. Strings always can be accessed as lists. Dates can be treated as strings and therefore are lists (usually delimited by slashes or hyphens). Arrays and structures, however, can never be accessed as lists.

2. A, C, and D. Because it is an empty string, B is not valid. (ColdFusion will not throw an error, but the list will always contain one element.)

3. A, B, C, and D. By default, the list has one element. If a space is used as a delimiter, the list has two elements. If two characters are used as delimiters (for example, `er` or `no`), the list has three elements. If the delimiter contains all the characters `Ben Forta`, the list has no elements at all, just delimiters.

Chapter 14

1. A and B. `ArrayNew()` is usually used to create an array, but `ListToArray()` can be used too. Neither C nor D is a valid function.

2. B. The `ArraySum()` function requires that all array members have numeric values; if one was empty (as is index `3`), an error would be thrown.

3. C and D. A is incorrect because no equals sign is required in a `<cfset>`. B is also incorrect since an array can be resized to any size. As the loop iterates, the size of the array decreases because of the deleted indexes.

4. A and C. A is false because an associative array is not an array (it is a structure). C is false because arrays can have more than three dimensions through the repetitive use of `ArrayNew()`. B and D are true.

Chapter 15

1. B. Remember that structures are pointers. Both of the structures (A and B) are the same structure, and each equals 2 after being set a second time.

2. B. The attributes that are used with a `<cfloop>` and a structure are `item` and `collection`. `#` must be used around the structure within the `collection` attribute.

3. A. `StructNew()` takes no parameters. The other three options are all valid.

4. B and C. A is invalid, because spaces are not allowed in key names when using dot notation. B is valid, as long as `lastname` is a variable containing a valid key name. C is standard dot notation. D is invalid, because quotes are not allowed in key names.

Chapter 16

1. A, B, and E. `<cfinput type="file">` is not supported, and `<cfslider>` is only supported as a Java applet, but not as Flash. (Although this will likely change in future releases).
2. C. A and B are valid tags but are not used for control alignment and placement, D is not a valid tag.
3. B and D. Bindings, embedded ActionScript expressions, and control styling are all supported by Flash Forms. Server-side events and the creation of custom controls requires the use of Macromedia Flash or Macromedia Flex.

Chapter 17

1. A, B, C, D and E. Any controls may be used, as long as the XSL skin used has been written to support them.
2. B. At a minimum, a file containing `<cfform>` and an `.xsl` file are needed.
3. B and C. The form action should not be in the `.xsl`, that is in the form itself. Similarly, no controls definitions (including submit buttons) belong in `.xsl` file.

Chapter 18

1. C and E. Client-side scripting is not supported by the print rendered, nor are browser plug-ins.
2. A and D. Margins can be set for the entire `<cfdocument>` as well at the `<cfdocumentsection>` level. B is not a valid tag, and C is incorrect because margins are not set using `<cfdocumentitem>`.
3. B and D. A (Excel) is supported by `<cfreport>` but not by `<cfdocument>`, C and E are not supported at this time.

Chapter 19

1. C. — `.cfr` files may be invoked directly, unless that functionality has been disabled.
2. B, C, D, E. — Queries may be passed to the query attribute, and all simple data types (including dates, numbers, and strings) may be passed as input parameters.
3. A, B and D. — C and E are not supported at this time.
4. A, B, C. — All of these return queries (they are not database queries, but any query object is usable), the other three do not return queries.

Chapter 20

1. B and C. — The rest are invalid.
2. A, B and F. — Although charts may be embedded in other formats (like PDF and FlashPaper), only Flash, JPEG, and PNG are directly supported.
3. B. — `$` symbols are used to delimit charting values.

Chapter 21

1. D and F. — The `<CFHTTP>` tag and custom tag interfaces have been exposed only through tag-based interfaces, so they cannot be used within a `<CFSCRIPT>` block. All the other options are accessible using functions. Remember that none of ColdFusion's services (query, HTTP, FTP, and so on) are available in a `<CFSCRIPT>` block.
2. D. — A is false because the same operators are used in CFML as in `<CFSCRIPT>` blocks. B is false because CFML is capable of doing things that `<CFSCRIPT>` blocks are not (such as database queries). C is false because `switch/case` statements are available in both syntaxes.
3. D. — As no `break` statement is used, both lines of code are executed.

Chapter 22

1. B and C. One of the purposes of `DE()` is to stop ColdFusion from evaluating an expression. This can be used in an `IIf()` function to return a literal rather than a value. Answer A is incorrect because `DE()` is not used only for output. Answer D is incorrect because `DE()` stands for *delay evaluation*.

2. C. The condition (`1 is 1`) is true and returns the first of the two arguments. The first argument has three expressions within it (`1,2,3` are three separate expressions). Because ColdFusion always returns the last expression, the rightmost one is returned (`3`).

3. B. The `Evaluate()` function can create expressions by concatenating strings and literals. The complete expression evaluates to `"p=ArrayNew(1)"`, which creates a new array.

4. A. It might appear that the answer is B (`y`). Because `x` is not equal to `y` (`x = "y"` and `y = "x"`), the second of the two expressions can run. The second expression is simply `"x"`. If the expression had quotation marks around it, then `x` would be evaluated as the value `"y"`. But because `x` has no quotes around it, it is actually evaluated twice. First, it is evaluated to see what it equals (`y`), and then that value is evaluated as an expression in itself, which equals `"x"`. It is doubtful that anything this difficult would be on the exam, but it is sure good practice!

Chapter 23

1. A, B, and D. Stored procedures are much faster than passing SQL or calling a view because they are precompiled in the database server. Therefore, A is correct. B is also correct, because stored procedures can hide certain columns and introduce layers of abstraction. D is correct, as stored procedures are indeed more powerful. C and E are not correct, because stored procedures can be difficult to create and are not standard across database platforms.

2. C. The TYPE attribute of <cfprocparam> is "inout" when a stored procedure gives a variable the same name as that of the parameter it returns. An example would be a stored procedure that takes a product's price (itemPrice) and returns the price (again as itemPrice), with all discounts applied.

3. B. <cfprocparam> can return arrays, but <cfprocresult> always returns queries.

Chapter 24

1. A, B, and C. The <cftransaction> tag has an isolation attribute. Whether the database respects this ISOLATION tag is beyond your control. Isolation levels can affect performance, with serializable the worst performer and READ UNCOMMITTED the best. Isolation levels also affect the way records are locked. D is the only answer that is false, because the database has full control over what is locked.

2. C. Answer A is incorrect because <cftransaction> supports rollbacks as well as commits. B is incorrect because a dirty read is possible, depending on the isolation level. D is also incorrect because <CFLOCK> has nothing to do with a database transaction per se.

3. B. If the inner <cftransaction> tag were terminated, the code would work.

4. A. A serializable read is the worst performer.

Chapter 25

1. A, C, and D. Local variables (VARIABLES) and ARGUMENTS, if present, are not exposed.

2. B and C. <cftimer> blocks and manual use of GetTickCount() are used to determine code execution time. <cflog> writes to log files, and there is no Debug() function.

3. B and D. Debug output is viewable within Dreamweaver and via a Web browser.

Chapter 26

1. B. When the type is `Validation`, `<cferror>` checks server-side form validation.

2. B and D. `Any` catches any exception, and `Application` is used specifically for this purpose.

3. C and D. `<cfscript>` supports only `try` and `catch`.

Chapter 27

1. B and E. To secure complete applications, the login code must be executed on each request, so it should be placed in an `Application.` file.

2. A and C. Users are logged out when a time-out occurs or when the browser closes (or when `<cflogout>` is invoked).

3. B. `401` triggers the display of a login form.

Chapter 28

1. B. By prefixing a variable with `Caller.` inside a Custom Tag, you tell ColdFusion to make the variable available to the calling page.

2. B and C. By default, A and D will not be seen. B is the first file that would be found. C is the default Custom Tags directory.

3. A. The code in B simply creates a variable, not a default value. C creates a hidden form variable, which has no direct effect on the Custom Tag. D explicitly passes a Custom Tag attribute and value, but it does not set a default.

Chapter 29

1. D. By default, none of the others exist.

2. B. `start` is typically not that useful for actual processing, because when the tag is executed it has no knowledge of any tag contents or children. C is impossible, because processing cannot occur when the tag is `inactive`.

3. C. `<cfassociate>` associates a child tag with a parent so as to pass any data up to it.

Chapter 30

1. B. `Arguments` is an array that contains every passed argument, regardless of whether it is enumerated explicitly.

2. A. You must use the `VAR` keyword to create a variable local to the UDF. Omitting `VAR` causes the variable to be created in the calling code's scope.

3. B and D. A is incorrect, as there is no difference in execution speed. C and E are incorrect, as the statements are true of both tag- and `<cfscript>`-based UDFs.

Chapter 31

1. A, C, and D. CFCs are designed to encourage code reuse and tiered development, and they can indeed be accessed outside of ColdFusion. B and E are false, as CFCs are not needed to access Java or implement error handling (although both can be performed inside of CFCs).

2. B. `empObj` is missing `#` characters, and so a string is being passed instead of the object. A is incorrect, as a path is not always needed. C is incorrect, as `method` is not used in `<cfobject>`. D is incorrect because `returnvariable` is always optional.

3. B. `name` is required. The other attributes are all valid but not required.

4. A. `access` is set to `"remote"` to allow remote access.

5. C, D, E, and G. `REQUEST`, `SESSION`, `SERVER`, and `VARIABLES` may contain complex data types, and if no scope is specified, then `VARIABLES` is the default.

Chapter 32

1. C and D. Web Service data is XML in a SOAP package.

2. B. `<cfinvoke>` is used to invoke ColdFusion Components and Web Services. A is incorrect, as `<cfinvoke>` handles its own HTTP calls internally. C is incorrect, as only CFCs can be instantiated as objects, not Web Services. D is incorrect, as all Web Services' XML processing is handled by ColdFusion internally.

3. A, B, and D. For a CFC function to be accessed as a Web Service, it must be named using `NAME`, access must be set with `access="remote"`, and the `RETURNTYPE` must be specified too.

Chapter 33

1. A. As ColdFusion runs on underlying Java internally, Java is the preferred extensibility option.

2. D. `<cfimport>` is used to import JSP Tag Libraries. A is incorrect, as `<cfobject>` is used to load objects (such as Java objects). B is incorrect, as `<cfmodule>` only works for CFML Custom Tags. And `<cfinvoke>` is also incorrect, as it is used to invoke ColdFusion Components and Web Services.

3. A and C. `<cfobject>` and `CreateObject()` are used to invoke Java objects.

Chapter 34

1. A and B. `<CFXML>` creates XML Document Objects, as does `XMLParse()` (by converting an XML document to a Document Object). C and D are valid functions but do not create XML Document Objects.

2. D. `ToString()` creates an XML document from an XML Document Object. `XMLParse()` is exactly the opposite. `XMLFormat()` creates XML-safe text, and `ToXML()` does not exist.

3. A and D. XML documents may indeed be case sensitive, and they must be well formed (which is why `ToString()` should be used to generate the XML document). XML is not in a binary format (it is plain text), and it does not (or should not) contain page-formatting information; XML describes data (not layout, as HTML does).

Chapter 35

1. A. The other three are valid.
2. A. By not declaring an `output` attribute, you are telling ColdFusion to write the results of the WDDX packet to the page.

Chapter 36

1. B. Invoked code could indeed call Custom Tags or UDFs, but these cannot be invoked directly from Flash.
2. A and C. `ARGUMENTS` will contain passed arguments if invoking a CFC; `FLASH` will contain passed arguments if invoking a `.cfm` file.
3. A and C. CFCs indeed encourage separation of content, and they provide the simplest integration. B is false because CFCs are not automatically faster than `.cfm` files. D is false, since CFCs have the same access to CFML that straight `.cfm` files do. E is false, as CFCs and `.cfm` files are equally portable.

Chapter 37

1. C. D is not a real function, and B is the name of the CFC method that is invoked to process gateway requests.
2. A and B. CFML performs local asynchronous processing, and JMS provides access to distributed and asynchronous processing via Java messaging.
3. A and E. Configuration file (D) is optional, B and C are incorrect.

Chapter 38

1. A, B, and D. The `NEAR` operator is available only in explicit search expressions.
2. A and B. `<cfcollection>` with the `action="optimize"` attribute is the preferred method for optimization. However, `<cfindex>` with the `action="optimize"` attribute is the old, deprecated method and is still backward-compatible.

Chapter 39

1. A, B, C, and D. Access to `<cffile>`, `<cfcontent>`, `<cfdirectory>`, and `<cfregistry>` can all be restricted through ColdFusion Administrator. You cannot restrict E and F, nor would you want to.
2. C. `<cffile>` reads and writes files but cannot return file information—for that, you need `<cfdirectory>`.
3. B. This option is not the default and is required for file uploads.

Chapter 40

1. A. Scheduled events are executed by using a `<CFHTTP>` agent.
2. B, C, and D. There is no `ADD` action; `UPDATE` will add if the task does not exist. `DELETE` and `RUN` are valid.
3. B and C. `weekly` is valid; `hourly` is not (to accomplish that, you'd need to specify `3600` as the number of seconds). `90` seconds is valid; `15` is not (`60` seconds is the shortest interval allowed).

Chapter 41

1. B and C. `<cfmailparam>` is used to attach files to an outbound message and to set SMTP headers if needed.
2. A, B, and D. ColdFusion has no integrated support for IMAP.
3. D. A period on its own line may terminate the message, causing you to lose any text that follows it.
4. A, C, and D. There is no `getattachments`. `getall` retrieves attachments if `attachmentpath` is specified.

Chapter 42

1. B. The distinguished name is used as the unique reference in LDAP hierarchies.
2. A. `start` nominates the directory branch for searching.

3. A and B. The distinguished name is a unique reference to a specific attribute. The distinguished name is made up of the relative distinguished name and all the attributes up to the root of the LDAP hierarchy.

Chapter 43

1. C. Ordinarily, you must specify `method="post"` with a relevant `<cfhttpparam>` tag to send variables. However, URL parameters can be sent in the `URL` attribute itself.

2. B. `<cffile>` is required to receive an uploaded file from a client browser. `<cfftp>` is used to manage a remote FTP connection and file transfer.

3. C. `Header` contains the headers sent back from the remote server. The other options are valid `CFHTTP` variables but will not contain server header information.

Chapter 44

1. B and D. A is used in `UPDATE` operations. C is not a valid keyword.

2. A and D. A is valid. Wildcard characters are actually not required when you use `LIKE`; the search is effectively an equality test. B is invalid; `NOT` must precede `LIKE`. C is invalid; wildcards can be used with strings, not with numbers. D is valid; there is no limit to the number of wildcard characters that you can use in a search.

3. B. You use `UPDATE` when columns (as opposed to rows) are affected. A, `DELETE`, deletes entire rows. C, `NULL`, is not a statement; it represents no value and can be used with `UPDATE` to set a column to no value.

4. B. Primary keys may indeed be made up of more than one column. All the other statements are false.

Chapter 45

1. A. `SELECT` is used to join two or more tables.

2. C. Using `=*` is equivalent to using the ANSI SQL `RIGHT OUTER JOIN`.

3. A, C, and D. No keyword is required for self-joins.

Chapter 46

1. B. `GROUP BY` is used to group aggregates. The other clauses are all valid but do not group data, which is required here.

2. D. `WHERE` and `ORDER BY` are not required, and neither is an alias (although an alias should ideally be used). The `HAVING` clause, however, must contain entries from the `SELECT` list.

3. B and D. The average function is `AVG`, and the function used to total values is `SUM`.

Chapter 47

1. A and B. Indexes are of significance only to data retrieval, and primary keys merely identify rows.

2. A and D. Many databases (especially nonclient/server databases) do not support the use of stored procedures, and stored procedures are fully supported in ColdFusion.

3. A, B, and C. `SELECT` does not change data and therefore does not support the use of triggers.

4. A. The use of stored procedures helps because they prevent users from passing explicit SQL code to be executed.

Chapter 48

1. A, D, and E. This is a trick question. Queries cannot be cached in `CLIENT` or `COOKIE` variables. They can, however, be stored in `VARIABLES` variables (in fact, that is what most queries are stored).

2. A and D. Query-based caching can be disabled in the ColdFusion Administrator, but there is no way to prevent users from caching queries to variables. Locking is an issue only with variable-based caching.

3. C. `CACHEDWITHIN` and `CACHEDAFTER` are used in query caching. Answer D does not exist.

4. D. Bind parameters will not allow extraneous characters in SQL statements.

Chapter 49

1. C. The `<cfswitch>/<cfcase>` tags are best used with many values of the same expression.
2. A. Includes perform better than custom tag calls.
3. D. `<cfform>` needs to write JavaScript code to the page head, which likely would have been flushed already.

Chapter 50

1. B, C, and D. The average ColdFusion execution time must be calculated from the other counters.
2. D. `Cache Pops/Sec` tells how many pages are taken out of the cache to make room for more.

INDEX

A

B

C

D

Q

R

S

U

X

Y